Visual Basic® 5
Training Guide

About the Training Guide Series

Computer training has become a billion-dollar business and a major problem for end users, workers, and corporations. Beginner training courses typically cost between $100 and $500. With this in mind, we at AP PROFESSIONAL decided to attack the problem and offer the best in training at a fraction of the cost. The goals were simple. We wanted to create a program that would:

- teach the subject quickly and easily
- provide the in-depth training that users expect
- be easy to use at or away from the computer

It seemed that an interactive CD-ROM, combined with an excellent book, would provide the most reusable and flexible training program. We decided to look at all the best CD training products on the market. After looking at the competition, we concluded that the LearnKey, Inc., products offer the best interface and use the best instructional methodology. Each instructor on the LearnKey videos is an excellent teacher. Each is also effective on camera. LearnKey was quite generous in adapting the content of their CDs to meet our needs.

With the LearnKey CD, we had the leverage to get some of the top writing talents in the computer business. The result is the best in CD/book training at an affordable price.

Now that you have bought this package, enjoy the CD, read the book ... whichever!

You may also want to purchase other books in the Training Guide series, including:

C++ Training Guide
Windows NT® Training Guide
Windows NT® Server Training Guide
Windows® 95 Training Guide
(We'll be doing many more, so watch for upcoming titles!)

For special deals on bulk orders, please call (619) 699-6477.
If you need technical support, you may contact LearnKey, Inc., at (801) 674-9733.

We at AP PROFESSIONAL and LearnKey, Inc., hope you enjoy this exciting training package.

Visual Basic® 5
Training Guide

William H. Murray & Chris H. Pappas

AP PROFESSIONAL
AP PROFESSIONAL is a division of Academic Press

Boston   San Diego   New York
London   Sydney   Tokyo   Toronto

This book is printed on acid-free paper. ∞

Copyright © 1997 by Academic Press.

All rights reserved.

AP Professional
1300 Boylston St., Chestnut Hill, MA 02167, USA
An Imprint of Academic Press
A Division of Harcourt Brace & Company
http://www.apnet.com

United Kingdom Edition published by
ACADEMIC PRESS LIMITED
24-28 Oval Road, London NW1 7DX
http://www.hbuk.cc.uk/ap/

Library of Congress Cataloging-in-Publication Data

Murray, William H.
  The Visual Basic 5 Training Guide / William Murray, Chris Pappas.
    p. cm.
  Includes index.
  ISBN 0-12-511905-4 (alk. paper). — CD-ROM ISBN 0-12-511906-2
  1. BASIC (Computer program language) 2. Microsoft Visual BASIC.
I. Pappas, Chris H. II. Title.
QA76.73.B3B59 1997
005.26'8—dc21   97-10938
                                                          CIP

Printed in the United States of America
97 98 99 00 IP 9 8 7 6 5 4 3 2

Dedication

CHP—*To Becky and Adam*
WHM—*To Bob and Lynn*

Contents

Introduction

Programming for Windows 95 and Windows NT will never be the same. Microsoft's Visual Basic 5 programming language has brought welcome relief to programmers. Gone are programming development cycles that are measured in days and weeks—you can now create real Windows applications in just minutes. Visual Basic 5 should receive an award for its power, ease of use, flawless performance, and well-written documentation. Microsoft has done an outstanding job in developing Visual Basic 5 for Windows 95 and NT and has left the competition in the dust.

This book was designed to complement the tools provided in the Visual Basic 5 package. In order to use this book and the programs on the enclosed diskette, you will need to run Microsoft Windows 95 or Windows NT and Microsoft's Visual Basic 5 package on your computer. We suggest setting up Visual Basic 5 in the default directories suggested by the setup program since many of the applications will look for the tools in these directories.

The first nine chapters of this book concentrate on the foundations of Visual Basic 5 programming. This material includes definitions, using tools, and creating simple applications. The remaining eight chapters concentrate on developing more involved applications. These applications illustrate most of the programming concepts related to Visual Basic 5, and are skillfully woven into application code that can serve as a template for your own projects. Chapter 10, for example, contains many simple programs designed to get you started. These examples include base conversions, statistical calculations, sorting, and techniques for creating tables. By Chapter 15, you'll be a pro at developing applications that include professional quality line, bar, and pie charts. Chapter 16 is a detailed look at how Visual Basic 5 programmers can access functions in Microsoft's WIN32API. Finally, Chapter 17 looks at how you can introduce common and custom controls into your Visual Basic 5 projects.

As you progress from chapter to chapter you'll learn Windows 95 and NT programming terminology, good programming techniques, and many secrets that will help you write fast and efficient Visual Basic 5 code. Prepare yourself for the most exciting programming event that you have ever experienced. Welcome to Microsoft's Visual Basic 5.

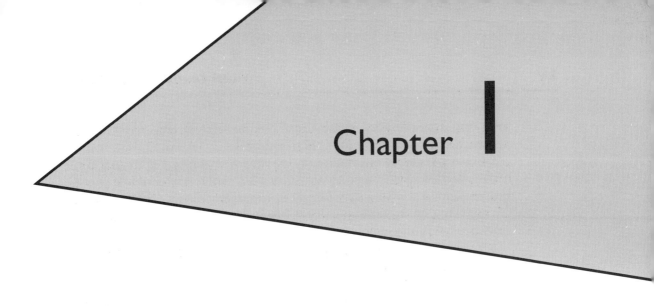

Chapter 1

Visual Basic 5 Fundamentals

With the success of Windows 95 and Windows NT more and more demand is being placed on the programmer to design applications for these graphics environments. Microsoft designed Visual Basic to make this type of Windows application development an easy process. With the latest release, Visual Basic 5, even more features have been added to take full advantage of the 32-bit Windows 95 and Windows NT environments. Instead of the steep learning curve encountered by C or C++ programmers, Visual Basic 5 offers the programmer a Toolkit that allows quick construction of very advanced applications. In this chapter, we will examine the events that have led to the development of the Visual Basic language, learn some basic definitions, and even develop a simple program.

THE RECENT PAST

Applications design has changed drastically over the past few years as a result of user demand and dramatic hardware improvements. The first challenge was to be able to run more than one program at a time. The solution for running multiple programs was a new breed of software involving DOS enhancers. Products like Quarterdeck's DESQVIEW and Microsoft's first version of Windows permitted several applications to be initialized and swapped to and from disk as needed. The problems with these environments, however, were that they would frequently lock up and crash the system. This major inconvenience often led to the loss of critical data.

DOS enhancers were obviously not the answer, but it would take both a hardware and a software solution to solve the problem. First, Intel designed a whole new family of microprocessors specifically for multitasking environments (80386, 80486, and Pentium). Now, only a software solution was needed.

Microsoft's Windows seemed to fit the solution to the software problem. The advantage of Microsoft Windows was that it presented both the user and the programmer with a common interface. The user got a graphical point-and-click environment that was the same across all applications. Programmers got a predefined set of tools, called the Microsoft Windows Software Development Kit (SDK), that enabled them to create this common look. Windows also freed the programmer from having to worry about the end user's unique hardware configurations, including printers, scanners, mice, and so on.

There was only one snag for the programmer: the Windows SDK had over 600 new functions to master along with the overlaid concept of event-driven programming. This was quite a problem for the traditional DOS command line programmer. Not only did the programmer have to master the philosophy of event-driven programming and the 600 functions, but also all this was written in C, and C was an emerging language at the time. Thus, the programmer had to master C before beginning the arduous task of mastering the Windows SDK! Something needed to be done to give the average programmer easy access to Windows.

Visual Basic from its inception was designed to make developing a graphical Windows application as easy as possible. Visual Basic 5 automatically takes care of the more tedious tasks of creating an application's graphical look. The programmer is free to concentrate more on an application's features rather than how to style it for Windows. All of this is accomplished by programming in the BASIC language.

Some programmers turn their noses up at the BASIC language, saying it is unstructured and procedure oriented. They often prefer object-oriented environments that use the Microsoft Foundation Class (MFC) library. Fine! Let them write their MFC applications, because you'll be developing robust Windows applications that contain all of the features of the MFC applications in 1/20 of the time!

WHY USE VISUAL BASIC 5?

Visual Basic 5 will probably be the most addicting Windows application development environment you will ever use! Visual Basic 5 comes with a complete set of graphical tools and high-level language constructs that make it easy and quick to go from an idea to a full-fledged running application.

Visual Basic 5 is not only easy to use but also fun to use. You will quickly be inventing and experimenting with new project designs. And, almost as quickly as you conjure these ideas up, you can implement them. You will also find Visual Basic 5's feedback and online debugging tools an invaluable coach when developing new applications.

Each Visual Basic 5 application you design will follow three basic steps. Note that no code is written for the first two steps:

- Draw the objects that make up the user interface.
- Set the properties for each object to change its appearance and behavior.
- Attach program code to each object.

THE BASIC LANGUAGE AND VISUAL BASIC 5

There are really only two prerequisites to using Visual Basic 5. First, you need to be comfortable using Windows, Windows 95, or Windows NT. This means that you must be comfortable with how to use a mouse, the selection of menus and menu features, use of dialog boxes, and so forth. Second, you need to understand certain computer language operations. For example, you should understand **If...Then...Else** selection statements, **For** loops, constants, variables, and subroutines.

If you have written code for Microsoft QuickBasic you are well on your way to programming with Visual Basic 5. Normal BASIC code, however, will require some tweaking before placing it in a Visual Basic 5 application.

PROGRAMMING BASED ON EVENTS

All Windows applications (Windows 3.x, Windows 95, and Windows NT) have a common graphical user interface called the GUI. Multiple

Windows applications all share the same hardware: computer, monitors, printers, and so on. Because of their concurrent nature, it is no longer possible for a single program to begin, execute, and terminate before the next application is loaded and run. Windows, therefore, requires that all applications respond to ever changing and unpredictable occurrences.

This is the world of event-driven programming. Instead of writing a program that executes from top to bottom, you design an application that responds to events. These events can be generated by the user, such as a key press. Windows, itself, generates other events. For example, when two applications want access to the modem at the same time, Windows has to decide which one uses the modem and which one waits. When the privileged application is finished communicating, Windows tells the idle application to get started.

While the idle application is waiting for an event, it remains in the environment. The user can run other applications; perform data entry; open, close, or resize windows; or customize system settings. But the idle application's code is always present and ready to be activated when the user returns to the program.

THE VISUAL BASIC 5 TOOLKIT

Visual Basic 5 comes complete with all the design tools necessary to efficiently create, debug, and test applications that will take full advantage of Microsoft Windows' capabilities. Visual Basic 5 features include or provide support for:

- a color palette for defining the colors of the user interface.
- a Menu Design window for creating a hierarchical menu bar with accelerator keys, keyboard access keys, and grayed or checked menu items. All of this can be achieved without writing any code!
- a property bar that makes it easy to edit the initial properties of each object without writing code!
- with a quick double-click on any object, automatic display of the associated code page that handles all the events for that item.
- entire toolboxes of objects for point, click, and drag creation of user interfaces.
- a complete math library.

- a currency data type for use in financial calculations.
- access to all Windows functions.
- direct system calls to Windows Application Programming Interface (API) functions.
- floating-point math data types and functions.
- icon library to add a professional look to every application. The icon library contains icons that you can use or modify with the icon editor.
- integer and long integer data types.
- online debugging and interpreting of each statement as it is being written, translating code immediately to runable form.
- predefined command objects that allow you to create CommandButton, OptionButton, CheckBox, TextBox, ListBox, ComboBox, Frame, and other controls. In addition, it is easy to add horizontal and vertical scroll bars and menus.
- sequential and random-access file support.
- static and dynamic arrays, including user-defined types.
- unique graphic statements.
- variable-length string data type.
- support for developing 16-bit or 32-bit code.
- development of (OCX) custom controls.
- ability to use common controls.

While this list is impressive to the experienced Windows programmer, it is by no means exhaustive. Visual Basic 5 is capable of much more.

INSTALLATION

Visual Basic 5 is shipped in both CD-ROM and diskette versions. The Visual Basic 5 setup is designed to guide you quickly through all of the installation options. The setup program not only installs Visual Basic 5 but also optionally loads the Help system, tutorials, sample applications, the icon library, and other tools.

For an optimal development environment, we recommend using Visual Basic 5 on a computer equipped with a Pentium processor with

16 MB of random-access memory (RAM) and Windows 95 or Windows NT as the operating system.

Run the Visual Basic 5 setup program from the Windows 95 or NT File menu's Run option or from the File Manager. Just follow the installation instructions to choose which subdirectories are to be created and which files are to be copied to your hard disk. The process is almost automatic.

We installed our copy of Visual Basic 5 in a subdirectory named VB5.

OPERATING UNDER VISUAL BASIC 5

The easiest way to start a Visual Basic 5 session is to click the Windows 95 or NT Start button, select Programs from the initial list, and then select the Visual Basic 5 icon from the list of installed applications.

Visual Basic 5 runs like all other applications. You will enter a complete development environment with your screen divided into many different programming categories.

GETTING VISUAL BASIC 5 HELP

Visual Basic 5 Help is installed during installation. You should spend time gaining familiarity with the online Help facility. Just about any question you have can be answered by a proper traversal of the Help database. However, to use this library efficiently requires a basic knowledge of how Help operates.

Activating Help

The Help utility is a context-sensitive system that knows exactly which Visual Basic 5 window you are in, which line of code you are currently on, or which Visual Basic 5 option you are trying to use. By pressing F1, any valid command or option description will be immediately displayed in the Help window. Figure 1.1 shows the Visual Basic 5 Help dialog box set to retrieve help on the Caption property.

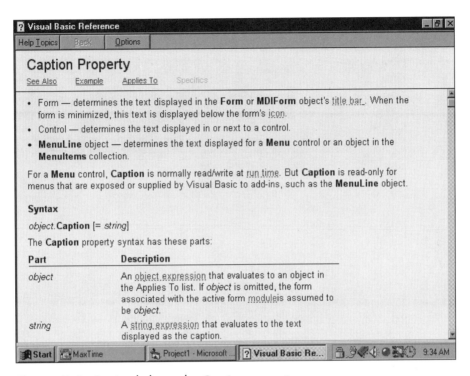

Figure 1.1 Getting help on the Caption property.

Scrolling a Help Window

The vertical and horizontal scroll bars allow you to scan up and down the support text explaining the particular feature in question. In many cases the Help window will reference a coded example that you can copy and run. Figure 1.2 shows a programming example from the Help screen for the Icon property.

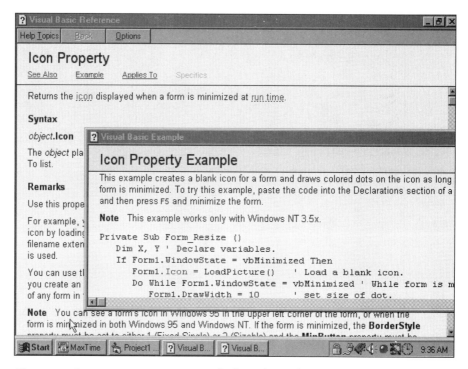

Figure 1.2 A programming example from the Help screen.

Using Index and Search

Another useful search method is to use the index of Topics. Here you select a category related to your question or again use the Search option. If you select the Search option, a dialog box will be opened that allows you to type in a search category. For example, you could type the word "operator," as shown in Figure 1.3. As you begin typing the search topic, the Search utility tries to match each new letter you type with all related topics. When this is completed, a list of related files is displayed in the Topics Found dialog box.

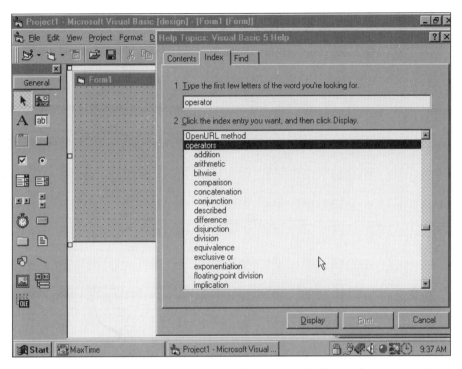

Figure 1.3 Using the Search engine to find topics dealing with "operator."

Help Supports Cross-References

Finally, any highlighted or underlined term displayed in any of the Help windows can be used as a topic cross-reference. If a term has a dashed underline, the cross-reference is simply a definition. Terms with solid underlines produce full cross-reference text. You select a term by tabbing to the highlighted term or by clicking on it with the mouse to open the subtopic's window, as illustrated in Figure 1.4. The two sets of buttons permit you to move forward or backward to the next or previous Help entry. The previous button takes you back to your previous query.

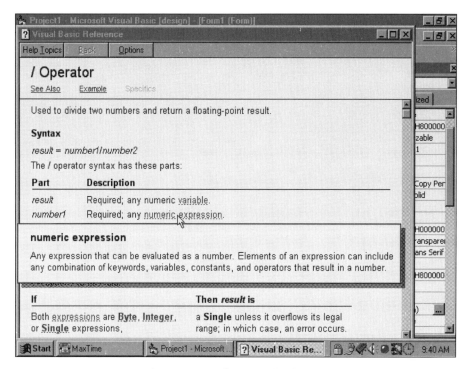

Figure 1.4 Preparing for a cross-reference check.

Using Help to Run Coded Examples

To run an example from within Help, Visual Basic 5 requires that a form be open. This form can be an existing form or one that is specifically opened to test the example code. For example, open the Help window and do a search for Line, then select Help on the Line Method. From the Help window click on the **example** keyword, as shown in Figure 1.5.

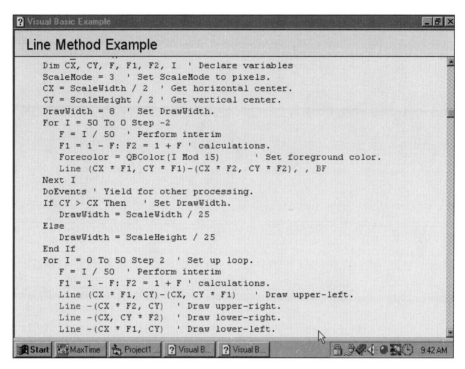

Figure 1.5 Selecting "example" from the Help window.

Once the coded example is displayed on the screen, highlight the code and then copy the code by using the Edit | Copy file selection or by clicking your right mouse button and selecting the Copy option. Now, return to the opened form for your project. Paste the code you just copied by selecting Edit | Paste or by using the right mouse button and selecting the Paste option. The code should be pasted under the form's click event. Figure 1.6 illustrates the result of the paste operation.

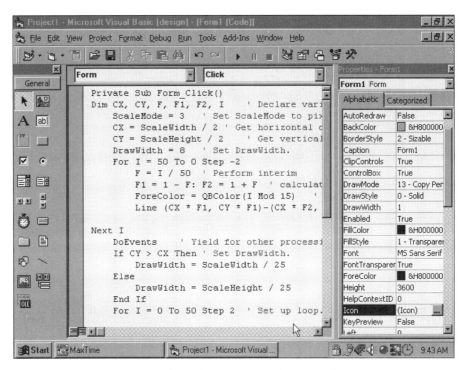

Figure 1.6 Pasting example code into a Visual Basic 5 form.

From the Visual Basic 5 <u>R</u>un menu, choose the <u>S</u>tart option, or press F5 to run the example. Click on the form to test the actual code. For this example, the results should be similar to those shown in Figure 1.7. When you are finished, choose the <u>R</u>un | <u>E</u>nd sequence from the Visual Basic 5 menu.

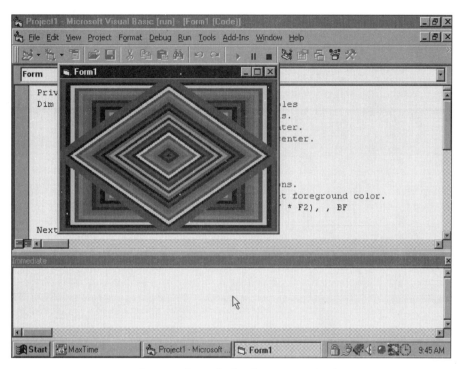

Figure 1.7 Running the sample code for the Line Method.

CREATING AN APPLICATION

In this section you will learn the fundamentals for creating a complete Visual Basic 5 application. When you start Visual Basic 5 you should see a screen similar to Figure 1.8.

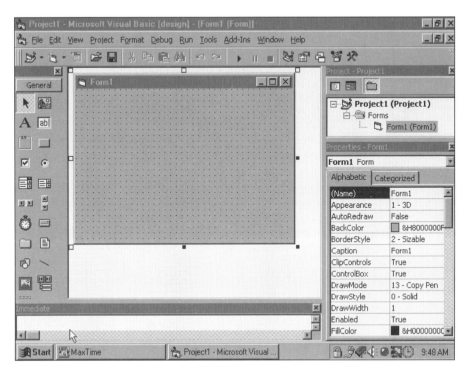

Figure 1.8 The initial Visual Basic 5 screen.

Forms and Modules

Every Visual Basic 5 application is composed of forms and modules. Forms are used to store the visual elements of an application along with any related code required by that element. Modules contain just programming code. Their information can be shared with other modules making up the whole application.

The Project Manager

Visual Basic 5 uses a Project Manager to keep track of all of the components that make up a complete application. To the right of your screen (refer back to Figure 1.8) you will see the **Project1** window. Notice that it already has at least one entry: **Form1.frm**. Every Visual Basic 5 application needs at least one form. This initial form, **Form1.frm**, is automatically entered into the **Project1** window and is displayed in the center of the screen.

Code Page and Controls

Every form has associated with it a *code page*. The code page contains the code that acts upon any of the controls placed on the form. A control can be a TextBox control that allows the program to output text or the user to enter data. It can be a CommandButton control that causes a particular action to take place, or many other frequently needed program-user interactions. You can get to any form's code page either by double-clicking on the form itself or by pressing F7.

To begin your first program, bring up **Form1**'s code page by double-clicking on **Form1**, as shown in Figure 1.9.

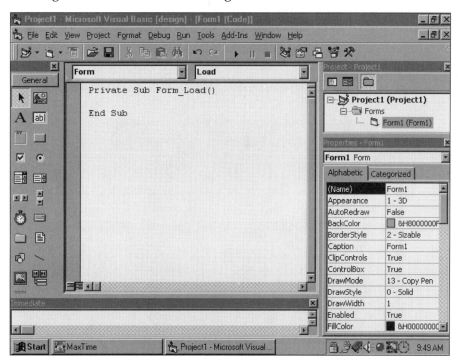

Figure 1.9 Form1's initial code page.

From the Form1.frm list of procedures, select **Click**.

*Note: If you do not see the **Click()** procedure, click on the second drop-down list found immediately above Form1.frm's code page. Scroll through the drop-down list until you see **Click**.*

You are now ready to enter the code that will be automatically executed whenever the form receives a mouse click. Notice that the name of the subroutine is **Form_Click()**. With the cursor on the code page, space over two spaces for good indentation and type: ***Print "Visual Basic 5 is fun and easy!"*** That's it! You are now ready to run your first program.

Running the Program

When you are inside Visual Basic 5 there are two ways to run a program; you can choose the Run | Start menu sequence or press F5. Press F5 now and click the mouse on the window. Your results should be similar to Figure 1.10.

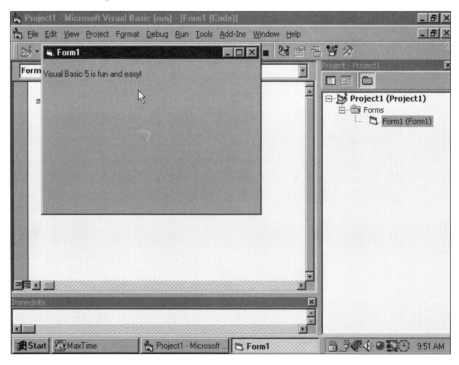

Figure 1.10 The window for the first application.

Consider the feat you just performed. You did not have to write any code to dimension and create the window; color it; label it; give it the ability to be moved, resized, iconized, and expanded; provide the ability to switch to another application; and on and on. All you did was concentrate on what you wanted to achieve, then typed one line of code, and Visual Basic 5 took care of all the rest! You did it all in record time—the C and C++ programmers are still trying to get their compilers booted!

The remainder of this book will teach you how to hone your programming skills and take advantage of a wide variety of Visual Basic 5 tools. However, before looking at these new features, you'll need to master a few new concepts.

STANDARD CONTROLS

For the purposes of Visual Basic 5, a standard control is a graphical object that is placed on a form. A CommandButton (sometimes called a radio button) or TextBox control is an example of a standard control. Every control has its own set of recognized properties and events. All Visual Basic 5 interfaces are designed using a combination of these controls and their related events.

Note: Visual Basic 5 also allows the use of custom controls. The user designs these controls. The controls' properties are not predefined, as they are for standard or common controls. They must be defined by the programmer. Chapter 17 discusses common and custom controls.

Table 1.1 summarizes the most frequently used controls from all of the controls that appear in the Visual Basic 5 toolbox. The toolbox is generally found to the left on your screen. Figure 1.11 shows the default Visual Basic 5 toolbox for the Enterprise version of the product. Your toolbox may have a similar appearance.

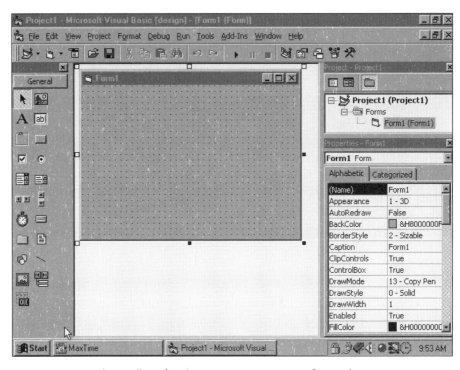

Figure 1.11 The toolbox for the Enterprise version of Visual Basic 5.

If you are using a different version of Visual Basic 5, you may have more or less controls in your toolbox, as shown in Figure 1.11. You can get information on any control by dragging the control to an open form, finding its name in the Properties dialog box, and using Help, as described earlier.

Table 1.1 Frequently Used Controls and Descriptions

Control's Function	Control's Name	Description
Checkbox	CheckBox	CheckBox controls provide the user with a yes/no, include/exclude option. When the option is selected, the checkbox control will display a check symbol. An unselected item has a clear checkbox. Multiple boxes can be checked.

(continued)

Table 1.1 *(continued)*

Control's Function	Control's Name	Description
Combo box	ComboBox	ComboBox controls combine the features of TextBox and ListBox controls. The **Style** property of a ComboBox control allows you to select any one of three styles: drop-down ComboBox (**Style** = 0), simple—list always displayed (**Style** = 1), drop-down list box (**Style** = 2).
Command button	CommandButton	The CommandButton control appears iconically as a keyboard. CommandButton controls are used to execute an instruction sequence when the user activates them. Sometimes these controls are called push buttons. CommandButton controls graphically depress when they are selected by the user. The CommandButton control is usually activated by its associated **command_Click ()** event. Two properties that are unique to CommandButton controls are **Default** and **Cancel**. These are used to create the frequently seen **OK** and **Cancel** buttons that respond to the ENTER and ESC keys, respectively.
Data control	Data	Provides access to data stored in databases using any one of three types of objects. The Data control enables you to move from record to record and to display and manipulate data from the records in bound controls. Without a Data control or an equivalent data source control like the RemoteData control, data-aware (bound) controls on a form can't automatically access data.

(continued)

Table 1.1 *(continued)*

Control's Function	Control's Name	Description
Directory list	DirListBox	A DirListBox control allows the user to browse through a disk's directory hierarchy. Directory list properties allow the application to determine which path the user has selected.
Drive list	DriveListBox	A DriveListBox control enables a user to select a valid disk drive at run time. Use this control to display a list of all the valid drives in the user's system. You can create dialog boxes that enable the user to open a file from a list of files on a disk in any available drive.
File list	FileListBox	The FileListBox control gives the user the ability to see all the files in a selected directory and to perform wild card searches for a file. The application can use the **FileName** property to determine which file the user has selected. This control is typically used in conjunction with a DirListBox control. The FileListBox control can enable the writing of a File Open procedure with a minimum amount of code overhead.
Frame	Frame	The Frame control provides a visual and functional grouping for related controls. Frame controls can be used to draw simple boxes. When additional controls are placed within a Frame control they form a group. During the design phase of a form, if the Frame control is moved, all the controls contained in the Frame control are moved with it. OptionButton controls placed within the Frame control form a single group.

(continued)

Table 1.1 *(continued)*

Control's Function	Control's Name	Description
Image	Image	Use the Image control to display a graphic. An Image control can display a graphic from a bitmap, icon, or metafile, as well as enhanced metafile, JPEG, or GIF files.
Label	Label	The Label control uses a large-looking letter "A" icon. Label controls are used to display text that will not change (static text). Thus, Label controls are used for labeling other controls that do not have their own caption property. Labels controls can, however, be changed by program code.
List box	ListBox	ListBox controls display a list of items from which the user can select one. A ListBox control is defined as a string array. You can access the **List** array using the **ListIndex**. The **ListCount** property returns the number of rows in the array. ComboBox controls and all the file-system controls use similar properties.
Option button	OptionButton	These controls are often referred to as radio buttons. OptionButton controls are used to select one option out of a group of related options. Unlike grouped CheckBox controls, which can have several items checked, related controls can have only one control selected at a time. They are often called radio buttons because, just as with a car radio, you can select only one station at a time.Selecting another OptionButton control cancels the previous control.

(continued)

Table 1.1 *(continued)*

Control's Function	Control's Name	Description
Picture box	PictureBox	The PictureBox control uses an icon that resembles a small desert scene. PictureBox controls are used to display graphics. The pixel information can come from an icon, bitmap, or metafile. PictureBox controls are also used to out put from graphics and **Print** methods.
Pointer	Pointer	The Pointer resembles a mouse pointer and is used to select, move, or resize any control in the toolbox.
Scroll bars	HScrollBar and VScrollBar	Horizontal and vertical scroll bar controls give the user a graphical means of moving through lists or selecting data ranges.
Shape	Shape	The Shape control is a graphical control displayed as a rectangle, square, oval, circle, rounded rectangle, or rounded square.
Text box	TextBox	A TextBox control is used to display text generated by the application or to receive input from the user. TextBox controls can be made multiline capable by turning on the control's **MultiLine** property. When in multiline mode, TextBox controls can take advantage of automatic word wrapping. The most impotant property of a TextBox control is the **Text** property, which returns the box's contents in string form.
Timer	Timer	Timer controls are used to activate a specific event at periodic intervals. Using the **Interval** property (specified in milliseconds), Timer controls can be used to create alarms, run procedures in the background, or coordinate other time-related events.

CONTROL PROPERTIES

Once the form's interface has been designed with the various control objects just described, you can alter their behavior and appearance. Figure 1.12 shows a Properties box for a TextBox control that gives you access to these control enhancers.

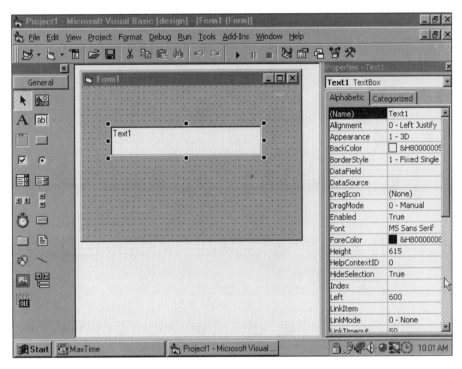

Figure 1.12 The Properties box for a TextBox control.

Every object you create in Visual Basic 5 has an associated set of characteristics called *properties*. The most common set of properties defines an object's size, screen location, and color. Each time you create an object, Visual Basic 5 assigns the appropriate properties to it and initializes them to a set of predefined values. The Properties box contains a list of properties appropriate to the selected object and allows you to change their values. For example, Figure 1.13 shows what happens when you change the type of font and Figure 1.14 shows what happens when you change the font size in the TextBox control by changing the font style in the Properties box.

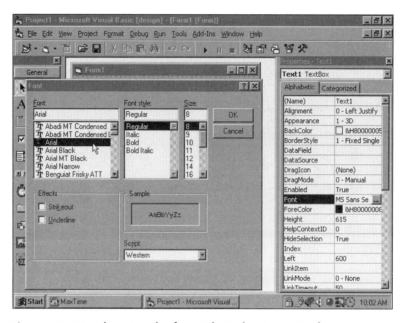

Figure 1.13 Changing the font style in the Properties box.

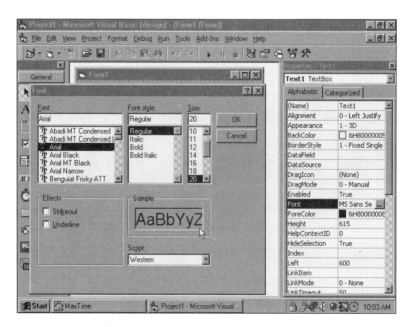

Figure 1.14 Changing the font size in the Properties box.

Each time a control is added to a form, Visual Basic 5 automatically type-names and sequentially numbers it for you. For example, if you use two timer controls, Visual Basic 5 will label and number them **Timer1** and **Timer2**, OptionButton controls are labeled **Option1**, CheckBox controls are marked as **Check1**, and so on.

CHANGING CONTROL PROPERTIES

To gain experience with control properties, open Visual Basic 5. With **Form1** in the center of the screen, move the mouse to the toolbox and place the pointer over a TextBox control. The TextBox control uses the icon with a lowercase "ab" in it. Now double-click the left mouse button and a copy of the control will automatically be transferred to **Form1**.

The newly installed TextBox control can be sized by grabbing its edges with the mouse. It can also be repositioned anywhere on the form. As you size or move the TextBox control, notice that certain numbers change in the Properties box for **Text1**.

Now, from the Properties box, use the mouse to select **Font** and click on it. The Properties box transfers the default font size of 8 to the edit window. Click on the edit window and you'll be able to type in a replacement font size. When you hit the return key, the control's text size changes immediately.

Did you notice any problem? Depending on the font size you chose, the control may not be wide enough to contain all the larger text. No problem, simply click on the control and resize it! You may have asked for a 24-point font and gotten only an 18-point font. Windows will give you the closest size available that matches your request.

A FAST METHOD OF CHANGING PROPERTIES FOR SEVERAL CONTROLS

Applications quickly become more complex with numerous controls on a form. It is possible, for example, that a form contains 20 TextBox controls. Changing the properties of each one of them could become very time consuming and error prone. Rather than selecting each control with the mouse and then changing the property in the Properties box, simply scroll down the list of controls from within the Properties box using the list box. The list box is at the top of the Properties box. When you have selected an object's property for one control, for example,

Font, the selected property remains highlighted as you move from one control to another.

If you want all the controls on your form to have the same property, say **Font**, select one of the controls and the new font size. Now select the other controls in order. The selected property will be highlighted in the properties edit window for each object, waiting for you to type in the new setting.

OBJECT NAMES AND LABELS

Each time a new control is added to a form, Visual Basic 5 automatically labels and numbers it for you. One of the properties that you can change for any control is its **Name**. This is how the control will be referred to by name throughout your application. A control's name is not the same as its label.

Click on the TextBox control you created earlier and go back to the Properties box. Slide down the list until you see **Name**. Now click on it. Notice that the edit box now displays **Text1**. Change the entry by clicking on the settings box and typing the word OPEN. Notice that the control's label didn't change, just the name of the control. To change the control's label you need to select the control, click on the Captions property, and immediately type the new label. Try changing the TextBox control's label from **Text1** to **OPEN**.

It is important to remember the difference between a control's label and its name. Controls, just like forms, have their own *code page*. A code page is an associated set of subroutines that are identified by the control's **Name** property. Trying to use a control's label in a coded reference can lead to unnecessary frustration. If you are a little uncertain of this distinction, create a control, change only its **Name** property, and then bring up the control's code page by pressing F7. Does the uncompleted subroutine have the new **Name** property attached to it or the default label supplied by Visual Basic 5? (Hint: The subroutine header will match the **Name** property.)

EVENT PROCEDURES

Forms and controls have not only a predefined set of properties but also a set of events to which they will respond. Typically these events are generated by the user, for example, a mouse click, but they can also be generated by the system itself. Whenever you want an object to respond to an event, you put the instructions in an *event procedure*. Figure 1.15 shows a list of events that an OptionButton control (radio button) can respond to.

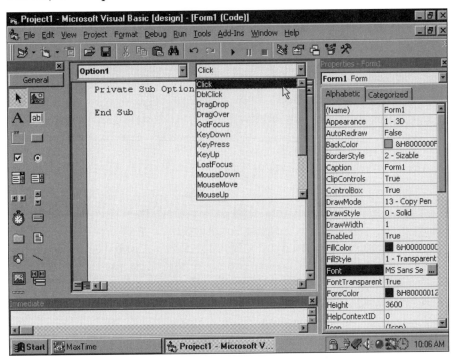

Figure 1.15 Events that an OptionButton control can respond to.

Notice that the top of the code page lists the form name **Form1**, then the object: **Option1**, and the Proc: **Click**. The procedure box lists all the events that are legal for the current object. The code page also displays a *code template* for the associated event procedure. What goes into the template is the code that will be executed when a form or control acknowledges that the particular event has occurred.

The procedure box will automatically show in boldface any event procedure that has code in it. This speeds up the debug cycle by enabling you to see quickly which events have already been written.

Go into the code template for the **Option1** control, select the dblClick event, and type: **Print "The party's over."** Now press F5 to run the program instantly. Double-click the mouse on the **Option1** control. The program responds by displaying "The party's over."

Visual Basic 5 knows which event procedure to execute by checking the *objectname_eventname* reference, in this case the **Option1_dblClick ()** event. Because of this close association, event procedures are said to be attached to controls and forms.

CHANGING PROPERTIES WITH CODE

Many of the properties listed in an object's property list can be changed while the application is executing. For example, instead of having the **Option1** control print "The party's over," you could change the caption on the button. All you would have to do is delete the print statement and add one line of code to the **Option1** button's **Option1_dblClick()** subroutine:

```
Option1.Caption = "The End"
```

The syntax for changing an object's properties using code is to use the object's name, followed by a period, then the property's name. On the right side of the assignment operator you put a legal substitute. Try entering the change described above and then run the program. Now when you run the program and click on the Option1 button its caption will change to "The End," as shown in Figure 1.16.

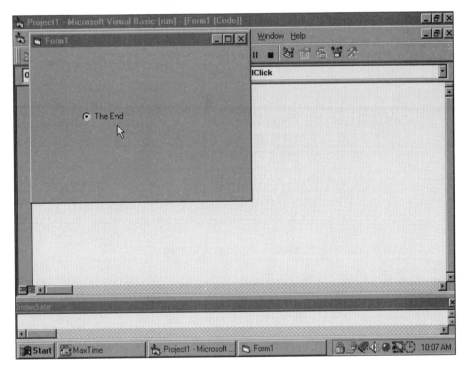

Figure 1.16 Changing a control's property from within a program.

SAVING FORMS AND PROJECTS

Every good programmer knows that you must save your work frequently. Visual Basic 5 has several save options shown in Table 1.2 that will allow you to manage a project selectively. All save options are listed under the File menu.

Table 1.2 Save Options

Save Option	Usage
Save Project	Saves all of the forms and modules for the current project, including the project file.
Save Project As...	Makes a duplicate project under the new name. Duplicates all forms, modules, and project files. The original project is left intact.

(continued)

Table 1.2 *(continued)*

Save Option	Usage
Save Form	Saves the current form or module.
Save Form As...	Makes a duplicate of the selected form or module. The original file is left intact. The newly created file will replace the original in the project file listing.

Files are saved in a binary format. In order to print the contents of a control, form, or module, use the File | Print menu sequence.

YOUR VISUAL BASIC 5 APPLICATIONS

When you combine imagination, programming expertise, and a few hours' time with Visual Basic 5, you will be able to design practical business applications like the example shown in Figure 1.17.

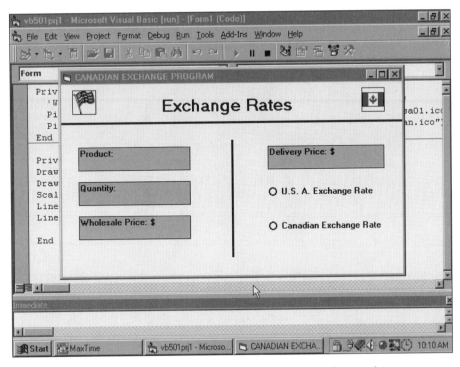

Figure 1.17 A simple business application designed with Visual Basic 5.

You might want to try your hand at a simple computer game, like the one shown in Figure 1.18.

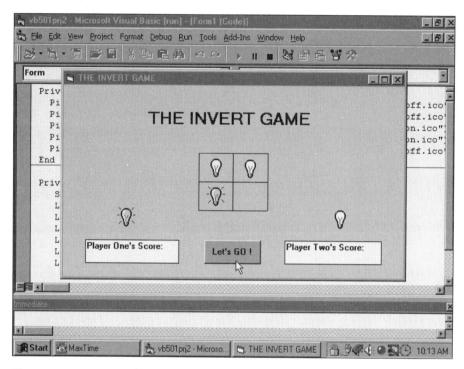

Figure 1.18 A simple computer game designed with Visual Basic 5.

As you begin your programming in Visual Basic 5, take time to enjoy this refreshing way to program. Visual Basic 5 is the better way to program for Windows 95 and NT!

Chapter 2

Creating User Interfaces

The user interface is the most important component of any application. To put it crudely, it is the user interface that is stuck in users' faces as they use your application. If the interface is well designed, your application will be easy, almost intuitive to use. Design the interface poorly, and users will start looking elsewhere for an easier-to-use product. It doesn't matter how slick the code is under the hood, if the visual appearance and ease of use aren't there, the product will be a flop. America Online (AOL) is a success story directly related to its user interface.

Visual Basic 5 includes a new Application Wizard that can aid in the creation of new Visual Basic projects. A special section is devoted to a discussion of the Application Wizard at the end of this chapter.

In this chapter, you will learn about the components that make up a good user interface. Many of these components were discussed briefly in Chapter 1.

ELEMENTS OF GOOD DESIGN

A well-designed software package almost anticipates your every move. Consider Visual Basic 5 itself. Here is software designed to be used!

You have probably also used software that was advertised as easy-to-use, only to find it impossible to cope with. We've thrown away word processors, communications software, and scanner software for this very reason; we're sure you have too.

The software had one fatal flaw, its visual appearance. The product gave you no hint of what you were supposed to do next. Cryptic commands, unclear instructions, and poorly written manuals make products a nightmare to use.

There are a couple of reasons for poorly designed products:

- The simplest yet most common reason for a design failure is one that we've all experienced: the deadline. How often have you said, "I could have…if only I had more time!"?

- Another reason involves the graphical interface. Once programmers leave the command-line prompt for the graphics interface, they have two programming chores: design the graphical interface and design the code to go with it. It can take the average programmer a considerable amount of time to learn a comprehensive palette of graphics subroutines. Then the programmer must typically learn how to write the code necessary for the end user's unique hardware configuration.

The sad truth is that good programmers can master all of this only to come up with a cluttered and confusing user interface. What happened? The average intelligent, well-trained programmer is not a commercial artist too. To design good interfaces, you need to understand the elements of a good graphical design.

In this and the next chapter you will be shown how to place various interface controls in forms using the elements of good design.

USING THE GRID

During the design of an application's interface the needed control objects are selected from the toolbox and placed on a form. If you looked closely at the blank forms used in Chapter 1, you probably noticed a background composed of dots. These dots form a user-definable grid. By using the optional grid you can visually align the controls as they are placed on the form.

Figure 2.1 shows the folder that is displayed when you select this option from the Tools | Options | General menu selection.

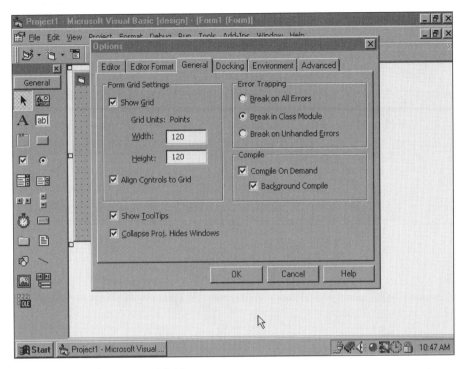

Figure 2.1 The General folder.

By changing the *Grid Width* and *Grid Height* parameters you can vary the distance between the dots. Larger values space the dots farther apart, smaller values do just the opposite. The *Show Grid* parameter determines whether the grid is displayed. The *Align Controls to Grid* parameter selects the grid's autoalignment mode. If you have selected this option, each time a new control is placed it will automatically jump to the nearest row-column marked by the grid.

Autoalignment can be a help or a hindrance depending on the types and sizes of your controls. Whenever you want to place a control between grid marks you have two options: You can turn autoalignment off or change the width and height settings for the grid dots. Turning autoalignment off leaves the grid displayed so that you can still orient yourself on the form. However, for critical applications, it's probably better to narrow the grid's dot settings so that each control lines up to the pixel.

CONTROL FUNDAMENTALS

Before starting this section, make certain that Visual Basic 5 is displaying a clean form. If Visual Basic 5 is not displaying a clean form, select File | New Project from the menu. We are going to work with a VB application, so do not select VB Application Wizard at this time. When you start Visual Basic 5, the toolbox is automatically displayed. Like any other window, it can be moved and closed as needed. Figure 2.2 shows the toolbox provided with the Enterprise version of Visual Basic 5. Your version of Visual Basic 5 may have a similar appearance.

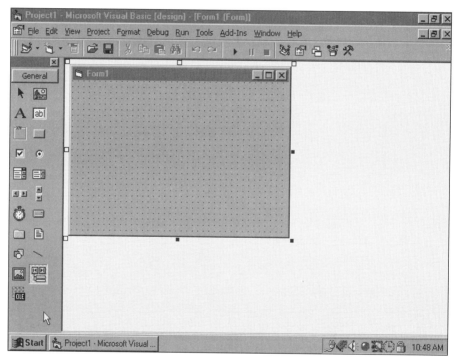

Figure 2.2 A toolbox of controls from the Enterprise version of Visual Basic 5.

Selecting a Control

Controls can be selected from the toolbox by using a single or double mouse click. Here is how the single-click technique works:

- Place the mouse pointer over the selected control and click once.
- Move the mouse pointer to the form.

- The mouse pointer will change into a cross hair.
- Move the cross hair to where you want the upper left corner of your control to begin.
- Press and hold the left mouse button.
- Drag the cross hair to the lower right corner of where you want the control to end.
- Release the mouse button.

The double-click technique has more to do with knowing ahead of time how many and what types of controls are needed. Here is how the double-click technique works:

- Place the mouse pointer over the selected control and press the left button twice.
- The control will automatically appear in the center of the form.
- Repeat the first two steps as needed.
- Each time you select a new control it will automatically appear in the center of the form, overlaying any previously created controls.
- Move to the center of the form, after you have selected all of the controls needed.
- Starting with the form's top control, move and size.
- The controls will be displayed in turn in reverse order from the way they were selected, similarly to removing cards from the top of a deck.

Although the double-click approach can save time by eliminating the back-and-forth movement of the mouse pointer between the tool-box and the form, it is usually confusing to the novice user. We suggest using the single-click technique.

Moving and Resizing Controls

After a control has been placed on a form it can be moved and sized by using the mouse pointer. Figure 2.3 shows a default size TextBox control that was placed on the form using the double-click technique. Recall that the TextBox control is the one with the "ab" in the icon. Now, notice that the frame of the control has a dark border with eight strategically placed "handles."

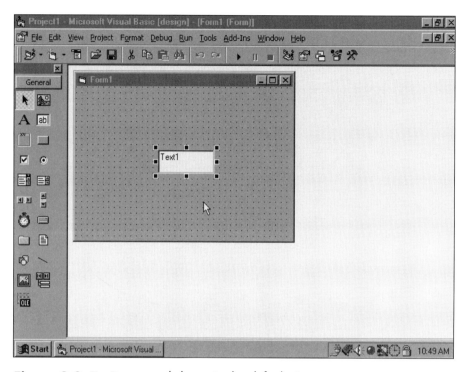

Figure 2.3 TextBox control shown in the default size.

The simplest action you can take with a control is to move it. By placing the mouse over the center of the control and holding down the left mouse button, you can move the control to a new location on the form.

Resizing a control is just about as easy. The handles in the center of the horizontal frame edges are used to change the height of the control. The handles in the center of the vertical frame edges are used to change a control's width. Handles on the diagonal corners are used to change a control's height and width simultaneously. At this point you should stop and practice both moving and resizing the TextBox control control.

The 1/4" Control

Windows almost demands that users adapt to the point-and-click graphical interface. There are a few complaints, however. These complaints are the result of a poor interface design rather than an inherent weakness in Windows.

One area that demands designer attention has to do with the ease of activating a program's control options. Complaints arise when control options are too small, are too hard to hit, or congest the screen. How much fun can it be for users to aim their roller ball mouse at a 1/4" square button labeled EXIT, while holding their laptops on the commuter plane?

The good design solution is obvious! Make your controls big enough to be easily activated and place controls in an uncluttered manner on the form.

Deleting a Control

If for some reason you decide that you do not want a particular control on the form, the control can easily be deleted. There are two ways to delete a control. The first technique for deleting a control involves selecting the control by clicking the mouse on it. Once the focus is on the control, press the **Del** key or choose the Edit | Delete menu option.

The second technique is also useful for deleting multiple controls at the same time. Here, the only difference needed to delete several controls is that the **Ctrl** key is held down as each unwanted object is selected. To remove the group of unwanted controls, either press **Del** or use the Edit | Delete menu sequence.

Duplicating Controls

When it is necessary to duplicate a control's design across forms or even across applications, Visual Basic 5 is designed to make this a simple process. First, the item(s) to be duplicated is selected. Next, use the Edit | Copy menu sequence followed by the Edit | Paste sequence. The item(s) will then be cloned into the target file.

A SIMPLE SALES TAX CALCULATOR

One of the most addicting features of Visual Basic 5 is the ease with which you can create an application's visual interface. Figure 2.4 shows a simple Sales Tax Calculator design that can be completed in less than 10 minutes.

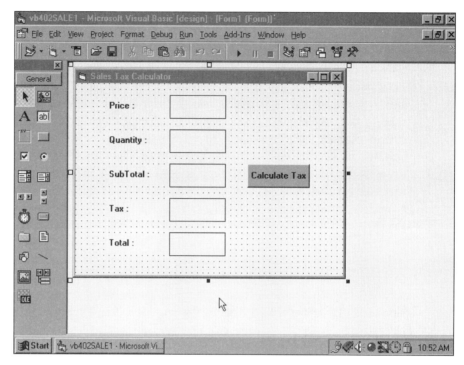

Figure 2.4 The design of a simple Sales Tax Calculator.

In the next sections you'll learn how to design this form, step by step. The Sales Tax Calculator design uses only three types of controls: one CommandButton control, five Label controls, and five TextBox controls. The first two TextBox controls are used to input an item's price and quantity sold. The last three TextBox controls are used to display a subtotal, tax for the item(s), and a total. Each of the five Label controls is used to identify clearly what each TextBox control contains. The CommandButton control signals the calculator to generate and display the final results. As you view Figure 2.4, notice that the size of the calculator's display has been designed to be smaller than the default form size.

Sizing a Form

To begin developing the calculator's interface, select the File | New Project menu sequence. The first step in a good design is to visualize the size of the final interface and then size the form appropriately.

It seems that no matter what project you are developing the application has a unique interface size. As an example, consider an event timer or calculator. An event timer could be used simply to flash an entire screen with the message "Meeting on Tuesday at 1:00 PM." The Sales Tax Calculator was designed with a small window size because there were only a few controls on its form.

It is recommended that a form be sized before placing controls. This is important because Visual Basic 5 treats a control's user-defined dimensions as an unchangeable parameter. Thus, resizing a form does not automatically adjust the form's contents. When a form is resized, the controls will have to be repositioned, manually, one at a time.

To size a form, place the mouse pointer over the appropriate form border and wait until the image changes to a bidirectional arrow. Click the mouse and pull the border to its new location.

To start your design process, start with a new form in Visual Basic 5 and size the form to the approximate shape of the form shown previously in Figure 2.4.

Selecting and Placing Label Control Controls

The first control to be placed is a Label control. This is the control with a large "A" for an icon in the toolbox. Click the mouse pointer over the Label control icon in the toolbox. Now, move the mouse pointer onto the form, placing the cross hair where you want the upper left corner of the Label control to begin. Next, hold the mouse button down while dragging the mouse to the lower right edge of the displayed rectangle until you have created and sized the Label control. Release the mouse button. Design your control so that your form now looks like Figure 2.5.

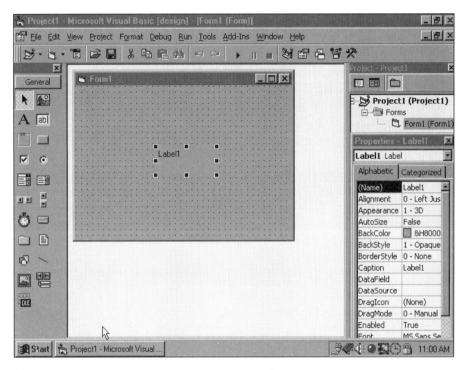

Figure 2.5 The Label control is placed on a form.

   The next four Label controls, needed by the calculator, are going to be designed using the double-click method. Move the mouse pointer back to the toolbox and double-click on the Label icon four times. Notice that each time you select the control it automatically appears labeled (**Label2..Label5**) in the center of the form. When you are finished, **Label5** will be the form's bottommost control. Now, simply move and size each control until it takes on the appearance of Figure 2.6.

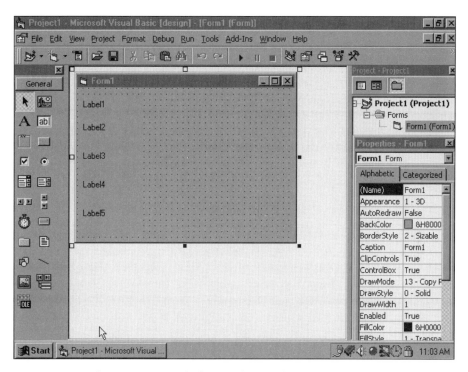

Figure 2.6 The remaining Label controls are placed.

Selecting and Placing TextBox Controls

The process for selecting a TextBox control (the control that uses the "ab" for an icon) or any other control in the toolbox is the same as the process used to place Label controls. Finish the Sales Tax Calculator by placing the remaining controls. Its final appearance should resemble Figure 2.4, shown earlier. You will need to add five TextBox control controls and one command control (a small empty rounded rectangle) to complete the form.

WORKING WITH ADDITIONAL CONTROLS

Before you can become proficient at designing a good interface you need to gain experience selecting, placing, and sizing other controls. In this section you will learn to select other popular controls, learn about any peculiarities in placing them, and learn what they are used for.

Remember, although the forms and controls are complete, no code has been attached to make the program operational. In Chapters 3 and 4 you will learn how to modify and link code to each control.

Frame Control

Frames are used either to group logically related controls graphically or to subdivide a form visually. When related controls are to be grouped, it is important to place the Frame control on the form first, then overlay the Frame control with other controls. If this technique is used, every time the Frame control is moved, all controls associated with it will move too.

To enable this synchronous movement of a Frame control and its associated controls you *must* use the single-click approach to place the controls in the Frame control. The single-click method allows you to create the control directly within the frame. The double-click method will not work because, by default, it places the control in the center of the form, not within the Frame control!

A proper Frame control design will also allow you to copy an entire group from one form to another with predictable results. If a control is placed with the double-click method, it will be left out of any duplicated Frame controls. Figure 2.7 shows a Frame control being used to group five related controls graphically.

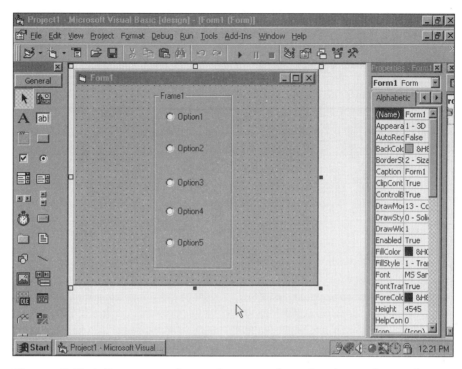

Figure 2.7 A Frame control is used to group five related controls on a form.

CheckBox Control

The CheckBox control (a rectangle with a check mark in it) is used to present the user with a list of items that can be individually selected. Figure 2.8 shows an example of how CheckBox controls can be used to obtain a user's boat preferences. The important characteristic to remember about this type of control is that any, all, or none of the listed items may be selected.

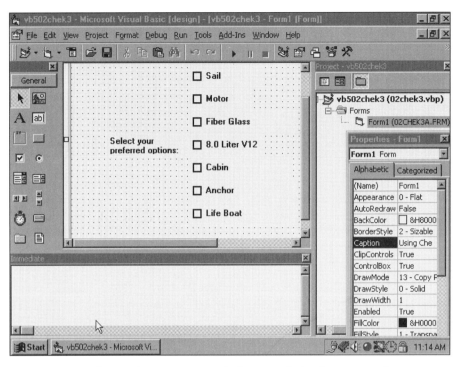

Figure 2.8 Selecting boat options with the use of CheckBox controls.

The key to good design when using CheckBox controls is to keep the check options to a minimum and make sure they are logically related. The form, shown earlier in Figure 2.8, would have been less effective if it had presented the user with 20 options.

You may ask, "Why not use a Frame control to group those CheckBox controls?" A Frame control could be a valid choice for a form that has two or three logically related categories of this type of control. Since the form, shown in Figure 2.8, had only one category of options, a Frame control was unnecessary.

Would a Frame control have hurt the form's design? Probably not! A well-designed form is like a well-documented program: There is neither too little information nor too much! Putting a Frame control around the CheckBox controls might have added little extra under-standing to the overall interface.

OptionButton Control

The OptionButton control (a radio button or "bull's-eye" icon) allows the user to make one choice in a group. This control is different from a CheckBox control, which allows the user to choose as many items as desired.

An OptionButton control, sometimes called a radio button, differs from a CheckBox control in one other area: One option must always be selected in the group. The analogy with a car's radio buttons works quite well. A radio always has one station selected, and any new selection cancels the previous one.

Rules for good design when placing OptionButton controls are the same as those for placing CheckBox controls. Keep the design simple and logical. Be careful not to use OptionButton controls whenever the application really needs CheckBox controls. Also, the first OptionButton control that is placed in a group will be the one the program chooses as its default (it receives the "focus"). The default can be changed, but you'll have to write a little code to do it. Figure 2.9 shows the proper use and a valid graphical layout for several OptionButton controls.

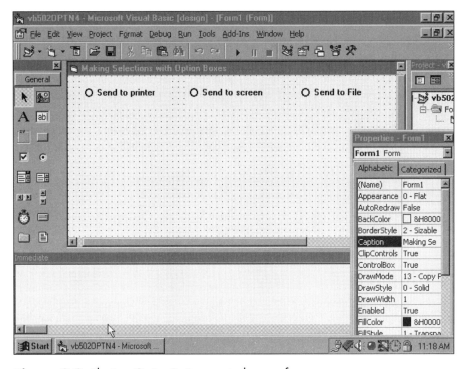

Figure 2.9 Placing OptionButton controls on a form.

ComboBox Control (Three Styles)

A ComboBox control (an icon with several small rectangular areas) combines the characteristics of a TextBox control and a ListBox control. With a ComboBox control the user can type in a selection or go to the list and pick an item directly.

ComboBox controls have three styles that allow you to tailor the application's interface. Figure 2.10 shows the three styles in order: Style = 0 (default), Style = 1, and Style = 2. Style = 0 creates a ComboBox control that has both an edit window and a drop-down list. Style = 1 is similar, with the exception that it simultaneously displays the edit window and the list. Style = 2 will produce a drop-down list only and has no editing capabilities. With this last style the user must choose one of the listed options.

Note: Only Style = 1 ComboBox controls can be resized horizontally and vertically. The other two styles will permit you to change their widths only.

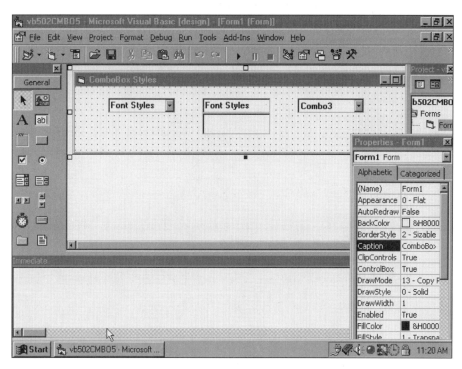

Figure 2.10 ComboBox controls come in three styles.

There are two considerations when creating a form that uses ComboBox controls. First, the appropriate style of ComboBox control must be selected for the particular application. Second, there must be enough room left, on the form (Style = 1) or later when the program is running (Style = 0, 2), to display the list. Care should be taken when placing the last two ComboBox styles so that at run time the displayed list will not cover critically important screen output.

ListBox Control

A ListBox control (the icon has four small rectangles grouped together) displays a catalog of items from which only one can be selected. If the list is longer than the dimensioned ListBox, Visual Basic 5 will automatically add a scroll bar. ListBox controls, unlike ComboBox controls, do not expand down the screen when active. This makes placing a ListBox control much simpler, because the size you see on the design form is the size displayed at run time. Figure 2.11 shows the use of a ListBox control.

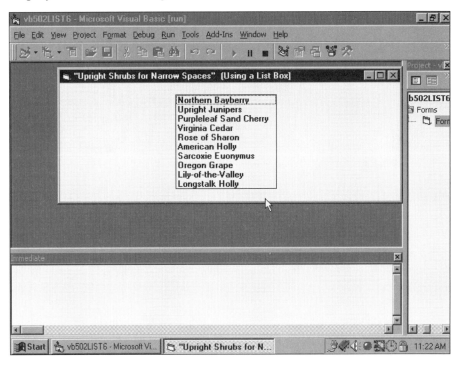

Figure 2.11 Using a ListBox control.

Horizontal and Vertical Scroll Bar Controls

Scroll bar controls, VScrollBar control and HScrollBar control (an icon with two vertical or horizontal rectangles containing arrows), allow the user to move graphically through a range of items. This range may be physical space as in word processor pages or values such as those used to describe colors for rendering a picture. Figure 2.12 shows several scroll bars with descriptive frames.

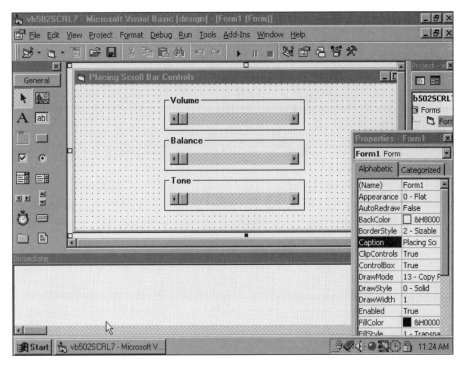

Figure 2.12 Several scroll bar controls placed on a form.

Horizontal and vertical scroll bar controls are placed on a form using the same design techniques as other controls. They can be resized in both width and height. They are better substitutes for TextBox controls whenever the input values are unknown by the user. For example, changing control colors with user-defined input requires a knowledge of system color codes. However, a scroll bar allows the user to make these selections without requiring any foreknowledge of valid code settings.

Timer Control

Figure 2.13 shows a Timer control (an icon with a clock face) on the form under design.

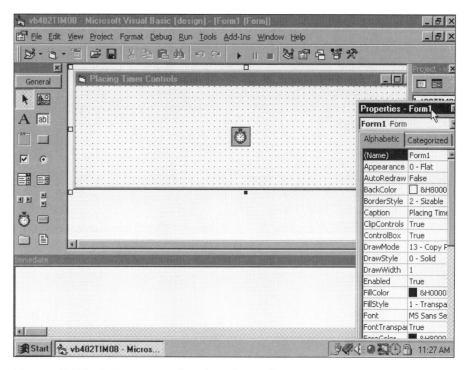

Figure 2.13 A Timer control is placed on a form.

When applications are run, Timer controls are not visible, as are other controls. Timer controls are used to respond to the timer **Interval** property, which represents the passing of time. They are used to execute code at regular time intervals.

DriveListBox Control

Figure 2.14 shows a DriveListBox control (an icon with the face of a disk drive).

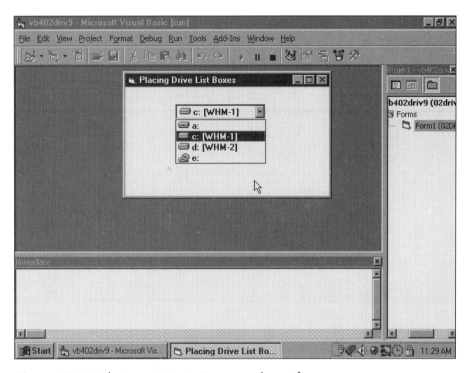

Figure 2.14 Placing a DriveListBox control on a form.

The DriveListBox control allows the user to select an active drive from the list displayed. DriveListBox controls are frequently used with directory and FileListBox controls to give a fully functional drive/directory/file view and selection capability to an application. Only the DriveListBox control's width can be changed at design time.

Care should be taken when designing a form with a DriveListBox control. DriveListBox controls use a drop-down list when activated, and it is possible for a poorly placed list to obscure important screen output.

DirListBox Control

Figure 2.15 shows a DirListBox control (an icon with the appearance of a file folder).

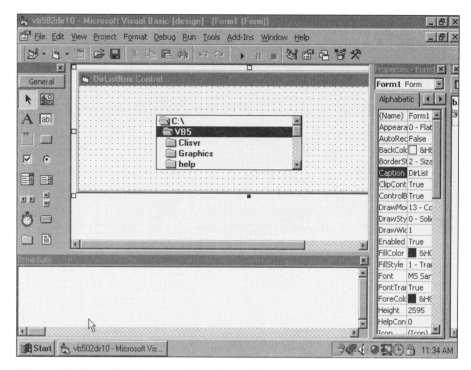

Figure 2.15 A DirListBox is placed on a form.

A DirListBox control is used to display the active drive's directories and paths at run time.

The DirListBox is sized on the form at design time. If the directory hierarchy will not fit in the predefined ListBox boundaries, Visual Basic 5 will automatically add scroll bars. A good form design will place the DirListBox control near the DriveListBox control, as shown in Figure 2.16.

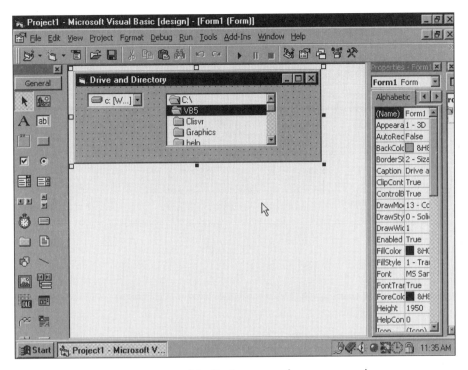

Figure 2.16 DriveListBox and DirListBox controls are grouped near each other.

FileListBox Control

Usually FileListBox controls (an icon that represents a piece of paper with a turned edge) are used with DriveListBox and DirListBox controls. FileListBox controls display the currently active drive/path's files, as shown in Figure 2.17.

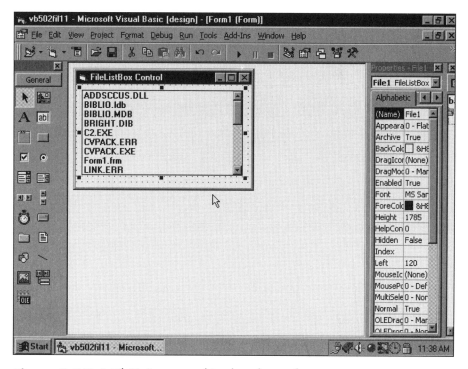

Figure 2.17 A FileListBox control is placed on a form.

In conjunction with a dialog box, the file's contents can be modified using the standard attribute wild card searches, such as *.EXE. Figure 2.18 shows a typical trio of DriveListBox, DirListBox, and FileListBox controls.

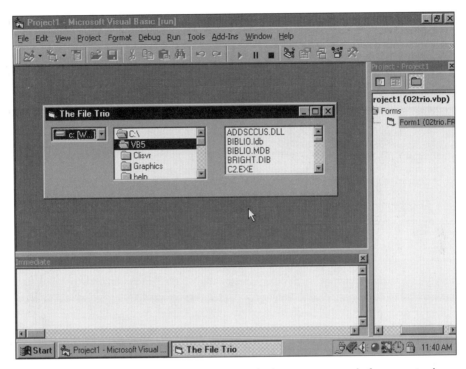

Figure 2.18 DriveListBox, DirListBox, and FileListBox controls form a trio that allows complete file selection capabilities.

VB APPLICATION WIZARD

The VB Application Wizard is a tool that can aid good user interface design when projects get large and complicated. You may even use it for simple applications.

The VB Application Wizard is an automated interface designer that makes it easy to create consistently styled projects containing single or multiple interfaces, a variety of menu options, World Wide Web (WWW) access, form control, and database access. During design time you may choose any or all of these options. When you design projects with the VB Application Wizard, each project's appearance (interface) will comply with Microsoft's standards for Windows applications.

To start the VB Application Wizard, use the File | New Project menu selection. Then select the VB Application Wizard as shown in Figure 2.19.

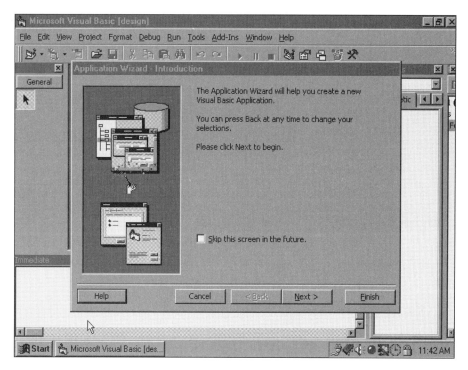

Figure 2.19 Use the VB Application Wizard to build projects automatically.

The VB Application Wizard will now present you with a series of choices in order to customize your project's design.

The first choice involves the interface type. In Figure 2.20, notice that we selected the Single Document Interface (SDI).

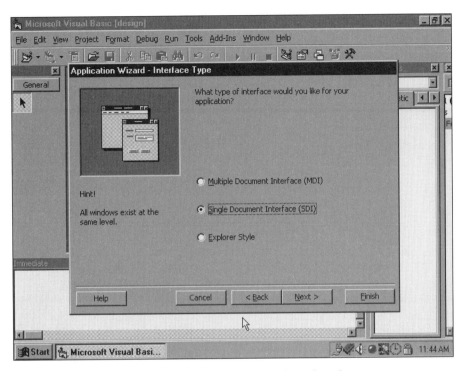

Figure 2.20 A Single Document Interface is selected as the project's interface type.

This is the best option for projects running under Windows 95 and Windows NT, since all windows will exist at the same level of precedence. Each of the other options is explained when the OptionButton control is selected for that option.

The second choice determines whether your project will have a menu. Several menu items can be included. In Figure 2.21, you will notice that we selected all of the menu options.

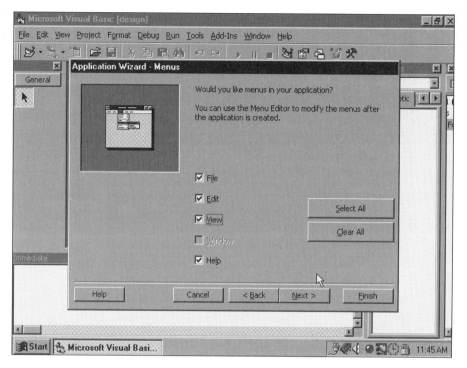

Figure 2.21 The project will include a menu bar with all of the checked drop-down menus.

If your project will contain large quantities of strings, you are given the option of placing those strings in a resource file. For small projects, this option does not need to be used. Figure 2.22 shows that we will not place strings in a separate file.

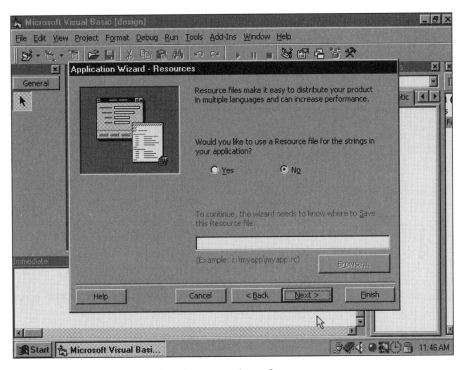

Figure 2.22 Projects with a large number of strings can use a separate resource file.

Projects that would benefit from a separate resource file for strings would be those involving word processing, databases, and so on.

Does the user of your application need access to the World Wide Web (WWW)? If so, support for that access can be built into your application. In this example, we declined WWW support, as you can see in Figure 2.23.

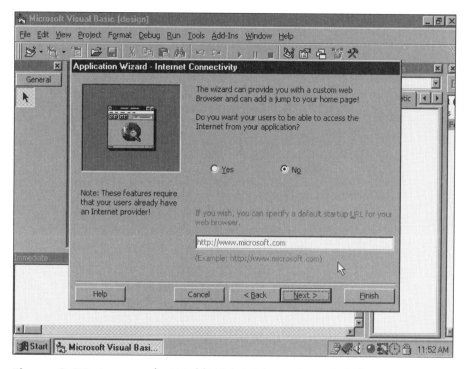

Figure 2.23 Access to the World Wide Web can be included in your project.

It is also possible to include a variety of forms. The Standard Forms dialog box lets you select from a number of predefined options. In our example, no forms are selected, as you can see in Figure 2.24.

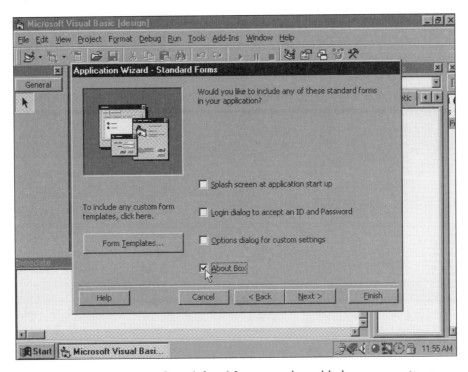

Figure 2.24 A variety of predefined forms can be added to your project.

Predefined forms allow a number of options including login screens, custom settings, and so on. Experiment with these forms. By using predefined forms you maintain consistency across all of your projects.

It is even possible to access various databases from within a Visual Basic application. The Data Access Forms dialog box permits the selection of a database, such as Access, for your project. In our example, no database access was requested, as shown in Figure 2.25.

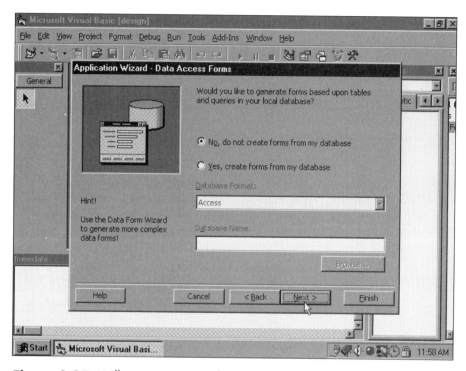

Figure 2.25 Will your project need to access a database? Let the Application Wizard include the necessary interface.

Finally, the VB Application Wizard has all of the information necessary to design your custom user interface. The last option allows you to name the project and view a summary report of the project that will be created when the Finish button is pushed. Figure 2.26 shows our selections for the sample project.

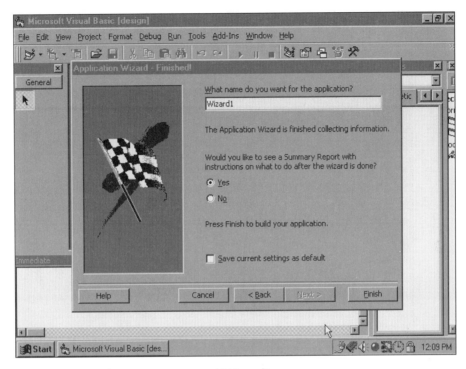

Figure 2.26 This project is named Wizard1.

Remember, to this point we have not seen a form or moved a control from the toolbox. When you select Finish, however, the VB Application Wizard will build a complete application with all of the interface features that you selected.

Figure 2.27 shows our project, designed to our specifications by the VB Application Wizard.

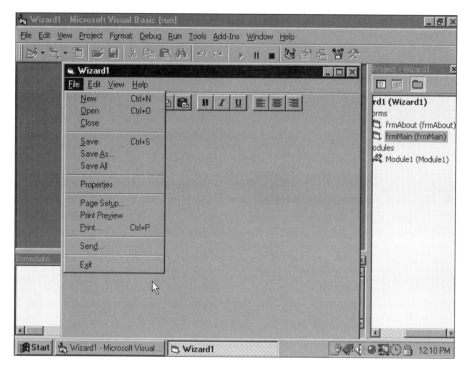

Figure 2.27 The user interface for the Wizard1 project designed completely by the VB Application Wizard.

Now run the application and make several menu selections. What do you mean, "Nothing works"? Well, of course it doesn't! You haven't written any code to respond to the menu selections or other project options. You'll learn how to do this in the next two chapters.

The VB Application Wizard is an interface design tool capable of designing consistent user interfaces from one project to another. You, however, must still provide the code for your project.

CREATING A "GOOD DESIGN"

Now that you are familiar with the most popular controls in the toolbox and the VB Application Wizard, experiment with other controls available in your Visual Basic 5 toolbox. Regardless of which controls you use, good design suggests the rules that follow.

When laying out an application's interface the most important rule to remember is: Keep it simple.

- Good form design should be similar to good subroutine design: It should do neither too much nor too little.
- Explain screen output by using labels, meaningful command names, and titled frames.
- Don't use cluttered forms. If necessary, break the interface down into two or more forms.
- Check that controls with run-time drop-down lists do not cover up critical screen output.
- Properly size and place each control—be consistent.
- Select the correct control for the task.
- Use as few controls as is absolutely necessary.

WHAT'S COMING

In the next two chapters you will learn how to modify control properties and add code to your applications in order to interface with controls.

Chapter 3

Altering Interface Properties

Interface properties describe the characteristics of a form or control. Forms and controls are provided with default properties that can be changed to enhance and customize an application.

In this chapter you will learn about properties and how to alter them to fit an application's particular needs.

PROPERTIES

In Chapter 2, you learned how to design forms and place controls in a Visual Basic 5 Windows application. The first step in designing an application is to lay out the application's visual interface. At this point the preliminary design is limited to three traits: the controls selected, their placement, and their initial size. Next, you will learn how to enhance a control's appearance and define its behavior.

Every form and control you create comes equipped with a predefined set of characteristics called properties. This property list is unique for each object (form or control) type. While many objects share common traits such as color, size, and screen position, they also have unique attributes. For example, only horizontal and vertical scroll bars have a **SmallChange** property that tells the application how far to scroll the screen image when the user clicks on the up or down arrow.

Default values are automatically assigned to each property when an object is created. For example, Label, Text, Frame, and Command controls are automatically assigned a font size of 8 points. Under most circumstances these initial values will work fine throughout the execution of an application. You do not need to change any or all of the properties on an object if the default values are acceptable.

PROPERTY DETAILS

If properties must be changed, use the Properties dialog box first discussed in Chapter 1. To customize an application's controls, however, you need to understand how the various properties are used.

The list in Table 3.1 briefly describes each property and shows any default values. It is important for you to study the descriptions. Properties are like little automatically invoked pieces of code. Good application design requires an understanding of how to use and set properties.

Table 3.1 Control and Form Properties with Descriptions

Property	Description
ActiveControl	This property is a read-only run-time property. It returns whichever control has the focus. It is invalid if all of the form's controls are disabled or invisible. It is not available at design time.
ActiveForm	This property is identical to the ActiveControl property except that the currently active form is returned. It is invalid if no forms are loaded.
Alignment	This property sets or returns the alignment of text in a label (default = 0, left justify). A value of 1 selects right justification, and 2 selects autocentering.
Archive, Hidden, Normal, ReadOnly, System	These properties are used for file list objects only. The prop erty determines whether a file list box contains files with the attribute selected (Archive, Normal, and ReadOnly, default = -1, display files with attribute set). A value of 0 turns off the listing of files with these attributes. For Hidden and System properties the default = 0, do not display files with these attributes.

(continued)

Table 3.1 *(continued)*

Property	Description
AutoRedraw	This property is used by forms and picture objects to set or return output from graphics methods (default = 0, disables automatic repainting of an object and writes graphics or print output only to the screen). A value of -1 enables automatic repainting of a form or picture object. Output is sent to the screen and to an image stored in memory. All repainting is done using this memory image.
Autosize	This property is used by label and picture controls. It is used to decide whether a control is automatically resized to fit its contents (default = 0, keep control's size constant, clipping any area outside the boundary). A value of -1 instructs Visual Basic 5 to resize the control automatically to fit its contents.
BackColor	This property is used by all controls except scroll bar and time objects. This property sets or returns the background color of an object.
BorderStyle	This property is a read-only property at run time. It is used to set the border style of forms, labels (run-time write), picture, and text objects (default = 2, a sizable border). A value of 0 specifies no border, 1 selects a fixed single-line border, and 3 draws a fixed double-line border.
Cancel	This property is for command object only. If a command button is the Cancel button on a form default = 0, turns this capability off. A value of -1 is returned when the command button is the Cancel button and the Default button for the form.
Caption	This property can be used by all forms and controls with captions that choose to display text in a way appropriate to each control. By setting or changing this property an application can vary a control's meaning.
Checked	This property is used with menus only. It determines whether a check mark is to be displayed next to a menu item (default = 0, does not display a check mark next to the item). A value of -1 draws the check mark.
ControlBox	This property is a run-time read-only property. It determines whether a control menu box appears on a form at run time (default = -1, display the control menu box). A value of 0 prevents the object from being displayed.

(continued)

Table 3.1 *(continued)*

Property	*Description*
CtlName	This property is used by all control objects. It identifies each object in code. All CtlNames must begin with a letter and can be a maximum of 40 characters, including underscore and alphanumeric characters.
CurrentX, CurrentY	These are run time-only properties. They set or return a form, picture box, or printer object's current horizontal (CurrentX) and vertical (CurrentY) screen or page coordinates.
Default	This property is used for command controls only. It decides which Command button is the default button on a form.
DragIcon	The property is used by all controls except timer objects. It sets or returns the image icon that is to be displayed during a drag-and-drop operation (default = none, uses the default pointer). An *.ICO file extension and format can be displayed if specified.
DragMode	This property is used by all controls except timer objects. DragMode selects automatic or manual dragging mode for a drag-and-drop operation (default = 0, manual). A value of 1 selects automatic mode. In this mode the control does not respond to mouse clicks in the usual manner. Instead, it allows the user to move the icon on the form.
DrawMode	This property is reserved for form, picture, and printer objects. It selects or returns the appearance of any output produced by a graphics method (default = 13, copy pen, output pen color matches selected ForeColor property). Here are the values for the DrawMode Property settings:

Value	Meaning
1	Blackness (all black output)
2	Not Merge Pen (inverse output to 15—Merge Pen)
3	Mask Not Pen (output combines colors in display and the inverse of the pen color)
4	Not Copy Pen (inverse of pen color)
5	Mask Pen Not (output combines colors in pen and the inverse of the display)
6	Invert (inverse of display color)

(continued)

Table 3.1 *(continued)*

Property	Description
	7 Xor Pen (output is colors in pen and in display but not in both)
	8 Not Mask Pen (output is the inverse of Mask Pen Color)
	9 Mask Pen (output is colors common to both the pen and display)
	10 Not Xor Pen (output is the inverse of Xor Pen colors)
	11 Nop (no operation—turns drawing off, output remains unchanged)
	12 Merge Not Pen (output is combination of inverse of the pen color and display color)
	13 Copy Pen (default—output color is determined by the ForeColor property)
	14 Merge Pen Not (output is combination of the inverse of the display and the pen color)
	15 Merge Pen (output is combination of display color and pen color)
	16 Whiteness (output is white)
	The DrawMode property is used to vary the visual effects created when drawing with the **Pset**, **Circle**, and **Line** methods.
DrawStyle	This property sets the line style graphics methods used by form, picture, and printer objects. Here are the values for the DrawStyle settings:
	Value Meaning
	0 Solid (Default)
	1 Dashed
	2 Dotted
	3 Dash-dot
	4 Dash-dot-dot
	5 Invisible
	6 Inside solid

(continued)

Table 3.1 *(continued)*

Property	Description
	Note however, that if the associated DrawWidth property is set to a value greater than one, DrawStyles 0 through 4 will produce only solid lines.
DrawWidth	This property is used for form, picture, and printer objects. It sets the line width for graphics output methods. The default value is 1, which equals one pixel's width.
Drive	This property is used only with drive list boxes and sets or returns the selected drive at run time. This property is not available during the design of a form. The property returns a string representing the floppy disk ("a:" or "b:", etc.), fixed disk ("c:[volume id]"), or network connection ("x:\\server\share").
Enabled	This property applies to all controls and forms. The property decides whether the form or control is allowed to respond to user-generated events such as keyboard entry or a mouse click (default = -1, signals that the object can respond to events). A value of 0 inhibits the object from responding.
FileName	This property is valid only for file list boxes. The property sets or returns the selected file from the list portion of a file list box.
FillColor	This property is only for form, picture, and printer objects. It can set the color used by the **Circle** and **Line** graphics methods to fill circles and boxes.
FillStyle	This property sets or returns the pattern to be used to fill circles and boxes that are created with the **Circle** and **Line** draw methods. The property is valid only for form, picture, and printer objects.
FontBold, FontItalic, FontStrikethru, FontTransparent, FontUnderline	These properties apply to all controls except scroll bars and timers. They determine the displayed font's characteristics: **FontBold**, *FontItalic*, ~~FontStrikethru~~, and <u>FontUnderline</u>. FontTransparent specifies whether background text or graphics are included along with the selected font. This last property is valid only for form, picture, and printer objects. FontBold and FontTransparent (default = -1, on). FontItalic, FontStrikethru, and FontUnderline (default = 0, off).
FontCount	This property is used only with screen and printer objects. It returns the number of available fonts for the selected output device. This is a read-only run-time characteristic.

(continued)

Table 3.1 *(continued)*

Property	Description
FontName	This property is valid for all form and control objects except scroll bars and timers. The property sets or returns the name of the output display font (default font is determined by the operating environment).
Fonts	This property is for screen and printer objects. It returns the available fonts for the selected device. This read-only run-time property returns a string array with from 0 to FontCount -1 entries.
FontSize	This property is used to set or return the selected font's point size. This property is valid for all form and control objects except timers and scroll bars.
ForeColor	This property is used by all form and control objects except commands, scroll bars, and timers. The property sets or returns the foreground color used to display the object's text or graphics.
FormName	This property is used only by form objects. It sets the identifier to be used when accessing a form within code. The string returned is not available at run time. The FormName is separate from a form's Caption property.
hDC	This property is a read-only run-time property. It is used by form, picture, and printer objects to return a device context handle used by Windows API calls.
Height	This property is used by all objects except timer controls and returns the control's height. For forms this includes the title bar. For printers this run-time read-only value indicates the physical dimensions of the paper. For screen objects this run time–only value returns the height of the screen.
Hidden	(see Archive property)
hWnd	This property is used by form objects only. It returns a handle to a form. This run-time read-only value is provided by the operating system.
Icon	This property is a write-only property at design time and a read-only property at run time. It returns the icon that is displayed whenever a form is minimized.

(continued)

Table 3.1 *(continued)*

Property	Description
Image	This property is used by form and picture boxes. It is a run-time read-only property that returns a handle to a persistent bitmap. This is an operating environment handle returned by Microsoft Windows.
Index	This property is a run-time read-only property. It is used by all controls to identify uniquely a control from within a control array.
Interval	This property sets or returns the number of milliseconds in a timer's countdown interval. A value of 0 disables the timer. If the timer's Enabled property is set to -1 (TRUE), every interval of 1000 equals one second. The maximum value allowed is 65,535 or just over one minute. You can have a maximum of 16 timers in Windows.
LargeChange, SmallChange	These properties are used by both vertical and horizontal scroll bars. When the user clicks the mouse between the scroll box and scroll arrow, LargeChange reports the amount of change. SmallChange returns the amount of change when the user clicks a scroll arrow (default = 1).
Left, Top	These properties are used by all controls except timers. They return the distance between the internal left and top edge of an object (respectively) and the left and top edge of its container. For controls, the value returned is measured in system coordinate units. Forms return a value that is expressed in twips.
LinkItem	This property is used by the label, picture, and text box controls. The property is used to specify what data is to be passed to a client control in a DDE communication with another application.
LinkMode	This property is used by form, label, picture, and text box controls to decide the type of link used for the dynamic data exchange (DDE) conversation.
LinkTimeout	This property is used by label, picture, and text box objects to decide the amount of time a control waits for a response from a DDE message.
LinkTopic	This property determines the name of the application and the subject of the DDE conversation link for form, label, picture, and text box controls.

(continued)

Table 3.1 *(continued)*

Property	*Description*
List	This property sets or returns the list of items contained in a combo, list, directory, drive, or file list box.
ListCount	This property is a run-time read-only property. It is used together with the List property. ListCount returns the number of items contained in a combo, list, directory, drive, or file list box.
ListIndex	This property is a run-time property that sets or returns the index of the currently selected item in a combo, directory, drive, file, or list box control.
Max, Min	These properties are used by both horizontal and vertical scroll bar controls to determine the bar's maximum and minimum value. The valid range specifies a value between - 32,768 and 32,767 inclusive (defaults = 32,767 Max and 0 Min).
MaxButton, MinButton	These properties are used by form objects only. They decide whether or not the Maximize and Minimize buttons are displayed (default = -1, which displays the button). A value of 0 turns the button off.
MousePointer	This property is used to set or return the type of mouse pointer that is displayed when the pointer is over the associated object at run time. Here are valid values for this property:

Value	Meaning
0	(Default) The shape is determined by the control
1	Arrow
2	Cross hairs
3	I-beam
4	Small square-within-square icon
5	Four-pointed arrow
6	Double arrow (northeast/southwest)
7	Double arrow (north/south)
8	Double arrow (northwest/southeast)
9	Double arrow (east/west)
10	Up arrow

(continued)

Table 3.1 *(continued)*

Property	Description
	11 Hourglass (wait)
	12 No drop
MultiLine	This property is a read-only property. It specifies whether a text box can display and accept multiple lines of text (default = 0, data must fit on one line, ignores carriage return). A value of 1 activates multiline mode.
Normal	(see Archive)
Page	This property is a read-only property at run time. It indicates which page is to receive output.
Parent	This property is a run-time read-only property. It is used by all controls to return the form on which the control is located.
Path	This property is used by list and file box objects. It sets or returns the current path.
Pattern	This property is for list box controls only. It specifies which files are to be displayed. The default search pattern is (*.*).
Picture	This property is for forms and picture controls only. This write-only property is used to indicate which graphic is to be displayed in the Selected control (default = none, no picture displayed).
ReadOnly	(see Archive)
ScaleHeight, ScaleWidth	These properties are used by forms and picture and printer controls. They set or return the range of the vertical (ScaleHeight) and horizontal (ScaleWidth) axes for an object's internal coordinate system.
ScaleLeft, ScaleTop	These properties are used by form, picture, and printer objects to set or return the horizontal (ScaleLeft) or vertical (ScaleTop) coordinates describing the left and top corners of an object's internal area.
ScaleMode	This property is used by form, picture, and printer objects to set or return the units in an object's coordinate system. Here are the valid settings:
	Value Meaning
	0 Indicates that the ScaleHeight/Width/Left/Top has been directly set by the user.

(continued)

Table 3.1 *(continued)*

Property	*Description*
	1 (Default) twip; there are 1440 twips per logical inch.
	2 Point; there are 72 points per logical inch.
	3 Pixel
	4 Character, with 120 twips in the x coordinate, 240 in the y coordinate.
	5 Inch
	6 Millimeter
	7 Centimeter
ScaleWidth	(see ScaleHeight)
ScrollBars	This property is a run-time read-only property. It is used to determine whether a text box has vertical or horizontal scroll bars (default = 0, none). A value of 1 sets horizontal, 2 vertical, 3 both scroll bars.
SelLength, SelStart, SelText	These properties apply only to combo and text box objects. Sel is an abbreviation for selected. SelLength sets or returns the number of characters selected. SelStart sets or returns the starting point of the selected text. SelText sets or returns the string holding the currently selected text.
SmallChange	(see LargeChange)
Sorted	This property is only for combo and list box controls that have the Sorted property. It selects automatic alphabetic sorting of the object's list (default = 0, do not sort). A value of -1 (True) activates sorting.
Style	(see description of Combo Box (three styles) in Chapter 2)
System	(see Archive)
TabIndex	This property sets or returns the control's position within the tab order of the parent form. The property is valid for all controls except timers.
TabStop	This property is used by all controls except frame and timer objects. The property decides whether tabbing stops with the selected control (default =-1, designating the control as a tab stop). A value of 0 ignores the control when the user is hitting the TAB key.

(continued)

Table 3.1 *(continued)*

Property	Description
Tag	This property is used by all Visual Basic 5 objects to store data uniquely with the selected object.
Text	This property sets or returns a combo, list, or text box's contents. For combo box style = 2, Text property sets or returns the selected item in the list box. Styles 0 and 1 set or return the text within the edit portion of the control.
Top	(see Left)
Value	This property is only for check, command, scroll bar, and option controls. It returns the state of the checkbox (default = 0, off; 1 is on, 2 is grayed). Value is not available at design time for com mand or option controls but at run time decides whether the control was selected (-1, True, selected; 0, not selected). For scroll bars, Value determines the current position of the scroll bar (Value is between –32,768, and 32,767).
Visible	This property is used by all objects except timers to set or return the visual state of the object (default = -1, display object). A value of 0 hides the object.
Width	(see Height)
WindowState	This property is a run time-only property. It sets or returns the visual state of a form (default = 0, normal). A value of 1 minimizes to an icon, while a value of 2 maximizes the form.

CHANGING PROPERTIES

All of the controls provided by the Visual Basic 5 Toolkit have features in common and a few features that are unique. In this section you will gain experience with setting control properties. Where possible, the examples have been selected to highlight each control's unique properties. This approach will allow you to see the parameters associated with these distinctive characteristics. After working through the examples you will better understand the nuances of each control. Knowing this information will enable you to choose the appropriate control for each situation.

PictureBox Control Properties

The only control to use the picture property is the PictureBox control (Note: form objects also have this property). To add a picture at design time you select the picture property from the Properties dialog box and click on the three dots to the right of the Settings box. Figure 3.1 displays the Load Picture dialog box. Notice that Visual Basic 5 expects a file with one of three extension types: *.BMP, *.WMF, *.ICO. You can only assign bitmap, Windows meta file, or icon file format-style pictures.

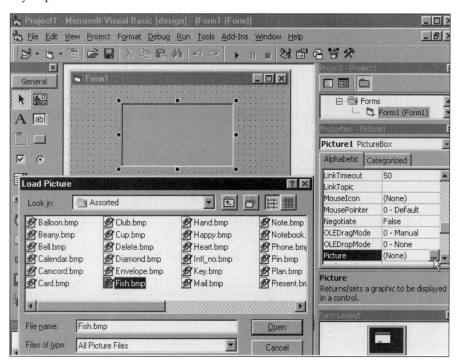

Figure 3.1 Selecting a picture for the Picture property.

Visual Basic 5 is shipped with a large collection of ready-to-use icons. Many of these predefined icons are designed to mimic frequently used program operations, like retrieving or saving a file. Figure 3.1, shown earlier, shows how to assign the Crdfle02.ico icon to the PictureBox control. Once you have selected the file and clicked on the dialog box OK button, Visual Basic 5 immediately displays the graphic. Crdfle02.ico displays a cardfile holder with cardfiles.

Label Control Properties

The function of a Label control is to display text. The displayed information can be used for titles, column headings, or for labeling input or output zones. Visual Basic 5 provides Label controls with a unique Alignment property. Labels can be left justified, centered, or right justified. Figure 3.2 shows Label1 with the Alignment property set to 2 - Center.

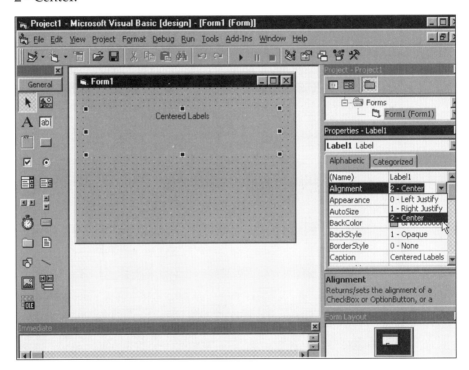

Figure 3.2 Using the Label control's Alignment property to center text.

TextBox Control Properties

A TextBox control is used to input or output information. It may be helpful to think of a TextBox control more as a small edit window. Visual Basic 5 provides TextBox controls with a unique MultiLine property. Figure 3.3 shows how you can turn this Boolean option on.

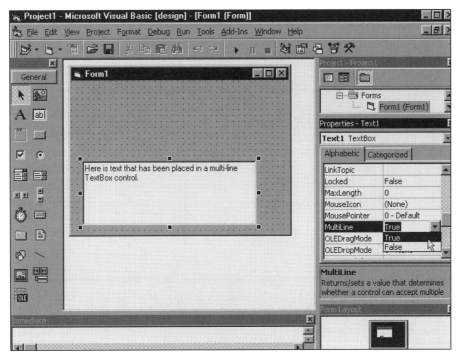

Figure 3.3 Setting a TextBox control's MultiLine property.

Frame Control Properties

A Frame control has no unique properties. Figure 3.4 shows that the Height property (common to most controls) has been changed to a value of 2000. This example brings up two very interesting points.

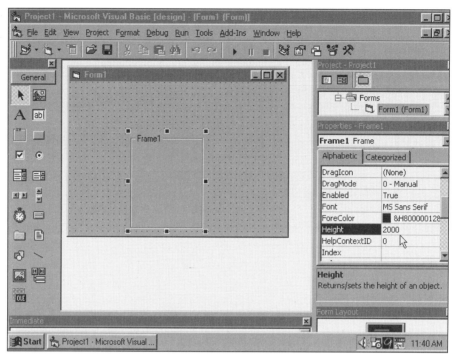

Figure 3.4 Changing the Height property on a Frame control.

Many control properties can be set while physically creating the control on the form. For example, clicking on Frame1's horizontal handle and dragging it automatically changes the height property. If this is true, you are probably asking yourself why you would want to change the height any other way. The answer to the question has to do with precision. To quickly create different types of controls with exactly the same height, it is easier to enter the exact value than to eyeball the control's size on the form.

The second subject of interest presented by this example has to do with when a control's properties are set. Some properties can be set at design time, some only at run time, and others either way. In this chapter you are being shown how to define a control's characteristics by using the Properties dialog box. Chapter 4 will demonstrate how to set or change a control's characteristics with programming code at design time and/or during execution.

A serious problem can arise when defining a control's characteristics with the Properties dialog box. The piece of the puzzle that is missing is programming code. Properties set with the Properties dialog box do not translate directly into code that can be listed or printed. Although you can copy the control in file form, the only way to verify the control's individual property settings is to view the control's properties in the Properties dialog box.

CommandButton Control Properties

CommandButton controls are used to present the user graphically with a panel of options and a means of activating various tasks. Within a displayed command group one option is usually selected more frequently than the others. Because of this fact, Visual Basic 5 provides CommandButton controls with a unique Default property. Only one button on a form can have this property set to a value of True.

Well-designed applications provide the user with the ability to undo a critical task selection. Visual Basic 5 also provides command buttons with a Cancel property. When this value is set, the Default property indicates which button on the form is the Cancel button. Again, only one command on a form can have this property set to True. Figure 3.5 shows how to turn this Boolean property on. Under many circumstances it is logically correct and syntactically legal to make the Cancel button the Default button.

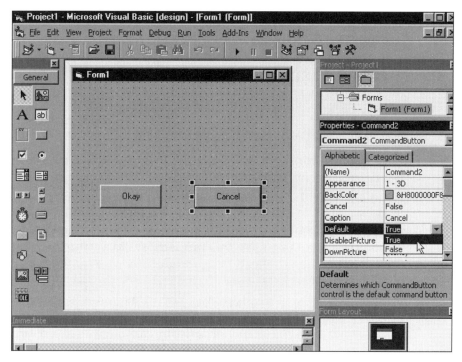

Figure 3.5 Making the Cancel button the Default button.

CheckBox Control Properties

CheckBox controls have no unique properties. However, they do share a very useful Visible property with other controls. By default, when you create a control the Visible property is automatically set to True. However, there are many instances when you will want a control to be displayed only if a certain option has been picked. For example, suppose you are writing a program that presents a customer with a list of boat options. It would be meaningless to ask for a roof color preference unless the customer has first chosen a boat with a cabin. Figure 3.6 shows a form with five checkboxes. In the Properties dialog box you can see the fourth CheckBox control's Visible property being set to False. (Why isn't a CheckBox control the best choice for this design problem? Answer: You could select more than one cabin roof color!)

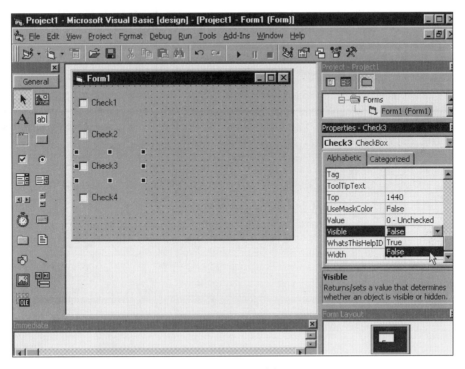

Figure 3.6 Setting a CheckBox control's Visible property.

OptionButton Control Properties

OptionButton controls do not have any distinguishing properties but they do share an Enabled property with other controls. The Enabled property is used to place a control visibly on the screen, but in a selectable/unselectable state. With a control's Enabled property set to False, users can still see the option although they cannot choose it. This can be a valid design approach because it leaves the user aware of other selection possibilities.

Figure 3.7 shows a group of OptionButton controls that use the Enabled property to set the control choices to False. This might be a better control type choice than CheckBox controls because only one item can be selected.

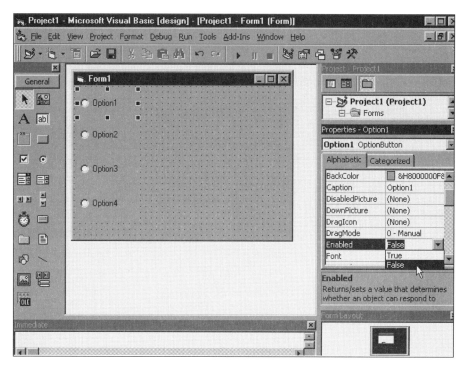

Figure 3.7 OptionButton controls with their Enable properties set to False.

ComboBox Control Properties

See a description of ComboBox controls, Three Styles, in Chapter 2.

ListBox Control Properties

ListBox and ComboBox controls share a unique Sorted property. When the Sorted property is set to True both control types will display a sorted list. By default this property is set to False. Figure 3.8 shows how to set the sorted feature to True.

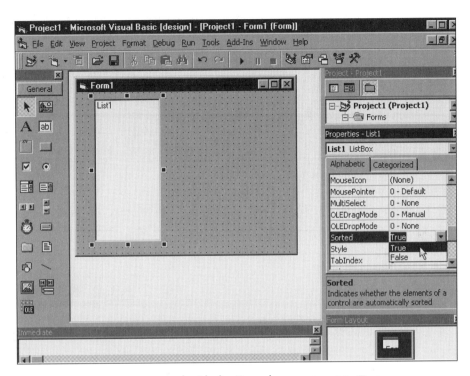

Figure 3.8 A ListBox control with the Sorted property set to True.

HScrollBar and VScrollBar Control Properties

HScrollBar and VScrollBar controls have four unique properties: LargeChange, SmallChange, Max, and Min. Min indicates the value returned by the scroll bar in its leftmost (horizontal) or topmost (vertical) position. Max returns a value from the opposite end of the range: rightmost (horizontal) or bottommost (vertical).

The LargeChange property tells the program how much to increment or decrement the value property when the user clicks between the "thumb" and the up/down arrow. SmallChange determines the value added or subtracted from the current value when the user clicks on the up/down arrow.

For example, imagine a horizontal scroll bar being used to represent a color intensity. There are 100 possible color intensity levels. Figure 3.9 shows how the control's Max property is being set. Note that Min = 0 and LargeChange = 1.

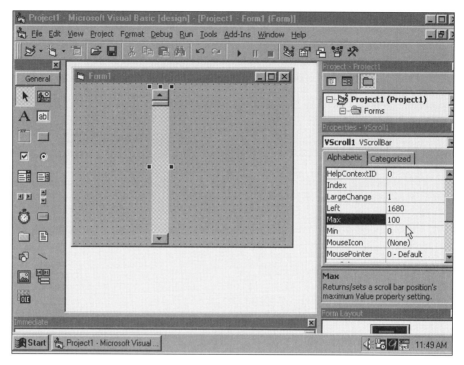

Figure 3.9 Setting the scroll bar properties.

Timer Control Properties

The only control object to use the Interval property is a timer. Figure 3.10 shows how to set a timer's interval property to 2000. The highest value permissible is 65,535. When Enabled, the timer will delay for approximately two seconds.

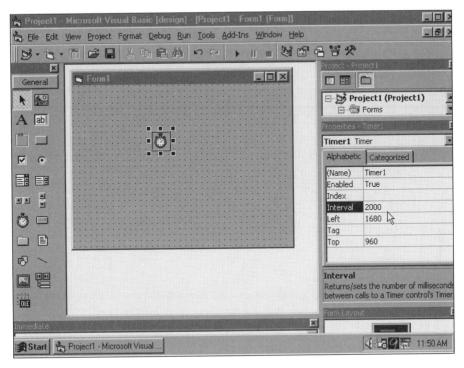

Figure 3.10 Setting a timer control's Interval property.

DriveListBox Control Properties

DriveListBox controls have a unique property called Drive that can be set only at run time. In Chapter 4 you will learn how to use this option.

DirListBox Control Properties

The Path property is shared by both DirListBox and ListBox controls. Like the Drive property, the Path property can be read/written only at run time. Chapter 4 will teach you how to access this useful property.

FileListBox Control Properties

FileListBox controls have five unique properties: Archive, Hidden, Normal, ReadOnly, and System. Each property selectively turns on or off the listing of files with that attribute. By default, the file list box controls display all Archive, Normal, and ReadOnly files. Figure 3.11 uses the Properties dialog box to include all help files (.hlp) in the control's output.

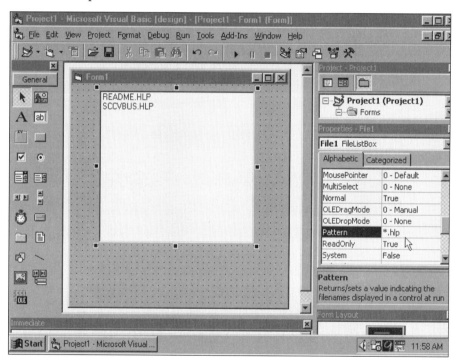

Figure 3.11 Changing the FileListBox control's property to display all .hlp files.

COLORS

Almost all Visual Basic 5 forms and controls allow you to select a ForeColor and BackColor. If the color selection is being made at design time it is suggested that you use the Color Palette window. Visual Basic 5 looks for an RGB (red, green, blue) value when deciding on a color. This value represents a percentage of each of the primary colors to be blended to create the chosen hue. The colors are specified by hexadecimal numbers that range from &H000000 to &HFFFFFF with each primary color taking two bytes. Red, for example, is &H0000FF.

Figure 3.12 shows the Visual Basic 5 Color Palette window that can be displayed by selecting the View | Color Palette menu option.

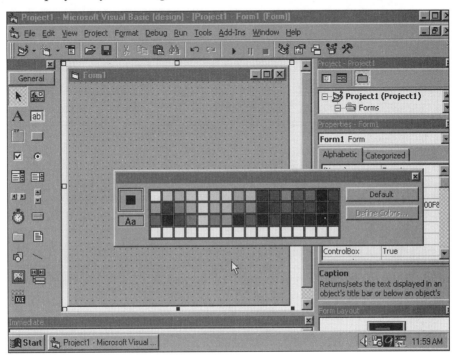

Figure 3.12 The Color Palette window for color selection.

With the Color Palette window open, select a control's Fore and BackColor. Simply click on either property for the selected control and then click on the desired color. Notice that Visual Basic 5 will automatically insert the correct RGB value into the BackColor box of the Properties dialog box, as shown in Figure 3.13.

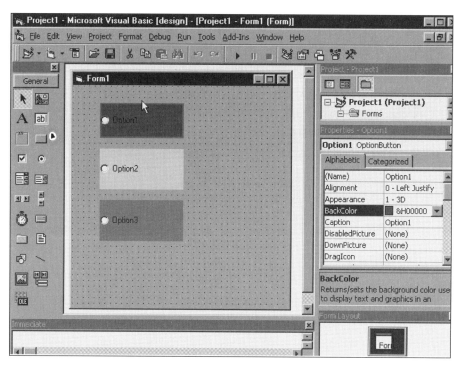

Figure 3.13 Changing a control's colors with the Color Palette.

SETTING THE SALES TAX CALCULATOR PROPERTIES

In order to gain experience with changing a control's properties let's modify the Sales Tax Calculator form from Chapter 2. Use the Properties dialog box to make the needed modifications. For each change listed, first click on the object and then select the required property. Finally, insert the new Setting value.

To alter the tax form, select each label box (Label1..Label5), in order, and change the Caption property. Change Label1 to read "Price:", Lable2 to read "Quantity:", Label3 to read "SubTotal:", Label4 to read "Tax:", and Label5 to read "Total:".

Next, delete every text box's Text1..Text5 labeling by changing the Text property. Select the Text1 text box, then choose the Text property from the Properties dialog box, and now backspace over the label. Repeat these steps for Text2 through Text5.

The final two changes involve the Caption property for forms and command controls. Change Form1's Caption to "Sales Tax Calculator" and Command1's Caption to "Calculate Tax."

With this little bit of experimentation you have now gained valuable experience in altering the properties of forms and controls.

Chapter 4

Writing Code

In the previous chapters you have learned how to design good forms and the details of controls and control properties. In this chapter, you will begin to learn how to write and include code in your Visual Basic 5 applications.

This chapter will concentrate on teaching good code design, just as Chapter 2 concentrated on good interface design.

CODING CONTROLS

You'll find there is more to creating a good application than just designing a good interface. Once an application's forms and controls have been created, something has to tell them how the interaction is to be accomplished. This communication is achieved with programming code.

Starting in this chapter and following throughout the remainder of the book you will be shown the best way to attach code. This is an important issue because of Visual Basic 5's unique approach to program development. New questions that need to be answered include:

- How do I share code with someone else?
- Once a control is added to a form, how do I decide which event to use?
- Are a control's properties best set at design time or run time?

- What rules of good program design must be used?
- When and why should a control's properties be changed?
- When code is designed for a control, which control should be used?
- When are stand-alone subroutines best used?
- When should global variables be used?
- When should a local variable be used?
- Where is my program? I have property settings hidden at design time, individual object events, a global file, stand-alone subroutines with their own window, etc.
- Is it better to attach code to a control or a form?

The answers to these common questions and more will be woven throughout the progressive topic discussions presented in each chapter.

PROPERTIES PLUS CODE

Before the advent of object-oriented programming, most application code written for the graphical interface was procedure-oriented code. Programmers had to be concerned about every aspect of the graphical environment. Many lines of code were written just to detect the graphics hardware and select the correct display mode. These programmers had to write whole subroutines to construct objects that Visual Basic 5 can create in a mouse click.

If the Sales Tax Calculator example had been developed in C or C++, hundreds of lines of code would have been needed to accomplish the same task. Now, with Visual Basic 5 you can simply slide the mouse pointer over to the Toolkit and place any variety of controls on a form in seconds.

Visual Basic 5 relieves the programmer from having to write this mundane code for placing and implementing controls and interfaces. Now the programmer is free to concentrate on the programming task itself. Visual Basic 5 even goes one step further in helping the programmer by automatically associating useful subroutine templates with each form or control in use. In Visual Basic 5 terminology, these subroutine templates are called *event procedures*.

In this chapter you will learn the syntax for writing event procedures. You will discover how the code page window helps you write

an event procedure by automatically creating the subroutine overhead. The discussion of the many types of event procedures will highlight how you can use these subroutines to control an object's
behavior. In addition, you will learn how to use the printer to make
hard copies of your code.

CREATING EVENT PROCEDURES

Objects, called forms and controls in Visual Basic 5, respond by invoking an appropriate event procedure whenever that particular event
occurs. Event procedures can be attached to forms and controls
because of this symbiotic relationship.

   All control event procedures use the same syntax for the header;
this includes the name of the control (defined by the Name property
—see the Properties dialog box), followed by an underscore and an
event name. For example, Option1's Click event looks like:

```
Option1_Click
```

   A similar syntax is used for form event procedures. The only difference is that a form name is used instead of a control. For example,
Form1's LinkOpen command looks like:

```
Form1_LinkOpen
```

   Here is a complete code template for a control event:

```
Private Sub ControlName_EventName ()
  'your code is written here
End Sub
```

   The template for a form event varies only in the procedure name's
object type:

```
Private Sub FormName_EventName ()
  'your code is written here
End Sub
```

   The reserved words **Private Sub** and **End Sub** are used by Visual
Basic 5 to indicate where a subroutine begins and ends. The procedure
header follows the word **Private Sub** along with the code that is executed when the event is triggered. For example, the following subroutine turns Command1's caption into a "Hello There!" message in a
bold font whenever the user clicks the command button.

```
Private Sub Command1.Click ()
 Command1.FontBold = True
 Command1.Caption = "Hello There!"
End Sub
```

The next example changes Frame1's BorderStyle into a nonsizable frame when the user clicks on the form.

```
Private Sub Form1_Click ()
 'Set to double BorderStyle
 BorderStyle = 3
End Sub
```

When the border style (BorderStyle = 3) is used, it prevents the user from shrinking or expanding the window. The setting also prevents the user from minimizing or maximizing the form. Many medical applications incorporate this feature to prevent the user from accidentally modifying a critical window. For example, how useful would a graphical heart monitor be if a medical attendant could shrink the display or reduce it to an icon?

THE CODE PAGE

Visual Basic 5 supports a drop-down code page window that allows easy viewing, entering, and editing the form and control code you are developing. When writing event procedures the code page will automatically construct the necessary overhead. This overhead is a template that follows the syntax described in the previous section.

Code Page Activation

There are three ways to display the code page:

- The first and simplest approach is to simply double-click on a form or control.
- The second approach requires that an object first be selected. Once it is selected, use F7 to view the code.
- The third approach requires the use of the View | Code menu option.

Code page windows are made up of three components: the Object and Procedure drop-down list boxes and the larger text editing area.

The Object list box, in the upper left of the code page window, provides easy access to a project's forms and controls. By clicking on the down arrow a scrollable point-and-click selection of each object is presented. An example object list is shown in Figure 4.1.

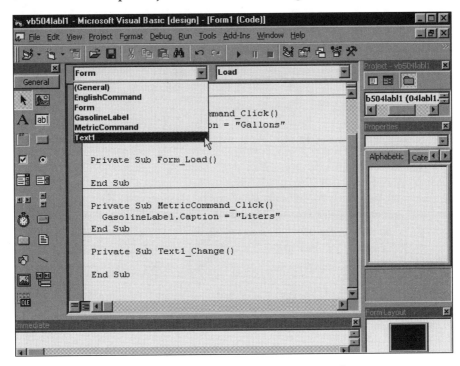

Figure 4.1 An example of the code window's Object list box.

The Procedure list box works the same way as its Object counterpart except that it displays the currently selected object's list of event procedures. The Procedure list box appears in the upper right corner of the code page window. When moving from one object to another, the Procedure box will automatically make Click the default event.

All Procedure list box entries that are bold in the list have programming code associated with them. Doesn't that feature make editing easier? By simply checking an object's list of bold events you know which procedures the object is using. Nonbold entries can be used by the developer as a reminder that the event code needs to be written. Figure 4.2 shows a form's event list with several bold entries.

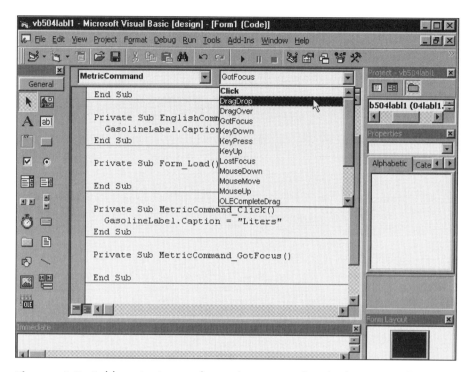

Figure 4.2 Bold entries in a code window's Procedure list box mean there is programming code associated with the item.

Attaching Code to Objects

To add new or additional programming code to an object, simply double-click on the object. The code window will open and move to the front of the display area. Next, select the desired event from the Procedure list box. Visual Basic 5 will immediately display the event's programming code or an empty template, if the code needs to be written. Finally, click the mouse inside the code window and begin entering or modifying the programming code.

EXAMINING EVENT TYPES

The purpose and use of each event type must be understood in order to write a correct Visual Basic 5 Windows application. In Table 4.1, you will find the event types grouped into six categories. Within each category you will find event types that are frequently used together. Study each category carefully—you will gain an appreciation for the types of actions a Visual Basic 5 program can perform.

Remember that no one object (control or form) has access to all event types, just as some properties are unique to certain controls or forms.

Table 4.1 Events and Descriptions

Event	Change to Control
Change	The meaning of this event depends on the type of control. Generally, the event indicates that the control's contents have changed:
	• Combo box control (Style = 0, 1) and text box control— contents have changed when user entered data or Text property altered.
	• Directory list box control—when new directory is selected or Path property is altered in code.
	• Drive list box control—when user selects a new drive or code changes Drive property.
	• Label box control—label contents changed via dynamic data exchange (DDE) link or Caption property modified.
	• Scroll bar controls—triggered when the "thumb" is moved or when code changes the Value property.
	• Picture box control—picture contents have changed via DDE link or Picture property altered.
DropDown	This event is used by combo box controls (Style = 0, 2) only; this event occurs when the list portion of a combo box is about to drop down.
PathChange	This event is used by file list box controls only; this event occurs when code changes the FileName or Path properties.
PatternChange	This event is used by file list box controls only; the event is triggered when code changes the FileName or Pattern properties.
	Drag and Drop
DragDrop	This event is triggered by either dragging a control over a form or Control and releasing the mouse button, or using the **Drag** method with an integer -2 argument action.

(continued)

Table 4.1 *(continued)*

Event	Change to Control
DragOver	This event occurs when the drag-and-drop operation is in progress.
Timer	This event is triggered when the preset Interval property has elapsed.
	Dynamic Data Exchange
LinkOpen	This event occurs when the DDE conversation is being launched.
LinkError	This event occurs whenever there is a DDE communications problem. There are numerous flagged error conditions:
	Attempt to open too many DDE links.
	Client selected wrong control array element in DDE conversation.
	Not enough memory for DDE link, conversation.
	Server code attempted to execute client operations in DDE conversation.
	Some other application attempted DDE without initiating a DDE.
	Some other application requested data in wrong format.
	Some other application requested data without first initiating a DDE.
	Some other application tried to change data for nonexistent DDE.
	Some other application tried to continue DDE after server switched LinkMode to 0 (none).
	Some other application tried to store data without initiating a DDE.
	String was too long and truncated before being sent through the DDE link.
	Unexpected DDE message was sent from some other application.
LinkExecute	This event occurs when a client application initiates a DDE conversation and it sends a command string. This string is used by the server application to activate the specified action. LinkExecute occurs when the client application sends the string.
LinkClose	This event is triggered when either the client or server application terminates the DDE conversation.

(continued)

Table 4.1 *(continued)*

Event	Change to Control
	Focus
GotFocus	This event is triggered when any object receives the focus. This can be accomplished by clicking the mouse, by tabbing, or by using the **SetFocus** method. A form can get the focus only if all of its controls are disabled. The event is frequently used to add additional screen output whenever a certain option is active.
LostFocus	This event is the opposite of GotFocus. Typically used to graphically undo a GotFocus event.
	Form and Picture Boxes
Paint	This event occurs whenever part or all of a control or form has been exposed because the object covering it has been moved, resized, or deleted. This event is not used whenever the form or control's AutoRedraw property is set to -1, TRUE. (Form and Picture box only.)
Resize	This event is triggered any time a form is resized. The event can be used to initiate the resizing of the form's contents.
Load	This event is used by forms only and is triggered whenever a form is loaded. The Load event is used to initialize any information within a form or its controls.
UnLoad	This event occurs when a form is about to be removed from the screen. Since this event is triggered just before the form is disposed of, it is a good place to do any last-minute checking. The UnLoad event can prompt the user for any last-minute instructions, like "File NOT Saved!"
	Keyboard Control
KeyDown, KeyUp	In this event, the KeyDown (a key is pressed) or KeyUp (a key was released) occurs when a control has the focus. The events detect all keys on the keyboard. The control with the focus receives the *Index*, *KeyCode*, and *Shift* arguments. The values returned uniquely identify the control within the control array, the key's key code found in CONSTANT.TXT, and the state of the SHIFT, ALT, and CTRL keys (SHIFT key, bit 0; CTRL key, bit 1; ALT key, bit 2).
KeyPress	In this event, the KeyPress is triggered whenever the user presses and releases an ASCII key. KeyPress uses two arguments: *Index* and *KeyAscii*. The first value uniquely identifies the control within a control array. *KeyAscii* returns a standard, numeric

(continued)

Table 4.1 *(continued)*

Event	Change to Control
	ASCII keycode. KeyPress deals only with standard printable keys, CTRL combined with standard alphabetic keys, and a few additional characters such as BACKSPACE and carriage return.
	Mouse Operations
Click	This event occurs when the user presses and releases the mouse button over an object. Form Click events occur when the user clicks on the blank area of the form or a disabled control. Control Click events occur with the mouse, selecting a combo or list box item with mouse or arrow keys, pressing SPACEBAR on an object with the Focus, or pressing ENTER on a command with Default set to TRUE (-1). Click events can be triggered with code by setting the control's Value property to TRUE (-1).
DblClick	This event occurs when the user quickly presses and releases the mouse button twice. The user must double-click the mouse within the system's double-click time limit to generate a DblClick event. DblClick is generated for command objects.
MouseDown, MouseUp	The MouseDown event occurs when the user presses the mouse button. The MouseUp event occurs when the user releases the button. The events return *Index, Button, Shift,* and *X,Y* values. Depending on the control, this information can be used to decide which control in the control array has been selected, which mouse button was used (left, bit 0 = set; right, bit 1 = set; middle button, bit 2 = set), whether the SHIFT, CTRL, or ALT key was depressed, and the location of the mouse pointer.
MouseMove	This event occurs whenever the user moves the mouse. MouseMove events return the same four parameters as MouseDown/Up.

Making Use of Event Procedures

In this section you'll combine your understanding of controls, forms, properties, and event procedures. The following examples are designed to answer some of the questions dealing with control properties, how to set them, and which events best apply to certain objects. The examples can also be used as models for writing your own Visual Basic 5 applications.

Label Controls

Several automakers have designed digital dashboards that display
information in either English or metric format. In a Visual Basic 5
interface this descriptive text could be represented by LabelBox controls. For example, based on the user input, a gauge could toggle any
appropriate designator. If a gas gauge was being used, it could be
labeled in either gallons or liters. Figure 4.3 shows an interface
where the appropriate label is selected on the basis of the user's command choice.

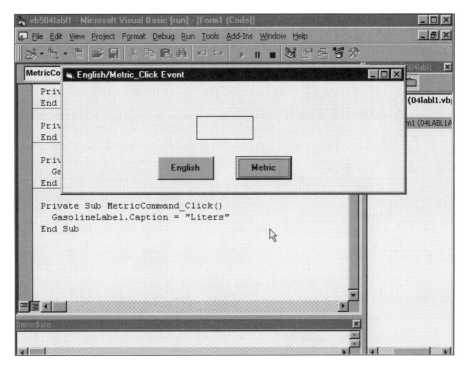

Figure 4.3 A label is selected, based on the user's command choice.

There are two steps to this interface design. First, the label's alignment property is set to two (2, center). This will automatically center
the information. Next, the label's border style (BorderStyle) is set to 0.
This means no border style is used. Both settings are changed with the
Properties dialog box at design time.

The second step of this design requires the use of each command's Click event procedure. The following line of code was added to the English command's Click event to change the gasoline label to "Gallons."

```
Private Sub EnglishCommand_Click ()
 GasolineLabel.Caption = "Gallons"
End Sub
```

A similar statement was added to the metric command's Click event to display "Liters."

```
Private Sub MetricCommand_Click ()
 GasolineLabel.Caption = "Liters"
End Sub
```

Here each event procedure will modify the label's caption property during run time. This is a correct use for an event procedure, since the application could not know ahead of time which labeling preference the user might select.

To answer the questions "When should a property be set? At design time or run time?" use the following general rule. If you know an object's property settings before the program is run, or if the property setting will never change, set them at design time. (However, this does not mean that a property set at design time can never be changed at run time.)

By using the Properties dialog box to define an object's characteristics you avoid two problems. First, you simplify the creation of the program by not wasting time entering the run time code equivalent. For a beginner this can be quite an advantage, since beginners often incorrectly select or misspell an object's properties.

A second advantage is the elimination of cluttered source code. This advantage is gained by setting an object's properties at design time. This allows the programmer to create or view only those lines of code necessary to get the job done.

PictureBox Controls

Imagine the following scenario: You are writing a portion of a Visual Basic 5 application that deals with file I/O. In keeping with good design principles you want to create an easy-to-use interface. You have an idea! Why not display a picture, representing the drive type selected by the user, in the program's interface?

Then you encounter a problem—you can't use the PictureBox control's Picture property at design time because you do not know which drive type (fixed or floppy) the user will choose. Your only option is to write the code necessary to assign the correct picture or icon at run time.

To do this, use the PictureBox control's **GotFocus** event, and write the following code:

```
Private Sub Picture1_GotFocus ()
 PictureStyle = 2
 If PictureStyle = 1 Then
  picture1.picture = LoadPicture("c:\VB5\Graphics\Icons\
        Computer\DISK07.ICO")
 ElseIf PictureStyle = 2 Then
  picture1.picture = LoadPicture("c:\VB5\Graphics\Icons\
        Computer\DISK08.ICO")
 ElseIf PictureStyle = 3 Then
  picture1.picture = LoadPicture("c:\VB5\Graphics\Icons\
        Computer\DRIVE01.ICO")
 End If
End Sub
```

 Note: Remember that line wraps are not permitted when you enter code. Each call to the LoadPicture() function must be entered on one line.

This portion of code assumes that the icons needed for the application reside on the C drive, in the c:\VB5\Graphics\Icons\Computer subdirectory. If your icons are in a different location, these portions of code will need to be changed.

Figure 4.4 demonstrates the effect of running this code.

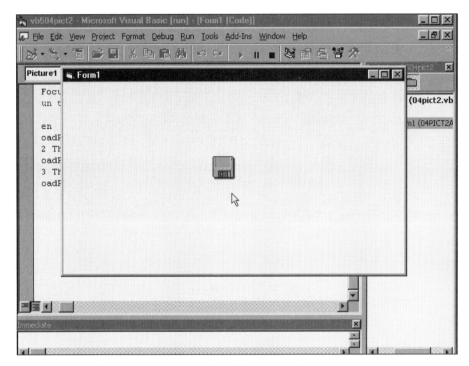

Figure 4.4 The correct icon is selected by using the Picture1_GotFocus event.

By using a nested If…Then…Else programming statement, the **LoadPicture** command can assign the correct image. (Note: The PictureBox control's **BorderStyle** has been set to zero (0, none) so that the displayed image is frameless.)

Timer Controls

Timer controls use unique Timer event procedures. This event procedure is triggered whenever the Timer's Interval has elapsed. One of the simplest and most useful features you can add to any application is a visual time display.

Figure 4.5 displays a readable LabelBox control showing the current time.

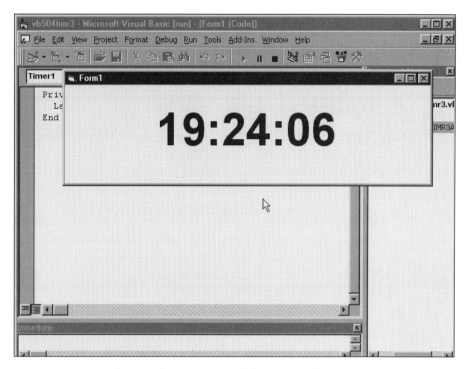

Figure 4.5 Displaying the time in a LabelBox control.

A LabelBox control can display the current time. Set the Timer control's Interval property to allow the Timer control to trigger the Timer event procedure. The **Time$** is assigned to the Label control's Caption property. This might sound complicated, but it isn't. The following programming code is all that is needed.

```
Private Sub Timer1.Timer ()
 Label1.Caption = Time$
End Sub
```

In this case, the clock's visual appearance is not controlled by the Timer event. As with most controls, its behavior and appearance is determined by a combination of coded events and design time properties.

When the label was created its FontSize was changed to a more readable TrueType Arial 48 point font and the Alignment property was set to 2 (center the label). Incidentally, if you are wondering why a label box was needed in this situation, it is because Timer controls do not directly have output capabilities.

The system's clock needs to trigger the Timer event, so the Timer control's Interval property was set to 1000. This invoked the Timer event once a second (1 second = 1000 milliseconds), keeping the clock's display accurate to within the second.

File, Directory, and Drive Controls

File, Directory, and Drive controls are designed to interface easily with one another. In the following example, you'll see just how simple it is to add the fundamentals of a file system to any application. The code is very brief because the controls themselves use values returned from the operating system to examine and display the information.

A Form_Load event procedure is automatically invoked whenever Form1 is loaded. For our example, it contains only one line of code that limits the File1 ListBox control's initial display to files with a *.FRM pattern. (Note: This overrides the controls default of "*.*") One valid reason for setting a control property at run time instead of design time is that it can flag another programmer to the importance of this change.

```
Private Sub Form_Load ()
  File1.Pattern = "*.FRM"
End Sub
```

The following Text1_Change event enables the user to alter the search Pattern dynamically while the program is running. Any text change within a TextBox control invokes the Change event procedure. This example assigns a new Pattern based on the text string automatically returned by Text1's Text property. The File1.Pattern property has a global scope and can be accessed from any appropriate event procedures.

```
Private Sub Text1_Change ()
  File1.Pattern = Text1.Text
End Sub
```

The Drive and Directory controls are linked together by their respective Change events. When the user clicks on a new drive, the Drive List box trips the Change event assigning the new drive's path to the Directory ListBox control. This allows the Directory ListBox control to update its contents.

```
Private Sub Drive1_Change ()
 Dir1.Path = Drive1.Drive
End Sub
```

The following Dir1_Change event synchronizes File1's display with the chosen directory:

```
Private Sub Dir1_Change ()
 File1.Path = Dir1.Path
End Sub
```

ANOTHER PASS AT THE SALES TAX CALCULATOR

In order to gain experience attaching code to controls, let's make another pass at the Sales Tax Calculator application. For this example, you will write programming code for a **Change** event and a **Click** event.

The **Change** event is a particularly good example to program because it is automatic. In other words, the user doesn't actually click on the control to activate the event. Instead, the **Change** event is triggered whenever the control's contents are modified.

The second event type, **Click**, is more typical of the kinds of controls you normally think of in a Visual Basic 5 application. This is an event where the application performs a specific task after the user has clicked on a command button, for example.

To implement this code, bring down the code page window for the Sales Tax Calculator's Text2 control. Remember, one way to do this is by double-clicking on the form's control and selecting the **Change** event from the Procedure ListBox control. Enter the following lines of code:

```
Private Sub Text2_Change ()
 SubTotal = Val(Text1.Text) * Val(Text2.Text)
 Text3.Text = Format$(SubTotal, "#,###,##0.00")
End Sub
```

Repeat the same process for Command1, only this time select the **Click** event from the Procedure list. Enter the lines of code shown in Figure 4.6.

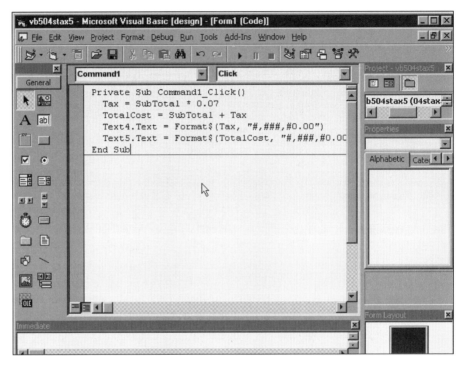

Figure 4.6 The Sales Tax Calculator's Command1_Click event.

One additional line of code is needed in order to get the program to execute properly. This application needs a variable that will be "visible" across the two types of events. In order to share this information and be visible, the variable must be declared **global**.

The declaration can be made by following these steps: Bring the Sales Tax Calculator's Project window to the front by clicking on it or selecting it from the View | Project window option. Next, open a module.bas file by using the Project | Add Module key sequence. Enter the following variable declaration in this module

```
Global SubTotal As Integer
```

We generally save this file by the same name as the project so in this case the file would be saved as 04STAX.BAS. Also, at this point you need to perform a very critical task—save the form. You would not want to lose all of this work should a test run of the application lock the computer system! To save a form you can choose the File | Save Project or File | Save Module option.

Remember, the Save Module option saves only the active module. To save all three code changes you would not only save the module but also execute a separate save for Form1. Since both the **Change** and **Click** events are bound to the controls on Form1, you do not need to execute a unique save for each event.

USING THE SALES TAX CALCULATOR

You are now ready to test the Sales Tax Calculator. There are two ways to execute a Visual Basic 5 application: Press F5 or select the Run | Start menu option.

The program begins by placing the input focus on the TextBox control labeled Price. Try entering 600.00. Next, tab down to the Text2 TextBox control (next to the Quantity label) and enter 4. Notice that the second you entered the 4, a SubTotal was generated. To finish testing the calculator, click on the Calculate Tax command. The program finishes by calculating both the Tax and the Total.

UNDERSTANDING HOW THE SALES TAX CALCULATOR FUNCTIONS

The Sales Tax Calculator is an excellent model for many Visual Basic 5 applications because it retrieves input from the user, performs calculations on the data, and formats screen output.

The program starts by allowing the user to enter a product price. This information is entered as text into the Text1 TextBox control. After this the user enters the quantity sold (Text2 TextBox control).

The second a value is entered, Text2's **Change** event is activated. This event gains access to the price and quantity sold by accessing each TextBox control's Text property. Because this data is in non-numeric format, the **Val()** BASIC function is used to convert the information into a numeric format:

```
SubTotal = Val(Text1.Text) * Val(Text2.Text)
```

The translated data is then assigned to the SubTotal variable. Printing the information to the SubTotal's associated TextBox control (Text3) is achieved with the following code statement:

```
Text3.Text = Format$(SubTotal, "#,###,#00.0")
```

In this equation you can see a solution to yet another formatting problem. Since the value in the SubTotal variable is a numeric value, its contents cannot be assigned to a TextBox control's Text property! The BASIC **Format$()** function converts a numeric value into a character string using a format template ("#,###,#00.0").

Finally, when the user clicks on the Calculate Tax command the **Command1.Click** event is triggered. In a manner similar to the event just discussed, this event calculates a Tax and Total and then outputs its formatted information. Of particular interest is the global reference to the SubTotal variable. Had SubTotal been defined only in Text2's **Change** event, it would have been an invalid reference for the **Click** event.

DO YOU HAVE A FINAL PRODUCT TO SHIP?

When a project file is run from within Visual Basic 5, Visual Basic 5 translates code line by line into executable format, line by line. In other words, the files saved on your work disk are useless to anyone not owning Visual Basic 5. To create an executable version of your program that will run under Windows you need to create an *.EXE file. To turn any Visual Basic 5 project into an executable *.EXE file:

1. Open the project file for the application.
2. Click on the File | Make… .exe, file option.
3. Often the drive:\path used for an application's development is different from where the final *.EXE file is saved. Check to see if the correct drive:\path has been selected; if not, select the correct route using the Directory ListBox control.
4. Make sure the file name is valid. You do not need to add the *.exe extension. Visual Basic 5 does this for you automatically.

Once you have converted your application to an executable file you can run it from Windows 95 or Windows NT by using the Run command from the Start popup. Now you can protect your programming by distributing only the executable version of your program; this way, no one can read or alter your programming code.

To ship executable copies of your program you will need to bundle your file with a copy of the Visual Basic 5 dynamic link library, VBRUN500.DLL. The 500 represents the version number of the product. This file should be located in your Visual Basic 5 subdirectory.

HARD COPIES OF YOUR WORK

Hard copies of a project are very useful for debugging the application, sharing ideas with a coworker, or publishing in magazines or books. Visual Basic 5 makes it easy for your printer to output single procedures or entire projects. If you need to share an interface design with someone, no problem, just print the information.

Printing Forms and Controls

To begin printing a single procedure or form you must first load the procedure into the code window. Now, select the File | Print... option. Visual Basic 5 will then display the Print dialog box shown in Figure 4.7.

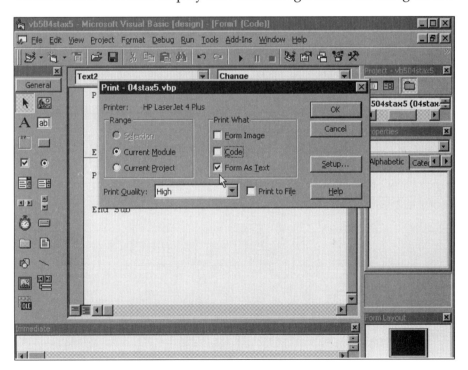

Figure 4.7 The Print dialog box.

Notice that the Current Module option box has been selected along with the Form as Text checkbox. Clicking on the OK button will cause the printer to print the object's interface (for forms) and the procedure.

Printing an entire project's design is no more complicated than clicking the Project option while in the Print dialog box (see Figure 4.7).

Copying Code to a Word Processor

There are many occasions when having the ability to pull a piece of code into a word processor, such as Microsoft Word, would be very useful. For example, you could be writing the documentation for your project. It would be handy to be able to insert pieces of project code into your final project report.

Since Microsoft Word and Visual Basic can be running at the same time, simply mark and copy the desired code with normal edit commands. Then paste the copied code directly into your word processor.

Figure 4.8 shows a portion of project code that was transferred to Microsoft Word by the Copy-Paste process.

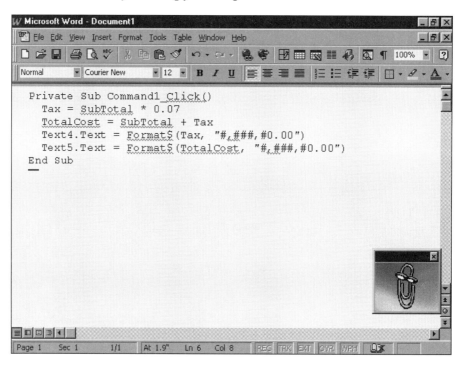

Figure 4.8 Copying and pasting program code in a word processor document.

WHAT'S COMING?

In this chapter you have learned how to write programming code and attach it properly to forms and controls. In the next chapter, we'll spend more time examining specific elements of the BASIC and Visual Basic 5 programming languages.

Chapter 5

Visual Basic 5 as a Programming Language

Most programmers agree that there is not one programming language that is ideal for every programming task. Real-world development environments consist of unique combinations of programmers' experience, hardware design, and application requirements. The language chosen by a novice programmer, using a limited hardware configuration, is just as good as the one chosen by a systems developer using the latest compiler technology. The key to a successful program design is to use the right tool at the right time. Visual Basic 5 stands alone as being the best tool for easily developing Windows applications!

Visual Basic 5 has launched 32-bit Windows 95 and Windows NT program development into a new era. Programmers familiar with BASIC will have the opportunity to rediscover familiar programming that now has a fresh look. Novice BASIC programmers will encounter a language that is clean, straightforward, and simple to use.

Effective use of Visual Basic 5 requires a good understanding of its language elements. This chapter is designed to give you this understanding by using the vocabulary of programmers. You will be shown the logic and syntax behind Visual Basic 5 comments, data types, variables, constants, control structures, mathematics operators, procedures, and scoping rules.

Historically, BASIC has to be given credit for introducing more people to computer programming than any other computer language. In 1963–1964, two Dartmouth professors, John Kemeny and

Thomas Kurtz, developed BASIC (Beginner's All-purpose Symbolic Instruction Code). Their goal was to design a language that required little familiarity with computers or mathematics.

Early in 1970 Bill Gates and Paul Allen developed a microcomputer-based BASIC. It has been in a maturation process ever since. Originally designed as an educational language, BASIC evolved into the hobbyist's language of choice. From there the language matured into a full-fledged professional programmer's language.

Most of Visual Basic 5's language elements are inherited from Microsoft's well-bred QuickBasic. However, there are a few important differences:

- Arrays must be explicitly declared with **Dim** or **ReDim**.

- **Function** procedure calls must include parentheses even if no arguments are being passed. (The parentheses can be omitted if the module or form includes a **Declare** statement for the **Function** procedure being called.)

- There is no line continuation character.

- Variable scope has changed. Earlier versions of BASIC made all variables global. In Visual Basic 5, variables are local by default.

- Visual Basic 5 manages the fractional portion of all **Currency** variables. This bypasses the usual rounding errors generated by floating-point numbers.

- Visual Basic 5 supports only the **Declare** statement for DLL (dynamic-link library) routines and **Function** procedures with no arguments.

Details of program conversion from various forms of BASIC to Visual Basic 5 can be found in the Microsoft Visual Basic 5 *Programmer's Guide* and by using the compiler's online help facility.

COMMENTS

Commenting source code is very important for the program developer. A terse, well-chosen explanation can turn an inscrutable code segment into an undeniably skillful problem solution. Comments should not be abused. They should not insult the intelligence of an experienced programmer nor assume too much. A comment in Visual Basic 5, as in regular BASIC, begins with a (') symbol. Anything to the right of this symbol is ignored by Visual Basic 5. Comments may occupy an entire line:

```
'Create a data file and fill with records
Open "NEW.DAT" For Random As #1 Len = Len(FileRecord)
```

or follow executable code as seen in the following example:

```
NL$ = Chr$(13) + Chr$(10) 'This defines a newline.
```

Notice that the syntax for a Visual Basic 5 comment does not require any closing symbol. All comments terminate at the end of each line. Separate comment symbols are required on each line to create the standard commercial comment block, for example:

```
'===========================================================
'Date:              06/January/97
'Authored by:       H. W. Longfellow
'Input:             NEWDAT.DAT - Regional Data File, User Input
'Output:            NEWDAT.DAT - Updated Regional Data File
'External Effects: ERR.DAT  - Copy of invalid input
'===========================================================
```

An easy way to decide whether a code segment needs commenting is to ask the question, "Who is the audience?" Code written for personal use typically has less internal documentation than algorithms destined to be maintained by other programmers. In both cases a brief comment is required by any code segment whose meaning would not be obvious when viewed weeks later.

RULES FOR IDENTIFIERS

A symbiotic relationship exists between comment blocks and meaningful identifiers. An *identifier* is used to represent constants, variables, labels, and procedures in your source code. Rules for selecting good identifiers include:

- The identifier must begin with a letter.
- After the first letter, the identifier may contain letters, numbers, and underscore (_) symbols.

- Identifiers have a maximum length of 40 characters.

- You cannot use a valid keyword for an identifier. For example, you cannot declare a video monitor's intensity variable *Dim*, since **Dim** is used by Visual Basic 5 to define identifiers and allocate storage. However, you can inlay keywords. For example, *Monitor_Dim* would be a syntactically legal combination.

Source code should be easy to read. Creating a program with these characteristics takes extra time. It is much easier and quicker to use uncommented cryptic variable names. However, if you take the time to create meaningful identifiers and comment obscure code, the result will be a reusable library of easily understood algorithms.

DATA TYPES

Visual Basic 5 supports the standard combination of data types along with a **Currency** type, as shown in Table 5.1.

Table 5.1 Visual Basic 5 Data Types

Data Type	Explanation	Symbol	Range
Integer	2-byte integer	%	-32,768 to +32,767
Long	4-byte integer	&	-2,147,483,648 to +2,147,483,647
Single	4-byte floating point	!	-3.37E+38 to +3.37E+38
Double	8-byte floating point	# (or none)	-1.67D+308 to +1.67D+308
String	1 byte per character	$	0 to approximately 65,535
Currency	8 bytes with fixed decimal	@	-9.22E+14 to +9.22E+14

Before a variable can be used, its data type must be declared with either the **Dim** statement or the **Global** or **Static** modifier. An alternative to using the **Dim...As** declaration syntax is to use the Visual Basic 5 type-declaration characters. You can define a variable's type simply by appending any of the type-declaration characters in column three of Table 5.1. For example, *Index%* is defined to be an **Integer** and *Salary@* is of type **Currency**.

If you leave a variable's type undefined, Visual Basic 5 assumes the variable is of type **Single**. Any form or module can change this default with a **Def***type* statement. The syntax for the **Def***type* statement takes on the following form:

```
DefInt alpha_range[,alpha_range]...
DefLng alpha_range[,alpha_range]...
DefSng alpha_range[,alpha_range]...
DefDbl alpha_range[,alpha_range]...
DefStr alpha_range[,alpha_range]...
DefCur alpha_range[,alpha_range]...
```

For example, the following statement defines all variables consisting of the letters A through H as type **Currency**:

```
DefCur A-H
```

Unlike the C or C++ programming language, Visual Basic 5 is not case sensitive. Therefore, the previous statement could have been written a–H, A–h, or a–h and still have the same effect. **Def***type* statements affect only the default type of variables defined in a specific file (global, form, or module); the default data type for other forms or modules is unaffected.

DEFINING CONSTANTS

A *constant* is a memory location that is assigned a meaningful identifier and an unchangeable value. They are used to make source code more readable and reliable. Constants are more readable because their labels say in English what they mean to the algorithm. They make the programs more robust because they can't be changed by programming code or the user. The syntax for a **Const** statement takes this form:

```
[Global] Const constant_identifier = expression
          [constant_identifier = expression]...
```

Visual Basic 5 uses several files to hold frequently used constants. For example, the Win32api.txt file holds constants, declarations, and so on for interfacing with Windows. The contents of the Win32api.txt file can be viewed in a word processor. Since this file is very large, there is an alternative method of viewing the file's contents with the use of the Application Programming Interface (API) Viewer.

The API Viewer can be started by running apiload.exe. This application is located in a subdirectory off your main Visual Basic 5 directory. The subdirectory is named winapi. Start the viewer by typing:

```
c:\Vb5\winapi\apiload.exe
```

You should see a screen similar to Figure 5.1.

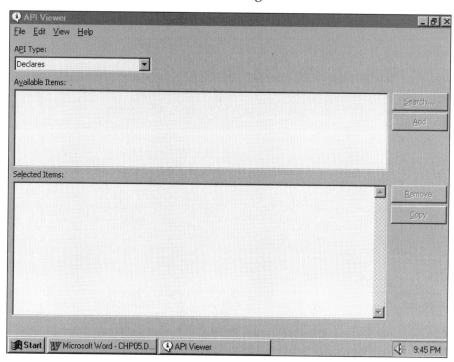

Figure 5.1 The API Viewer's initial screen.

The Win32api.txt file is a text file, so the Load Text File… item is selected from the File menu as shown in Figure 5.2.

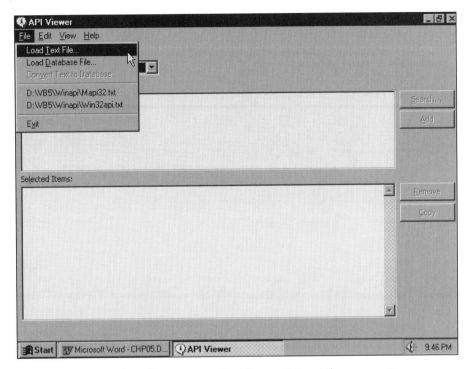

Figure 5.2 Use the File menu to select the Load Text File... menu item.

A list of text files, present in this subdirectory, is then displayed, as shown in Figure 5.3.

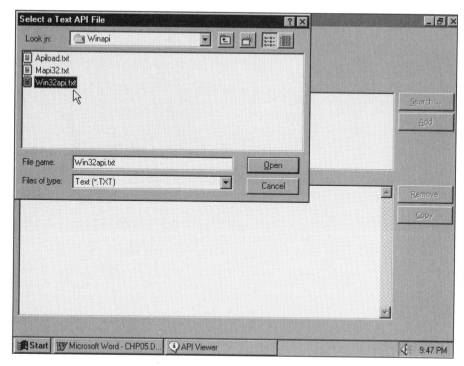

Figure 5.3 A list of available text files, in this subdirectory, is displayed in a dialog box.

Select the Win32api.txt file for viewing. The API Viewer will now load the Win32api.txt file and allow you to view various API types. Figure 5.4 shows several API constants that have been selected.

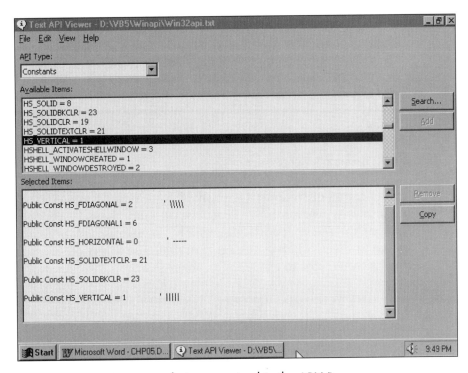

Figure 5.4 API constants being examined in the API Viewer.

DEFINING VARIABLES

Visual Basic 5 uses the **Dim** statement to declare the data type of a variable and allocate storage (except for dynamically allocated arrays). The syntax, including all possible parameters, takes on the following form:

```
Dim[Shared] identifier[([subscript])][As type][,
     identifier[([subscript])][As type]]...
```

The **Shared** keyword maintains compatibility with other dialects of BASIC (such as Microsoft's QuickBasic and the Microsoft BASIC Compiler). Subscripts are used to dimension single or multidimensional array variables. The identifier's data type follows the reserved word **As**. The following listing demonstrates how to define variables in Visual Basic 5:

```
Dim Airplane As Integer
Dim PayCheck As Double
```

```
Dim CustomerAddress As String
Dim BankBalance As Currency
```

It is also syntactically correct to include multiple definitions on the same line. This can save space by allowing you to do away with duplicate **Dim** instructions:

```
Dim Velocity As Double, Acceleration As Integer
```

ASSIGNMENT STATEMENT

The assignment statement is probably the most frequently used statement in any programming language. Its purpose is to assign the contents of the *source* (constant, variable, expression, or function return value) to the *destination* storage variable. The direction of information flow is from right to left:

```
destination = source
```

As an example, the following assignment statements set Command2 properties:

```
Command2.BackColor = Red
Command2.Caption = "DELL"
Command2.FontBold = TRUE
Command2.Enabled = FALSE
```

ARRAYS

If you have been programming with other languages, you are probably familiar with the concept of an array. An array is a structure that allows you to store homogeneous data types in consecutive memory locations. Visual Basic 5 uses an index into the array structure to locate individual elements. The syntax for an array declaration takes on the following form:

```
Dim ArrayName ([UpperBound]
        [LBound to UBound]
        [LRBound to LUBound,LCBound to UCBound]
        [PlaneUpperBound,LRBound to URBound,
                LCBound to UCBound]
        [PlaneUpperBound,RowUpperBound,ColUpperBound]
        ) As data_type
```

Vectors and Matrices

The following listing contains two lines of code. These statements illustrate how to define vectors (one-dimensional arrays) and matrices (two-dimensional arrays): *StoneCount* as an array of 200 elements indexed from 0 (default) through 199 and *PaySheet* as a two-dimensional array with rows numbered 1 through 20, columns numbered 1 through 40.

```
Dim StoneCount (199) As Integer
Dim PaySheet (1 to 20, 1 to 40) As Currency
```

Index Base Changes

Visual Basic 5 allows any form or module to change an array's initial index value by using the **Option Base** instruction. For example:

```
Option Base 2
```

   This instruction changes an array's first index from a default value of 0 to 2. **Option Base** changes affect only array declarations that include a number-of-elements parameter. Had this statement been executed prior to the two array declarations, shown previously, Visual Basic 5 would have seen *StoneCount* as having 199 elements indexed from 2 to 201. Visual Basic 5 would continue to interpret *PaySheet* as having 20 rows (indexed from 1 to 20) and 40 columns (indexed from 1 to 40).

Multidimensional Arrays

Visual Basic 5 allows you to declare arrays with up to a maximum of 60 dimensions! For each dimension you can specify just the upper bound or include the lower bound. Try to guess the sizes of the following two arrays:

```
Option Base 1
Dim SocialSecurity (6, 1 to 150, 1 to 10) As Integer
Dim BalancedBudget (1 to 5, 1 to 2, 1 to 15, 1 to 20) As Double
```

   The *SocialSecurity* array contains six planes, 150 rows, and 10 columns (9000 elements). Notice that the first dimension specified an upper bound only. With this syntax there would have been seven planes had the **Option Base** statement been eliminated. The other two dimensions would remain unchanged.

The second declaration uses a lower and an upper bound to designate all four dimensions. Using time as an example for BalancedBudget's fourth dimension, the array contains five time sectors, two planes, 15 rows per plane, and 20 columns per plane (3000 elements).

Dynamic Arrays

Dynamic arrays allow a programmer to delay the physical allocation of an array's storage until the program is actually executing. This can be critical to the efficient use of memory. Here are several simple rules that need to be considered when dealing with dynamic arrays:

- Declare the array using the **Dim** or **Global** statement (in the Global module), with an empty dimension list.
- Declaring a dynamic array with the **Dim** statement as just described (empty dimension list) limits the array to eight dimensions.
- **ReDim** statements may appear only within procedures. These statements are used to change the range of an array's dimensions, never the number of dimensions.
- To avoid the eight-dimension limit, do not use the **Dim** statement. Create the array directly using just the **ReDim** instruction. This method supports the normal limit of 60 dimensions.
- It is best to use a **ReDim** statement to create the array.
- Use the same array declaration syntax previously defined.
- Multiple **ReDim** statements can be used to alter a previously created array's dimension bounds.
- Do not use **ReDim** to alter the number of dimensions in a previously created array.
- Variables may be used to dimension an array.

For example, the following statement, placed at the form level, tells Visual Basic 5 that *Coordinates* is the name of a dynamically allocated array:

```
Dim Coordinates () As Integer.
```

Later on in the program a procedure is used to allocate storage:

```
Sub InputCoordinates ()
     .
     .
     .

ReDim Coordinates (49, 99)
```

The variable, *Coordinates*, now contains 500 elements, 50 rows by 100 columns. One option would be to allow the user to delineate the boundaries while the program is executing. The application would then use the variable's contents to dimension the array:

```
ReDim Coordinates (UserDefinedRows, UserDefinedColumns)
```

Of course, the application could later alter the number of rows and columns:

```
ReDim Coordinates (29, 29)
```

This next statement is illegal because it tries to change *Coordinates* from a two-dimensional to a four-dimensional array:

```
ReDim Coordinates (Cars, Planes, Boats, Motorcycles)
```

Remember, **ReDim** statements are used to change the range of an array's dimensions, never the number of dimensions.

USER-DEFINED TYPES (RECORDS)

User-defined types are unique combinations of standard data types. They are used to customize an application's data declarations. These original combinations are declared in the global module with a **Type** statement. **Type** declarations do not allocate storage, they are only format templates. The syntax for **Type** declarations takes on the following form:

```
Type identifier
  field_identifier As data_type
  [field_identifier As data_type
     .
     .
     .

  ]
End Type
```

For example, the following user-defined type defines the storage format required by *Worker* records:

```
Type Worker
 Name As String * 50
 Address1 As String * 40
 Address2 As String * 40
 Department As String * 10
 HoursWorked As Single
 HourlyWage As Single
 OvertimeRate As Single
 WeeklyPay As Double
End Type
```

The type *Worker* includes fixed-length string and numeric fields. This type of declaration is excellent for random-access file operations because all strings are defined as fixed length.

Once the type has been declared in the global module, you can use it as part of a variable declaration:

```
Dim One_Worker As Worker
Dim All_Workers (99) As Worker
```

The first statement creates one variable (*One_Worker*) of the new type *Worker*. The second statement allocates an array-of-records. *All_Workers* contains 100 rows of *Workers*.

To access the individual fields of a record you use the following syntax:

```
variable_name[index].field_identifier
```

To access *One_Worker*'s name field you would write:

```
One_Worker.Name = "Jeff Salt"
```

The only syntax change required when accessing a field within an array-of-records is the inclusion of a row selector. To access the first worker's name in *All_Workers* you would write:

```
All_Workers(0).Name = "Cindy Susquehanna"
```

OPERATORS

Visual Basic 5 provides a complete set of arithmetic, relational (comparison), and logical operators. Some operators are unique; others, though not unique in function, use unique symbols. Table 5.2 lists the operators from highest precedence level to lowest.

Table 5.2 Frequently Used Visual Basic 5 Operators

Category	Operation	Symbol
Arithmetic	Exponentiation	^
	Unary minus	-
	Multiplication and division	*,/
	Integer division	\
	Modulo arithmetic	**Mod**
	Addition	+
	Subtraction	-
	String concatenation	&
Relational	Equal, greater than, less than,	=,>,<
	not equal, less than or equal,	<>,<=
	greater than or equal	>=
Logical	Negation	**Not**
	Logical AND	**And**
	Logical OR	**Or**
	EXclusive OR	**Xor**
	Equivalence (EXclusive NOR)	**Eqv**
	Implication	**Imp**

Most of these operators are probably familiar, except perhaps for Implication (**Imp**). Table 5.3 and the explanatory example are included to help you understand this function.

Table 5.3 Implication Truth Table

Bit 1	Bit 2	f
0	0	1
0	1	1
1	0	0
1	1	1

The following example can be used to test the implication truth table:

Assume $A = 18$, $B = 16$, $C = 14$, and D = null:
$A > B$ Imp $B > C$ returns 1
$A > B$ Imp $C > B$ returns 0
$B > A$ Imp $C > B$ returns 1
$B > A$ Imp $C > D$ returns 1

The second test case is the only instance in which the function returns a 0 (False). This is when the implication that $A > B$ implies $C > B$. All other test cases result in a 1 (True).

LOGIC FLOW

The logic flow of a Visual Basic 5 application is controlled by decision, selection, and loop statements. Each control structure works the same as its C or C++ counterpart. The following examples present the syntax for each structure. As you study each structure pay attention to the format style. A consistent indentation scheme is the best way to convey a program's logic flow.

If...Then

You use **If...Then** statements to execute conditionally one or more statements. The syntax for the two forms takes on the following form:

```
If condition Then statement[s]
```

or

```
If condition then
  statement
```

```
statement
    .
    .
    .
End If
```

Although the first form could also be used to execute multiple statements, the second approach is more common:

```
If Value% = 6 Then
 Put FileNum%, Index%, CustEntry
 Index% = Index% + 1
End If
```

If...Then...Else[ElseIf]

The **If...Then...Else** decision statement allows the application to select one of several logically related options. There is one catch to the control structure: the use of the keyword **ElseIf**. **ElseIf** is used to create nested **If...Then...ElseIf**s. The syntax takes on the following form:

```
If test_1 Then
 test_1_statement[s]
[ElseIf test_2 Then
 test_2_statement[s]]
[ElseIf test_n Then
 test_n_statement[s]]
[Else
 default_statement[s]]
End If
```

The following example uses a nested **If...Then...ElseIf...Else** to update a plotting *YCoord* variable:

```
If YCoord > 40 Then
 YCoord = 0
ElseIf YCoord < -40 Then
 YCoord = -10
ElseIf YCoord > 0 Then
 YCoord = YCoord + 1
Else
 YCoord = YCoord - 1
End If
```

Select Case

The **Select Case** structure can be used to replace deeply nested **If...Then...ElseIf...Else** statements. The syntax presents a programmer with a more easily entered and read choice structure:

```
Select Case test
 Case option_match_1
  option_match_1_statement[s]
 [Case option_match_2
  option_match_2_statement[s]]
 [Case option_match_n
  option_match_n_statement[s]]
 [Case Else
  default_option_statement[s]]
End Select
```

Notice that the **Select Case** statement has an optional **Else** clause and must be terminated with an **End Select** instruction. The following example uses the **Select Case** structure to rewrite the nested **If...Then...ElseIf...Else** in the previous example:

```
Select Case YCoord
 Case 41
  YCoord = 0
 Case -41
  YCoord = -10
 Case 1 To 40
   YCoord = YCoord + 1
 Case Else
   YCoord = YCoord - 1
End Select
```

For Loops

A **For** loop is used to repeat one line or several lines of code a predetermined number of times. **For** loops work with a *loop_control* variable that is initialized once and then automatically incremented or decremented with each pass through the loop. **For** loops are pretest loops. They may be entered from 0 to many times depending on *loop_control*'s initial value. The syntax takes on this form:

```
For loop_control = start_value To end_value [Step increment]
 statement[s]
Next [loop_control]
```

When using a For loop in Visual Basic 5, consider:

1. Copying the *start_value* into the *loop_control* variable.
2. Loops that increment: Test to see if *loop_control* is less than or equal to *end_value*.
3. Loops that decrement: Test to see if *loop_control* is greater than or equal to *end_value*.
4. Enter the loop if either test evaluates to True.
5. After executing the statement(s) in the loop, the **Next** instruction automatically increments (count up) or decrements (count down) the *loop_control* variable. (If you leave off the variable in the **Next** statement, **Next** will be paired with the closest **For** statement.)
6. Repeat steps 2, 3, and 4 until the *loop_control* exceeds (count up) or is below (count down) *end_value*.
7. **For** loops default to an automatic increment (+1) or decrement (-1) of one.
8. An optional **Step** can be used to change the default increment value—for example, +2 for increment and -5 for decrement loops.

Here is an example in which the loop sums up the first 101 even integers from 100 to 200:

```
Dim I, GrandTotal As Integer
For I = 100 To 200 Step 2
 GrandTotal = GrandTotal + I
Next I
```

Do While...Loop

Unlike **For** loops, which always execute a predetermined number of iterations, **Do** loops execute an indefinite number of times. **Do While...Loops** are pretest loops. As with **For** loops, this means that the condition for entering or not entering the loop is examined before any statements within the loop are executed. **Do While...Loops** execute while the test condition evaluates to true. They may execute from zero to many times. Their syntax takes on the following form:

```
Do While test_condition
  statement[s]
Loop
```

Care must be taken when writing the code for **Do While...Loops** to make certain that at some point the *test_condition* evaluates to False, terminating the loop.

The following code segment uses a **Do While...Loop** to generate the sum of even integers from 2 to 200.

```
Dim I, GrandTotal As Integer
I = 2
Do While I <= 200
  GrandTotal = GrandTotal + I
  I = I + 2
Loop
```

Do...Loop While

Do...Loop Whiles are called posttest loops. This is because the statements nested within the loop structure are executed at least once before the *test_condition* is checked. The loop then repeats as long as the *test_condition* evaluates to True. The syntax for a **Do...Loop While** takes on the following form:

```
Do
  statement[s]
Loop While test_condition
```

Do Until...Loop, Do...Loop Until

Visual Basic 5 supports two logical inverses of the **Do** loops just described. **Do Until...Loops** and **Do...Loop Untils** execute while the *test_condition* evaluates to False. With this exception, both loop structures perform like their positive counterparts. The **Do Until...Loop** is a pretest loop, **Do...Loop Until** is a posttest loop. The syntax for a **Do Until...Loop** takes on this form:

```
Do Until test_condition
  statement[s]
Loop
```

The syntax for a **Do...Loop Until** takes on this form:

```
Do
 statement[s]
Loop Until test_condition
```

PROCEDURES

Most programming code in a Visual Basic 5 application takes place inside procedures. These procedures are called event procedures and are portions of code that are executed when a form or control recognizes that a particular event has occurred. As efficient as event procedures are, they are not perfect for all situations, and for this reason Visual Basic 5 supports **Sub** and **Function** procedures.

Take, for example, a database program that always maintains a sorted list. The user has three click options: create original list (Command1), insert into list (Command2), and merge lists (Command3). Potentially, each operation can shuffle the order of the list. Without procedures you would be required to replicate the sort algorithm three times, once for each click event. Figure 5.5 illustrates the correct relationship.

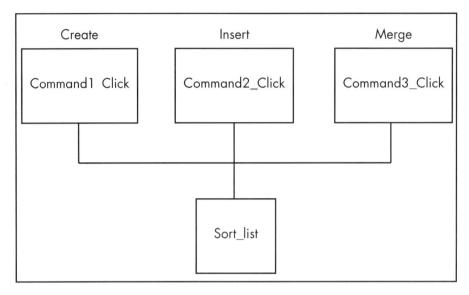

Figure 5.5 The relationship between general procedures and event procedures.

Sub Procedures

Sub procedures are different from **Function** procedures in that they can return from zero to many values. **Function**(s) must always return one value. The syntax for a **Sub** procedure takes on the following form:

```
Sub procedure_identifier ([argument][,argument...])
 statement[s]
End Sub
```

The *argument* list defines the name for each argument and, optionally, its *data_type*. To identify an *argument*'s data type you can either use the **As** keyword or append a *TDC*, type-declaration character (% (Integer), & (Long Integer), ! (Single), # (Double), @ (Currency), $ (String), or none (defaults to Double)). The syntax for each *argument* takes on the following form:

```
[ByVal] variable_identifier [TDC][As data_type]
```

The **ByVal** keyword is explained in the section Passing Arguments Call-By-Value later in this chapter.

Calling a **Sub** procedure from within a Visual Basic 5 application is syntactically different from the method in most high-level programming languages. A Visual Basic 5 calling statement does not need parentheses around the argument list. The syntax for calling a **Sub** procedure takes on the following form:

```
procedure_identifier [arg1][arg2...argn]
```

By default, Visual Basic 5 passes all arguments (*arg1..argn*) as *call-by-variable*. This means that the address of each argument is passed to the procedure, not a copy of argument's contents. Call-by-variable allows the procedure to change the variable's contents permanently.

Function Procedures

Unlike **Sub** procedures that are called, **Function** procedures are invoked from within expressions. They always return one value. Because of this, their syntax is slightly different:

```
Function procedure_identifier[TDC] ([argument]
                 [,argument...]) [As data_type]
  statement[s]
End Function
```

The syntax for defining **Function** *arguments* is identical to that for **Sub** procedures. The **As** keyword is optional and can be used to define the **Function's** return type. If it is omitted, the **Function's** return type must be indicated with an appended *TDC*. **Function** procedures are said to be "invoked" and require the argument list to be surrounded with parentheses.

CREATING PROCEDURES

General procedures are created by first opening a form and selecting the View | Code window. Next, the Tools | Add Procedure... option is selected. Visual Basic 5 displays a dialog box that allows you to enter the procedure's name and click on its type, as seen in Figure 5.6.

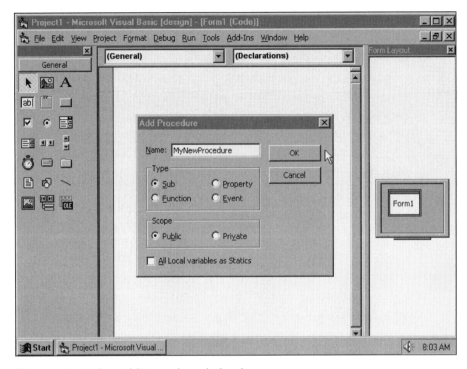

Figure 5.6 The Add Procedure dialog box.

PASSING ARGUMENTS CALL-BY-VALUE

By preceding a procedure parameter with the **ByVal** keyword, you instruct Visual Basic 5 to accept a copy of the passed value. Passing a parameter call-**ByVal** prevents the invoked procedure from making any permanent changes to the original data.

Sometimes the **ByVal** keyword is needed to pass values that would otherwise invoke a translator complaint. For example, a form's control properties are global to any procedure bound to the form. Trying to pass them to a bound subroutine invokes a "Parameter type mismatch" error. The **ByVal** keyword allows you to pass a copy of these values, not the address of where they are stored. This can be very useful when trying to write generic procedures that are not hardwired to a particular control.

The following function header passes the *WorkerSalary* **ByVal.** This allows the function to have access to the value but prevents it from altering the original base value:

```
Function CalculatePay (ByVal WorkerSalary As Long) As Double
```

IDENTIFIER SCOPE

The *scope* of an identifier delimits where the constant, type, variable, or procedure is visible. Visible, in this sense, means where it can affect the outcome of an event. The correct placement of an identifier's declaration can make all the difference in making an algorithm easy to understand.

The basic rule of thumb is to keep an identifier's declaration as close to the code that uses it as possible. Visual Basic 5 identifiers can have one of four levels of visibility: global, form or module, and local. Figure 5.7 illustrates their relationship.

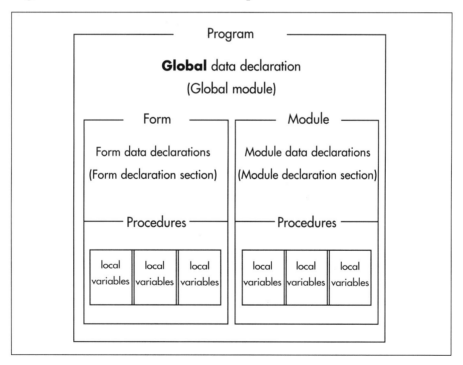

Figure 5.7 Scope levels for identifiers.

Global Identifiers

Any constant, type, or variable can have global accessibility if it is defined in an application's global module. The **Global** modifier is used instead of the standard **Dim** keyword. The **Global** modifier automatically initializes numeric variables to 0 and strings to null or empty string.

Sometimes global scope is referred to as file scope. This means that the identifier can be accessed by any form, module, or procedure. In addition, global variables retain their currently assigned values from one procedure to another.

The following code section defines a global count *(Max_Values)*, an 8-element array of hours worked *(DailyHoursWorked)*, and a 200-element array *(ForeignDictionary)* of a user-defined type *(BiLingualStorage)*.

```
Global Max_Values As Integer
Global DailyHoursWorked(7) As Long
Type BiLingualStorage
 Russian As String
 Spanish As String
End Type
Global ForeignDictionary(199) As BiLingualStorage
```

Form- and Module-Level Identifiers

A *form-level identifier* is used to create identifiers that are visible across all event, **Sub**, and **Function** procedures within a form. This is achieved by using the code page window to edit the form's "general" Object "declarations" Procedure.

Form-level identifiers are global to all of the form's procedures but they are local to the form. Form-level identifiers are not accessible by other forms or modules.

Module-level identifiers are similar to their form-level counterparts except that the identifiers are defined in the module's "declarations" section. Module-level identifiers are global to all nested procedures but local to the module. Module-level identifiers are not accessible by other modules or forms.

Local Identifiers

Local variables have the most restricted visibility. They are declared using the **Dim** statement at the beginning of the event, **Sub**, or **Function** procedure or for the subprocedure itself. Storage is allocated for local identifiers when the procedure is entered. When the procedure is finished executing the local identifier returns to bit oblivion.

The following procedure creates the loop control variable *Index* when the procedure is entered. After the procedure has finished execution, the variable is removed from the run time stack.

```
Private Sub Command1_Click ()
 Dim Index As Integer
 For Index = 1 to MaxValues
   Print ForeignDictionary(Index).Spanish
 Next I
End Sub
```

The Private Modifier

The Private modifier is used to indicate that the **Sub** procedure is accessible only to other procedures in the module where it is declared.

The Public Modifier

The Public modifier is used to indicate that the **Sub** procedure is accessible to all procedures in all modules.

The Static Modifier

The **Static** modifier gives a local identifier, global lifetime, while retaining local visibility. The **Static** modifier replaces the **Dim** keyword when defining the variable.

Normally a procedure's variables have local scope. They are created when the procedure is entered, automatically initialized (0, numeric; NULL-string, string), and destroyed when the procedure is exited. The following Click procedure would forever print "Starting" were it not for the **Static** modifier:

```
Private Sub Command1_Click ()
Static Index As Integer
```

```
If Index = 0 Then
 Command1.Caption = "Starting"
 Index = Index + 1
Else
 Command1.Caption = Format$(Index, "##")
 Index = Index + 1
End If
End Sub
```

The most frequent and valid reason for using **Static** local variables is to create accumulators. An *accumulator* is a variable that maintains some sort of running total within the procedure. The value it stores is meaningless to any other piece of code outside the procedure.

With *Index* defined as **Static** it is initialized only once the first time the procedure is entered. A persistent value change is made by any statement, within the procedure, that modifies *Index*. The variable, while having a global lifetime, can be accessed only within Command1_Click!

Index's value could have been retained by defining the identifier at the global level. However, this would have been a bad design decision. A global definition would have left a programmer confused, since such a placement implies that the variable is used by several forms, modules, or procedures.

Identifiers with the Same Name

Visual Basic 5 allows you to reuse variable names. This means that you can define an array *Index* in an input procedure and another *Index* in an output procedure. Visual Basic 5 resolves the conflict by always searching the nearest level of scope.

Any statement accessing a variable is checked against the procedure declarations first, followed by form or module and global definitions. The following guidelines can be used when deciding whether a variable should be declared globally, avoiding repeated local declarations, or locally:

- Under certain circumstances code readability may be sacrificed for execution speed by declaring a variable globally instead of using repeated local definitions.

- Use global file declarations to represent specifically data that is needed in multiple procedures, forms, or modules.

- Variable declarations should appear at the level closest to the statements using the identifier.
- Variables declared at the local level unclutter the global file.

LOOKING AHEAD

In the next chapter, we'll look at ways to add the programming elements, from this chapter, to various Visual Basic 5 controls.

Chapter 6

Interfacing with Controls and Menus

In the previous chapter you learned about key Visual Basic 5 programming language elements. In this chapter you'll learn how to incorporate those elements into programming code that will, well, "control" the operation of various Visual Basic 5 controls. Many Visual Basic 5 controls can be added at design time from the Toolbox. The Toolbox can be placed on your design screen from the <u>V</u>iew | <u>T</u>oolbox menu selection, as shown in Figure 6.1.

Figure 6.1 Visual Basic's Toolbox.

A control is placed in a form by dragging it from the Toolbox to the form with the mouse. Once the control is placed on the form it is visible but nonfunctional. In Chapter 3 you learned about the various controls shown in the Toolbox and studied their properties. In this chapter you will learn how to write programming code to interface with controls to make them fully functional.

HANDLING A USER'S RESPONSE

CommandButton and Menu controls, for example, are controls that are used by almost all Windows 95 and Windows NT applications. CommandButton controls are visible in the Toolbox, whereas Menu controls must be added with the Menu Editor. These controls allow you to create a clean, professional looking, and easily understood interface. Controls prevent a user from entering incorrect information by permitting only a point-and-click selection. This approach streamlines the programming algorithm and makes for smooth program execution.

Visual Basic 5 allows the inclusion of shortcut and access key activation. These shortcut and access key activations are one- or two-key combinations that allow users to keep their fingers on "home row" when making command or menu selections.

Visual Basic 5 makes it very easy for you to add commands, menus, and access keys to an application. In previous chapters you have worked with placing and activating controls. The combination of the Toolbox control selection and Command_Click () events took only minutes to learn and construct. You'll find that creating Menu controls with the Menu Editor's Design window is just as easy.

In the next sections you will learn the mechanics and syntax of programming CommandButton and Menu controls. Each example presents a new feature of Visual Basic 5 that you can begin to use in your own designs. Most other controls, in the Toolbox, can be programmed in a similar manner.

COMMANDBUTTON CONTROLS

A CommandButton control is designed to emulate visually a push button (similar to the operation of a doorbell button). Clicking the mouse on a CommandButton control produces the visual effect of pressing a button. When the mouse button is clicked, the button visually pushes in on the screen. As soon as the mouse button is released, the button pops back up.

Useful CommandButton controls are created with a combination of three characteristics: proper size, correct screen location, and a meaningful Caption property. For example, Figure 6.2 shows a CommandButton control with the Caption set to "Turn Sound ON."

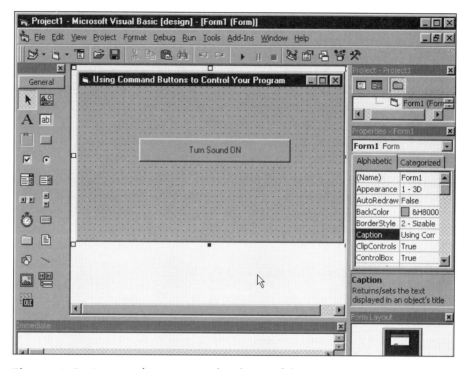

Figure 6.2 CommandButton control with a useful Caption.

Sound cues are only one of the many useful environment options a program can have. A "Turn Sound ON" CommandButton control can be used to toggle the selection of audible reminders.

Visual Basic 5 provides four ways (one mouse, three keyboard) to access a CommandButton control. All four approaches cause Visual Basic 5 to invoke the Command_Click () event. The easiest approach, for nontypists, is to use the mouse to click on the button.

A second approach is to choose a CommandButton control by pressing the SPACEBAR. The use of the SPACEBAR automatically selects the control with the current focus. Only one CommandButton control can have the focus at any given moment. *Focus* determines which control will receive the user's response. Focus can be changed by using the TAB key. During execution, the control caption that is surrounded with a faint dashed rectangle has the focus.

The remaining two methods for choosing a CommandButton control are linked to the ENTER and ESC keys. Setting a CommandButton control's Default property to TRUE (-1) at design time allows the user to activate the option by pressing ENTER. Pressing ENTER automatically invokes the Default command regardless of which control has the focus.

In a similar way, setting a command's Cancel property to TRUE (-1) at design time allows the user to select the option with the ESC key. Pressing ESC automatically invokes the Cancel command, overriding any control having the focus.

PICTUREBOX CONTROLS

PictureBox controls also recognize Click events. They are the preferred alternative to CommandButton controls when designing a language-independent interface. You can use a picture box anywhere you can use a CommandButton control. Figure 6.3 shows a picture box replacement for Figure 6.2's CommandButton control.

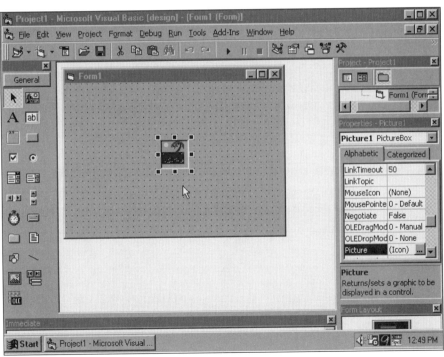

Figure 6.3 Picture1.Picture="c:\Vb5\Graphics\Icons\Misc\misc31.ico".

A PictureBox control is also considered the most user-friendly alternative when designing children's applications. PictureBox controls should, therefore, be chosen carefully and be appropriate for the text they are replacing.

PROGRAMMING COMMANDBUTTON CONTROL RESPONSES

It is common in business applications to work with large databases. Most database programs use some sort of search procedure for locating information. If you have ever written a search procedure, in another programming language, you are aware of some of the technical difficulties that can be encountered. These difficulties often entail the case (upper- or lowercase characters) of the search string along with its length. These are critical factors when attempting to find a perfect match in a search.

Many databases store their information in mixed case. A good search procedure must take this into consideration. For example, the words Washington, WASHINGTON, and washington are different only because of the case of the letters they contain. In its most robust sense, the search procedure should be written in such a way that it really doesn't matter how the data is stored. It should also be impervious to the user's input format, in terms of case.

A simple solution is to force all characters to upper- or lowercase in both the search string and source string. Although today's applications are far more sophisticated, that is a simple solution that is easy to implement. Figure 6.4 shows an interface that can be used for this purpose. The user enters the search string in any cAsE. Pressing the Correct button causes the corresponding Click event to display the **UCase$**ed (all uppercase) string along with its length.

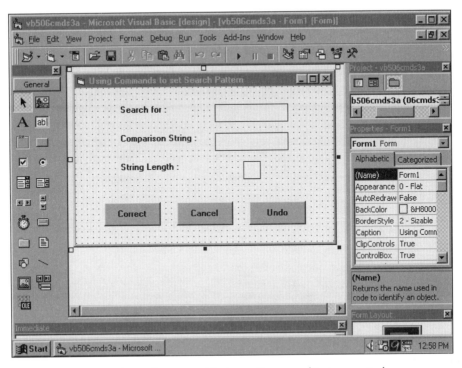

Figure 6.4 Search application with three CommandButton controls.

 Note: Ucase$ will produce errors if it is used with case-sensitive data. That is not the case in this simple example, however.

The Cancel button is used to remove an incorrect entry. The convenient Undo command allows a user to back up easily from a hasty decision.

There are nine controls in the interface: three Label controls, three TextBox controls, and three CommandButton controls. All of the form's actions are controlled by the Command1_Click(), Command2_Click(), and Command3_Click () events. Let's examine how the control code might be written for the Correct button:

```
Dim PastResponse As String

Private Sub Command1_Click ()
  Text2.Text = UCase$(Text1.Text)
  Text3.Text = Format$(Len(Text1.Text), "00")
End Sub
```

PastResponse was defined in Form1's general declarations section. This allowed the variable to be global to the three Click events and local to the form.

The first statement in the procedure uses Visual Basic 5's built-in **UCase$()** function (or BIF) to convert the user's input to UPPERcase. This is displayed in the Comparison String's Text2 box control.

The string's length is displayed by invoking two additional BIFs. The **Len()** function returns a numeric value representing the string parameter's length. **Format$()** converts this numeric representation back into a string format so that it can be assigned to the Text property of Text3.

Pressing the Cancel button invokes the Command2_Click() event. Here is how code can be written to handle this event:

```
Private Sub Command2_Click ()
   PastResponse = Text1.Text
   Text1.Text = ""
   Text2.Text = ""
   Text3.Text = ""
   Text1.SetFocus
End Sub
```

The first statement takes care of remembering the user's current entry. The next three statements erase the user's previous responses.

The last statement uses Visual Basic 5's **SetFocus** instruction to automatically place the input focus back on Text1. This causes the I-beam cursor to flash in the *Search for:* window. Redirecting a form's control focus can be one of the simplest design decisions you can make to help guide the user. When this is done the user is reminded to enter a new search word.

The Undo button allows the user to reenter the previous search word. Here is how the Command3_Click() event is coded:

```
Private Sub Command3_Click ()
   Text1.Text = PastResponse
   Command1.Value = -1         'TRUE
End Sub
```

The first statement sets the *Search for:* text back to the user's previous choice. The second statement uses the command's Value property. This property can be read or set and reflects the control's activated state. Assigning a TRUE to the property is the equivalent, in code, of having the user click on the button. The statement invokes the Correct button's Click event. When the code is executed the user's past entry in UPPERcase along with its length will be displayed.

WORKING WITH COMMANDBUTTON CONTROLS AT EXECUTION TIME

CommandButton controls, as you know, have many properties that can be controlled at execution time. These include Cancel, Default, Enabled, and Visible. Which of these properties should you use? In answering the question, remember that all Windows applications are very visual. For example, to run an application, the user clicks the mouse on the Run command. The Run control may even be a graphical swimmer icon if the application is a Swimmer's Lap Time/Distance Analyzer!

Two command properties that help manage a form's visual clarity are Visible and Enabled. Visual Basic 5 can be instructed to display (Visible = -1, TRUE) or hide (Visible = 0, FALSE) a CommandButton control by assigning the appropriate value. CommandButton controls should be displayed only if their selection is important to the current operation in a user interface.

Enabled (Enabled = -1, TRUE) controls have a bold font appearance, whereas disabled controls (Enabled = 0, FALSE) have a faint gray Caption property. Unlike an invisible CommandButton control property, a disabled control property allows the user to see, but not access, options that are available under certain circumstances.

For example, Figure 6.5 shows a visible but disabled Undo button. This state tells the user that it is not currently active but is functionally available when the right conditions exist. The control was set to inactive, during the design phase, by resetting the control's Enabled property to FALSE.

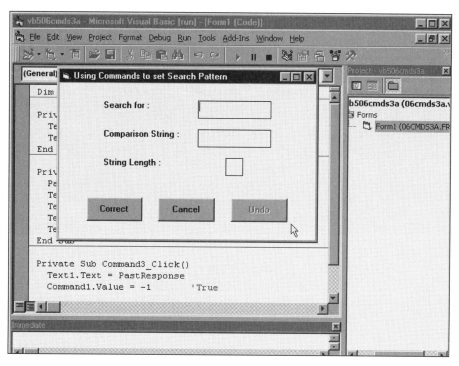

Figure 6.5 Disabled Undo CommandButton controls.

The Undo button remains visible but inactive until the user enters the first search string. The event is acknowledged when the user clicks on the Correct button. The program uses this action to enable the Undo button. Only one line of code was necessary to update the Command1_Click event:

```
Private Sub Command1_Click ()
  Command3.Enabled = -1   'Enables the Undo command
  Text2.Text = UCase$(Text1.Text)
  Text3.Text = Format$(Len(Text1.Text), "00")
End Sub
```

To create a fully functional search window interface, combine the previous change with your understanding of Default and Cancel properties. Reset the Default property on the Cancel button to TRUE. This allows the user to invoke the Correct button's Click event by pressing the ENTER key.

Do the same thing with the Cancel button's Cancel property. Now the interface will respond to the ESC key as if the user had clicked on the Cancel button.

CONTROLLING THE TAB ORDER

Any form using more than one control has a tab order by default. The tab order determines which control will get the focus when the user presses the TAB key. The tab order can be controlled at design time and/or run time. All controls except Timer controls and Menu controls are a part of the tab order. Disabled or invisible controls are not part of the tab order.

The TabIndex and TabStop properties manage a form's tab order. TabIndex defines the route. TabStop indicates whether a control is in or out of the tab order. By default, a form's tab order is set by the control creation sequence. A TabIndex of 0 is assigned to the first control placed on the form. The second control is given TabIndex = 1, and so on. An application's source code can be streamlined by a predetermined control placement order. This eliminates all need for tab order assignment statements but requires insight into the design of the user interface.

When a control is placed on a form, its TabStop property is automatically set to TRUE. This means that it can be reached with the TAB key at run time.

If you have entered and executed the code for the search window described earlier, you might have been annoyed that you had to tab past the uppercase and length output TextBox controls (Text2, Text3). To improve the window's performance, go back to the form's design window and change the TabStop property for these controls to FALSE. Now when you execute the program the TAB key will bypass these controls.

Did you notice that the Undo CommandButton control was not in the tab order until the Correct button was pressed? Visual Basic 5 takes care of changing the TabStop property whenever an inactive control becomes active. The inactive control's TabIndex is set at design time and can be changed at run time.

Changing the Tab Order

The following statement illustrates how to change a control's TabIndex:

```
form.control.TabIndex = [0,-1]
```

Changing one control's TabIndex has the rippling effect of updating all successively created form controls.

For example, if the original form design had sequentially created Text1, Text2, Command1, and Command2, their respective TabIndex values would go from 0 to 3. Table 6.1 illustrates what would happen to the tab order if Command1's TabIndex was changed to 0 with the following run-time code:

```
Command1.TabIndex = 0
```

Table 6.1 Effects of Changing One Tab Index

Control	Original Form Design TabIndex	Final Order
Text1	0	2
Text2	1	3
Command1	2	0
Command2	3	1

Since TabIndex numbering begins at 0, the highest TabIndex setting is always one less than the number of controls in the tab order. When in doubt, an application can always set a control's TabIndex to a value larger than the number of controls; this effectively moves the control to the end of the tab order. However, setting a control's TabIndex to a value less than 0 generates an error.

USING PROPERTY VALUES AT EXECUTION TIME

Many control properties can be accessed at run time. This access allows an application to monitor user input constantly and respond with a visual prompt. The following statement uses the current value of the Enabled property to activate selectively a background color choice:

```
If Text1.Enabled Then
   Text1.BackColor = BLUE   '&HFF0000
Else
   Text1.BackColor = Form1.BackColor
End If
```

This brief example shows how you can highlight an active control with color. The **Else** part of the statement camouflages an inactive control by making it blend with the form's background.

By the way, since all logic control statements must evaluate to a TRUE (nonzero value) or FALSE (0) and the Enabled property fits this description, there is no need for a logical test. The statement does not have to read as shown next to be syntactically correct:

```
If Text1.Enabled = TRUE
```

Just remember, as far as Visual Basic 5 is concerned any positive or negative nonzero value is considered a logical TRUE.

DEVELOPING MENU-DRIVEN APPLICATIONS

Adding a hierarchical menu to a Visual Basic 5 application is just as easy as adding controls to a form. A *hierarchical* menu is one that has menu items linked to nested menus (*submenus*) with their own set of related commands.

Visual Basic 5 sees each menu item as a separate command control with its own Click event procedure. Figures 6.6 and 6.7 show the BOOLEAN Calculator's two menus.

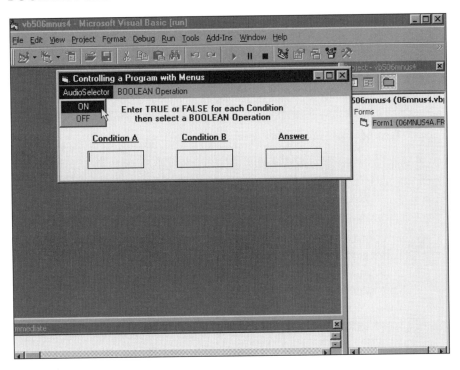

Figure 6.6 AudioSelector menu.

This BOOLEAN Calculator is also designed to teach and review Visual Basic 5's five logical operators. In addition, it demonstrates how to add an audible cue to a program's execution and make the option user selectable.

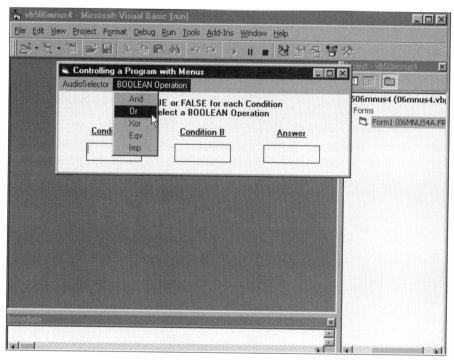

Figure 6.7 BOOLEAN operation menu.

Adding a Menu

The Menu Editor's Design window is used to create a program's menus. It controls the number of menu items and their hierarchical arrangement and initializes the restricted set of command control properties.

Although it is true that Visual Basic 5 interprets menu items as command control objects, it does not give them the usual full set of command control properties. The only properties valid for a menu item are Caption, Name, Shortcut, Window List, HelpContextID, Checked, Enabled, Index, and Visible.

The Menu Editor is started by selecting Tools | Menu Editor... from the Visual Basic 5 menu bar. Figure 6.8 shows the completed BOOLEAN Calculator menu definition.

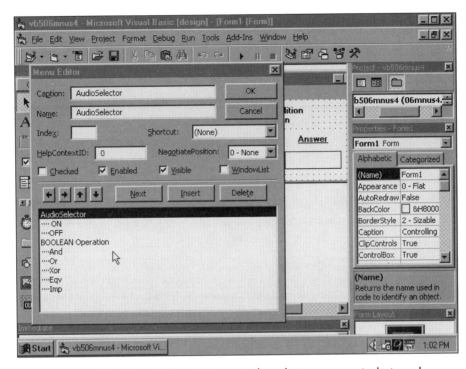

Figure 6.8 The Menu Editor Design window during a menu's design phase.

Items placed in the Menu Editor's Design window can be a command, menu name, separator bar, or submenu. Here are the steps for adding a menu entry:

1. Enter the Caption for the entry.
2. Give the entry a Name (CtlName) so that you can refer to the item in code.
3. Use an Index value to help determine a control's position within a control array. (This doesn't refer to the screen position.)
4. A Shortcut will allow the use of a shortcut key for each command.
5. The HelpContextID can be used to assign a numeric value for context ID help via the HelpFile property.
6. Use NegotiatePosition when the menu's NegotiatePosition property is selected (determines whether the menu appears in a container form).

7. Decide whether the entry's original appearance should be Checked (displayed with a check mark), Enabled (alert to responses), and Visible.

8. Use Enabled if the menu item is to respond to events. Use clear if you want the item to be unavailable and grayed.

9. Use Visible to allow the menu item to appear on the menu.

10. The use of WindowList determines whether the menu control contains a list of open MDI child forms. This is for MDI applications.

Once the new menu is specified, you'll want to add menu names and menu items. These are added with the help of the Menu Editor's arrow keys, in the following manner:

1. Use the editor's left and right arrow icons to decide the entry's level (these are located in the middle of the previous figure). An entry that is not indented is a top-level menu. A menu item is inserted (appears indented) by clicking on the right arrow icon. Menu items are often called sub-menu items.

2. Five levels of indentation are permitted. A menu can have as many as four levels of submenus. The fifth level is unique because it can use only commands and separator bars. No additional submenu items are permitted at the fifth level.

3. During the design phase, submenu items appear in the Menu Editor's Design window with leading dashes. The number of dashes is related to their level.

4. Additional menu items are added by using ENTER or selecting the Next command.

5. A separator bar can be added to a menu by entering a single hyphen (-). Separator bars can have names (CtlName). Using this reference, they can be activated or deactivated with programming code.

To give the user keyboard access to a menu item, insert an ampersand (&) before a letter. At run time, this letter is underlined (the ampersand is not visible), and the user can access the menu or command by pressing ALT and the letter. If you need an ampersand to show in the menu, put two consecutive ampersands in the caption.

All menu items except separator bars recognize their own Click event. The Click event procedure is invoked when the user chooses it.

Once a menu design is completed, the Menu Editor can be closed by clicking on the OK button. When the Menu Editor is closed, Visual Basic 5 will add the fully functional menu hierarchy to your form's design. The only thing left to do is to add the Click event source code to the application's code. This code will tell your application what is to take place when a particular menu item is selected.

Coding Menu Items

Visual Basic 5 automatically creates a Click event for each menu item you enter (except separator bars). To add code to a menu command, make certain that the Menu Editor's Design window is closed by clicking on the OK button.

To get to a menu command's Click event, simply double-click on the menu item. If the menu item is in a submenu, follow the command sequence needed to select that option.

The following declaration was added to the BOOLEAN Calculator's general form declarations. This gave each menu item's Click event global access to the identifier:

```
Dim Sound As Integer
```

The BOOLEAN Calculator's audible response is determined by the AudioSelection's ON and OFF Click event procedures. The procedure names match the CtlName given to each command:

```
Private Sub ONSelector_Click ()
   Sound = TRUE
End Sub

Private Sub OFFSelector_Click ()
   Sound = FALSE
End Sub
```

The application automatically turns the sound response ON whenever it is started. The following code was added to the form's Load event procedure:

```
Private Sub Form_Load ()
   Sound = TRUE
End Sub
```

Form Load events are used frequently to set up an interface's initial characteristics.

The BOOLEAN Calculator operates by letting the user enter TRUE or FALSE for Condition A and Condition B. As soon as the user selects the Logical Operator the result of the operation appears in the Answer box. The following five operator events generate this value:

```
Private Sub AndOpr_Click ()
   If Text1.Text = "TRUE" And Text2.Text = "TRUE" Then
     Text3.Text = "TRUE"
   Else
     Text3.Text = "FALSE"
   End If
   If Sound Then
     Beep
   End If
End Sub


Private Sub OrOpr_Click ()
   If Text1.Text = "FALSE" And Text2.Text = "FALSE" Then
     Text3.Text = "FALSE"
   Else
     Text3.Text = "TRUE"
   End If
   If Sound Then
     Beep
   End If
End Sub


Private Sub XorOpr_Click ()
   If Text1.Text <> Text2.Text Then
     Text3.Text = "TRUE"
   Else
     Text3.Text = "FALSE"
   End If
   If Sound Then
     Beep
   End If
End Sub
```

```
Private Sub EqvOpr_Click ()
  If Text1.Text = Text2.Text Then
    Text3.Text = "TRUE"
  Else
    Text3.Text = "FALSE"
  End If
  If Sound Then
    Beep
  End If
End Sub

Private Sub ImpOpr_Click ()
  If Text1.Text = "TRUE" And Text2.Text = "FALSE" Then
    Text3.Text = "FALSE"
  Else
    Text3.Text = "TRUE"
  End If
  If Sound Then
    Beep
  End If
End Sub
```

Notice, in the previous listing, how each event takes advantage of *Sound's* global setting.

The following two Change event procedures were added to prevent the user from associating a past Answer with an altered Condition A or B input:

```
Private Sub Text1_Change ()
  Text3.Text = ""
End Sub

Private Sub Text2_Change ()
  Text3.Text = ""
End Sub
```

TextBox control Change events are triggered whenever the user alters the control's contents. If the user changes the input in either Text1 or Text2, the application blanks out the Answer box's display.

PLACING CHECK MARKS ON MENU SELECTIONS

It is often confusing to have to remember which of an application's menu options have been selected and which have not. Check marks can be placed next to active options to make this clear to the user. A menu option's check mark can be set at design time by clicking on the Checked option in the Menu Editor's Design window. This approach is usually used to flag system presets—values that are initially turned on.

The Foreign Language Calculator program, shown in Figure 6.9, shows the Language | English command Checked property set at design time.

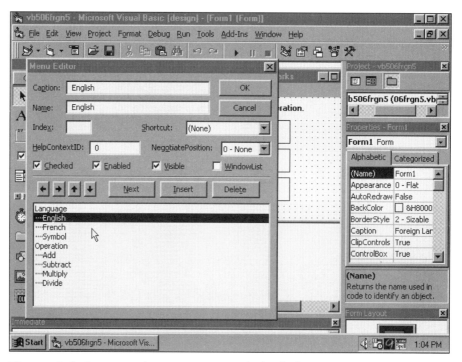

Figure 6.9 Presetting the menu command Checked property.

As the program executes the check mark moves to reflect the user's current language preference. Figure 6.10 indicates the selection of a French language interface.

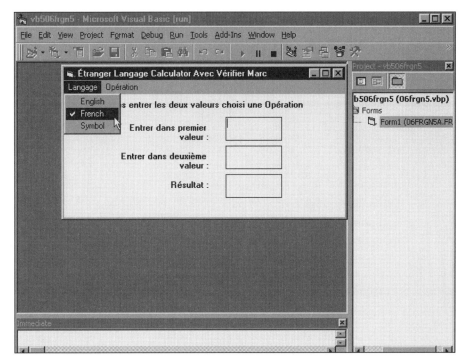

Figure 6.10 Changing check marks at execution time.

The syntax for accessing a menu command's Checked property takes on the following form:

```
command.Checked = [0,-1]
```

The following listing has the same three lines of code highlighted for each language Click event. This will help you to concentrate on the lines of code necessary to manipulate check marks:

```
Private Sub French_Click ()
   English.Checked = FALSE
   French.Checked = TRUE
   Symbol.Checked = FALSE
   Form1.Caption = "Étranger Langage Calculator Avec Vérifier
Marc"
   Language.Caption = "Langage"
   Operation.Caption = "Opération"
   Add.Caption = "Ajouter"
   Subtract.Caption = "Soustraction"
```

```
    Multiply.Caption = "Multiplier"
    Divide.Caption = "Diviser"
    Label1.Caption = "Entrer dans premier valeur :"
    Label2.Caption = "Entrer dans deuxième valeur :"
    Label3.Caption = "Résultat :"
    Label4.Caption = "Après entrer les deux valeurs choisi une
                       Opération"
End Sub


Private Sub English_Click ()
    English.Checked = TRUE
    French.Checked = FALSE
    Symbol.Checked = FALSE
    Form1.Caption = "Foreign Language Calculator that uses
                       Check Marks"
    Language.Caption = "Language"
    Operation.Caption = "Operation"
    Label1.Caption = "Enter first value :"
    Label2.Caption = "Enter second value :"
    Label3.Caption = "Result :"
    Label4.Caption = "After entering both values select an
                       Operation"
End Sub


Private Sub Symbol_Click ()
    English.Checked = FALSE
    French.Checked = FALSE
    Symbol.Checked = TRUE
    Form1.Caption = "A  [ +, -, *, / ]  B  =  ?"
    Language.Caption = "Language"
    Operation.Caption = "[ +, -, *, / ]"
    Add.Caption = "+"
    Subtract.Caption = "-"
    Multiply.Caption = "*"
    Divide.Caption = "/"
    Label1.Caption = "A "
    Label2.Caption = "B "
```

```
Label3.Caption = " = "
Label4.Caption = "1) A <- ?,        2) B <- ?,
                   3) [ +, -, *, / ]"
```

End Sub

Each event procedure is responsible for turning ON the check mark associated with its menu command and turning OFF any previously selected option. It also takes care of changing the form's prompts to the selected language.

Figure 6.11 shows the four Operation menu commands for this example. Each has its own Click event procedure:

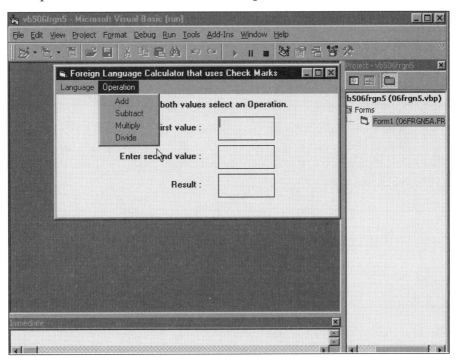

Figure 6.11 Operation menu commands.

```
Private Sub Add_Click ()
  Text3.Text = Format$(Val(Text1.Text) + Val(Text2.Text))
End Sub

Private Sub Subtract_Click ()
  Text3.Text = Format$(Val(Text1.Text) - Val(Text2.Text))
End Sub

Private Sub Multiply_Click ()
  Text3.Text = Format$(Val(Text1.Text) * Val(Text2.Text))
End Sub

Private Sub Divide_Click ()
  Text3.Text = Format$(Val(Text1.Text) / Val(Text2.Text))
End Sub
```

Each Operation event uses the **Val()** BIF to convert the user's response into a numeric value. Once the result has been calculated **Format$()** converts it back to a string. The assignment statement takes the string representation and assigns it to the appropriate text box control.

Here is a challenge: See if you can write the four lines of code needed by each procedure to add a check mark to the four menu commands. (Hint: Each event procedure has to turn its Check ON and all others OFF.)

Figure 6.12 displays the program's Symbol Language mode.

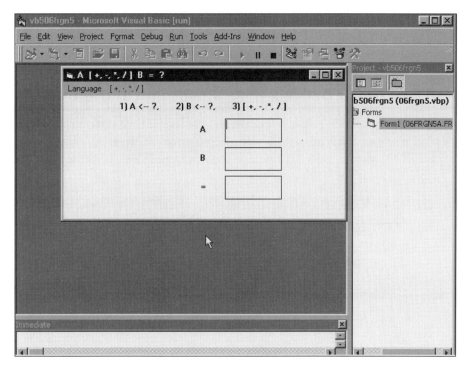

Figure 6.12 Foreign Language Calculator in Symbol mode.

This simple application demonstrates how easy it is to modify a program's interface so that it can respond to users of different backgrounds and experience.

ADDING OR DELETING MENU COMMANDS AT EXECUTION TIME

Visual Basic 5 allows a program to add and delete menu items at the time of execution. This ability permits the menu commands to reflect the current state of the application. All of this functionality is made possible by a structure called a *control array*.

Control Arrays

A *control array* is a set of similar controls that all share the same CtlName and Click event procedure. They are similar to regular arrays that hold collections of homogeneous data types. Command control arrays have elements that are functionally homogeneous.

If an application wishes to add menu options dynamically, the new control must be part of a control array. In this manner, the added control can syntactically link to executable code.

Adding or Deleting Color Commands at Execution Time

The display's color selection is a useful feature that can be easily incorporated into an application. The form's interface, shown in Figure 6.13, shows a menu with two commands that allow the user to select the monitor's DisplayMode.

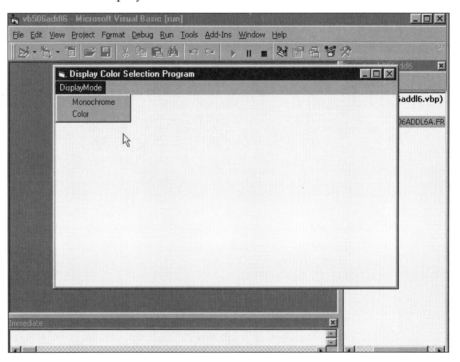

Figure 6.13 The Display Color Selection Program.

When the user clicks on the Monochrome command, a separator bar and two monochromatic display options are added to the menu, as seen in Figure 6.14.

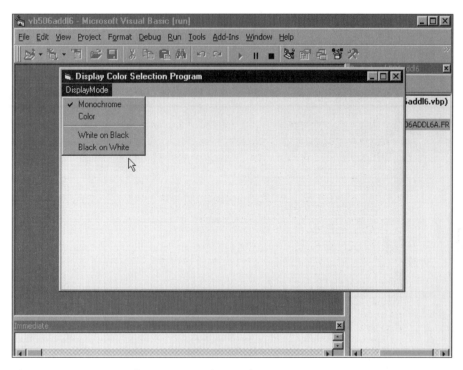

Figure 6.14 Monochromatic DisplayMode options.

Notice that the program also adds a check mark to the DisplayMode that is selected.

An alternative chromatic list is added to the menu when the user selects the color DisplayMode, as seen in Figure 6.15.

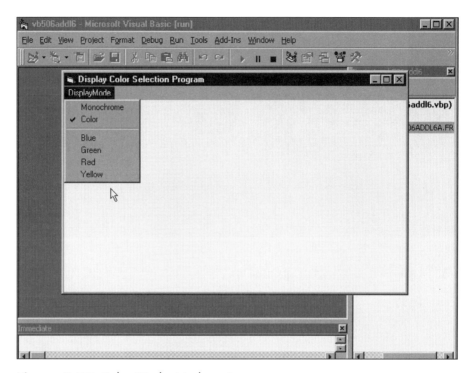

Figure 6.15 Color DisplayMode options.

The first step in creating a menu that can change dynamically is to create the command control array. Figure 6.16 highlights the last element added to the Display Color Selection Program. Notice that the menu command uses DisplayMode as the caption and the Visible and Enable properties have been checked.

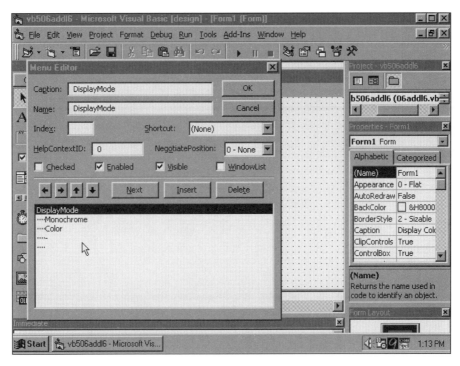

Figure 6.16 Creating a control array with the Menu Editor.

Visual Basic 5 understands that this new entry is the first element in the control array because the Index property has been assigned a value of 0. In addition, the menu command's Name (CtlName) has been set to ChromaticChoice. Any menu command created while the application is running will share this Click event procedure.

The following statement shows the syntax necessary to add a control dynamically at run time:

```
Load CtlName[(index)]
```

Visual Basic 5 sequentially indexes each newly loaded **(Load)** control. However, there are circumstances in which you may want to designate a specific *index*.

The **Unload** statement is used to remove control elements that were created with the **Load** instruction:

```
Unload CtlName[(index)]
```

If you try to **Unload** a deleted control element, an error message will be generated.

Monochrome and Color Click Event Procedures

Code must be written to respond to the various menu events. Consider the following portion of code:

```
Private Sub Monochrome_Click ()
  Dim Index As Integer
  If Monochrome.Checked = TRUE Then      'Cancel same mode
    Monochrome.Checked = FALSE
    SeparatorBar.Visible = FALSE
    Unload ChromaticChoice(1)
    Unload ChromaticChoice(2)
    NumEntry = 0

  Else
    If Color.Checked = TRUE Then        'Switching modes
      Color.Checked = FALSE
      For Index = 4 To 1 Step -1
        Unload ChromaticChoice(Index)
        NumEntry = NumEntry - 1
      Next Index
    End If

    Monochrome.Checked = TRUE
    SeparatorBar.Visible = TRUE
    NumEntry = NumEntry + 1             'Creating chroma choices
    Load ChromaticChoice(NumEntry)
    ChromaticChoice(NumEntry).Caption = "White on Black"
    ChromaticChoice(NumEntry).Visible = TRUE
    NumEntry = NumEntry + 1
    Load ChromaticChoice(NumEntry)
    ChromaticChoice(NumEntry).Caption = "Black on White"
    ChromaticChoice(NumEntry).Visible = TRUE
  End If
End Sub

Private Sub Color_Click ()
  Dim Index As Integer
  If Color.Checked = TRUE Then          'Cancel same mode
```

```
      Color.Checked = FALSE
      SeparatorBar.Visible = FALSE
      For Index = 4 To 1 Step -1
        Unload ChromaticChoice(Index)
        NumEntry = NumEntry - 1
      Next Index

   Else
      If Monochrome.Checked = TRUE Then   'Switching modes
        Monochrome.Checked = FALSE
        Unload ChromaticChoice(1)
        Unload ChromaticChoice(2)
        NumEntry = 0
      End If

      Color.Checked = TRUE
      SeparatorBar.Visible = TRUE
      For Index = 1 To 4                  'Creating chroma choices
        Load ChromaticChoice(Index)
        ChromaticChoice(Index).Visible = TRUE
        NumEntry = NumEntry + 1
      Next Index
      ChromaticChoice(1).Caption = "Blue"
      ChromaticChoice(2).Caption = "Green"
      ChromaticChoice(3).Caption = "Red"
      ChromaticChoice(4).Caption = "Yellow"
   End If
End Sub
```

The two event procedures, in this listing, are responsible for:

- Deciding whether the user is canceling the same display mode.
- Deciding whether this is a midapplication display mode change.
- Deciding whether this is the first time the display mode has been selected.
- If the user is canceling the same display mode, removing the separator bar and **UnLoad**ing the chromatic commands.

- If this is a midapplication display mode change, deleting all previously loaded **(Load)** chromatic commands.
- If this is the first time the display mode has been selected, creating the original set of chromatic commands.
- Setting and resetting the menu's Checked properties.

When a new control array element is loaded it inherits all of the property settings from the lowest existing element in the array. This is always true, except for the Visible, Index, and TabIndex properties. As a result of this fact, it is not sufficient just to **Load** the element. The menu's Visible property must be set to TRUE in order for the command to show up on the menu.

You may be wondering what happened to ChromaticChoice(0), the first element in the control array. It could have been used to assign the first chroma command for each DisplayMode. However, this would have prohibited the use of the **For** loop when unloading **(Unload)** the chroma options. Control array elements that are created at design time, in this case ChromaticChoice(0), cannot be unloaded **(Unload)** at run time.

Sharing Event Procedures

One of the easiest approaches to understanding control arrays is to examine the shared CtlName_Click event procedure. Whenever the user clicks on a menu command that is part of a control array, Visual Basic 5 invokes the common Click event procedure and sends the control element's *Index* value. The following listing shows how the Display Color Selection Program changes the screen's **ForeColor** and **BackColor**.

```
Private Sub ChromaticChoice_Click (Index As Integer)
  Select Case Index
    Case 1
      If Monochrome.Checked = TRUE Then
        Form1.ForeColor = WHITE
        Form1.BackColor = BLACK
      Else
        Form1.ForeColor = YELLOW
        Form1.BackColor = BLUE
      End If
```

```
   Case 2
     If Monochrome.Checked = TRUE Then
        Form1.ForeColor = BLACK
        Form1.BackColor = WHITE
     Else
        Form1.ForeColor = BLACK
        Form1.BackColor = GREEN
     End If
   Case 3
     Form1.ForeColor = WHITE
     Form1.BackColor = RED
   Case 4
     Form1.ForeColor = BLUE
     Form1.BackColor = YELLOW
 End Select
 Form1.CurrentX = 2600
 Form1.CurrentY = 1700
 Print "ForeColor  : "; ColorConvert(Form1.ForeColor)
 Form1.CurrentX = 2600
 Print "BackColor : "; ColorConvert(Form1.BackColor)
End Sub
```

In this example, the *Index* value is used to activate the appropriate **Case** statement.

The two print statements serve an interesting purpose. These statements convert the **ForeColor** and **BackColor** constants to string equivalents so that the application can tell the user, in English, which colors have been selected:

```
Function ColorConvert (ByVal HexNumber As Long) As String
  Select Case HexNumber
    Case &H0&
      ColorConvert = "Black"
    Case &HFFFFFF
      ColorConvert = "White"
    Case &HFF0000
      ColorConvert = "Blue"
    Case &HFF00&
      ColorConvert = "Green"
```

```
    Case &HFFFF&
       ColorConvert = "Yellow"
    Case &HFF&
       ColorConvert = "Red"
    End Select
End Function
```

The code was entered into Form1's general procedure window. The color **Const** is a hexadecimal value, returned by the function **ByVal()**. Many form properties are globally accessible. If these form properties are passed to a **Sub** procedure, an error message will be generated. If, instead, information is passed by using the **ByVal()** function, Visual Basic 5 copies the value instead of using its memory address.

A global access of Form1's **ForeColor** and **BackColor** would have made the function too complicated. Here the problem centers on the fact that the application wants to print both the current **ForeColor** and **BackColor**. If the **Select Case** statement had read:

```
Select Case Form1.ForeColor
```

with the previous statement, there would have been no need to have a function parameter list. The property would have been accessed globally. However, if this were the case, the function would have been rendered useless for converting the **BackColor**. It then would have required either a Boolean flag or a duplicate function with the **Select Case** statement hardwired to Form1.BackColor.

Executing the Display Color Selection Program

In order to run the Display Color Selection Program you will need to add the following definitions to Form1's general declarations.

```
Dim NumEntry As Integer

' Copied from Win32api.txt file.
' BackColor, ForeColor, FillColor (standard RGB colors: form,
' controls)
Const BLACK = &H0&
Const RED = &HFF&
Const GREEN = &HFF00&
Const YELLOW = &HFFFF&
Const BLUE = &HFF0000
```

```
Const MAGENTA = &HFF00FF
Const CYAN = &HFFFF00
Const WHITE = &HFFFFFF
```

 Note: The Win32api.txt file is contained in the Winapi subdirectory.

The integer variable, *NumEntry*, was globally defined so that all of the form's Click events would have access to its current value.

USING SHORTCUT AND ACCESS KEYS

Shortcut and access keys can speed program operation. *Shortcut* keys allow the user to execute a menu command simply by pressing a function key or using a CTRL key combination, such as CTRL + R, for Run.

Access keys permit the user to select a control or menu command by pressing the ALT key together with a highlighted command letter. In the case of submenu items the user simply presses the highlighted letter.

Figure 6.17 shows the Menu Editor that is displayed when the user selects the Ctrl+E key combination while the Foreign Language Calculator is loaded.

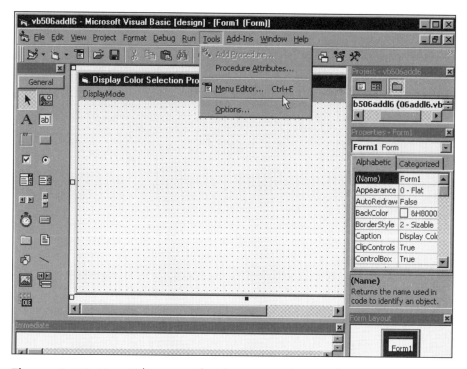

Figure 6.17 Menu Editor started with an access key combination.

An access key is designed by placing an ampersand (&) in front of a letter in a menu command's Caption. The ampersand is not displayed, at execution time, but causes the letter that follows it to be bold. For example, the following Caption entry will make the letter "R" bold:

&Run

Make certain when selecting access keys that they are unique for all menu entries. For example, *Save File* and *Save File As* menu commands should not share the same &S access key.

ACCESS KEY ASSIGNMENT FOR TEXTBOX AND PICTUREBOX CONTROLS

Can an access key be used with a TextBox or PictureBox control, since neither has a Caption property? The answer is yes if a LabelBox control is linked with the TextBox or PictureBox control.

Although LabelBox controls cannot receive the focus, they do have Caption properties. If you try to TAB to a LabelBox control you will skip to the next control in the tab order. Visual Basic 5 uses these two disjoint characteristics to give these controls access keys.

To assign an access key to either control you must first create a LabelBox control and assign an access key to the Caption property. Next, you have to create and place the control (TextBox or PictureBox) that will be linked to the LabelBox control. With this sequence, Visual Basic 5 will assign the LabelBox's access key to the control object. This may be an indirect route, but it is the only solution to the problem.

WHAT'S AHEAD

You should now be very comfortable in designing forms, placing controls, changing properties, and implementing control programming code. In the next two chapters, you will learn how to make your programs more interactive by controlling input and output.

Chapter 7

Input

In the previous chapters, you have learned how to design forms, place controls, and set properties and program responses. Truly interactive programs allow user input information at the time of program execution. This input can range from simple control interaction to text and numeric information. In this chapter you will learn how to write programming code to gather information from the user of your application.

APPEARANCES ARE EVERYTHING

Have you already asked yourself the following question: "Why would I want to program in any language other than Visual Basic 5?" As you have read through the earlier chapters and tried the examples, you have discovered that Visual Basic 5 provides a totally new approach to Windows program development. Not only does it make designing your application fun but also the final product has the look and feel of a professionally designed software package!

Part of this professional appearance comes from the standard Visual Basic 5 input mechanisms supported by Windows 95 and Windows NT:

- CheckBox controls
- ComboBox controls (three styles)

- ListBox controls
- MultiLine TextBox controls
- OptionButton controls
- HScrollBar and VScrollBar controls

Let's begin a study of controls that can be used for user input. Each of the examples in the chapter has been selected to highlight a unique feature of a control's characteristics and proper usage.

A CLOSER LOOK AT TEXTBOX CONTROLS

TextBox controls present the user with an input mechanism that can accept any type of data entry. Single-line or multiline input can include any combination of alphanumeric entries.

A TextBox control's interaction with a user is greatly determined by the MultiLine and ScrollBars design time properties. When a TextBox control's MultiLine property is set to TRUE (-1), the application can display multiple lines of text and accept a multiline user response. Note, however, that you cannot use the Properties bar to enter multiple lines of text at design time.

TextBoxes and Form_Load

One way to enable a TextBox control to display multiple lines of text, at startup, is to use the control's Form_Load event procedure. The placement of line breaks can be controlled by defining a carriage return, Chr$(13), and linefeed character, Chr$(10), as NL$. The following Form_Load procedure uses NL$ to instruct Visual Basic 5 to put the second sentence on its own line.

Note: Visual Basic 5 has no line continuation character. In some cases, examples have been justified to fit within the typesetter's boundaries for this book. They will not execute as they are indented. If you are entering each example manually, make certain that each statement is completed on its own line.

Here is an example of code in which Text1.Text is formatted for the book on two lines but must be on one line when written in your Visual Basic 5 application:

```
Private Sub Form_Load ()
 Changed = 0
 NL$ = Chr$(13) + Chr$(10)
 Text1.Text = "Here is an illegal word wrap" + NL$ +
        "that must be edited to one line only!"
End Sub
```

When trying this example, make certain that the TextBox control's MultiLine property is set to TRUE (-1). Otherwise, you will see the two lines joined by a strange double-bar graphic symbol with the last sentence truncated by the control's border.

TextBox ScrollBars

The TextBox control's ScrollBars property should not be confused with HScrollBar and VScrollBar controls, which are not attached to TextBox controls. These controls have their own characteristics. When a TextBox control's Scroll Bars property is set to TRUE (-1) the user sees the selected scroll bar(s).

Horizontal scroll bars allow the user to enter text that is wider than the box's boundaries. This can be done without creating a word wrap with up to a maximum of 255 characters per line. When the ScrollBars property is turned off (0), user input is automatically word wrapped to fit within the TextBox control.

Normally, a TextBox control's contents are scrolled up and down with the cursor keys. If the vertical scroll bar has been turned on, the user has the additional advantage of being able to advance quickly forward or backward through the displayed information with the mouse.

SPEEDING? WHO ME?

A MultiLine TextBox control should be used in your program design whenever the user can respond with varying-length input strings. For example, a Car Buyers Database program could have one field that allows the agent to enter an automobile description. This would naturally vary in length from one car to another.

As an example, the following program uses a similar response mechanism to accept a speeder's reason(s) for exceeding the speed limit (07MLTI1 example). If you have ever been stopped for exceeding the speed limit, this program might be just the ticket. (Yes, a pun was intended.)

The program starts by requesting the speeder to enter a 45-word excuse. As soon as the user begins to present his or her case (i.e., enter the excuse), the TextBox control's initial contents are erased, and a stoplight is displayed, along with a display of "Words left in your excuse:" in the label field.

As the user continues to enter the plea, the lights on the stoplight remind the user of the word limit. Initially, the stoplight glows green. When the user has entered approximately half of the allotted words, the light changes to yellow.

Correlated with this visual effect is the word count. When the speeder attempts to exceed the word limit, the word count decrements to 0 and displays a red light. Figure 7.1 shows the program's original screen.

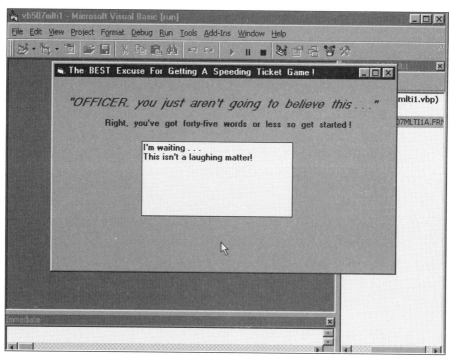

Figure 7.1 The speeding excuse game.

The following Form1 general declarations are used to set up the program's constants and global variables:

```
Const MaxWords = 45
'Storage needed, approximately (Max_Words * 5) bytes
'Dim AnExcuse As String * 225
Dim Changed As Integer
```

MaxWords defines the maximum number of words allowed for the speeding excuse. The Dim AnExcuse statement is commented out because it would apply only to applications that have been coded to store individual excuses in a random-access file. This application does not include that code.

Random-access files require that each record be of a fixed length. This allows a record, physically placed on a disk between two other records, to be entered, edited, and deleted without affecting the surrounding data.

The variable *Changed* is global to the form and will keep track of the number of times the Text1_Change event procedure is called. All of the program's action takes place in the Text1_KeyPress and Text1_Change event procedures.

Which Event Procedures Should Be Used?

Learning to write a good Visual Basic 5 application can require some practice. One of the frequent questions involves a decision on which event procedure should be used for a particular effect. One approach to discovering the answer is to ask this question: "What do users do to indicate they've responded?" Do they click the mouse, drag an icon, press any ASCII key on the keyboard, or press a particular key—cursor, function, CTRL, or special (like Break)? Often the answer to this question will indicate which event procedure to code.

The Text1_Change and Text1_Keypress event procedures control all of the action in the speeder's excuse game. Take a minute to study the code for Text1_Change:

```
Private Sub Text1_Change ()
 Dim CurrentLength As Integer
 If Changed > 0 Then
```

```
CurrentLength = Len(Text1.Text) \ 5 'avg chars per word
Label1.Caption = Format$(MaxWords - CurrentLength)
Label4.Caption = "Words left in your excuse :"
If CurrentLength = 0 Then
 Picture1.Picture =
  LoadPicture("c:\VB5\Graphics\Icons\Traffic\TRFFC10A.ICO")
 ElseIf CurrentLength = MaxWords \ 2 Then
  Picture1.Picture =
   LoadPicture("c:\VB5\Graphics\Icons\Traffic\TRFFC10B.ICO")
 ElseIf CurrentLength = MaxWords Then
  Picture1.Picture =
   LoadPicture("c:\VB5\Graphics\Icons\Traffic\TRFFC10C.ICO")
 End If
End If
'AnExcuse = Text1.Text
End Sub
```

Text1_Change

The TextBox control's Change event procedures are automatically invoked anytime the user or code changes the contents of the TextBox control. This automatic invocation can be used to your advantage or it can create a control nightmare!

The variable *CurrentLength* keeps track of the number of excuse words entered. It does this by invoking the **Len()** function on the TextBox control's Text property. This returns the number of characters currently in the excuse. The returned value is then divided by the average number of characters per word (five) to approximate the number of words entered.

The **If** *Changed* > 0 statement takes care of executing the code within the Change event procedure only *after* the user has responded. Without this control statement the Form_Loaded text would have executed the Change event. This would have caused the Change event to display the stoplight and word count even before the user had typed anything.

Once the plaintiff begins entering the story the procedure continues by calculating and assigning a "words left count to" value to the Label1 control's Caption property along with a clarifying statement (Label4.Caption), as seen in Figure 7.2.

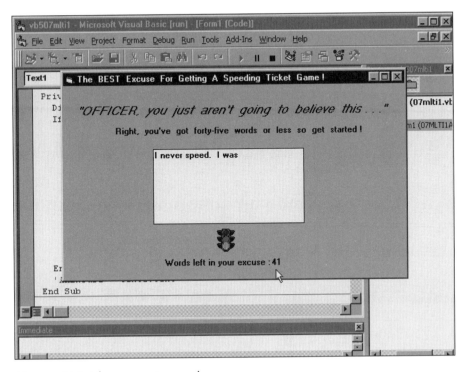

Figure 7.2 The user enters a plea.

The visual selection of which stoplight to display is controlled by the **If...ElseIf...** statement, as seen in Figures 7.3 and 7.4. By using *CurrentLength*, the algorithm decides which of Visual Basic 5's three stoplights is needed (TRFFC10A, TRFFC10B, or TRFFC10C).

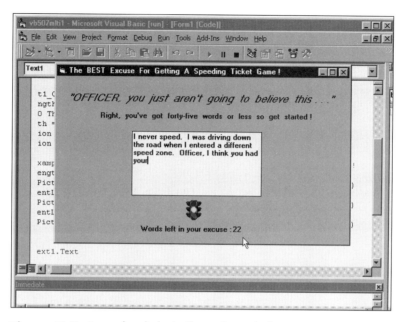

Figure 7.3 An amber light halfway through the excuse.

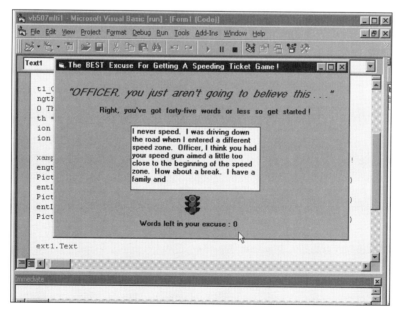

Figure 7.4 A red light at the end of the excuse.

If the speeder's excuses were being stored in a random-access database Text1.Text could be assigned to the fixed-length string variable *AnExcuse*. This variable could then be used by an appropriate Insert procedure. Another alternative would be for the Insert procedure to access Text1.Text globally. This would completely do away with the need for the variable *AnExcuse*.

Text1_KeyPress

A KeyPress event is triggered anytime the user presses a standard ASCII character. This is in contrast to the KeyDown and KeyUp events, which respond to CTRL and function key entries. The KeyPress event is ideal for handling standard TextBox control input. It is the focal point for the successful execution of the program. The KeyPress procedure prevents the Form_Load event from falsely triggering the Text1_Change event:

```
Private Sub Text1_KeyPress (KeyAscii As Integer)
 Changed = Changed + 1
 If Changed = 1 Then
  Text1.Text = ""
 End If
End Sub
```

The *Changed* variable was defined back in Form1's general declarations. This makes it globally accessible to all of the form's controls and event procedures.

The Form_Load event initialized its value to 0. When the Form_Load event triggered the display of its contents in Text1, the Text1_Change event was triggered. Because *Changed* was 0, the code in Text1_Change was ignored. However, when the user started typing the excuse, Text1_KeyPress incremented *Changed* to 1. This caused the procedure to erase Text1.Text, deleting the trooper's initial (and final) warning.

However, much more is happening in the programming code. When Text1_KeyPress changes Text1's contents, the Text1_Change event is immediately invoked. Since KeyPress has incremented the variable *Changed* to 1, all the code in the Text1_Change event procedure is executed. The user now sees the appropriately lit traffic light along with the "words left" prompt and number.

Limiting Data Entry

The program's interface suffers from one flaw. The speeder can ramble on with the excuse. This problem can be solved by using the *KeyAscii* argument to the KeyPress event procedure. *KeyAscii* represents the numeric equivalent (ASCII) of all printable characters. Most of the time *KeyAscii* needs to be converted before the program can make any use of it.

The following Text1_KeyPress event procedure has been modified to prevent the defendant from exceeding the 45-word limit (07MLTI2 example):

```
Private Sub Text1_KeyPress (KeyAscii As Integer)
 Static NoMoreEntries As Integer
 Changed = Changed + 1
 If Changed = 1 Then
  Text1.Text = ""
 End If
 If((MaxWords - CurrentLength=0) And (Chr$(KeyAscii)=" ")) Then
  NoMoreEntries = -1
 End If
 If NoMoreEntries Then
  KeyAscii = 0
  Beep
 End If
End Sub
```

User input is controlled by adding a flag, *NoMoreEntries*, to the event procedure. It is declared to be a **Static** variable, so that its current contents persist after the procedure is exited. Visual Basic 5 initializes its value to 0, as it does with all numeric variables.

The procedure keeps track of two events: when the number of words left equals 0 (MaxWords - CurrentLength) and when the character the speeder has typed is a blank (" "). The second test looks for a blank by using Chr$(KeyAscii) = " ". This test permits the user to finish typing the entire 45th word. Without this test the algorithm could stop the user typing in midword—something only the judge is permitted to do.

When these two test conditions are met, the variable *NoMoreEntries* is set to TRUE (-1). This allows program execution to enter the last **If** statement. Setting *KeyAscii* to 0 effectively cancels the keystroke, leaving the input bar at the same spot. The **Beep** function sends the speeder a warning tone, alerting the speeder to wait for the judge's decision.

Test your understanding of the KeyPress event and its associated *KeyAscii* argument by rewriting the program to actually count the number of words entered. (Hint: Count the number of times the speeder presses the SPACEBAR.)

USING AN OPTIONBUTTON CONTROL WHEN MAKING SELECTIONS

Programs use OptionButton controls to present the user with a set of mutually exclusive choices. Figure 7.5 illustrates a program's interface that uses three OptionButton controls.

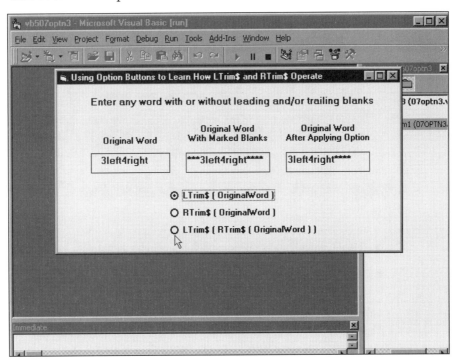

Figure 7.5 Program using three OptionButton controls—LTrim$ selected.

The application uses Visual Basic 5's **LTrim$** and **RTrim$** functions to demonstrate visually their effects on a user-supplied word.

OptionButton controls always work in a group. Selecting one OptionButton control from the group effectively cancels out any other conflicting choice. If a form has multiple option groups, they must be physically tied to a frame or picture box. Otherwise, all of the OptionButton controls placed directly on a form constitute a single group. Figure 7.6 shows **RTrim$** selected.

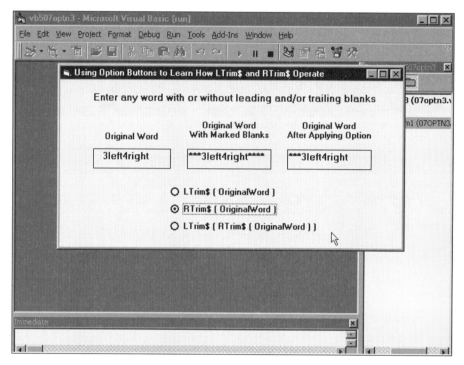

Figure 7.6 RTrim$ is selected.

The Value property of an OptionButton control determines whether the button has been selected, TRUE (-1), or not, FALSE (0). OptionButton controls can be selected directly by a user's mouse click or by tabbing to the control and pressing SPACEBAR. An OptionButtonN_Click event is triggered when the button is chosen.

The program begins by defining a few variables global to Form1 (07OPTN3 example):

```
Dim LTrimmedWord As String
Dim RTrimmedWord As String
Dim LRTrimmedWord As String
```

Each variable will hold the modified string created by invoking the associated string function.

Text1_LostFocus

Here is an application in which most of the programming action takes place in the Text1_LostFocus event procedure. This procedure is automatically invoked whenever the control loses the input focus. For this program, this code takes care of generating the display string combinations to be used by Text2.Text and Text3.Text controls:

```
Private Sub Text1_LostFocus ()
 Dim CharIndex As Integer
 Dim OriginalWord As String
 OriginalWord = Text1.Text
 Text2.Text = AddStars(OriginalWord)
 LTrimmedWord = AddStars(LTrim$(OriginalWord))
 RTrimmedWord = AddStars(RTrim$(OriginalWord))
 LRTrimmedWord = LTrim$(RTrim$(OriginalWord))
End Sub
```

OriginalWord is used to store the unmodified response entered by the user (Text1.Text) and for clarity of meaning.

The AddStars() Function

Function **AddStars()** is used to replace leading and trailing blanks with an asterisk "*" because blanks, leading or trailing, are pretty hard for the average eye to see:

```
Function AddStars (AWord As String) As String
 Dim CharIndex As Integer
 Dim PaddedWord As String
 For CharIndex = 1 To Len(AWord)
  If Mid$(AWord, CharIndex, 1) = " " Then
   PaddedWord = PaddedWord + "*"
  Else
   PaddedWord = PaddedWord + Mid$(AWord, CharIndex, 1)
  End If
 Next
 AddStars = PaddedWord
End Function
```

The function is called for the *OriginalWord* and all other modified string combinations *(LTrimmedWord, RTrimmedWord,* and *LRTrimmed Word)*. Notice that Text1_LostFocus takes care of sending the function an already truncated string:

```
LTrimmedWord = AddStars(LTrim$(OriginalWord))
RTrimmedWord = AddStars(RTrim$(OriginalWord))
```

There is no need to pass *LRTrimmedWord,* since it has no leading or trailing blanks. Figure 7.7 shows the results of using LTrim$ and RTrim$.

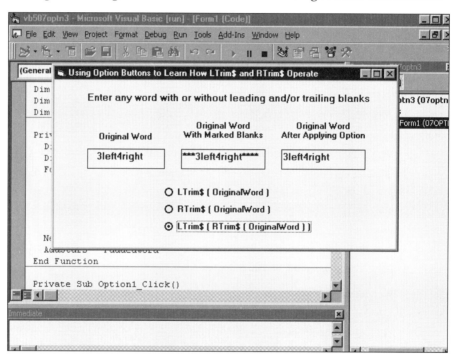

Figure 7.7 LTrim$ and RTrim$ together.

Option1_Click(), Option2_Click(), Option3_Click() Click Events

The three OptionButton Click events are responsible for the Text3.Text control's contents, as shown earlier in Figures 7.6 and 7.7:

```
Private Sub Option1_Click ()
 Text3.Text = LTrimmedWord
End Sub

Private Sub Option2_Click ()
 Text3.Text = RTrimmedWord
End Sub

Private Sub Option3_Click ()
 Text3.Text = LRTrimmedWord
End Sub
```

Text1_GotFocus

A control's GotFocus event procedure is invoked anytime the object has the Focus. The example program uses this event to clear out any previously entered word and option selection whenever Text1 receives the Focus:

```
Private Sub Text1_GotFocus ()
 Text1.Text = ""
 Text2.Text = ""
 Text3.Text = ""
End Sub
```

CHECKBOX CONTROLS USED TO MAKE SELECTIONS

CheckBox controls are used whenever the user can concurrently select from several option choices. The Value property of a CheckBox control has three states (Table 7.1).

Table 7.1 A CheckBox Control's Value Property States

Value	Meaning
0	Check box is not selected or has been canceled by a second click.
1	Check box is selected and displays a check mark in the check box.
2	The check box caption has been grayed, indicating that it cannot be selected (Enabled = FALSE).

The following program uses all three values to control the application's visual appearance. Figure 7.8 shows the program's initial screen appearance. Notice that the fourth option, Electronic Mail, has a grayed appearance. This was set at design time by setting Check4's Enabled property to FALSE (0).

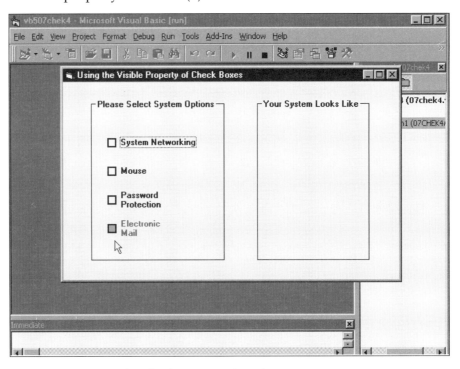

Figure 7.8 Using the CheckBox control's Value property.

First, two constants are declared in the program (07CHEK4 example):

```
Const Notselected = 0
Const Selected = 1
```

Next, the program waits for the user to select the system's configuration. Each time an option is selected, the application displays an appropriate graphic icon. The user can also cancel an option by clicking on a selected item:

```
Private Sub Check2_Click ()
 If Check2.Value = Selected Then
  Picture2.Visible = Selected
 Else
  Picture2.Visible = Notselected
 End If
End Sub


Private Sub Check3_Click ()
 If Check3.Value = Selected Then
  Picture3.Visible = Selected
 Else
  Picture3.Visible = Notselected
 End If
End Sub


Private Sub Check4_Click ()
 If Check4.Value = Selected Then
  Picture4.Visible = Selected
 Else
  Picture4.Visible = Notselected
 End If
End Sub
```

The only Click event that varies slightly is the one associated with the Networking option (Check1). The Check1_Click event has an additional responsibility of activating or deactivating option 4, Electronic Mail, since electronic mail is possible only with a networked system:

```
Private Sub Check1_Click ()
 If Check1.Value = Selected Then
```

```
  Picture1.Visible = Selected
  Check4.Enabled = Selected
Else
  Picture1.Visible = Notselected
  Picture4.Visible = Notselected
  Check4.Enabled = NotSeledected
  Check4.Value = Notselected
 End If
End Sub
```

The Check1_Click event switches the active state of the Check4 control by enabling or disabling Check4's Enabled property, as seen in Figure 7.9.

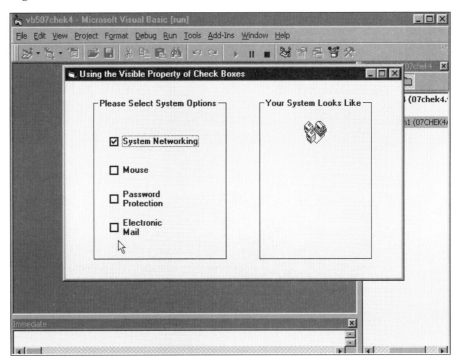

Figure 7.9 System Networking enabled.

Figure 7.10 shows screen output when all four check boxes have been selected.

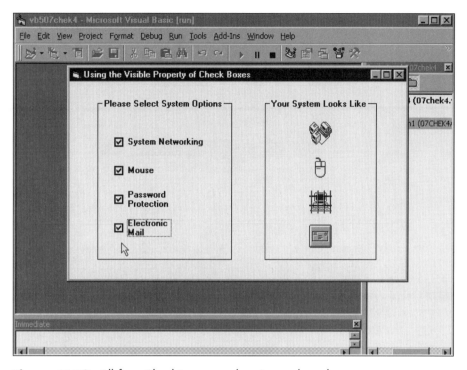

Figure 7.10 All four CheckBox control options selected.

LISTBOX CONTROLS USED TO MAKE SELECTIONS

A ListBox control allows the user to select from a list of related items. Once the item has been selected it is quite common for the program to supply explanatory information. For example, the following program uses a gardening ListBox control.

When the user selects "Sarcoxie Euonymous" the Plant Description box gives additional details about the plant, as seen in Figure 7.11.

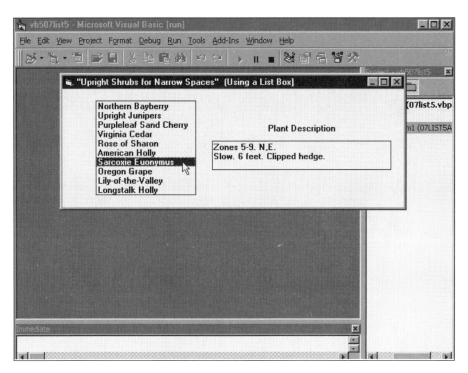

Figure 7.11 Using ListBox control selections.

Adding and Deleting Listed Items

You cannot add items to a ListBox control at design time by setting a property. Typically, ListBox control items are generated by the Form_Load event procedure. The syntax for adding an item to a list box at execution time takes on the following form:

```
ListControl.AddItem item [,index]
```

ListControl selects the ListBox control. The variable *Item* represents the data to be added. Since *index* is bracketed, it is optional. If it is included, *index* specifies which entry to add. When *index* is set to 0 it automatically makes the *item* the first list entry. The following listing demonstrates how the Upright Shrubs program initializes List1 (07List5 example):

```
Private Sub Form_Load ()
 List1.AddItem "Northern Bayberry"
```

```
List1.AddItem "Upright Junipers"
List1.AddItem "Purpleleaf Sand Cherry"
List1.AddItem "Virginia Cedar"
List1.AddItem "Rose of Sharon"
List1.AddItem "American Holly"
List1.AddItem "Sarcoxie Euonymus"
List1.AddItem "Oregon Grape"
List1.AddItem "Lily-of-the-Valley"
List1.AddItem "Longstalk Holly"
End Sub
```

Removing an item from a ListBox control is just as easy with the **RemoveItem** statement:

```
ListControl.RemoveItem index
```

In this case *index* indicates which element to remove.

Access to List Elements

Visual Basic 5 provides every ListBox and ComboBox control with four very useful properties (Table 7.2).

Table 7.2 ListBox and ComboBox Control Properties

Property	Description
Text	Contains the currently selected item stored in string format. For combo box Styles 0 and 1, the Text property may contain an entry that is not found in the list. This is because combo box Styles 0 and 1 have an edit window that allows the user to enter any text, not just copies of list items.
List	List is a string array that contains all items in the list.
ListCount	Contains the number of list entries.
ListIndex	Contains the index number of the selected item. The first element in the list is at index position 0. The last element in the list is at index position ListCount -1.

The ListBox control's Click procedure is usually the preferred choice for attaching execution code. The following List1_Click event procedure demonstrates how the Upright Shrubs program displays the selected plant's statistics:

```
Private Sub List1_Click ()
 NL$ = Chr$(13) + Chr$(10)
 If List1.Text = "Sarcoxie Euonymus" Then
  Text1.Text = "Zones 5-9. N,E." + NL$ + "Slow. 6 feet.
       Clipped hedge."
 End If
End Sub
```

Now it is your turn to rewrite the procedure so that it uses List1.ListIndex to enter a **Select Case** statement. Have each **Case** display some additional information about the plant. (Hint: Consider using **Case**s 0..9.)

Table 7.3 HScrollBar and VScrollBar Control Properties.

Property	Description
Min	This is the numeric value that will be returned in the scroll bar's Value property whenever the user moves the "thumb" to the extreme top (vertical) or left (horizontal).
Max	Similar to Min except that the numeric value returned in the scroll bar's Value property will reflect the bar's maximum value. This happens when the user moves the "thumb" to the extreme bottom (vertical) or right (horizontal).
SmallChange	This is the value that is added to or subtracted from the control's Value property whenever the user clicks on either arrow at the end of the bar.
LargeChange	This is the value that is added to or subtracted from the control's Value property whenever the user clicks between the "thumb" and the arrow at either end of the bar.

SCROLL BAR PROPERTIES

The HscrollBar and VScrollBar controls provide the user with an easy-to-use point-and-click range selection. They are frequently used as a visual substitute for numeric data entry. There are four properties associated with these controls (Table 7.3).

By using these properties a program can quickly adjust itself to the user's preferences. Consider an example that uses computer-controlled stereo receiver controls. The form is shown in Figure 7.12.

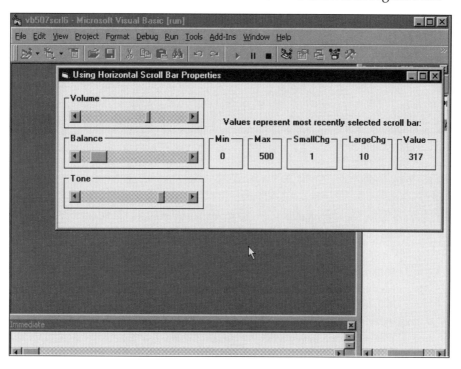

Figure 7.12 Scroll bar receiver controls.

The program begins by initializing the control's original properties to a previously determined range and setting (07SCRL6 example):

```
Private Sub Form_Load ()
 Hscroll2.SmallChange = 1
 Hscroll2.LargeChange = 2
 Hscroll2.Max = 5
 Hscroll2.Min = -5
 Hscroll2.Value = 0
 Hscroll3.SmallChange = 1
 Hscroll3.LargeChange = 3
 Hscroll3.Min = -20
 Hscroll3.Max = 20
 Hscroll3.Value = -5
 Hscroll1.SmallChange = 1
 Hscroll1.LargeChange = 10
 Hscroll1.Max = 500
 Hscroll1.Min = 0
 Hscroll1.Value = 50
End Sub
```

Notice the wide variation in ranges and increment/decrement values. For example, Hscroll2 is associated with the Balance scroll bar. Typically, stereo balance controls have a negative (-5) and positive (5) range, with most people settling on a happy middle (Hscroll.Value = 0).

A similar situation exists for a stereo's tone control (Hscroll3). Most people prefer a wider range to their tone preferences (-20 to 20) than is needed for balance. Volume, on the other hand, has the widest range, from 0 to 500, with the biggest LargeChange value (10).

Do you know why Hscroll1's Load_Form initializations were left until last? Here is a hint:

```
Private Sub HScroll1_Change ()
 Text1.Text = Format$(Hscroll1.Min)
 Text2.Text = Format$(Hscroll1.Max)
 Text3.Text = Format$(Hscroll1.SmallChange)
```

```
  Text4.Text = Format$(Hscroll1.LargeChange)
  Text5.Text = Format$(Hscroll1.Value)
End Sub

Private Sub HScroll2_Change ()
 Text1.Text = Format$(Hscroll2.Min)
 Text2.Text = Format$(Hscroll2.Max)
 Text3.Text = Format$(Hscroll2.SmallChange)
 Text4.Text = Format$(Hscroll2.LargeChange)
 Text5.Text = Format$(Hscroll2.Value)
End Sub

Private Sub HScroll3_Change ()
 Text1.Text = Format$(Hscroll3.Min)
 Text2.Text = Format$(Hscroll3.Max)
 Text3.Text = Format$(Hscroll3.SmallChange)
 Text4.Text = Format$(Hscroll3.LargeChange)
 Text5.Text = Format$(Hscroll3.Value)
End Sub
```

From the earlier discussion of TextBox controls, what happens to trigger the Change event procedure? It is triggered whenever a control's Text property is altered.

By placing the Hscroll1 control's definitions last, the program automatically places the Volume's current values into the TextBox controls, 1 through 5. This was done on purpose, because most users change the volume control more frequently than other stereo options.

COMBOBOX CONTROLS USED TO MAKE SELECTIONS

ComboBox controls are very similar to ListBox controls except that Style 0 and 1 properties provide the user with an edit option. A ComboBox control's Style 2 works exactly like a ListBox control except that it displays only the selected item once it has been chosen.

The following program interacts with users by allowing them to determine the display text's **FontName**, as seen in Figures 7.13 and 7.14.

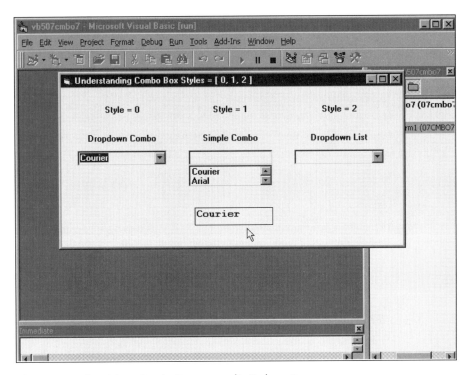

Figure 7.13 Using ComboBox control's Style = 0 property.

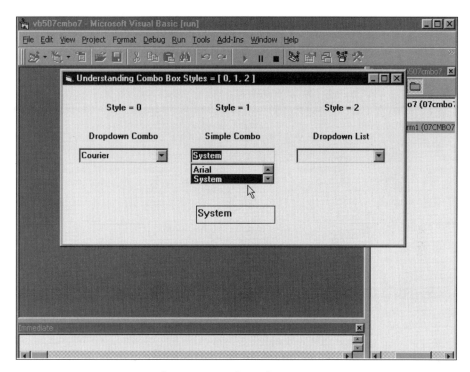

Figure 7.14 Using ComboBox control's Style = 1 property.

The first thing the application does is to load the lists into the combo box controls at run time by using the Form_Load event procedure (07CMBO7 example):

```
Private Sub Form_Load ()
 Combo1.AddItem "Courier"
 Combo1.AddItem "Roman"
 Combo1.AddItem "System"
 Combo2.AddItem "Courier"
 Combo2.AddItem "Roman"
 Combo2.AddItem "System"
 Combo3.AddItem "Courier"
 Combo3.AddItem "Roman"
 Combo3.AddItem "System"
End Sub
```

Program execution is controlled by each ComboBox control's Click event:

```
Private Sub Combo1_Click ()
 SetFontName (Combo1.ListIndex)
End Sub


Private Sub Combo2_Click ()
 SetFontName (Combo2.ListIndex)
End Sub


Private Sub Combo3_Click ()
 SetFontName (Combo3.ListIndex)
End Sub
```

Notice how each Click event takes care of sending the function *SetFontName* the ListIndex of the selected item.

Function *SetFontName* uses this numeric value and enters a **Select Case** statement that sets the Text1 control's FontName property to the user's preference. It also assigns the FontName to the Text property:

```
Private Sub SetFontName (ComboListIndex As Integer)
 Select Case ComboListIndex
  Case 0
   Text1.FontName = "Courier"
   Text1.Text = "Courier"
  Case 1
   Text1.FontName = "Roman"
   Text1.Text = "Roman"
  Case 2
   Text1.FontName = "System"
   Text1.Text = "System"
 End Select
End Sub
```

The application runs smoothly until the user enters a nonlisted font name in the first ComboBox control (Style = 0) or the second ComboBox control (Style = 1). Both combo boxes provide the user with an edit window. To add this feature, the program needs to have a validation procedure. The following code segment illustrates how this might be done for the second ComboBox control:

```
Private Sub Combo2_Change ()
 Dim Matches As Integer, Index As Integer
 Select Case UCase$(Combo2.Text)
  Case "COURIER"
   Matches = -1     'TRUE
   Index = 0
  Case "ROMAN"
   Matches = -1
   Index = 1
  Case "SYSTEM"
   Matches = -1
   Index = 2
  Case Else
   Matches = 0
   Index = -1
 End Select
 If Matches Then
  SetFontName (Index)
 End If
End Sub
```

Now, if the user types in a font name that matches, the procedure sets a *Matches* flag to TRUE (-1) and calculates an appropriate list *Index*. The **SetFontName()** function is invoked with a valid *Index* whenever there is a font name match.

USING INPUTBOX$ FOR SIMPLE INPUT CONTROL

An InputBox$ control is the easiest form of input control to use and master. With just a single programming statement, your application can tell the user what you're looking for and return the user's response. All of this takes place in a slick-looking dialog box format. The syntax for an **InputBox$** statement takes on the following form:

**InputBox$**(prompt$ [,boxtitle$ [,default_response$ [,X% ,Y%]]])

Only the *prompt$* string is required. This is the message that will be printed inside the dialog box. The optional *boxtitle$* labels the dialog box. The *default_response$* string determines the default response displayed in the TextBox control. The *X%* and *Y%* coordinates can be used to determine the box's display coordinates. The value is specified in twips (1/20 of a pixel) and represents the distance from the left and top edges of the screen, respectively.

The following programming example demonstrates just how easy it is to use this type of control to add password protection to a program. The control is shown in Figure 7.15.

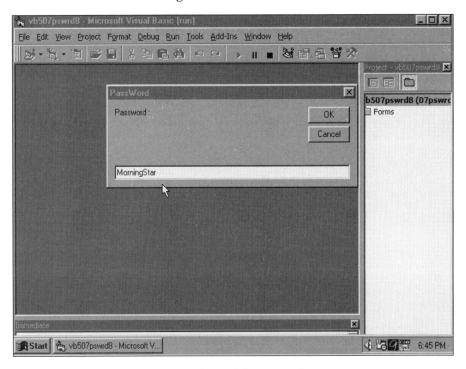

Figure 7.15 Using an InputBox$ to add password protection.

Program security can be added to your application with as little as four lines of code:

```
Private Sub Form_Load ()
 password$ = InputBox$("Password: ", "PassWord")
 If password$ <> "#$@JONES" Then
  End 'or UnLoad Form1
 End If
End Sub
```

The Form_Load procedure begins by displaying a password entry control, **InputBox$**. If the string returned from the control does not match the stored password, Visual Basic 5's **End** or, alternatively, **UnLoad Form** statement is executed. Either way, a mismatched entry terminates the program.

OUTPUT

Output is just as important as input for a well-written interactive application. In the next chapter, you'll be introduced to many techniques for sending information to the user.

Chapter 8

Output

This chapter deals with information returned by the application or computer to the user. This information is typically passed to the monitor's window or to a printer. In this chapter you will learn techniques for designing well-formatted output that will enhance your application.

OUTPUT

You have heard the saying "A picture is worth a thousand words." An application's screen and printer output can say just as much with a combination of graphics and text. Poorly labeled and formatted information can mean instantaneous death to the most eloquent programming code. Visual Basic 5 provides the programmer with a wide variety of formatting tools for creating meaningful output.

The example programs in this chapter demonstrate the variety of ways information can be displayed. The Visual Basic 5 output formats discussed include:

- date formatting
- enhancing forms and picture boxes with text
- label boxes used for output
- MsgBox output
- numeric formatting
- sending information to the printer

- tabular output
- time formatting
- using fonts

MsgBox Output

The Visual Basic 5 MsgBox, function or statement, is used to print brief explanatory or warning messages to the user. When activated, a dialog box with the specified message, along with an optional title, icon, number of buttons, and their type(s), is displayed. The syntax for the MsgBox statement takes on the following form:

```
MsgBox message$[,type%,[,type[,MsgBoxTitle$]]]
```

The *message$* contains the string to be displayed and can be up to 1024 characters. The *type%* parameters are used to give the number and type of buttons, the icon type, and default button. Tables 8.1, 8.2 8.3, and 8.4 define the various groups of button options. Group 1 has values from 0 to 5 and describes the number and type of buttons displayed in the dialog box.

Table 8.1 MsgBox Button Selection

Value	Description
0	Display OK button only
1	Display OK and Cancel buttons
2	Display Abort, Retry, and Ignore buttons
3	Display Yes, No, and Cancel buttons
4	Display Yes and No buttons
5	Display Retry and Cancel buttons

Group 2's values, as shown in Table 8.2, go from 16 to 64 and select the optional icon to be displayed in the MsgBox.

Table 8.2 MsgBox Icon Selection

Value	Description
16	Display Critical Message icon
32	Display Warning Query icon
48	Display Warning Message icon
64	Display Information Message icon

The third group, shown in Table 8.3, contains values that select the MsgBox's default button.

Table 8.3 MsgBox Default Button Selection

Value	Description
0	Selects the first button as the default
256	Selects the second button as the default
512	Selects the third button as the default

Table 8.4 lists the possible **MsgBox** function return values used to indicate which button the user selected.

Table 8.4 MsgBox Function Return Values

Value	Description
1	OK button
2	Cancel button
3	Abort button
4	Retry button
5	Ignore button
6	Yes button
7	No button

The following Form_Click event procedure creates the MsgBox shown in Figure 8.1 whenever the user clicks on the form.

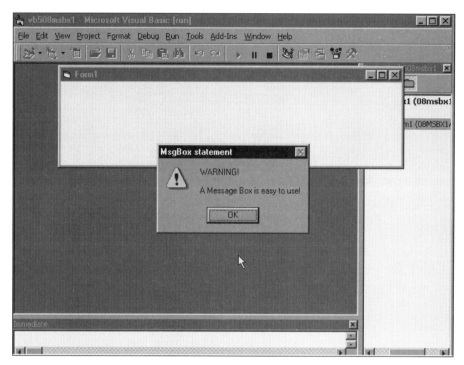

Figure 8.1 Experimenting with a simple MsgBox.

Normally, a MsgBox will automatically break lines at the right of the dialog box. However, you can manually format the box's display contents with carriage returns, Chr$(13), and linefeed characters, Chr$(10), as seen in the 08MSBX1 example:

```
Private Sub Form_Click ()
 NL$ = Chr$(13) + Chr$(10)
 MsgBox "WARNING!" + NL$ + NL$ + "A Message Box is easy to
     use!", 48, "MsgBox statement"
End Sub
```

MsgBoxes are *modal*. A modal dialog box or warning retains its focus until closed. Figure 8.1, shown earlier, displays the default OK button, which the user can click on, or accept by pressing the ENTER key, to close the dialog box.

OUTPUT FROM LABELBOX CONTROLS

Why would a programmer use a LabelBox control for output? First, think of the difference between LabelBox and TextBox controls in terms of output. The user cannot directly alter a LabelBox control's output. LabelBox controls are therefore the control of choice when displaying information that you do not want the user to change.

Normally, a LabelBox control's BorderStyle is set to 0 or None. However, by changing it to 1 or Single, the LabelBox control can visually mimic a TextBox control. Figure 8.2 uses one TextBox control and one LabelBox control with the BorderStyle set to 1.

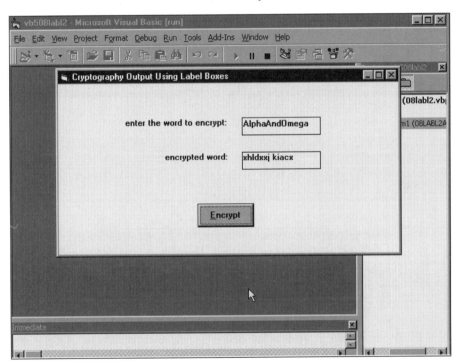

Figure 8.2 Experimenting with LabelBox output.

This example program allows the user to enter any word into Text1. After the Encode button is pressed, the program encrypts and displays the cloaked word in Label1. In a normal encryption program the user has no idea how the information is encoded. Since the encoded word is displayed in a LabelBox control, the user cannot click the mouse on the control and jumble its contents!

The Command1_Click event procedure performs the actual encryption (08LABL2):

```
Private Sub Command1_Click ()
 Dim Substitutes As String * 27
 Dim OriginalWord As String
 Dim EncodedWord As String
 Dim Index As Integer
 Dim Alphabet As String
 Dim SubstitutesIndex As Integer
 Dim OneChar As String

 Alphabet = "ABCDEFGHIJKLMNOPQRSTUVWXYZ "
 Substitutes = "xyz abcdefghijklmnopqrstuvw"
 OriginalWord = UCase$(Text1.Text)
 For Index = 1 To Len(OriginalWord)
  OneChar = Mid$(OriginalWord, Index, 1)
  SubstitutesIndex = InStr(Alphabet, OneChar)
  OneChar = Mid$(Substitutes, SubstitutesIndex, 1)
  EncodedWord = EncodedWord + OneChar
 Next Index
 Label3.Caption = EncodedWord
End Sub
```

The encryption process is started by first defining an *Alphabet* and *Substitutes* character set. Next, the *OriginalWord* word is uppercased (**UCase$**) to shorten the number of compare options. The algorithm works by isolating each character in the *OriginalWord* (using **Mid$**) and finding its *Index* position within the *Alphabet* (using **InStr**). A *OneCharacter* replacement is extracted from the *Substitutes* string using the *Index* value (using **Mid$**). The *EncodedWord* is built *OneCharacter* at a time using the string concatenation operator. Concatenation operations can use either the + or & operator. This process is repeated for the entire length (**Len**) of the *OriginalWord*. Once the encryption process is complete the *EncodedWord* is assigned to the Label3 Caption property and then displayed.

The execution of the program is enhanced by the following Text1_Change event:

```
Private Sub Text1_Change ()
 Label3.Caption = " "
End Sub
```

This short one-liner takes care of erasing any previously encrypted words if the user begins to enter a new one into Text1.

FORM AND PICTUREBOX CONTROLS ENHANCED WITH TEXT

Form or PictureBox control's output can be clarified with descriptive text. For example, the full-screen image displayed in Figure 8.3 shows a family picture. The message was created by printing text, with **Print**, to Form1.

Figure 8.3 Enhancing forms with text.

The following Form_Load event procedure creates the form's initial appearance (08PCTX3):

```
Private Sub Form_Load ()
 NL$ = Chr$(13) + Chr$(10)
 Print NL$ + NL$ + "   Family pictures are great"
End Sub
```

To automatically force the form's screen size to full screen, the form's WindowState was set equal to 2 or maximized at design time.

Normally, Visual Basic 5 places any text printed to a form behind any controls that have been placed on the form. For this reason, programs usually create blank forms specifically designed to hold text.

One solution to this problem is to set the form or picture box's AutoRedraw property to -1 (True). This enables automatic control repainting. This causes all graphics and **Print** output to be written to the screen and to an image stored in memory.

The property can be turned ON and OFF at run time, creating interesting results. For example, any text written to a form can be made a permanent part of the form by subsequently turning AutoRedraw OFF.

Another solution to this behind-the-scenes text placement is to use picture box controls. A picture box control supports graphics, bitmaps, and **Print** text. Any text printed with **Print**, to a form's PictureBox control, overlays the form.

The syntax for the **Print** method takes on the following form:

```
[object].Print [expression_format][;|,]
```

The optional *object* can designate a specific form or picture box. If it is omitted, Visual Basic 5 applies the **Print** method to whichever form has the code attached. The *expression_format* can be as simple as a single literal like, "Family pictures are great," or it can contain variables:

```
Print "The Final result is : "; Result
```

In this case, the semicolon is required to separate the literal from the variable holding the value to be printed.

Semicolons can also combine multiple string/variable combinations:

```
Print "Test 1 Score : "; Test1 ; Test 2 Score : "; Test2
```

They are also used to make code more readable by allowing long *expression_formats* to be broken up into separate lines. The following two statements have the same effect as the previous line of code:

```
Picture1.Print "Test 1 Score : "; Test1;
Picture1.Print "Test 2 Score : ", Test2;
```

WORKING WITH FONTS

One way to vary a form's impact and visual appeal is to use different font types and sizes. Figure 8.4 demonstrates the use of two Windows TrueType fonts. Standard Windows fonts can also be used.

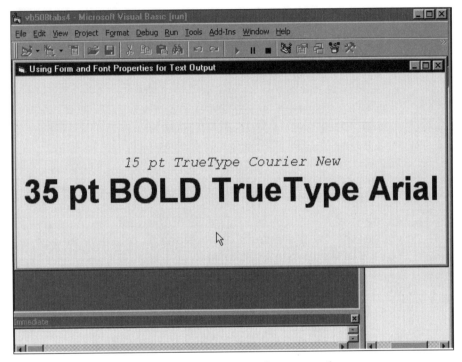

Figure 8.4 Enhancing form appearance with TrueType fonts.

The form's output is controlled by the following Form_Resize event procedure (08FNTS4):

```
Private Sub Form_Resize()
  AutoRedraw = -1
  Cls
  String1$ = "15 pt TrueType Courier New"
  String2$ = "35 pt BOLD TrueType Arial"
  FontName = "Courier New"
  FontSize = 15
  FontBold = 0
```

```
    FontItalic = -1
    Midx = TextWidth(String1$) / 2
    StringHeight = TextHeight(UserString$)
    CurrentX = ScaleWidth / 2 - Midx
    CurrentY = ScaleHeight / 2 - StringHeight
    Print String1$
    FontName = "Arial"
    FontSize = 35
    FontBold = -1
    FontItalic = 0
    Midx = TextWidth(String2$) / 2
    CurrentX = ScaleWidth / 2 - Midx
    Print String2$
End Sub
```

All of the previous code was placed inside the Form_Resize event procedure so that it is automatically executed whenever the user changes the form's size. This is important because the algorithm checks the form's current dimensions to calculate and print the two strings in the *center* of the form.

After turning AutoRedraw ON, the procedure clears any previous form output with the **Cls** method. It then defines the two expository strings (*String1$, String$2*).

Visual Basic 5 supports multiple fonts such as Courier New, Modern, System, and Times New Roman. Most fonts can be represented in different point sizes (8.25, 9.75, 12, 13.5, 24, etc.) and with different characteristics (FontBold, FontItalic, FontUnderline). However, not all fonts can support each and every font attribute. We recommend the use of Microsoft's TrueType font technology for the greatest flexibility when working with font characteristics.

A particular font is selected by using the FontName property at either design or run time. The same options exist for selecting FontSize, FontBold, FontItalic, and FontUnderline. The last two sections of the Form_Resize procedure begin by setting several of these attributes.

String1$'s horizontal and vertical positions are calculated using a combination of Visual Basic 5 BIFs (built-in functions), such as **TextWidth()**, **TextHeight()**, **ScaleWidth()**, and **ScaleHeight()**. **TextWidth()** and **TextHeight()** return the string's width and height display requirements. The functions' return values take into consideration the selected FontName and FontSize:

```
Midx = TextWidth(String1$) / 2
StringHeight = TextHeight(UserString$)
```

By knowing how much vertical and horizontal display space is required, the algorithm can calculate where to place the string. **ScaleWidth()** and **ScaleHeight()** are two BIFs that return an object's horizontal and vertical range. The return values take into consideration the object's internal coordinate system, set by the **ScaleMode()** property (0, User; 1, Twip; 2, Point; 3, Pixel; 4, Character; 5, Inch; 6, Millimeter; 7, Centimeter). For this example **ScaleMode()** was set to 4, Character:

```
CurrentX = ScaleWidth / 2 - Midx
CurrentY = ScaleHeight / 2 - StringHeight
```

CurrentX() and **CurrentY()** set or return an object's horizontal (**X**) and vertical (**Y**) screen or page coordinates using the object's coordinate system. In this example, **CurrentX()** is set equal to the horizontal center of the form (ScaleWidth/2) minus *String1$*'s width (Midx). **CurrentY()** is set equal to the form's vertical center (ScaleHeight/2) minus *String1$*'s StringHeight.

The entire process is repeated a second time, selecting a new FontName, FontSize, and new attributes to display *String2$*. The **Print** statement automatically advances the output pointer to the beginning of the next line. Therefore, only a new **CurrentX()** is calculated to center the second string.

TABULAR OUTPUT

Tab stops are a quick method for neatly formatting output. Figure 8.5 shows a portion of a program with several vacation packing options all formatted with tab stops.

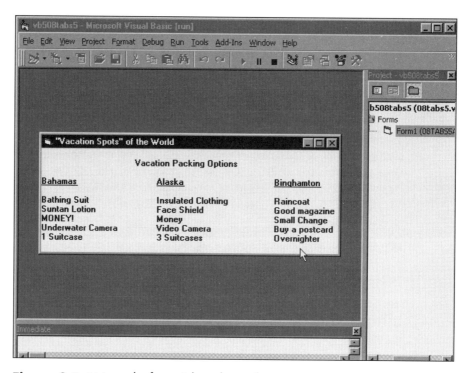

Figure 8.5 Using tabs for quick and neat formatting.

Visual Basic 5 has built-in print zones. Each print zone is 14 columns wide and is based on the currently active FontName and FontSize. A comma placed between **Print** strings instructs Visual Basic 5 to **Print** each item beginning at the next zone. The following Form_Load event procedure uses this default spacing (08TABS5):

```
Private Sub Form_Load ()
 Print
 Print , "      Vacation Packing Options"
 FontUnderline = -1
 Print
 Print "Bahamas", , "Alaska", , "Binghamton"
 FontUnderline = -0
 Print
 Print "Bathing Suit", , "Insulated Clothing", "Raincoat"
 Print "Suntan Lotion", "Face Shield", , "Good magazine"
 Print "MONEY!", , "Money", , "Small Change"
```

```
Print "Underwater Camera", "Video Camera", "Buy a postcard"
Print "1 Suitcase", , "3 Suitcases", , "Overnighter"
Print
End Sub
```

Consecutive commas (, ,) skip the designated number of columns to space items farther apart.

There will be occasions when the default 14 column spacing will be restrictive. This is true when the tabbed output will vary as the application adds and deletes displayed items. Under these circumstances it is best to use manual tab stops.

The following Form_Load event procedure produces the same output as the one just discussed except that it uses manual tab settings:

```
Private Sub Form_Load ()
 Print
 Print Tab(24); "Vacation Packing Options"
 FontUnderline = -1
 Print
 Print Tab(3); "Bahamas"; Tab(32); "Alaska";
      Tab(59);"Binghamton"
 FontUnderline = -0
 Print
 Print "Bathing Suit", , "Insulated Clothing", "Raincoat"
 Print "Suntan Lotion", "Face Shield", , "Good magazine"
 Print "MONEY!", , "Money", , "Small Change"
 Print "Underwater Camera", "Video Camera", "Buy a postcard"
 Print "1 Suitcase", , "3 Suitcases", , "Overnighter"
 Print
End Sub
```

The tab value represents the number of columns to move from the left edge of the object, *not* the number of columns to skip from the last tab stop specified.

NUMERIC, DATE, AND TIME FORMATTING

Visual Basic 5 provides a wide array of predefined data output formats for numbers, dates, and time. Figure 8.6 shows the initial screen appearance for the example program. The program is designed to allow you to experiment with the different international output formats (08FRMT7A).

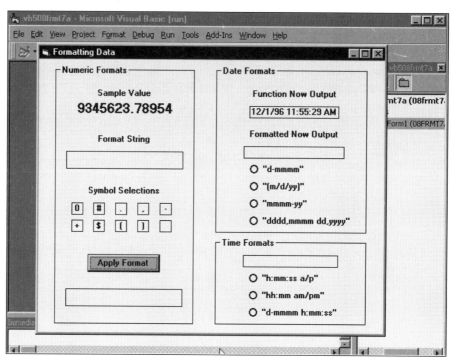

Figure 8.6 Experimenting with output formats.

Formatting Numbers

The **Format$()** function is used to convert numeric values into strings. **Format$()** is more sophisticated than the **Str$()** function because it converts the value to a string and allows it to overlay a format template. The template sets the converted value's number of decimal places, leading and trailing 0s, and the appearance of special symbols such as $, (,), +, and -. The syntax for a **Format$()** statement takes on the following form:

```
Format$(numeric_expression[,format_template$])
```

The *numeric_expression* specifies the value to be converted. The *format_template$* defines the format to be applied to the conversion. Table

8.5 lists some of the more frequently used format symbols and their meanings.

Table 8.5 Frequently Used Format Symbols

Symbol	Meaning
0	The 0 is a digit placeholder. It is placed to the left or right of other format symbols. The 0 can cause Visual Basic 5 to print leading and trailing 0s if the *numeric_expression* is smaller than the number of 0 digit placeholders.
#	The # is a digit placeholder. Unlike 0, it suppresses leading and trailing 0s. If the *numeric_expression* is smaller than the number of # placeholders, only the converted value is printed.
.	Defines where the decimal is to be placed.
,	The comma is used for thousands, hundred thousands, and millions separators.
Special	Symbols like $, (,), +, -, and spaces are printed exactly the way they appear in the template.
:	Time separator.
/	Date separator.
\	Instructs Visual Basic 5 to display the following character. This is used to print those format symbols that are usually part of a format template. For example, to print a #, include the following two symbols in the format template: \#
E+, E -, e+, e -	Scientific format.

The *format_template$* can have a maximum of three sections. If only one is present the same template is used for both positive and negative values. If the *format_template$* has two sections, the first section applies to positive values, the second to negative values. Three-section *format_template$*s go one step further by specifying how zero values are to be formatted.

For example, the following template has three sections and uses the same format for positive and negative values:

```
Format$(Balance,"$#,###,###.##")
```

Figure 8.7 shows the Sample Value formatted with the first section from the **Format$()** function.

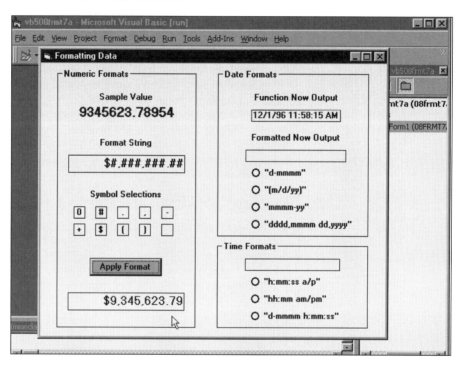

Figure 8.7 Formatting numbers.

This section of the program begins by printing a Sample Value. This is the number that will be formatted using the template created while the program is running. The following Click events are assigned to each one of the **Format$()** template symbols and are used to build the template:

```
Private Sub Label5_Click ()
 If Applied Then
  Applied = 0
```

```
  Label15.Caption = " "
  Label16.Caption = " "
 End If
 Label15.Caption = Label15.Caption + "0"
End Sub
Private Sub Label6_Click ()
 If Applied Then
  Applied = 0
  Label15.Caption = " "
  Label16.Caption = " "
 End If
 Label15.Caption = Label15.Caption + "#"
End Sub

Private Sub Label7_Click ()
 If Applied Then
  Applied = 0
  Label15.Caption = " "
  Label16.Caption = " "
 End If
 Label15.Caption = Label15.Caption + "."
End Sub

Private Sub Label8_Click ()
 If Applied Then
  Applied = 0
  Label15.Caption = " "
  Label16.Caption = " "
 End If
 Label15.Caption = Label15.Caption + ","
End Sub

Private Sub Label9_Click ()
 If Applied Then
  Applied = 0
  Label15.Caption = " "
  Label16.Caption = " "
```

```
  End If
   Label15.Caption = Label15.Caption + "-"
 End Sub


 Private Sub Label10_Click ()
  If Applied Then
   Applied = 0
   Label15.Caption = ""
   Label16.Caption = ""
  End If
   Label15.Caption = Label15.Caption + "+"
 End Sub


 Private Sub Label11_Click ()
  If Applied Then
   Applied = 0
   Label15.Caption = ""
   Label16.Caption = ""
  End If
   Label15.Caption = Label15.Caption + "$"
 End Sub


 Private Sub Label12_Click ()
  If Applied Then
   Applied = 0
   Label15.Caption = ""
   Label16.Caption = ""
  End If
   Label15.Caption = Label15.Caption + "("
 End Sub


 Private Sub Label13_Click ()
  If Applied Then
   Applied = 0
   Label15.Caption = ""
   Label16.Caption = ""
```

```
  End If
  Label15.Caption = Label15.Caption + ")"
End Sub


Private Sub Label14_Click ()
  If Applied Then
   Applied = 0
   Label15.Caption = ""
   Label16.Caption = ""
  End If
  Label15.Caption = Label15.Caption + " "
End Sub
```

Applying the template is a simple matter of clicking on the Apply Format command button and invoking its Click event:

```
Private Sub Command1_Click ()
  Label16.Caption = Format$(Val(Label2.Caption), Label15.Caption)
  Applied = -1
End Sub
```

Command1.Click begins by converting the string representation of Sample Value into a number by using **Val**. Then it applies the user-defined template stored in Label15.Caption. The *Applied* variable (defined in the form's general declarations) determines whether or not the **Format$** Click events build the template or erase a previous specification.

Was there anything that bothered you when you examined the previous section of code? Did you notice the identical code repeated in all the label control (5–14) Click events? A better approach to this coding might have been to make each label control (5–15) part of a control array.

One technique for creating the control array is to give each label control (5–15) the same CtlName, *FormatSymbols*. This tells Visual Basic 5 that they are homogeneous elements with the same *CtlName_Click* event procedure. The following *FormatSymbols_Click* event shows how the *FormatSymbols* control array index can be used to build the format template (08FRMTB):

```
Private Sub FormatSymbols_Click (Index As Integer)
  If Applied Then
```

```
 Applied = 0
 Label15.Caption = ""
 Label16.Caption = ""
End If
Select Case Index
 Case 0
  Label15.Caption = Label15.Caption + "0"
 Case 1
  Label15.Caption = Label15.Caption + "#"
 Case 2
  Label15.Caption = Label15.Caption + "."
 Case 3
  Label15.Caption = Label15.Caption + ","
 Case 4
  Label15.Caption = Label15.Caption + "-"
 Case 5
  Label15.Caption = Label15.Caption + "+"
 Case 6
  Label15.Caption = Label15.Caption + "$"
 Case 7
  Label15.Caption = Label15.Caption + "("
 Case 8
  Label15.Caption = Label15.Caption + ")"
 Case 9
  Label15.Caption = Label15.Caption + " "
 End Select
End Sub
```

While this might seem very complicated initially, the technique is built on the knowledge you have learned in the previous chapters of this book.

Formatting Dates

There is only a small difference between formatting numbers and formatting dates. The difference is the template symbols themselves. Table 8.6 lists some of the more frequently used date format symbols.

Table 8.6 Frequently Used Date Format Symbols

Symbol	Meaning
Day	d Display Day as a number without leading zeros (1–31). dd Display Day as a number with leading zero (01–31). ddd Display Day as (Sun–Sat). dddd Display Day as (Sunday–Saturday). ddddd Display a date number (in serial format) as a complete date (day, month, and year) formatted according to the short date string (sShortDate=) in the international section of the WIN.INI file. The default date format is mm/dd/yy if no sShortDate is defined.
Month/Minute	m Display Month as a number without leading zeros (1–12). Used immediately following h or hh, the minute (without leading zeros) rather than the month is displayed. mm Display Month as a number with leading zero (01–12). Used immediately following h or hh, the minute (with leading zeros) rather than the month is displayed. mmm Display Month as (Jan-Dec). mmmm Display Month as (January–December).
Year	yy Display Year as a two-digit number (00–99). yyyy Display Year as a four-digit number (1900–2040).

The *Dates Format section* of the Formatting Data example program works with a value returned by Visual Basic 5's **Now()** function. **Now()** returns a serial number representing the current system time and date. The following Form_Load event is responsible for the form's Function Now Output value:

```
Private Sub Form_Load ()
 Label18.Caption = Str$(Now)
End Sub
```

The procedure takes **Now()**'s numeric value, converts it to a string with the **Str$() function**, and assigns it to the Caption property of Label18. This prevents the user from changing its value, as you have already learned. The following four Option Click events are responsible for applying the selected **Format$()** template:

```
Private Sub Option1_Click ()
 Label20.Caption = Format$(Now, "d-mmmm")
End Sub
```

```
Private Sub Option2_Click ()
 Label20.Caption = Format$(Now, "(m/d/yy)")
End Sub


Private Sub Option3_Click ()
 Label20.Caption = Format$(Now, "mmmm-yy")
End Sub


Private Sub Option4_Click ()
 Label20.Caption = Format$(Now, "dddd,mmmm dd,yyyy")
End Sub
```

Figure 8.8 shows Option4's **Format$()** template applied to **Now()**.

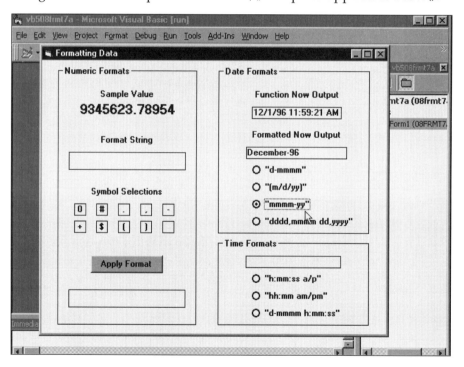

Figure 8.8 Experimenting with date formats.

Formatting Time

Table 8.7 shows popular **Format$()** template symbols used to define time formats.

Table 8.7 Frequently Used Time Format Symbols

Symbol	Meaning
Hour	h Display Hour as a number without leading zeros (0–23). hh Display Hour as a number with leading zeros (00–23).
Minutes	See Date **m**.
Second	s Display Seconds as a number without leading zeros (0–59). ss Display Seconds as a number with leading zeros (00–59).
Time	ttttt Display Time serial number as a complete time (hour, minute, and second) formatted with time separator defined by (sTime=) in the international section of the WIN.INI file. Default time format is h:mm:ss.
AM/PM	am/pm. Use the 12-hour clock displaying AM with AM/PM, any hour before noon; display PM with any a/p, hour between noon and 11:59 PM.

Figure 8.9 shows the results of applying the Option7 Click event **Format$()** template.

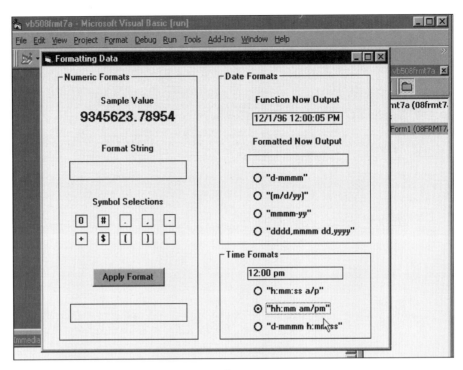

Figure 8.9 Experimenting with time formats.

Here is a portion of code responsible for formatting time in various manners.

```
Private Sub Option5_Click ()
 Label21.Caption = Format$(Now, "h:mm:ss a/p")
End Sub


Private Sub Option6_Click ()
 Label21.Caption = Format$(Now, "hh:mm am/pm")
End Sub


Private Sub Option7_Click ()
 Label21.Caption = Format$(Now, "d-mmmm h:mm:ss")
End Sub
```

SENDING OUTPUT TO A PRINTER

There are two basic methods for sending output to a printer; directly or by first "printing" to a form and then printing the form.

Direct Output to Printers

To print directly to the printer, precede the **Print()** statement with the **Printer** object. The general syntax takes on the following form:

```
Printer.Print literal[;]
```

Printer objects support all of the graphics methods necessary to draw points, lines, and circles. You can also use all the font properties described throughout the previous chapters (FontName, FontBold, etc.). You can even use **Printer.CurrentX()** and **Printer.CurrentY()** to designate which column and row the printer output is to begin on.

The *NewPage* method instructs the printer to advance the paper to the beginning of a new page. You dump the output buffer and advance the paper to the top of a clean page with the **EndDoc** method.

Each time you begin a new document, Visual Basic 5 automatically tracks the number of pages printed. You can access this internal value with the **Page** property. The following statement would print the current page number to the printer:

```
Printer.Print Printer.Page
```

Indirect Output to Printers

You can send output to the printer by first printing it to a form and then printing the form. The syntax **PrintForm()** takes on the following form:

```
[form].PrintForm
```

If *form* is omitted, Visual Basic 5 prints the current form. **PrintForm()** prints the entire form's contents by doing a pixel-by-pixel dump. Because of this, text output may appear to be of lower resolution than the output obtained by printing directly to the printer. To dump a form's graphics images to the printer you must set the form's AutoRedraw property to -1 (True).

The GUI

In Windows 95 and Windows NT all output is sent to a graphics window. This GUI, or graphical user interface, is also the perfect spot to draw images, create bitmaps, and play back video images.

In the next chapter, you will begin to explore the GUI environment and learn about many graphics fundamentals.

Chapter 9

Graphics Fundamentals

This chapter is the last in a group of chapters designed to acquaint you with specific elements of the Visual Basic 5 programming environment. The purpose of this chapter is to present the graphics programming elements provided with Visual Basic 5. By studying this chapter you will learn about coordinate systems and drawing scales, where and how to draw graphics elements, how to use color, techniques for making graphics permanent, and so on.

In Chapters 11 and 15, you will learn how to combine the individual concepts from Chapters 1 to 9 into complete Windows 95 and Windows NT graphics applications.

COORDINATE SYSTEMS

Have you ever watched a person handle a road map? If you ask how to get from one city to another, they fumble with the map just trying to find which way is up. However, once they learn that maps are always drawn with north at the top, they can usually find how to get from one location to another.

The Visual Basic 5 coordinate system is very much like reading a map. Once you establish up, down, left, and right it is much easier to use graphics commands correctly.

Many early languages used the smallest screen elements possible to describe screen coordinates and drawing scales. These elements, called pixels, are usually measured from the top left of the screen. Various graphics standards increased the resolution or the number of pixels in any given direction. For example, CGA (Computer Graphics Accelerator) monitors had color resolutions of 320 x 200 pixels. That is, 320 pixels starting with 0 on the left and ending with 319 on the right, 200 pixels starting with 0 at the top and ending with 199 on the bottom. VGA (Video Graphics Accelerator) monitors increased the resolution to 640 x 480, and now SVGA (Super Video Graphics Accelerator) and other standards have made another quantum jump. When Microsoft designed Windows they decided to make it device independent. That means that when you ask for a circle with a fixed radius, it will appear the same on CGA and VGA monitors without additional programming overhead for the programmer.

Device independence does not mean, however, that a single coordinate system or drawing scale will be used for all graphics. If graphics are to be sent to a printer, plotter, or other output device, it might be desirable to have the coordinate system and drawing scale in inches, centimeters, or millimeters instead of pixels. After all, there is no such thing as a pixel on a plotter.

The Default Coordinate System and Drawing Scale

Visual Basic 5 provides a default coordinate system and drawing scale that may be adequate for all of your graphical programming needs. By default, the **ScaleMode** function sets the drawing scale to *twips*. The resolution of this coordinate system is 1440 twips per inch. If an 8-inch line is drawn, then the line is 11,520 (8 x 1440) twips in length. Using this coordinate system results in very large numbers being passed to various graphics commands. Table 9.1 shows other additional drawing scales that can be used in Visual Basic 5. For example, to change the drawing scale to pixels, the following constant could be used:

```
ScaleMode = 3
```

Visual Basic 5 automatically adjusts **ScaleWidth** and **ScaleHeight** when **ScaleMode** is set to a new scale. Likewise, if **ScaleWidth** and **ScaleHeight** are set by the user, **ScaleMode** will be set to 0.

Table 9.1 Visual Basic 5 Scale Modes

ScaleMode	Constant	Description
0	vbUser	A user-defined drawing scale Entered by setting **ScaleWidth** or **ScaleHeight**
1	vbTwips	(1440 twips/inch)
2	vbPoints	Points (72 points/inch)
3	vbPixels	Pixels (VGA is 640 x 480)
4	vbCharacters	Characters (1/6 inch high, 1/12 inch wide)
5	vbInches	Inches
6	vbMillimeters	Millimeters
7	vbCentimeters	Centimeters

By default, the coordinate system places the origin (0, 0) at the top left of the drawing surface. If the drawing surface measures 7 inches across and 5 inches down, then Figure 9.1 represents the coordinate values for each corner.

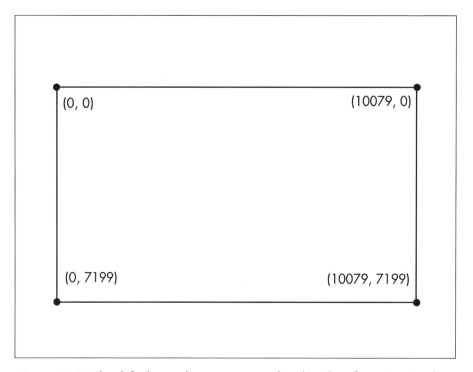

Figure 9.1 The default coordinate system and scale values for a 7 x 5 inch drawing surface.

In Figure 9.1, the origin is at 0, 0 (upper left) and the drawing scale is set to twips (1440 twips/inch).

The number of twips for any given drawing surface is dependent on the size of the drawing surface. **ScaleWidth** and **ScaleHeight** are measures of the actual drawing surface available to the user in scale units determined by the coordinate system of the object. The **Width** and **Height** properties, on the other hand, specify the size of the container in scale units that match the container's coordinate system. The container is the drawing surface plus any borders surrounding the surface.

Designing Custom Coordinate Systems

Many times the values provided by default will not be sufficient for your application's needs. If the default coordinate system is not satisfactory, it is possible to create a custom coordinate system and drawing scale. Imagine that a scientist wants to plot an equation on the screen. The values plotted horizontally vary between 0 and 4000. If only pixels can be addressed, the mathematician must scale the data points to the screen size. Every calculated point, on a VGA screen, must be multiplied by 640/4000 in order to fit the window. In Visual Basic 5 it is possible to create a custom coordinate system and drawing scale so that the horizontal extent of the window is 4000! This means that individual points from the mathematician's equation can be plotted directly without the need to scale. The next three examples will show you sample coordinate systems and drawing scales that might be useful for plotting equations and drawing charts.

Moving the Origin to the Bottom Left Corner Visual Basic 5 places the origin (0, 0) at the upper left of the window by default. This de facto standard is probably related to the fact that the pixel in the upper left corner is in the first column of the first row or the fact that the pixel in the upper left corner is hit by the cathode ray beam first. Regardless of the reason, we learned to graph in mathematics with the origin in the lower left corner for first-quadrant plots. How can the origin be changed?

The coordinate system and thus the drawing scale are changed with the use of four functions: **ScaleTop**, **ScaleLeft**, **ScaleHeight**, and **ScaleWidth**.

Assume for an instant that a form uses the following program code:

```
ScaleTop = 1000
ScaleHeight = -1000
ScaleLeft = 0
ScaleWidth = 1000
```

Examine Figure 9.2 to see a complete sketch of these values and the coordinates of the four corners of the drawing surface.

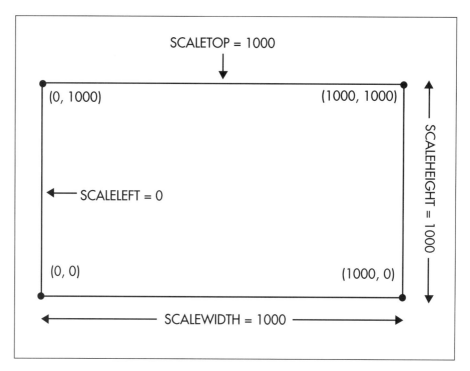

Figure 9.2 A custom coordinate system places the origin at the bottom left of the window.

    ScaleTop's value is the actual coordinate value for the top of the drawing surface. Likewise, **ScaleLeft** specifies the actual left coordinate value for the drawing surface. **ScaleHeight** and **ScaleWidth** do not describe coordinate points but instead describe the distances measured from **ScaleTop** and **ScaleLeft**, respectively. For example:

```
ScaleTop     + ScaleHeight   = Y value at bottom of drawing
                               surface
   1000      + -1000         = 0
ScaleLeft    + ScaleWidth    = X value at right of drawing
                               surface
      0      + 1000          = 1000
```

    ScaleHeight is considered a negative value because you are moving down from the top of the drawing surface.

    From these derived and calculated numbers, the coordinate points for the four corners of the drawing surface and the drawing scale can be derived. They are shown in Figure 9.2.

Moving the Origin for Charting Imagine that a business executive wants to draw a bar chart. The upper left corner on the chart is to be 0. Further, the extent of each chart axis is to be 500. The executive wants a border around the chart (for labels, etc.) 100 units in each direction. How are the values for the Visual Basic 5 functions determined?

First, draw the executive's chart on a piece of paper and label the values, as shown in Figure 9.3. Only the values given in the original specification are shown.

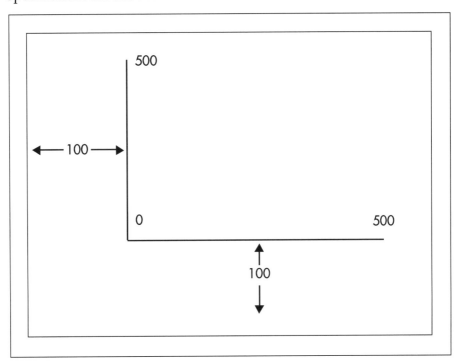

Figure 9.3 Determining function parameter values.

Remember that these values are based on bar chart coordinates that offset the origin point on a custom coordinate system.

By using Figure 9.3, the following values can be determined:

```
ScaleHeight   =    top margin   +  Vert. extent   + bottom margin
              =       100        +      500        +      100
ScaleHeight   =       700
ScaleWidth    =  left margin     +  Horz. extent   + right margin
              =       100        +      500        +      100
ScaleWidth    =       700
```

Once **ScaleHeight** and **ScaleWidth** are known, the equations (shown earlier) can be used to calculate **ScaleTop** and **ScaleLeft**.

```
ScaleTop    +   ScaleHeight    =     Y value at bottom of drawing
                                     surface
ScaleTop    +       -700       =    -100
                ScaleTop       =    -100 + 700 = 600
ScaleLeft   +   ScaleWidth     =     X value at right of drawing
                                     surface
ScaleLeft   +       700        =    600
                ScaleLeft      =    600 - 700 = -100
```

The executive's custom coordinate system and drawing scale can be realized with the following portion of code:

```
ScaleTop      =    600
ScaleHeight   =   -700
ScaleLeft     =   -100
ScaleWidth    =    700
```

Figure 9.4 shows the original specifications and the calculated coordinate points for the drawing surface's four corners.

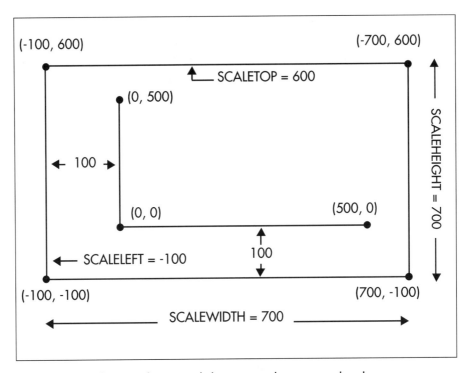

Figure 9.4 The coordinate and drawing scale are completed.

Once the values for **ScaleHeight** and **ScaleWidth** are found, **ScaleTop** and **ScaleLeft** can be calculated. The executive's bar chart coordinates and drawing scale are now fully specified, as shown in Figure 9.4.

Remember, working with coordinate systems and drawing scales can be a little tricky until you get the hang of it.

Moving the Origin to the Center Now imagine that the drawing surface is to be divided into four equal rectangles. This is to be done so that a graph can be drawn with points in all four quadrants of a rectangular coordinate system. The X axis will extend from -1000 to +1000 and the Y axis from +900 to -900. This places the origin at the center of the drawing surface. Figure 9.5 shows a sketch of the required coordinate system and drawing scale.

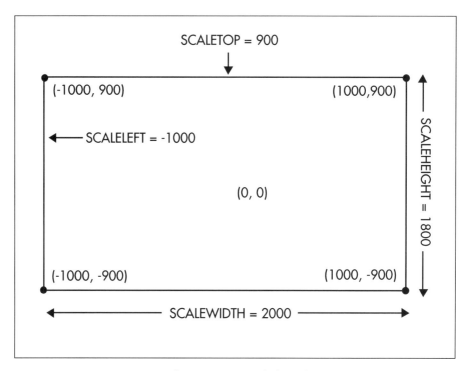

Figure 9.5 A custom coordinate system with four drawing quadrants.

Before you assume this might be an easy task, look at the values
derived from Figure 9.5.

```
ScaleHeight = top margin  +  vert. extent  +   bottom margin
            =      0       +      1800      +         0
ScaleHeight =    1800
ScaleWidth  = left margin +  horz.extent   +    right margin
            =      0       +      2000      +         0
ScaleWidth  =    2000
```

Once these values are known, the equations shown earlier can be
used to calculate **ScaleTop** and **ScaleLeft**.

```
ScaleTop   + ScaleHeight       = Y value at bottom of drawing
                                   surface
ScaleTop   +   -1800           = -900
             ScaleTop          = -900 + 1800 = 900
ScaleLeft + ScaleWidth         = X value at right of drawing
                                   surface
ScaleLeft +    2000            = 1000
             ScaleLeft         = 1000 - 2000 = -1000
```

The custom coordinate system and drawing scale can be achieved with the following code:

```
ScaleTop = 900
ScaleHeight = -1800
ScaleLeft = -1000
ScaleWidth = 2000
```

You will gain more experience with custom coordinate systems and drawing scales in Chapters 11 and 15.

DRAWING SURFACES

The drawing surface in Visual Basic 5 is an object such as a form, PictureBox, or printer. This section will teach you how to use each of these drawing surfaces. In our examples, if a drawing surface isn't specified, assume a form is used.

Forms Object

If the **ScaleMode** function isn't used to alter the coordinate system or drawing scale, a scale mode of 1 is assumed. This mode uses 1440 twips per inch.

For example, to draw a line on **Form1**, proceed as follows:

1. Open a new project. **Form1** will be created. Select View | Code from the menu.
2. Use the object ListBox control (upper left, just above the code display area) to view the code of the form.
3. Use the procedure ListBox control (upper right, just above the code display area) to select "Paint."

Now, program code can be entered into the Paint event procedure as follows:

```
Private Sub Form_Paint()
  DrawWidth = 10
  Line (500, 1500)-(3000, 3500)
End Sub
```

An alternative form of entry is to specify the object's name:

```
Private Sub Form_Paint
  DrawWidth = 10
```

```
Form1.Line (500,1500)-(3000,3500)
End Sub
```

Both pieces of code will draw a wide diagonal line on the **Form1** when the <u>S</u>tart option is selected from the main Visual Basic 5 <u>R</u>un menu. In the first case, the **Line** method assumes **Form1** because no object was specified and that **Form1** contains the Paint event procedure. In the second case, **Form1** was the object specified as the drawing surface. **DrawWidth** sets the width of lines when using graphics functions.

Give this example a try in Visual Basic 5. You should see a figure similar to Figure 9.6 on **Form1**.

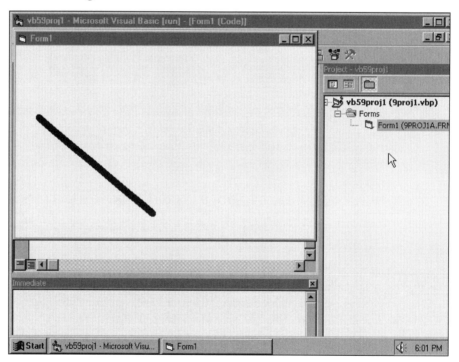

Figure 9.6 Drawing a wide diagonal line on a form's drawing surface.

If a second or third form is opened at design time, graphics can be sent to the specific form by using the form name as the object in the graphics method. For example, try this variation:

```
Private Sub Form_Paint
  Form3.Line (1000,1500)-(3000,4000)
End Sub
```

PictureBox Objects

Graphics methods can also be used to draw in PictureBox controls.

To draw a line on a picture box, **Picture1**, contained in **Form1**, proceed as follows:

1. Open a new project. Form1 will be created.
2. Select a PictureBox control from the Toolbox.
3. Place and size the picture box on Form1. The PictureBox is assigned the name Picture1.
4. Set the PictureBox control's AutoRedraw property to True.
5. Double-click the mouse on the object to view the object's code.
6. Use the procedure ListBox control to select "Paint" (the Paint event procedure for the form).

Now, program code can be entered into the Paint event procedure as follows:

```
Private Sub Form_Paint
  DrawWidth = 10
  Picture1.Line (500, 1500)-(3000, 3500)
End Sub
```

A diagonal line is drawn in the PictureBox control of **Form1** when the Start option is selected from the main Visual Basic 5 Run menu. Figure 9.7 shows the form and PictureBox control we created. Remember, the object's name must precede the graphics method. Your program's output should be similar.

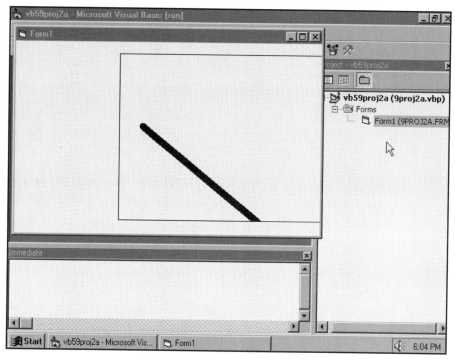

Figure 9.7 Drawing a line in a PictureBox control requires the object's name to precede the graphics method.

If a second or third PictureBox control is created at design time, graphics can be sent to the new PictureBox control in a similar manner. For example:

```
Private Sub Form_Paint
  DrawWidth = 5
  Picture2.Line (100, 500)-(300, 600)
End Sub
```

Printer Objects

Graphics methods can also be used to draw to the printer. To draw a line on a printer object proceed as follows:

1. Open a new project. Form1 will be created.
2. Double-click on the form to view the form's code.
3. Use the procedure ListBox control to select "Paint" (the Paint event procedure for the form).

Enter the following variation of program code into the Paint event procedure:

```
Private Sub Form_Paint()
   Printer.Line (1000, 1000)-(2000, 2000)
   Printer.EndDoc
End Sub
```

A diagonal line will be drawn on a Windows installed printer when the Start option is selected from the main Visual Basic 5 Run menu. Nothing new will be sent to the screen. The **EndDoc** method sends pending output to the printer or spooler and advances the page.

GRAPHICS PROPERTIES

Graphics properties include colors, line styles, line widths, fill styles, and graphics persistence. The correct combination of colors and styles creates a pleasing visual effect for graphs and charts. Visual Basic 5 also provides a **DrawMode** property that allows special effects to be performed when drawing. These effects include Xor, Not, Invert, etc. You can experiment with **DrawMode** properties as you learn how to use other useful Visual Basic 5 graphical properties.

Colors

Visual Basic 5 allows drawing and fill colors to be specified by two methods. The simpler method utilizes a color scheme from QuickBasic and the **QBColor** function. The second method uses the **RGB** function; RGB stands for red, green, and blue. In this function, three integer values specify the proportions of the colors that are mixed to produce a final result. Although the **RGB** function is more complicated, 256 x 256 x 256 = 16,777,216 color combinations are possible as compared with **QBColor**'s 16.

QBColor Options The **QBColor** function allows integer numbers, in the range 0 to 15, to specify a color from the QuickBasic palette. For example, a light red line can be drawn to a form with the following programming code:

```
Private Sub Form_Paint
  'draw a light red line on a form
  Line(1000,1000)-(2000,2000),QBColor(12)
End Sub
```

Table 9.2 list colors that can be used for drawing or filling closed shapes.

Table 9.2 QBColor Palette

Integer	Color	Integer	Color
0	Black	8	Gray
1	Blue	9	Lt. blue
2	Green	10	Lt. green
3	Cyan	11	Lt. cyan
4	Red	12	Lt. red
5	Magenta	13	Lt. magenta
6	Yellow	14	Lt. yellow
7	White	15	Bt. white

Although the palette is limited, simple applications can take advantage of a method that requires only one integer number to specify a color.

RGB Color Options   The **RGB** function allows three integer numbers, in the range 0 to 255, to specify a wide range of colors by mixing combinations of red, green, and blue. More precisely:

```
256 x 256 x 256 = 16,777,216 colors
```

The display of this range of colors is limited only by your graphics card and monitor. A yellow line, for example, can be drawn to a form with the following code:

```
Private Sub Form_Paint
  'draw a yellow line on a form
  Line(1000,1000)-(2000,2000),RGB(255,255,0)
End Sub
```

Table 9.3 list several colors that can be created with the **RGB** function.

Table 9.3 Several RGB Color Combinations

Color	Integers		
	R	**G**	**B**
Black	(0,	0,	0)
Blue	(0,	0,	255)
Green	(0,	255,	0)
Cyan	(0,	255,	255)
Red	(255,	0,	0)
Magenta	(255,	0,	255)
Yellow	(255,	255,	0)
White	(255,	255,	255)

Other combinations can be formed by specifying other integer values in the range 0 to 255.

Choosing the correct RGB color combination, experimentally, is a difficult task. That is why a project named 9Colr1.vbp is included with this book. Figure 9.8 shows the project form.

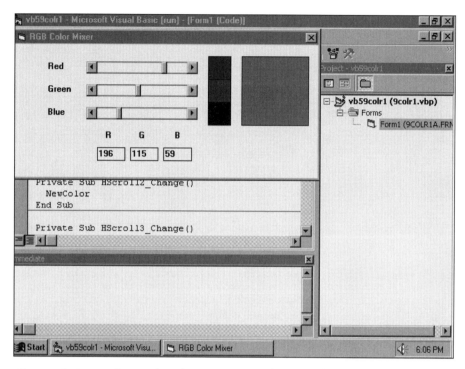

Figure 9.8 Use the 9Colr1.vbp project to pick RGB values.

This application program will allow you to mix red, green, and blue color combinations. The form paints the background color of PictureBox controls with the appropriate RGB color value and reports the numeric value to a TextBox control.

Load this application into Visual Basic 5 and click on the Start menu option in the main Run menu. By sliding one or all of the scroll bars, various combinations of red, green, and blue colors can be mixed in the PictureBox control. When you find color combinations you like, write the RGB numbers down for future reference.

Line Drawing Styles

Visual Basic 5 uses a solid line as the default line drawing style. Other combinations such as dash-dot are available as shown in Table 9.4.

Table 9.4 Line Drawing Styles

Integer	Constant	Description
0	vbSolid	Solid
1	vbDash	Dash
2	vbDot	Dot
3	vbDashDot	Dash-dot
4	vbDashDotDot	Dash-dot-dot
5	vbInvisible	Invisible
6	vbInsideSolid	Inside solid

The syntax for using the **DrawStyle** property involves the use of a single integer. For example, a line drawn with dashes can be programmed with the following code:

```
Private Sub Form_Paint
   'draw a dashed line on a form
   DrawStyle = vbDash
   Line(1000,1000)-(2000,2000)
End Sub
```

Drawing styles 1 through 4 work only with drawing widths equal to 1. If the drawing width is greater than 1, a solid line will be used as the drawing style.

Line Drawing Width

The thickness of a line can be changed with the use of the **DrawWidth** property. By default, the drawing width is set to 1. With a drawing with of 1, drawing styles other than solid lines can be used.

The syntax for using the **DrawWidth** property is straightforward:

```
Private Sub Form_Paint
   'draw a thick line on a form
   DrawWidth = 10
   Line(500,1500)-(3000,3500)
End Sub
```

The most pleasing effects for line widths involve small integer numbers, in the range 0 to 20.

Fill Color and Styles

Closed shapes such as boxes, rectangles, circles, and ellipses can be filled with a color. The color can be specified with the **QBColor** or **RGB** function. The fill style can vary from a solid brush to a diagonal cross. Table 9.5 lists the fill style properties. Color options were discussed earlier in this chapter.

Table 9.5 Fill Styles

Integer	Description
0	Solid
1	Transparent (default)
2	Horizontal lines
3	Vertical lines
4	Diagonal (downward, \ )
5	Diagonal (upward, /)
6	Cross (+)
7	Diagonal cross (x)

The following program segment will draw a circle on a form and fill it with a red diagonal pattern.

```
Private Sub Form_Paint
  'draw and fill a circle on a form
  FillStyle = 4
  FillColor = RGB(255,0,0)
  Circle (2000,2000), 1000
End Sub
```

Take a minute to experiment with this group of commands. Try various colors and fill styles.

Persistent Graphics

In Visual Basic 5 overlapping windows can be used for many purposes. These purposes include multiple forms, pictures, and menus. When graphics information is sent to an object, it can be sent in a persistent or nonpersistent form.

In persistent form, if the graphics in an object are temporarily covered with another form, the graphics will be restored when the overlapping form is removed. This can be done automatically because the graphics image is saved in memory. The persistent form is slower than its nonpersistent counterpart and places a burden on system memory. You'll know when you need this option, because your graphics images will be "eaten" by overlapped forms and pictures.

In nonpersistent form, the graphics are not saved in memory and cannot be restored if an overlapping form is removed. The nonpersistent form is fast and does not place an additional memory burden on the system.

The **AutoRedraw** property is used to determine persistence. If **AutoRedraw** is set to TRUE (-1), automatic repainting (persistent) is enabled. Graphics information is sent to the window and to memory. When **AutoRedraw** is FALSE (0), automatic repainting is disabled and graphics information is sent only to the window.

GRAPHICS DRAWING PRIMITIVES

Visual Basic 5 offers the following graphics methods: **Cls**, **PSet**, **Point**, **Line**, and **Circle**. At first glance, this seems like a limited set of graphics primitives. However, many of these Visual Basic 5 methods have modifiable parameters that allow them to, in turn, produce other graphing primitives. The **Line** method, for example, can be modified to draw a box or rectangle. The **Circle** method can be used to draw an ellipse, an arc, and pie wedges.

Cls, as you might suspect, is a method for clearing text and graphics from a form or PictureBox control. **Cls** resets the **CurrentX** and **CurrentY** of the form or PictureBox control to 0.

Drawing and Reading Point Information

Visual Basic 5 makes use of two methods for reading and writing point information. One is **Pset** and the other is **Step**.

Drawing Points PSet can be used with forms, PictureBox controls, or the printer, and uses the following syntax:

```
[object].PSet [Step](x!,y!)[,color&]
```

The use of the keyword **Step** causes the coordinate points x, y to be relative to **CurrentX** and **CurrentY** rather than absolute screen positions. For example:

```
'places point +50 twips from CurrentX and
'100 twips from CurrentY
  PSet Step(50,100)
```

If the **Step** keyword is not used, the position is absolute. For example:

```
'places point at +50 twips from left edge
'and 100 twips from top of form
  PSet (50,100)
```

A color can be specified using the **QBColor** or **RGB** function.

Reading Point Information Information can be returned about a point by using the **Point** method. **Point** uses the following syntax:

```
[object].Point (x!,y!)
```

The object can be a form, PictureBox control, or printer. The coordinate points (x, y) specify absolute positions based on the current coordinate system and drawing scale.

Lines and Rectangles

Visual Basic 5 provides the **Line** method for drawing lines and rectangles. Rectangles are closed shapes and can be filled with color. The syntax for the **Line** method is involved:

```
[object].Line [[Step](x1!,y1!)]-[Step](x2!,y2!)[,
               [color&],B[F]]]
```

The object can be a form, PictureBox control, or printer. The **Step** keyword indicates that the following values are measured relative to the **CurrentX** and **CurrentY** rather than specifying absolute window positions. Color values give the drawing color of the line or rectangle. **QBColor** or **RGB** color functions can be used. If a color value is not specified, the current **ForeColor** is used. **B** specifies that a rectangle is to be drawn rather than a line. In this case, the coordinates represent opposite corners of the rectangle. If, and only if, **B** is used, **F** can be used to specify that the rectangle is to be filled with the current **FillColor** and **FillStyle**.

Here are some **Line** examples that you can experiment with:

```
Private Sub Form_Paint()
  'DRAW SEVERAL LINES TO A FORM
  'draw diagonal line from (10,10)
  'to (1000,1000)
  Line (10,10)-(1000,1000)

  'draw diagonal line from (20,40)
  'to (70,140)
  Line (20,40)-Step(50,100)

  'draw a vertical green
  'line from (500,100) to (500,200)
  Line (500,100)-(500,200),QBColor(2)

  'DRAW SEVERAL RECTANGLES TO A FORM
  'draw a rectangle with one corner
  'at (10,10) and the other at (1000,
  '1000)
  Line (10,10)-(1000,1000),,B

  'draw a rectangle with
  'one corner at (20,40) and another
  'at (70,140). Drawing color is blue
  'fill color is whatever the current
  'fill color and style were set to
  Line (20,40)-Step(50,100),QBColor(3),BF
End Sub
```

The complicated syntax is a result of putting so much functionality into a single method. You'll find, however, that the **Line** method provides you with a lot of programming flexibility.

Drawing Circles, Ellipses, Arcs, and Pie Wedges

Visual Basic 5 provides the **Circle** method for drawing circles, ellipses, arcs, and pie wedges. Circles, ellipses, and pie wedges can form closed shapes that can be filled in the current style and color. The syntax for the **Circle** method is also involved:

```
[object].Circle [Step](x1!,y1!),radius![,[color&][,[start!][,
                        [end!][,aspect!]]]]
```

The object can be a form, PictureBox control, or printer. The **Step** keyword indicates that the following values are measured relative to the **CurrentX** and **CurrentY** rather than specifying absolute window positions. The **radius** value determines the size of the circle, ellipse, arc, or pie wedge. Color values give the drawing color for the selected shape. **QBColor** or **RGB** color functions can be used. If a color value is not specified, the current **ForeColor** is used. If the shape drawn is closed, it can be filled by first setting **FillColor**. The **start** and **end** values are used for arcs and pie wedges. They specify the starting and ending angle measured in radians. There are 2 x pi radians in 360 degrees. Values can be converted from degrees to radians with a simple proportion. The **aspect** value used for ellipses indicates how "squashed" the circle becomes. Integer values such as 2, 3, 4 indicate a smaller x axis compared to y. Fractional values, .5, .333, .25 mean that the x axis is longer than the y axis.

The use of the **Circle** method can be best demonstrated with several examples:

```
Private Sub Form_Paint()
  'Set all line widths to 5 pixels
  DrawWidth = 5

  'DRAW SEVERAL CIRCLES TO A FORM
  'draw a circle centered at (1000,
  '1000) with a radius of 800 twips.
  Circle (1000, 1000), 800

  'draw a red circle at
  'CurrentX+500 and CurrentY+100.
  'radius is 1500 twips.
  CurrentX = 2000
  CurrentY = 2000
  Circle Step(500, 100), 1500, RGB(255, 0, 0)

  'DRAW SEVERAL ELLIPSES TO A FORM
  'draw an ellipse centered at (4500,
  '4500) with a radius of 1000 twips
```

```
'and an aspect of 4. (y is 4 times
'x extent)
Circle (4500, 4500), 1000, , , , 4

'draw a green
'ellipse at CurrentX+50 and
'CurrentY+100. Radius is 800 twips.
'(x is 4 times y extent)
CurrentX = 1000
CurrentY = 2000
Circle Step(50, 100), 800, RGB(0, 255, 0), , , 0.25

'DRAW SEVERAL ARC SEGMENTS TO A FORM
Const PI = 3.14159

'draw an arc between 0 and
'180 (PI/4) degrees. Radius is 700 twips.
Circle (2000, 1000), 700, , 0, PI / 4

'draw a yellow arc from 90 (PI/8) to 180 (PI/4)
'degrees. Radius is 500 twips.
Circle Step(2000, 500), 500, RGB(255, 255, 0), PI / 8, PI / 4

'DRAW SEVERAL PIE WEDGES TO A FORM

'draw a pie wedge between 0 and
'180 (PI/4) degrees. Radius is 400 twips.
'minus signs extend a line to center of pie
'pie wedge - start angle < end angle
Circle (7000, 5000), 400, , -0#, -PI / 4

'draw a blue pie with a wedge removed!
'Radius is 500 twips.
'minus signs extend a line to center of pie
'pie with wedge removed - start angle > end angle
Circle (7000, 6000), 500, RGB(0, 255, 255), -PI / 4, -PI / 8
End Sub
```

Figure 9.9 shows the screen you should see if you create a form and place the previous code in the Paint event procedure.

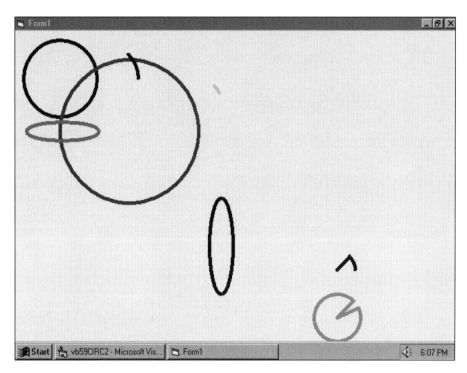

Figure 9.9 Using the Circle method for drawing a variety of graphics shapes.

The **Circle** method seems to be the Swiss Army knife of graphics commands.

What's Coming?

In the previous nine chapters you have learned the terminology, fundamentals, and techniques for using Visual Basic 5. In the remaining chapters of this book, these principles will be put to use developing applications with a truly professional flair. In Chapter 10, for example, we'll start building applications like a base change calculator.

Chapter 10

Numeric Examples

In previous chapters you have learned the fundamentals of using Visual Basic 5. In the remaining chapters of this book you will learn how to apply that information by creating useful working examples. These examples can be viewed as templates—code that can be used or modified in your own projects. Each remaining chapter focuses on a different category of programs. For example, this chapter will teach you how to create projects involving mathematical calculations from the areas of computer science, business, and mathematics.

In addition to the stated primary goal of each programming example, you will learn many Visual Basic 5 tips and shortcuts. For example, you may not be interested in obtaining a table of sine and cosine values, but you should find the technique for creating a table with a vertical scroll bar useful in your own projects.

GOOD PROJECT STYLE

Projects can contain global declarations, a variety of different forms, and user-defined modules. Because of this, a technique is needed to organize the various components of each example in this book.

For example, suppose that a project contains a global module, a module, and several forms. If the files are found in Chapter 11 we will start the related file names with an eleven (11). The chapter number will be followed by a four-letter alphanumeric mnemonic cryptically describing the project. Another number follows, designating the example number in the chapter. A project's first form will then have the letter "A" just preceding the file extension. Second and third forms will have the letters "B" and "C," and so on. For example:

```
11Icon3.bas      <- Global module
11Icon3A.frm     <- Form 1
11Icon3B.frm     <- Form 2
11Mod3.bas       <- User module
```

It is also possible to have a Project file and an Executable file in your directory.

```
11Icon3.vbp      <- Project file
11Icon3.exe      <- Executable file
```

These files must be present when a project is loaded in Visual Basic 5. They can reside on diskette or a subdirectory of your hard disk. We suggest transferring the files you are working with to the Visual Basic 5 subdirectory. Editing, compiling, and running projects will be much faster from a hard disk.

DESIGNING A BASE CHANGE CALCULATOR

The first project for this chapter will be named 10Calc1. To load all of the associated files from your reference disk or CD-ROM, use 10Calc1*.*, as a wild card to copy them to your working subdirectory on your hard disk. As you have read your Visual Basic 5 manuals, we're sure you have noticed a heavy reliance on hexadecimal number notation. Actually, hexadecimal and binary formats are the numeric bases most frequently used by programmers. Most Basic compilers, including Visual Basic 5, include formatting commands for converting decimal numbers to hexadecimal (base 16) and octal (base 8). Perhaps you are familiar with the **Hex$** and **Oct$** functions. The use of octal notation is somewhat passé, but it is an operation that is easy to perform with the built-in **Oct$** function. We are going to design a better base change calculator than the examples found in most books. Our base change calculator will allow conversion between decimal, hexadecimal, and binary formats. Now this will be a useful calculator when doing work in Visual Basic 5!

Figure 10.1 shows the data entry form **(Form1)** for this project.

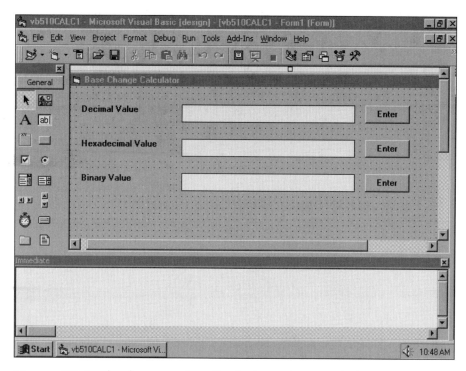

Figure 10.1 The data entry form for the base change calculator program.

 Note: We will use the default command and box names wherever possible in our examples. Thus, the control name for the first CommandButton control will be **Command1** *and that of the first TextBox control will be* **Text1**.*)*

You'll note from the figure that this form uses three labels, three TextBox controls, and three command buttons. The operation of the calculator is simple enough: Enter the number to be converted in the appropriate TextBox control and click on the corresponding command button. The program will calculate the remaining two numbers in the corresponding bases and return the values to the appropriate TextBox controls. What could be easier? For example, if the decimal number 1234 is entered as the decimal value, the program will return 4D2 as the hexadecimal result and 10011010010 as the binary answer. Let's look at the program code, section by section.

The Global Module

Several global declarations for data types are saved in this global module, 10calc1.bas. The global module makes these values available to all forms and modules of the project.

```
Global I As Integer
Global Decval As Double, Power As Double, Tempval As Double
```

Visual Basic 5 relies heavily on the global module when complicated projects are involved.

Converting to Decimal (Command1)

Each command button has its own corresponding code. If a decimal conversion is requested by pushing **Command1**, then a hexadecimal and a binary number must be calculated. Several command buttons, in this example, share identical portions of code. This code could have (should have) been placed in a subroutine and called when needed by a command button. However, to keep the programming as straightforward as possible, in this first example, we chose not to do this. Observe the code that responds to a click of the **Command1** button.

```
Private Sub Command1_Click ()
  'Input Decimal Value
  Decval = Val(Text1.Text)

  'Convert Decimal To Hexadecimal
  Text2.Text = Hex$(Decval)

  'Convert Decimal To Binary
  Binval$ = ""
  Do While Decval <> 0
    Binval$ = Format$(Decval - (Decval \ 2) * 2) + Binval$
    Decval = Decval \ 2
  Loop
  Text3.Text = Binval$
End Sub
```

The decimal value entered, in the TextBox control **(Text1)**, is retrieved as a string. It is converted to a decimal value with the **Val** function and stored in the variable *Decval.* The hexadecimal conversion is a piece of cake. Just call the **Hex$** function, with the decimal value (*Decval*) as the argument, and the function returns the hexadecimal equivalent as a string. This string value is sent directly to the second TextBox control (**Text2**), which displays the value to the user. The conversion from decimal is binary is a little more involved.

Conversion from decimal to binary can be achieved by dividing the decimal value and its successive quotients by 2. For each division, the remainder will be 0 or 1. These values are grouped together to form the binary result. For example, convert 12 to binary.

```
                quotient    remainder
12/2    =       6               0    (lsb)
 6/2    =       3               0
 3/2    =       1               1
 1/2    =       0               1    (msb)
```

The binary result is read as 1100, since the most significant bit is at the bottom of the division. In our conversion code, a binary result will be held in a string named **Binval$**. Notice that as the program loops around the conversion routine, the binary string is being built one character at a time by catenating the previous value of **Binval$** to the new value. New characters are generated with the division process just explained and converted to a character string. **LTrim$** ensures that all leftmost spaces are removed from the string. As you examine this code, remember that the division being performed is integer division.

Converting to Hexadecimal (Command2)

In order to perform this conversion a decimal and a binary value must be calculated. The binary value is obtained by first converting the hexadecimal value to decimal and then proceeding with the conversion routine from the previous command button. The hexadecimal conversion is unique code.

```
Private Sub Command2_Click ()
  'Input Hexadecimal Value
  Hexchar$ = "123456789ABCDEF"
  Hexval$ = UCase$(Text2.Text)

  'Convert Hexadecimal To Decimal
  Decval = 0
  For I = 1 To Len(Hexval$)
    Power = 16 ^ (Len(Hexval$) - I)
    Tempval = InStr(Hexchar$, Mid$(Hexval$, I, 1))
```

```
      Decval = Decval + (Tempval * Power)
   Next I
   Text1.Text = Format$(Decval)

   'Convert Decimal To Binary
   Binval$ = ""
   Do While Decval <> 0
     Binval$ = LTrim$(Str$(Decval - (Decval \ 2) * 2)) + Binval$
     Decval = Decval \ 2
   Loop
   Text3.Text = Binval$
End Sub
```

As you examine this code, notice that **Hexchar$** is an ordered string of hexadecimal characters. The decimal position of the character in the string corresponds directly to the hexadecimal value attached to the character. The hexadecimal value is read from TextBox control, **Text2**, as a string. The **UCase$** is used because hexadecimal characters must be uppercase, corresponding to those found in **Hexchar$**. The position of a digit in a hexadecimal number, as with any weighted number system, carries a weighting factor. For example, the hexadecimal number 4D2 is weighted in this manner:

```
2    ->     2 x 160    or     2 x    1
D    ->    13 x 161    or    13 x   16
4    ->     4 x 162    or     4 x  256
```

Decimal results are obtained by adding up the sum of the products. In this case:

```
 2 x    1  =      2
13 x   16  =    208
 4 x  256  =   1024
           _____
            1234    (decimal)
```

The conversion routine calculates each of these individual sums while in the **For** loop and accumulates a final answer by adding the previous decimal sum (*Decval*) to the newly obtained sum (*Tempval* * *Power*). *Tempval* is found by determining the positional value, in decimal, of the hexadecimal character from **Hexval$**. This magic is performed with a combination of the **Mid$** and **InStr** functions. If you are not familiar with these Basic functions, use the Help facility to examine each one for additional details.

Converting to Binary (Command3)

If you examine the code for the last command button, you should notice that the binary-to-decimal conversion routine looks strangely familiar. It is! This routine is the same as the last routine we examined, but adjusted for binary conversions.

```
Private Sub Command3_Click ()
  'Input Binary Value
  Binchar$ = "1"
  Binval$ = Text3.Text

  'Convert Binary To Decimal
  Decval = 0
  For I = 1 To Len(Binval$)
    Power = 2 ^ (Len(Binval$) - I)
    Tempval = InStr(Binchar$, Mid$(Binval$, I, 1))
    Decval = Decval + (Tempval * Power)
  Next I
  Text1.Text = Format$(Decval)

  'Convert Decimal To Hexadecimal
  Text2.Text = Hex$(Decval)
End Sub
```

Can you determine how this binary conversion is performed?

How Bases Are Changed

Once you have loaded this program, you are ready for action. Try a few examples of numbers that you know the equivalent results for to test your skills. Figure 10.2 shows one such conversion.

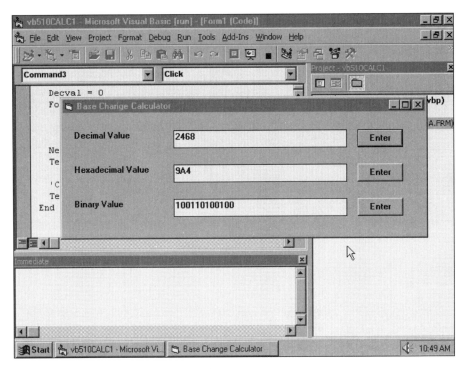

Figure 10.2 Performing a base change conversion.

Table 10.1 contains a few additional values you can experiment with.

Table 10.1 Numbers in Various Bases

Decimal	Hexadecimal	Binary
4321	10E1	1000011100001
877	360	1101101101
65535	FFFF	1111111111111111
17	11	10001
317	13D	100111101
3278	CCE	110011001110
200	C8	11001000
11	B	1011

You will find this program useful as you work through the remaining examples in the book and while developing your own code. If you create an executable version of the program, you can install it in

Windows and run it at just the click of a button. As a matter of fact, why not create a Windows group box just for the programs you want to use frequently from this book?

STATISTICS: FINDING THE MEAN AND STANDARD DEVIATION

The technique for data entry, shown in the previous example, is fine when small amounts of data are involved, but what if the user must enter 10 or 20 values? This project, named 10Stat2, will show you how to approach this problem. It would be impractical to have a separate TextBox control for every corresponding data value. One possible alternative involves using one TextBox control and entering a series of numeric values separated by a space, comma, or other delimiter. Remember, the information entered in a TextBox control is in the form of a character string. If the string contains multiple numeric representations separated by a delimiter, the program itself can separate the individual data elements.

In addition to performing some simple statistics, the next example will show you how to process a large group of data values entered in a TextBox control. Figure 10.3 shows the data entry form (**Form1**) for this project.

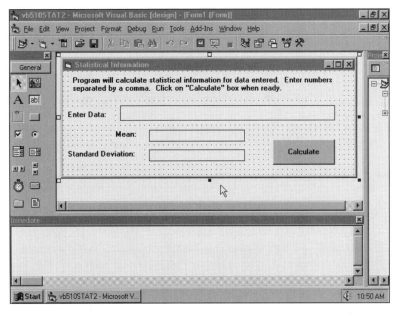

Figure 10.3 The data entry and answer form for statistical calculations.

First, the global module, 10stat2.bas, contains several data type definitions:

```
DefDbl A-Z
Global NArray(250), TSum, Mean, SOS, StdDev
Global I As Integer, TNums As Integer
Global SPos As Integer, FPos As Integer, NLen As Integer
```

All of the remaining project code is placed under the control of the **Command1** button. Once data is entered in the TextBox control (**Test1**) a simple click on "Calculate" will start the application. Examine the following piece of code:

```
Private Sub Command1_Click ()
  'Numbers in string equal commas + 1
  TNums = 1
  For I = 1 To Len(Text1.Text)
    Ch$ = Mid$(Text1.Text, I, 1)
    If Ch$ = "," Then TNums = TNums + 1
  Next I
```

The delimiter chosen for this example is a comma. One important piece of information that must be obtained immediately is the number of data values entered by the user. This can vary from run to run. The number of data values entered equals the number of delimiters (commas) plus one. The piece of code just shown examines the string, character by character, and reports the total number of data values in *TNums*.

The next piece of code separates the input, in individual numeric strings, and converts them to actual numeric values and saves them in *NArray*.

```
'Convert each group to a number
NewStr$ = Text1.Text + ","
SPos = 0
For I = 1 To TNums
  FPos = InStr(SPos + 1, NewStr$, Chr$(44))
  NLen = (FPos - SPos) -1
  NArray(I) = Val(Mid$(NewStr$, SPos + 1, NLen))
  SPos = FPos
Next I
```

Just before starting the string processing, a comma is catenated to the end of the string. This is necessary, since our routine will count all characters between leading and trailing commas as possible numeric data. If the last comma was not attached, the routine wouldn't know where the last entry ended. Exactly *TNums* numbers will be extracted from the string. The starting position for each numeric value is kept in *SPos*. Actually, a 1 is added to this value because *SPos* needs to point to a leading comma. *FPos* points to the trailing comma. *NLen* represents the number of characters making up the numeric representation. The number to be placed in *NArray* is determined with the use of the **Mid$** function. A string (just the characters for this numeric value) is returned by **Mid$** and converted to a numeric value with the **Val** function.

Remember, this example is also going to calculate some statistical values. It is possible to enter a large group of real or integer values in the data entry box. Once entered, the program will calculate the mean and standard deviation for the numbers and return the answers to the appropriate TextBox controls (**Text2** and **Text3**).

The mean or average is a relatively simple calculation to make.

```
'determine Mean
TSum = 0
For I = 1 To TNums
   TSum = TSum + NArray(I)
Next I
Mean = TSum / TNums
Text2.Text = Str$(Mean)
```

This piece of code reads each array entry and adds it to *TSum*. Once the total of all values is known, the mean can be calculated by dividing the total by the number of entries (*TNums*).

In order to find the standard deviation for the data, the variable *SOS* (sum of squares) is used. The sum of squares is determined by reading each *NArray* element, squaring it, and accumulating a running sum in *SOS*. When the **For** loop is complete, *SOS* will contain the sum of the squares for each value in *NArray*. Several variations of the equation exist for calculating the standard deviation. In this example:

```
s.d. = sqrt((SOS - (n*(mean^2)))/(n-1))
```

The extra parentheses are added for clarity.

```
'determine Standard Deviation
SOS = 0
For I = 1 To TNums
   SOS = SOS + NArray(I) ^ 2
Next I
StdDev = Sqr((SOS - TNums * (Mean ^ 2)) / (TNums -1))
Text3.Text = Str$(StdDev)
End Sub
```

Figure 10.4 shows several values in the data box and the corresponding mean and standard deviation.

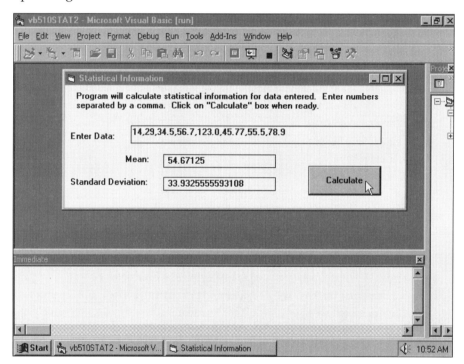

Figure 10.4 Calculating the mean and standard deviation.

Trigonometry: A Table of Sine and Cosine Values

As you know, TextBox controls are usually used to enter individual numeric values. The previous example showed you how to expand a TextBox control's capability so that large amounts of data can be entered with a single TextBox control. But what about output? The TextBox controls that we've used so far allow only one value to be shown at a time.

The second example expanded the range of data values that could be easily entered in a form. Project 10Trig3 will show you how to output larger amounts of data.

One technique for increasing the amount of data output to a single TextBox control involves catenating individual string elements together to form a longer string. That longer string can then be sent to the TextBox control. This might be an acceptable technique for single lines of information, but what about tabular data? A better approach is to switch to a clean form and print the data there. Now that's simple enough! Well, not quite. Since the range of data does not exceed the size of the form, there will be no problem. However, if the range of data is larger than the form, means must be provided for scrolling. Now the solution is a little more involved but well worth investigating. This is another template that you will find useful as you build your own examples.

In this example, the project will allow the user to print a formatted table of sine and cosine values. The angular range can be started and stopped at any integer angle. The step size can also be controlled. Thus, you can print a trigonometric table for the angles from 0 to 90 degrees in 1-degree steps or from 30 to 180 degrees in 5-degree steps. Figure 10.5 shows a relatively simple data entry form (**Form1**).

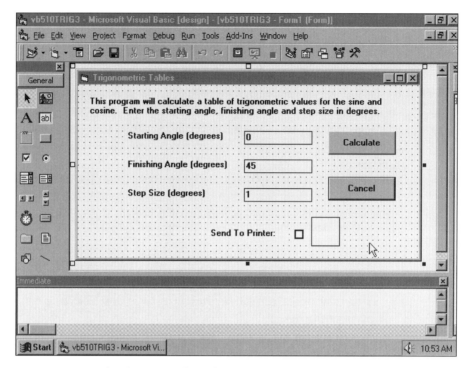

Figure 10.5 The data entry form for calculating sine and cosine values.

As you view this form, notice that several default values were entered, as text, when the form was created. A click on the Calculate (**Command1**) button will generate a table of sine and cosine values for the range 0 to 45 degrees in 1-degree steps. You also should note the presence of a checkbox if you desire a hard copy of the table from your printer. The checkbox places an icon on the form, and you'll need to make sure that the icon is present at the described location or the project will bomb.

The Cancel (**Command2**) button will replace any user-entered values with the original default values.

Global Declarations

The data values entered by the user are integer values giving the starting, finishing, and step size in degrees. The global file 10Trig3.bas describes these data values.

```
DefInt A-Z
Global I, StartAngle, FinishAngle, StepAngle
Global SinValue As Single, CosValue As Single
Global Const PI = 3.14159265
```

Since all trigonometric functions work with radians, it will be necessary to convert the angles, in degrees, to radians. There are pi radians in 180 degrees. This is why the global module contains the definition for **PI**. This project also contains code in **Form1** and **Form2**.

Processing Form1 Controls

Calculations begin with a click of the Calculate (**Command1**) button. The **Command1** button's action serves to collect data and pass the information along to other subroutines.

```
Private Sub Command1_Click ()
  StartAngle = Val(Text1.Text)
  FinishAngle = Val(Text2.Text)
  StepAngle = Val(Text3.Text)
  If ((FinishAngle - StartAngle) \ StepAngle) > 160 Then
    Call MsgBox1
    Call Cancel_Click
    Else
      Form2.FontSize = 12
      Form2.VScroll1.LargeChange = FontSize * 120
      Form2.VScroll1.SmallChange = FontSize * 23
      Form2.Show
  End If
End Sub
```

When the data values are in range, **Form2** is shown on the screen. The default font size is set to 12 and the **LargeChange** and **SmallChange** parameters for scroll bar movement are sized to change in proportion to the font. References to forms other than the current form are preceded by the form's name. For example, the scroll bars appear on **Form2**, so **Form2.VScroll1.LargeChange** is used.

When the data values are out of range, however, a call is made to a message box routine warning the user and then canceling the values entered. This is a polite method of performing range checking on data values.

```
Private Sub Cancel_Click ()
  Text1.Text = Str$(0)
  Text2.Text = Str$(45)
  Text3.Text = Str$(1)
End Sub
```

The message box routine consists of several parameters including a constant for establishing an OK button, a message box title, a message box message, and a call to the **MsgBox** function.

```
Private Sub MsgBox1 ()
  Const MB_OK = 0
  Title$ = "Message Box"
  Msg$ = "Decrease Range of Values or Increase Step Size"
  MBType% = MB_OK
  Response% = MsgBox(Msg$, MBType%, Title$)
End Sub
```

If the data values are in an acceptable range, the font size and scroll range sizes are set and **Form2** is ready to receive formatted output.

The Components of Form2

It is possible that the list of output values can exceed the size of the output form. To handle this possibility a vertical scroll bar has been included in **Form2**. A vertical scroll bar is placed on the form at design time by selecting the option from the Visual Basic 5 toolbox.

VScroll1 Change, Focus, or Paint   This example generates trigono-metric information any time the vertical scroll bar receives focus, when its position bar is changed, or when a Paint request occurs. Focus is achieved when a user clicks or tabs to the object.

```
Private Sub VScroll1_Change ()
  Call MyData
End Sub


Private Sub VScroll1_GotFocus ()
  Call MyData
End Sub
```

```
Private Sub Form_Paint()
  Call MyData
End Sub
```

In this program, new values are calculated by calling the **MyData** subroutine.

The MyData Subroutine When either scroll event occurs, a call is made to a subroutine called **MyData**. **MyData** is a subroutine created at design time. Subroutines can be added to the General Object of a form. Place your program in the general form and click the Code option from the Visual Basic 5 menu. Select the New Procedure option, specify a name, and begin code entry. You may add any number of new subroutines and procedures in this manner.

```
Private Sub MyData ()
  ScaleTop = VScroll1.Value
  Cls
  Print "Angle                  Sin";
  Print "                                  Cosine"
  Print
    .
    .
    .
```

VScroll1.Value returns the value of the vertical scroll bar's position. This value can be constrained between the **Max** and **Min** parameters specified by the programmer. Recall that the size of the vertical scroll bar's movement was set earlier by **LargeChange** and **SmallChange**. The **VScroll1.Value** is used to set the value of **ScaleTop**. The **ScaleTop** value sets the vertical coordinates for the top of the object's internal area. As the form is scrolled downward, the form's top adjusts accordingly. It is next necessary to refresh the screen so that when the screen is cleared (**Cls**) and updated, during a scroll or resizing, the new data will not be written on the top of old data. Finally, a title bar describing the table's entries is printed to the form.

The next piece of code is responsible for calculating and printing the data to the screen. The variable *I* represents the current angle. It varies from *StartAngle* to *FinishAngle* in steps of **StepAngle**. The angle is converted from degrees to radians before the sine or cosine functions are called. The appropriate values are returned to *SinValue* and *CosValue*.

```
        .

        .

        .

For I = StartAngle To FinishAngle Step StepAngle
  SinValue = Sin(PI * I / 180)
  CosValue = Cos(PI * I / 180)
  Print I; Tab(15); Format$(SinValue, "0.0000");
  Print Tab(35); Format$(CosValue, "0.0000")
Next I

  .

  .

  .
```

Tabs are always recommended for formatting tabular data. The angle value, *I*, is printed against the left-hand edge of the form, while **Tab(15)** positions the *SinValue* and **Tab(35)** the *CosValue* in fixed columns. Sine and cosine values vary between 0 and 1. To force neat columns of data, the **Format$** function specifies the precision of the answer and fills blanks in data with zeros.

If the printer checkbox has been marked, we also want to send a similar table to the printer. For the sake of clarity, here is some code shown earlier.

```
  .

  .

  .

'If checked, send to printer
If Form1.check1.Value = 1 Then
  Print "Angle                  Sin";
  Print "                              Cosine"
  Print
  For I = StartAngle To FinishAngle Step StepAngle
  SinValue = Sin(PI * I / 180)
  CosValue = Cos(PI * I / 180)
  Printer.Print I; Tab(15); Format$(SinValue, "0.0000");
  Printer.Print Tab(35); Format$(CosValue, "0.0000")
  Next I
  Printer.EndDoc
```

```
     End If
End Sub
          .

          .

          .
```

Output can be directed to the printer with **Printer.Print**. Once the program finishes generating data, **Printer.EndDoc** will release the results to the printer or spooler.

Scaling the Scroll Bar It is necessary to scale the vertical scroll bar to the form's current size. The height of the form is determined with the **Height** property. The value returned by this function is the height that we want the vertical scroll bar to be set to. So **VScroll1.Height** is set equal to the returned size.

```
Private Sub Form_Resize ()
  VScroll1.Height = ScaleHeight
  VScroll1.Left=ScaleWidth-VScroll1.Width
End Sub
```

Whenever a form resizing occurs, the vertical scroll bar will also be adjusted to fit the window.

Figure 10.6 shows a portion of the screen for the default values mentioned earlier.

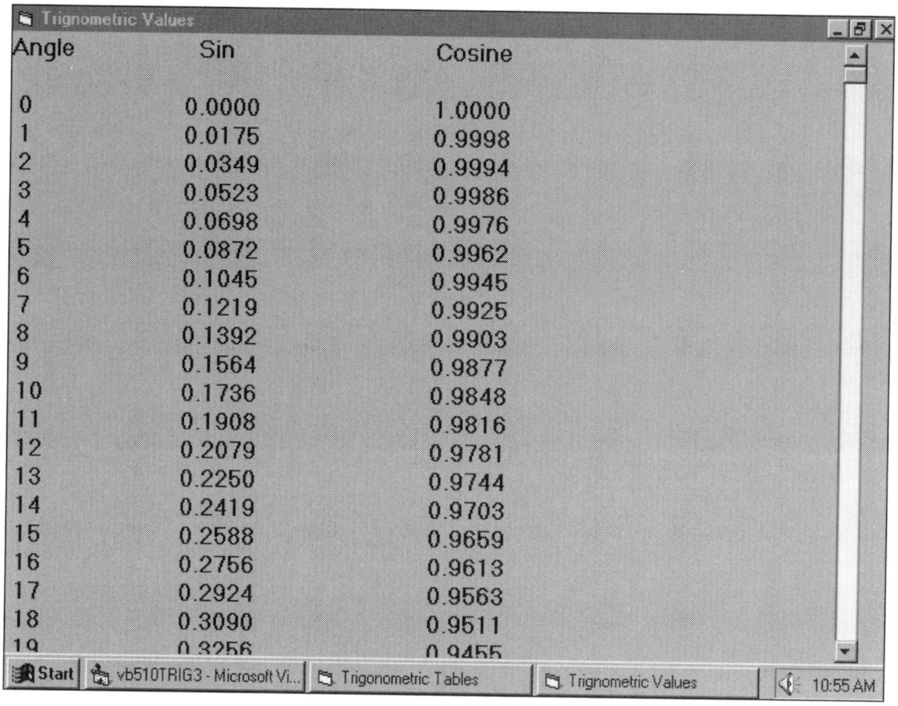

Angle	Sin	Cosine
0	0.0000	1.0000
1	0.0175	0.9998
2	0.0349	0.9994
3	0.0523	0.9986
4	0.0698	0.9976
5	0.0872	0.9962
6	0.1045	0.9945
7	0.1219	0.9925
8	0.1392	0.9903
9	0.1564	0.9877
10	0.1736	0.9848
11	0.1908	0.9816
12	0.2079	0.9781
13	0.2250	0.9744
14	0.2419	0.9703
15	0.2588	0.9659
16	0.2756	0.9613
17	0.2924	0.9563
18	0.3090	0.9511
19	0.3256	0.9455

Figure 10.6 Trigonometric table printed to Form2.

SORTING: A SHELL SORT TO ORDER DATA

This project, 10Sort4, uses a familiar sorting technique for ordering data. Sorts are used in all areas of computing. Students taking computer science courses often study a variety of sorting techniques and their relative efficiencies in a data structures class. In this example, our sort algorithm is a shell sort. In terms of efficiency, shell sorts fall between bubble sorts and quick sorts. Shell sorts can be used to sort a group of numbers in ascending or descending order, and that's what this example will allow. Figure 10.7 shows the initial form (**Form1**). Notice that this form uses two option buttons. These were installed to respond to double clicks from the mouse.

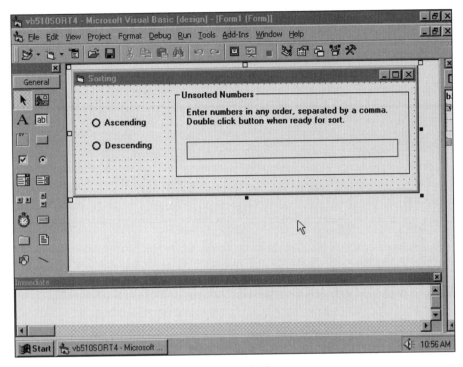

Figure 10.7 The data entry form for a shell sort program.

Global Declarations

This project will allow the ordering of real numbers stored in NArray. The group of numbers to be sorted will be obtained from a TextBox control on the initial form. The global file, 10Sort4.bas, specifies a number of global variables.

```
DefInt A-Z
Global TNums, I, SPos, FPos, NLen, DirFlag
Global IdxOffset, Elements, SwapFlag
Global NArray(50) As Double, Temp As Double
```

Option Buttons

The two option buttons for this example allow the user to select an ascending or descending sort. The code for both options is similar, with the differences occurring in the text sent to the screen and the direction flag (**DirFlag**) value.

```
Private Sub Option1_DblClick ()
  Call MyData

  Form2.Show
  Form2.Cls
  Form2.Print "Numbers in Ascending Order"
  Form2.Print
  DirFlag = 0

  Call MySort

  For I = 1 To TNums
    Form2.Print NArray(I)
  Next I
End Sub



Private Sub Option2_DblClick ()
  Call MyData

  Form2.Show
  Form2.Cls
  Form2.Print "Numbers in Descending Order"
  Form2.Print
  DirFlag = 1
  Call MySort

  For I = 1 To TNums
    Form2.Print NArray(I)
  Next I
End Sub
```

Both option buttons call the subroutines **MyData** and **MySort**. **MyData** is a routine for entering data that you are already familiar with—it was borrowed from the second example. (We told you this would be a useful routine for data entry.)

```
Private Sub MyData ()
   'total numbers = commas+1
   TNums = 1
   For I = 1 To Len(Text1.Text)
      Ch$ = Mid$(Text1.Text, I, 1)
      If Ch$ = "," Then TNums = TNums + 1
   Next I


   'separate, convert and store in array
   NewStr$ = Text1.Text + ","
   SPos = 0
   For I = 1 To TNums
      FPos = InStr(SPos + 1, NewStr$, Chr$(44))
      NLen = (FPos - SPos) -1
      NArray(I) = Val(Mid$(NewStr$, SPos + 1, NLen))
      SPos = FPos
   Next I
End Sub
```

This routine accepts a string of characters from the TextBox control with groups of characters separated by a comma. The routine finds the number of data values by counting commas. The **InStr** function finds the start and end of each group of characters for an individual number and sends the information to the **Mid$** function, which, together with **Val**, converts it to an actual number. Each number is stored in a unique location in *NArray*.

How Shell Sorts Work

The shell sort is a variation on a simple insertion sort. In a shell sort the data is divided into groups. Initially, each group is approximately half the size of the total array elements. *IdxOffset* contains the initial size of each group, and is found by dividing *TNums* by 2 and obtaining an integer result. The variable *I* serves as the index to the first group, and *IdxOffset* + *I* serves as the index to the second group. Comparisons are made between the elements in each group. Thus, the first number in group one is compared to the first number in group two. Depending on whether it is a descending or ascending sort, these elements may be exchanged in the respective groups. This continues until all elements in the groups have been compared. At the conclusion, the two groups are sorted a little better than they were initially found. Next, the group size is divided in half and elements in adjacent groups are compared again. When this is complete, the ordering is even better. However, the sort will not be complete until the group size has been reduced to one. Here is BASIC code for doing a fast Shell sort.

```
Private Sub MySort ()
  IdxOffset = TNums \ 2
  Do
    Elements = TNums - IdxOffset
    Do
      SwapFlag = 0
        For I = 1 To Elements
          If DirFlag = 0 Then
            If NArray(IdxOffset + I) < NArray(I) Then
              SwapFlag = I
              Temp = NArray(IdxOffset + I)
              NArray(IdxOffset + I) = NArray(I)
              NArray(I) = Temp
            End If
          End If

          If DirFlag = 1 Then
            If NArray(IdxOffset + I) > NArray(I) Then
              SwapFlag = I
              Temp = NArray(IdxOffset + I)
              NArray(IdxOffset + I) = NArray(I)
              NArray(I) = Temp
            End If
          End If
        Next I
    Loop While SwapFlag <> 0
    IdxOffset = IdxOffset \ 2
  Loop While IdxOffset > 0
End Sub
```

If you are an experienced BASIC programmer you might notice that this sort algorithm does not make use of Basic's **Swap** function. Visual Basic 5 does not provide this function, so our routine must do the swapping itself. The variable *Temp* is used to store one group element during the swapping process.

Figure 10.8 shows a group of numbers sorted in ascending order while Figure 10.9 shows a group of numbers sorted in descending order.

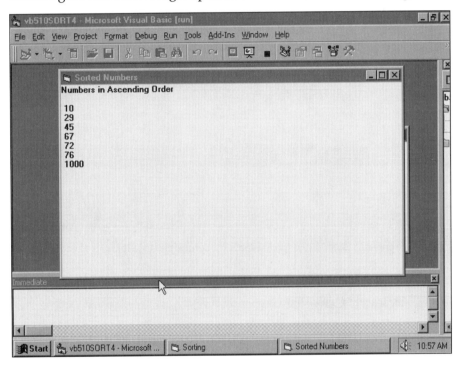

Figure 10.8 Sorting numbers in ascending order.

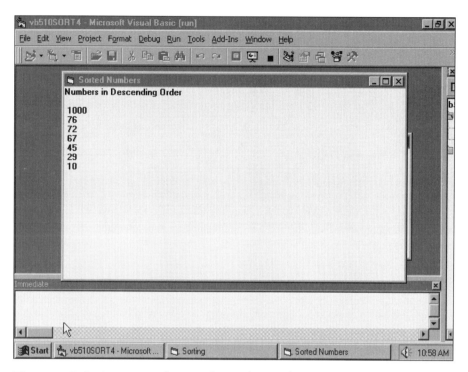

Figure 10.9 Sorting numbers in descending order.

WHAT'S COMING?

Visual Basic 5 is a graphical environment. In the next chapter you'll learn how to best take advantage of this environment by adding pictures and graphics to your projects.

Chapter 11

Pictures and Graphics

Windows makes using a computer easy because of its graphical interface. Windows 95 and Windows NT free the user and programmer from the mundane and boring text mode interface of past generation operating systems. They also give an exciting visual approach to application programs that was never before possible. Now, text, icons, pictures, and graphics can exist not only in the same application but also on the same screen.

In this chapter you will learn just how easy it is to bring icons and pictures into your Visual Basic 5 applications. You'll be able to create bitmap images in Windows 95 Paint or Windows NT Paintbrush and import them into your own applications. You'll also learn a technique for calling Windows Graphics Device Interface (GDI) graphics functions from within Visual Basic 5. Access to Windows functions, from Visual Basic 5, adds a new dimension of programming power.

INSTALLING A PICTURE WITH YOUR CODE

Two techniques are used to bring pictures into an application. One technique is to "hardwire" the picture to your application as you write your code. The second technique is to load the specified picture at run time. This first example will show you how to install a picture with your application code.

First, start Visual Basic 5 and create a project with a new form (**Form1** is okay). Now start Microsoft's Paint or Paintbrush application. Draw some artwork on the canvas, and click the **Edit** option to transfer the image to the clipboard. The artwork to be clipped must be surrounded with the scissors "cut" outline. Figure 11.1 shows a simple sketch in Microsoft Paint awaiting transfer to the clipboard.

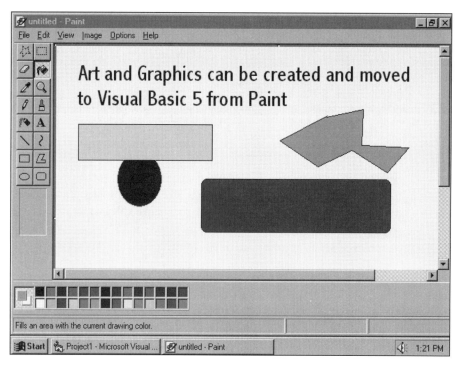

Figure 11.1 Creating a picture in Microsoft Paint.

Transfer to the clipboard takes place by selecting **Cut** or **Copy** from this menu. Now switch your focus back to **Form1** in Visual Basic 5 and from the Edit option choose Paste. The Microsoft Paint or Paintbrush image should now be transferred to your form in Visual Basic 5, as shown in Figure 11.2.

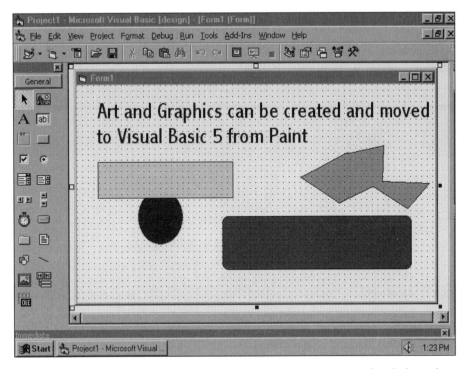

Figure 11.2 Transferring a Paint image to Visual Basic 5 via the clipboard.

If you save your project at this point and create an executable file, your artwork will be displayed on the screen whenever the application is run.

Installing pictures in your Visual Basic 5 forms has advantages and disadvantages.

The advantages include:

- pictures that are embedded in applications don't require an additional file on the disk at execution time.
- artwork that is part of the application cannot be changed by the user.

The disadvantages include:

- increased file size for the application file.
- inability to change or upgrade images without altering the original code.

A Desert Scene

Give this example a try if the last example didn't impress you. This project is named 11Pict1 on the diskette or CD-ROM. You can copy all of the associated files from the diskette to your Visual Basic 5 directory by specifying 11Pict1*.*. If you want to do your own work, create two forms, **Form1** and **Form2**. For the first form, just install the **Form2.Show** command under the **Command1_Click** option.

```
Private Sub Command1_Click ()
   Form2.Show
End Sub
```

As a guide see our example form shown in Figure 11.3.

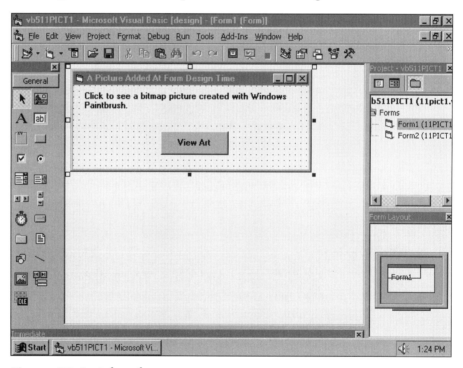

Figure 11.3 A form for viewing a picture.

Figure 11.3 is a form that allows you to view a picture loaded and saved in **Form2** at the time the application was created.

We created a desert scene image in Windows 95 Paint and transferred it, via the clipboard, to **Form2**. When this project is saved and an executable file is created, the user will be informed of what will happen when the command button is pushed. Figure 11.4 shows our desert scene for this example.

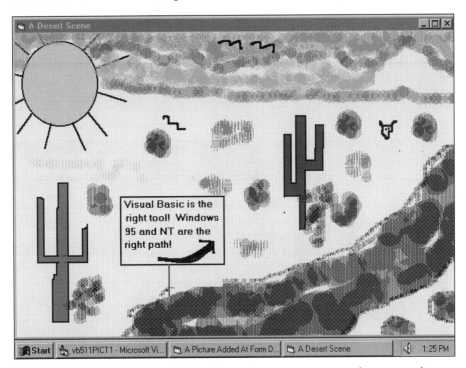

Figure 11.4 A picture created with Windows 95's Paint application and transferred to Form2 via the clipboard.

It is possible to create tasteful art on forms, on which controls and other user options can be overlaid. This is comparable to the difference between stock bank checks and fancy checks available with a variety of backgrounds.

LOADING A PICTURE FROM YOUR PROJECT

In this project, 11Pict2, you will learn how to load pictures into a window at run time. This approach has the advantage of being dynamic in its ability to change picture information. Since the picture is not part of the application, file size is also reduced.

In Visual Basic 5, pictures can be used if created in bitmap (.Bmp), icon (.Ico), or Metafile (.Wmf) formats. Icons, in reality, are just small bitmap images. Metafiles are a special file format developed for Windows.

Microsoft's Paint and Paintbrush applications allow files to be saved in the bitmap format from the 8dit command. For the next example, three bitmap images have been created and saved in the bitmap format: flower.bmp, house.bmp, and surprise.bmp. There is nothing special about these pictures, and you are free to create your own artwork for this project if you desire. Figure 11.5 shows **Form1** for this example.

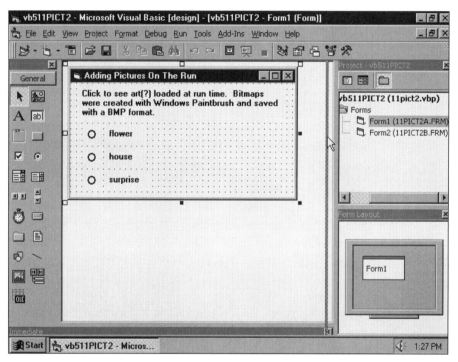

Figure 11.5 Multiple bitmap images loaded at run time.

The form uses three option buttons for viewing art in the art gallery. A double click on the first button will load and draw a flower bitmap. The second, a house. The third is a surprise, so you'll have to load the image from the diskette or CD-ROM disk and give it a try. Note that the application expects to find the bitmaps in the root directory of drive C.

```
Private Sub Option1_DblClick ()
  Form2.Show
  Screen.MousePointer = 11
  Form2.Picture = LoadPicture("c:\flower.bmp")
  Screen.MousePointer = 0
End Sub

Private Sub Option2_Click ()
  Form2.Show
  Screen.MousePointer = 11
  Form2.Picture = LoadPicture("c:\house.bmp")
  Screen.MousePointer = 0
End Sub

Private Sub Option3_Click ()
  Form2.Show
  Screen.MousePointer = 11
  Form2.Picture = LoadPicture("c:\surprise.bmp")
  Screen.MousePointer = 0
End Sub
```

In this example, each option button uses the **LoadPicture** function to bring in a previously saved bitmap image. Visual Basic 5 also has a **SavePicture** function that will allow you to save a bitmap image of a form.

Bitmap files can become quite large and require substantial time when loading. Consequently, it is considered good practice to place the hourglass icon figure on the screen to notify the user that action is being taken. Visual Basic 5 provides several stock cursor or pointer images, listed in Table 11.1.

Table 11.1 Visual Basic 5 Stock Pointers

Value	Constant	Shape
0	VbDefault	Arrow (default pointer)
1	VbArrow	Arrow
2	VbCrosshair	Crosshair
3	VbIbeam	I-beam
4	VbIconPointer	Icon
5	VbSizePointer	Arrow (four points)
6	VbSizeNESW	Arrow (two points, NE & SW)
7	VbSizeNS	Arrow (two points, N & S)
8	VbSizeNWSE	Arrow (two points, NW & SE)
9	VbSizeWE	Arrow (two points, W & E)
10	VbUpArrow	Arrow (up)
11	VbHourGlass	Hourglass (wait)
12	WbNoDrop	No drop
13	VbArrowHourglass	Arrow and hourglass
14	VbArrowQuestion	Arrow and question mark
15	VbSizeAll	Size all
99	VbCustom	Custom icon via MouseIcon property

The hourglass figure replaces the stock arrow pointer with a call to **Screen.MousePointer** and specifying the integer value 11. Once the picture is loaded, the pointer is reset with a similar call but with the integer value set to 0, the default.

Figure 11.6 and Figure 11.7 show two of the art gallery's selections.

Figure 11.6 A flower bitmap loaded at run time.

Figure 11.7 A house bitmap loaded at run time.

A SIMPLE ANIMATION EXAMPLE

It's easy to animate an application. In this example, small iconic images will be moved across the window. These iconic images can be loaded into a form, just like the bitmap pictures of the last examples. Their small size allows the user to place them anywhere on the form. As a matter of fact, their position can even be changed, dynamically, at run time.

This project is named 11Icon3. The project will show you how to move several icon images on the screen at run time. This appearance of motion can be applied to any icon, bitmap, or graphics images you create.

The technique for achieving this animation effect is a classical approach. First, the image is drawn on the screen at a given position. After a short time, a new position is specified for the image and it is quickly moved to the new location. Small increments of distance give smoother motion effects but require more time. Larger increments give a choppy movement but allow you to speed images across the screen. You'll have to decide what values work best for you.

All of the action takes place on **Form1** in this example.

The Global Module

Four variables are needed for this example, and they are declared in the global module as type integer. This file is named 11Icon3.bas.

```
DefInt A-Z
Global deltax1, deltax2
Global deltax3, deltax4
```

The delta values represent the incremental distance each of the four images will change at a given time. Movement in this example is constrained along the x axis, but two-dimensional movements can also be achieved.

Loading Image Information

Before images can be moved, they must be loaded onto the form. In this example we chose the USA flag icon from the Visual Basic 5 Icon Library.

 Note: If your icons are not at the specified location, change the path statement before attempting to load the picture.

```
Private Sub Form_Load ()
  picture1.picture =
LoadPicture("c:\Vb5\Graphics\Icons\Flags\flgusa01.ico")
  picture2.picture = picture1.picture
  picture3.picture = picture1.picture
  picture4.picture = picture1.picture
  Icon = picture1.picture
  deltax1 = 110
  deltax2 = -120
  deltax3 = 130
  deltax4 = -140
End Sub
```

Since animation will begin when the form is loaded, this programming code is placed in **Form_Load**. Notice that the icon needs to be loaded only once; the other three images are then copied from it.

Also note that the application's icon is also changed to the same image. When the application is shrunk to iconic size, the flag image will replace Visual Basic 5's stock icon.

This is also a good place to initialize the step sizes for all four images. If they are set to the same values, they will move at equal speeds across the screen. The larger the delta value, the faster (and more choppy) the motion. Positive values show an initial left-to-right movement while negative values are used for a right-to-left motion.

Move—But Not Too Fast

If a control wasn't used to set the pace for the animation, the images would be nothing more than a blur. They would be drawn-moved-drawn at such a pace that your eyes couldn't keep up. What is needed is a timer that will allow the image to remain at a given position for a specified amount of time.

Visual Basic 5 provides a **Timer** control that sets the execution pace of any form at run time. The timer is installed on a form, during creation, by selecting the **Timer** control from the Visual Basic 5 toolbox. The timer can be placed, like any other control, at any location on the form. The location is not critical, because the timer will not be visible at run time. Figure 11.8 shows the timer control and the initial locations for the four images (the places where the dots are missing!).

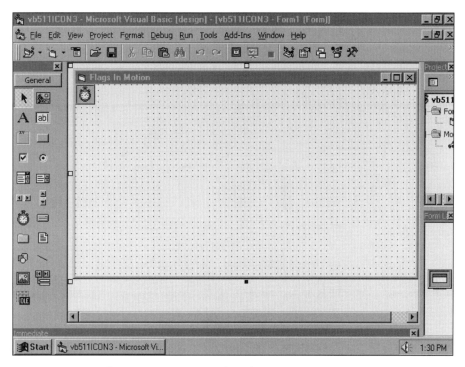

Figure 11.8 Placing a Timer control and icon pictures on Form1.

This is also the moment you set the timer's timing interval from the timer's Properties window. For this example, the timing interval was set to 1/4 second. Since values are specified in milliseconds, 250 was entered at this time.

It is now possible to chose **Timer1_Timer** from **Form1** and place the control code. Here is the code required to move each of the four images across the screen each time the timer signals.

```
Private Sub Timer1_Timer ()
  If picture1.Left < ScaleLeft Then deltax1 = 110
  If picture1.Left + picture1.Width > ScaleWidth + ScaleLeft
Then
     deltax1 = -110
  End If
  picture1.Move picture1.Left + deltax1

  If picture2.Left < ScaleLeft Then deltax2 = 120
  If picture2.Left + picture1.Width > ScaleWidth + ScaleLeft
Then
     deltax2 = -120
  End If
  picture2.Move picture2.Left + deltax2

  If picture3.Left < ScaleLeft Then deltax3 = 130
  If picture3.Left + picture3.Width > ScaleWidth + ScaleLeft
Then
     deltax3 = -130
  End If
  picture3.Move picture3.Left + deltax3

  If picture4.Left < ScaleLeft Then deltax4 = 140
  If picture4.Left + picture4.Width > ScaleWidth + ScaleLeft
Then
     deltax4 = -140
  End If
  picture4.Move picture4.Left + deltax4
End Sub
```

Essentially the same code is used for all four images. Since the image hasn't bumped into the left- or right-hand edge of the form, it will be moved in the same direction each time the timer signals. If an edge is encountered, the direction of movement is reversed and the image is sent back in the opposite direction.

This example moves flag images around on the screen, so an appropriate message is painted at the bottom of the form with **Form_Paint**.

```
Private Sub Form_Paint ()
  Fontsize = 48
  Msg$ = "God Bless America"
  CurrentX = 400
  CurrentY = 5000
  Form1.Print Msg$
End Sub
```

Figure 11.9 shows a snapshot of the screen while the flags are in motion.

Figure 11.9 Simple animation: flag icons in motion.

Remember, pictures or graphics images that you create can be substituted for the icon image. If you draw a circle and fill it with a color, you'll have a bouncing ball program.

A SIMPLE BAR CHART

In Chapter 15 you will learn how to create presentation-quality line, bar, and pie charts. These programs will allow you to input several values and then automatically scale the data to the chart. This example, named 11Bar4, will not take you quite that far. The range of bar values is set between 0 and 100, and because no range checking is employed, it is possible to chart off the graph. However, you will learn how to apply some information from Chapter 9 that dealt with Visual Basic 5's graphing options, how to fill rectangles with color and print text to a graphics screen. Visual Basic 5 is so easy to use that it was difficult to stop adding more features! Figure 11.10 shows the features for this charting program drawn on **Form1**.

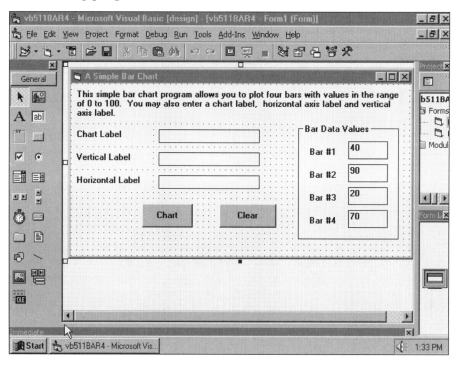

Figure 11.10 A simple bar chart.

Frame controls focus the user's attention on a group of related options. Examine Figure 11.10 and notice that a frame labeled Bar Data Values surrounds the bar input area. Notice, too, the four default values for viewing an initial chart.

The Global Module

Even though this program is complex, the data declarations in the global module are relatively simple. Here are the contents of the file 11bar4.bas.

```
DefInt A-Z
Global HBar1, HBar2, HBar3, HBar4, Temp
Global LabelWidth, LabelHeight, I, Length
Global Title$, XLabel$, YLabel$, Digit$
```

The heights of the bar chart bars are saved in *HBar1* through *HBar4*. *LabelWidth* and *LabelHeight* will be used to return information regarding the axis labels and chart title. The variable *I* will be used in a **For** loop that will help print the vertical axis label. *Length* will hold the number of characters in a particular string. The remaining values, all string variables, hold their respective axis labels and titles.

Starting Initial Charting

Form1 uses two command buttons to start the initial charting. If Chart (**Command1**) is clicked, a data gathering procedure is started.

```
Private Sub Command1_Click ()
  Title$ = Text1.Text
  YLabel$ = Text2.Text
  XLabel$ = Text3.Text
  HBar1 = Val(Text4.Text)
  HBar2 = Val(Text5.Text)
  HBar3 = Val(Text6.Text)
  HBar4 = Val(Text7.Text)
  Form2.Show
  Call MyPlot
End Sub
```

Information entered by the user or default chart values are read into the respective string and data variables. Then **Form2** is shown on the screen and a call is made to the **MyPlot** subroutine.

When the user decides to start over, during the process of data entry, a click on the Clear button (**Command2**) will reset all strings to null values.

```
Private Sub Command2_Click ()
   Text1.Text = ""
   Text2.Text = ""
   Text3.Text = ""
   Text4.Text = ""
   Text5.Text = ""
   Text6.Text = ""
   Text7.Text = ""
End Sub
```

This action, in effect, blanks out all data in the various text boxes.

Sizing the Bar Chart

It's possible to resize the chart's window to suit your needs. When the form is resized, it will be necessary to send a message to redraw the bar chart to the new form's dimensions. From **Form2** it is just a matter of calling the **MyPlot** subroutine whenever the form is resized.

This form can be sized all the way down to an icon! That means that if you have produced a chart, the chart will appear in miniature if the application is reduced to icon size. This is one technique for creating dynamic and meaningful icons for applications.

This means that every item on the form is scaled to the new form's dimensions. Well, almost everything! Graphics images scale very well, but fonts generally do not because they are available in fixed sizes. Windows will make a concerted effort to give you the font size you request, but if it doesn't exist, and you are not using a scalable font technology such as TrueType, the font size closest to your request will be selected. If the smallest font size is 6 point, you'll never get a font any smaller. When the chart is reduced to an icon, the graphics reduce correctly, but you'll be left with some very large axis labels. In this example, we chose to eliminate them when the form was scaled beyond a certain size. They are restored when the chart is enlarged.

```
Private Sub Form_Resize ()
   If (ScaleWidth < 50 Or ScaleHeight < 50) Then
      Title$=""
      YLabel$=""
      XLabel$=""
      Else
         Title$=Form1.Text1.Text
```

```
          YLabel$=Form1.Text2.Text
          XLabel$=Form1.Text3.Text
   End If
   Call MyPlot
End Sub
```

This action takes place on **Form2,** so it is necessary to specify the location of **Text1** through **Text2** for the restoration. They, of course, are on **Form1**.

The MyPlot Module

Visual Basic 5 allows you to define new modules for your application from the Visual Basic 5 File option. **MyPlot** is responsible for scaling, colors, graphics, and labels.

```
Private Sub MyPlot ()
   'draw & scale everything to form size
   Form2.Cls
   Form2.BackColor = QBColor(15)
   Form2.ScaleWidth = 120
   Form2.ScaleHeight = 120

      .
      .
      .
```

Whenever **MyPlot** is called the form is cleared, the background color is set (white), and the vertical and horizontal scale widths are established (120, 120).

Now the vertical and horizontal axes are drawn. The drawing width is set to a value of 2.

```
      .
      .
      .

   'draw axis
   Form2.DrawWidth = 2
   Form2.Line (20, 110)-(100, 110)
   Form2.Line (20, 20)-(20, 110)

      .
      .
      .
```

The **Line()** function is used here. The first pair of points gives the starting position of the line, the second pair the ending position.

Rectangular objects can also be drawn and filled with the **Line()** function. The starting position and the width of each of the four bars is fixed during the development of the application. The only user variable is the height of the bar (*HBar1 to HBar4*).

```
        .

        .

        .

'draw four bars in color
Form2.DrawWidth = 1
Form2.Line (21, 109 - HBar1)-(39, 109), QBColor(12), BF
Form2.Line (40, 109 - HBar2)-(59, 109), QBColor(9), BF
Form2.Line (60, 109 - HBar3)-(79, 109), QBColor(14), BF
Form2.Line (80, 109 - HBar4)-(99, 109), QBColor(10), BF

        .

        .

        .
```

Recall that the default coordinate system increases as you move down the chart. To plot the bar heights correctly, their values are subtracted from the bottom chart position. For this special form of the **Line()** function, the final two parameters specify the fill color (**QBColor**) and the desire to fill the rectangle (**BF**). Recall from Chapter 9 that colors can be specified as RGB values or QuickBasic values. In this chart, we chose the QuickBasic values for simplicity.

By this point, the vertical and horizontal axes and chart bars have been drawn. It is now necessary to draw any axis labels.

```
        .

        .

        .

'print horizontal axis label
Form2.FontSize = Form2.Height / 500
LabelWidth = Form2.TextWidth(XLabel$) / 2

LabelHeight = Form2.TextHeight(XLabel$) / 2
Form2.CurrentX = Form2.ScaleWidth / 2 - LabelWidth
Form2.CurrentY = (Form2.ScaleHeight * (61 / 64)) -
LabelHeight
```

```
Form2.Print XLabel$
      .
      .
      .
```

The horizontal label is positioned, centered, and scaled on the chart. The font size is determined experimentally by determining the form height and dividing it by 500. The system's default font is used in this example. The variable contents in *LabelWidth* and *LabelHeight* are used to decide where and how the label is printed. Proportions are used, rather than fixed values, because the screen can be resized. Thus, the horizontal label will be plotted near the bottom of the form, 61/64 of the form's size measured from the top of the form. (This value was also determined experimentally.)

The vertical axis label for the chart presents a little bit more of a programming challenge. Visual Basic 5 does not provide functions for rotating whole strings or individual characters. Our only option, at this point, is to divide the label into characters and plot them one at a time as we move down the vertical axis.

```
      .
      .
      .
'string characters for vertical axis label
Form2.FontSize = Form2.Height / 500
LabelWidth = Form2.TextWidth(YLabel$) * 3 / 2
LabelHeight = Form2.TextHeight(YLabel$) / 2
Form2.CurrentX = Form2.ScaleWidth / 7 - LabelHeight
Temp = Form2.CurrentX
Form2.CurrentY = (Form2.ScaleHeight * (32 / 64)) - LabelWidth
Length = Len(YLabel$)
For I = 1 To Length
   Digit$ = Mid$(YLabel$, I, 1)
   Form2.Print Digit$
   Form2.CurrentX = Temp
Next I
      .
      .
      .
```

The approach is the same as for the horizontal label until we get to drawing the individual characters. Here a **For** loop is used with the help of the **Mid$** function to extract individual characters from the string.

There are, however, a few flaws remaining in this project. First, the default font is a proportional font. This means that characters such as "i" take up less space that characters such as "w." This makes the vertical axis waver. This could be fixed by choosing a fixed font, such as Courier. Changing the font is an easy task. The second problem is that we chose to center the vertical axis based on the width of the string, when it really should have been based on the height of the string times the number of characters in the string. Can you figure out why? See if you can alter the programming code to achieve perfect centering on the vertical axis.

Windows offers functions that allow strings and individual characters to be rotated. Wouldn't it be nice if we could get to those Windows functions from Visual Basic 5?

The chart title will be a little larger than the other labels and printed in a different color.

```
         .

         .

         .

   'print title in color
   Form2.ForeColor = QBColor(13)
   Form2.FontSize = Form2.Height / 200
   LabelWidth = Form2.TextWidth(Title$) / 2
   LabelHeight = Form2.TextHeight(Title$) / 2
   Form2.CurrentX = Form2.ScaleWidth / 2 - LabelWidth
   Form2.CurrentY = (Form2.ScaleHeight * (5 / 64)) - LabelHeight
   Form2.Print Title$
   Form2.ForeColor = QBColor(0)
End Sub
```

The algorithm for centering and positioning the title is the same as for the horizontal axis label, except for the change in size and color. Notice that the title is drawn 5/64 of the form's size from the top of the window.

The Bar Chart

Figure 11.11 shows an example of the type of bar chart you can produce with this application.

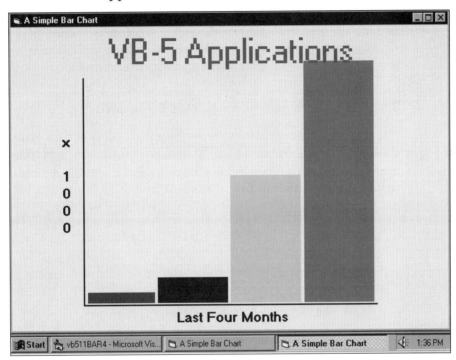

Figure 11.11 This bar chart can be sized down to an icon!

Once this application is running, experiment by resizing the chart from maximum to minimum. We'll use this application as the basis for developing an improved bar chart program in Chapter 15.

ACCESSING WINDOWS GDI GRAPHICS PRIMITIVES

Visual Basic 5 can also directly access many Windows functions. This feature expands our graphics drawing ability by including new and useful drawing primitives, as you will see in our application named 11GDI5. Among the more useful drawing functions included are: **Arc()**, **Chord()**, **Ellipse()**, **LineTo()**, **MoveToEx()**, **Pie()**, **Polygon()**, **Polyline()**, **Rectangle()**, **RoundRect()**, and **SetPixel()**. These functions can be "mixed and matched" with regular Visual Basic 5 functions. The **hDC** property is used to obtain a handle for the device context. Functions are used for routines that return a value; subroutines are used for those that do not return values. For the drawing primitives used in the next example **Long** values are returned by the functions and are used to indicate the success of the function call.

Additional information on Windows GDI graphics primitives can be found in the Microsoft Software Development Kit.

The Door to Powerful Windows Functions

The use of Windows functions requires that all function properties be passed by value. For functions with long parameter lists, the declaration for the function becomes quite long. For example, here is how you would declare the Windows **LineTo()** function:

```
Private Declare Function LineTo Lib
        "gdi32" (ByVal hDC As Long,
                ByVal X1 As Long,
                ByVal Y1 As Long) As Long
```

Important Note: Because of the width of a book page, each variable was declared on its own line. However, Visual Basic 5 requires these variables to be entered on the same *line as the declaration statement, without line breaks!*

Most Windows GDI primitives are drawn within a bounding rectangle. The **Pie()** function, for example, uses an invisible rectangle to bound the figure as described with upper left coordinates at **X1, Y1** and lower coordinates at **X2, Y2.** The pie wedge is drawn from the center of this bounding rectangle with the arc starting at **X3, Y3** and ending at **X4, Y4.** The parameters for the remaining functions in this example will not be discussed at this time; however, they work in the same manner. Remember there are hundreds of Windows functions, and most of these are now available to you.

You can find all the declarations for Windows functions in a Visual Basic 5 file named Win32api.txt. This is probably located in the Winapi subdirectory off the root Visual Basic 5 directory. Now, you can simply cut and paste the definitions you need directly into your project's code.

Viewing Several Windows Functions

Figure 11.12 shows the form that will be used for this example.

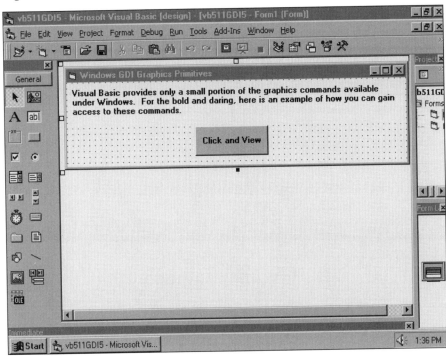

Figure 11.12 Drawing with Windows GDI graphics primitives.

The Click and View option triggers the **Command1** button. The figures that are drawn on **Form2** were declared in the general declaration section of **Form1**.

```
Private Declare Function Arc Lib
        "gdi32" (ByVal hDC As Long,
                ByVal X1 As Long,
                ByVal Y1 As Long,
                ByVal X2 As Long,
                ByVal Y2 As Long,
                ByVal X3 As Long,
                ByVal Y3 As Long,
                ByVal X4 As Long,
                ByVal Y4 As Long) As Long
```

```
Private Declare Function Chord Lib
        "gdi32" (ByVal hDC As Long,
                 ByVal X1 As Long,
                 ByVal Y1 As Long,
                 ByVal X2 As Long,
                 ByVal Y2 As Long,
                 ByVal X3 As Long,
                 ByVal Y3 As Long,
                 ByVal X4 As Long,
                 ByVal Y4 As Long) As Long
Private Declare Function Ellipse Lib
        "gdi32" (ByVal hDC As Long,
                 ByVal X1 As Long,
                 ByVal Y1 As Long,
                 ByVal X2 As Long,
                 ByVal Y2 As Long) As Long
Private Declare Function MoveToEx Lib
        "gdi32" (ByVal hDC As Long,
                 ByVal X1 As Long,
                 ByVal Y1 As Long,
                 ByVal Z1 As Long) As Long
Private Declare Function LineTo Lib
        "gdi32" (ByVal hDC As Long,
                 ByVal X1 As Long,
                 ByVal Y1 As Long) As Long
Private Declare Function Pie Lib
        "gdi32" (ByVal hDC As Long,
                 ByVal X1 As Long,
                 ByVal Y1 As Long,
                 ByVal X2 As Long,
                 ByVal Y2 As Long,
                 ByVal X3 As Long,
                 ByVal Y3 As Long,
                 ByVal X4 As Long,
                 ByVal Y4 As Long) As Long
Private Declare Function Rectangle Lib
        "gdi32" (ByVal hDC As Long,
                 ByVal X1 As Long,
```

```
                        ByVal Y1 As Long,
                        ByVal X2 As Long,
                        ByVal Y2 As Long) As Long
Private Declare Function RoundRect Lib
        "gdi32" (ByVal hDC As Long,
                        ByVal X1 As Long,
                        ByVal Y1 As Long,
                        ByVal X2 As Long,
                        ByVal Y2 As Long,
                        ByVal X3 As Long,
                        ByVal Y3 As Long) As Long
```

Remember that for each declaration, all code must be on the same line without a line break. Line breaks are inserted here only because of the limited line width of the book.

The parameter values for each function call are given as **Long** within the function. These values decide the size and placement of the shape drawn.

```
Private Sub Command1_Click ()
Form2.Show
  Form2.DrawWidth = 5

  'draw a line
  r% = MoveToEx(Form2.hDC, 10, 20, 0)
  r% = LineTo(Form2.hDC, 120, 170)

  'draw an arc
  r% = Arc(Form2.hDC, 95, 95, 205, 205, 150, 175, 175, 150)

  'draw a chord
  r% = Chord(Form2.hDC, 445, 20, 530, 80, 455, 25, 525, 70)

  'draw an ellipse
  r% = Ellipse(Form2.hDC, 190, 190, 275, 250)

  'draw a circle
  r% = Ellipse(Form2.hDC, 110, 50, 150, 110)

  'draw a pie wedge
```

```
r% = Pie(Form2.hDC, 310, 50, 410, 150, 310, 50, 310, 100)

'draw a rectangle
r% = Rectangle(Form2.hDC, 345, 190, 550, 300)

'draw a rounded rectangle
r% = RoundRect(Form2.hDC, 55, 230, 110, 275, 25, 25)
End Sub
```

Calling several Windows functions might not make for the most exciting graphical program in the book, but you have just learned a very powerful technique for accessing functions beyond those included in Visual Basic 5. Using these functions intelligently will require additional reference sources and patience when programming, but the rewards can be outstanding.

Figure 11.13 shows the screen output for this program.

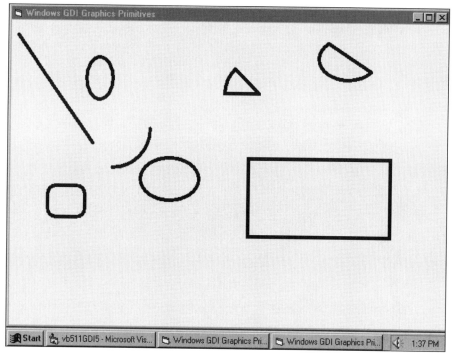

Figure 11.13 Graphics shapes drawn by Windows GDI graphics primitives.

A SIMPLE VIDEO PLAYER

If your version of Visual Basic 5 contains a Multimedia Control, you will be able to create a simple multimedia player in minutes. This player can be used to play any multimedia files, including WAVE files and AVI files.

Start a new project and open a form in the normal manner. With the Toolbox window visible, click on the Data Control and open its Components window, as shown in Figure 11.14.

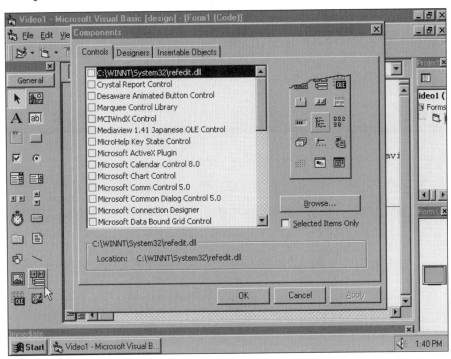

Figure 11.14 Viewing the components available to the Visual Basic 5 Data Control.

Tab down the list of controls in the Control Folder until you get to the Microsoft Multimedia Control 5. Check that control, as shown in Figure 11.15.

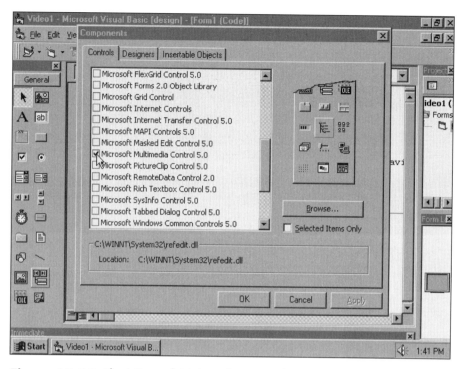

Figure 11.15 The Microsoft Multimedia Control 5 is added to the Toolbox.

The multimedia control will be added to the Toolbox icons when you close the Control folder. The multimedia control can now be moved and sized on your form. Figure 11.16 shows the multimedia control sized on this project's **Form1**.

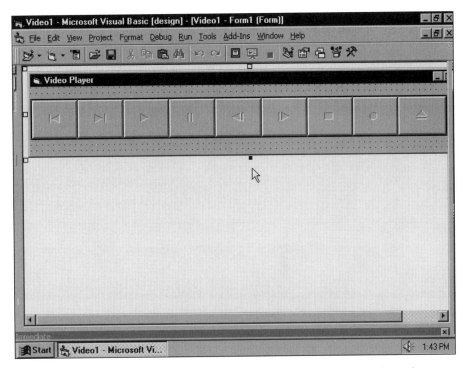

Figure 11.16 The Microsoft Multimedia Control 5 is placed and sized on Form1.

Now, simply add the following control code to the form:

```
Private Sub Form_Load()
    ' Set properties needed by MCI to open.
    MMControl1.Notify = False
    MMControl1.Wait = True
    MMControl1.Shareable = False
    MMControl1.DeviceType = "AVIVideo"
    MMControl1.filename = "C:\Vb5\Graphics\AVIs\Count24.avi"

    ' Open the MCI AVIVideo device.
    MMControl1.Command = "Open"
End Sub
```

```
Private Sub Form_Unload(Cancel As Integer)
    MMControl1.Command = "Close"
End Sub
```

The Count24.avi is a video clip supplied with Visual Basic 5. However, any AVI video clip can be used. Figure 11.17 shows the execution of the Count24.avi from our multimedia player.

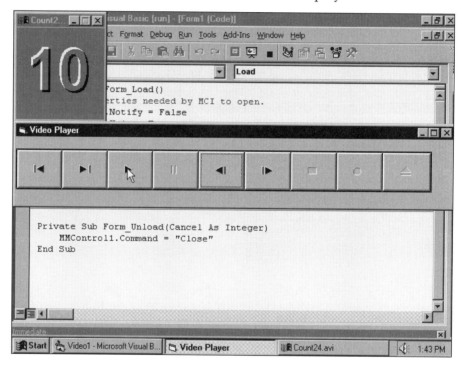

Figure 11.17 The Count24.avi video clip playing from our multimedia player project.

You can find additional information on the multimedia player control by using the built-in Visual Basic Help facility and looking up "Multimedia MCI Control." For example, to play WAVE files, you will need to change only two lines of code:

```
MMControl1.DeviceType = "WaveAudio"
MMControl1.filename = "C:\mywavefile.wav"
```

The file, mywavefile.wav, is any sound file you identify or create with WAVE file characteristics.

What's Coming?

With the skills you have developed in this and the previous chapter, you should be ready to tackle many Visual Basic 5 programming projects. In this next chapter you will learn how to obtain system information. This information will give you the ability to write projects that can access specific features of whatever computer hardware is available to them.

Chapter 12

System Resources and Utilities

Windows 95 and Windows NT provide a carefully crafted 32-bit environment where new programming rules apply. In order to access information about your system, you will have to tap into one of the hundreds of Windows functions that provide this type of information. For the programmer the problem is discovering which Windows functions are available and how to pass the required parameters to those functions. In this chapter you'll learn techniques for checking system resources such as memory, version number, key status, device capabilities, and much more. You'll also learn how to write several interesting utility programs that will teach you how to use the Visual Basic 5 timer control to place the time on the screen and produce a ticker tape program that will flash a message to you at a designated moment. You will even learn how to use the mouse and Visual Basic 5 menus to produce a Mouse-A-Sketch program for drawing on the screen.

OBTAINING SYSTEM INFORMATION

Many applications require information regarding the system on which they are being run. This information includes which processor is being used, how many processors are available, and the amount of memory that is available for the programs. Our first project will report all of this information and also return the operating system and version number.

This project, named 12CPU1, requests and returns the system information to a single form, shown in Figure 12.1.

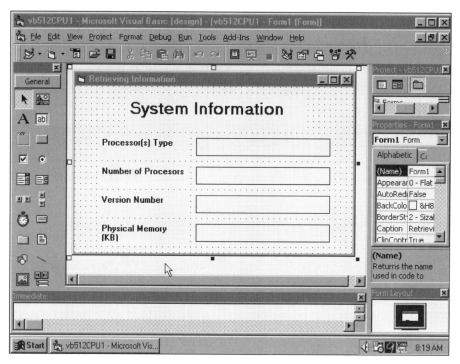

Figure 12.1 The System Information form used to report system information to the user.

The program gathers information from several sources. A call will be made to three Windows functions: **GetSystemInfo()**, **GlobalMemoryStatus(), and GetVersion()**.

Project Code for System Information

When this application is executed, a form will pop up on the screen and provide the user with the requested information. No further user interaction is necessary because the form contains no option or command buttons.

A module1 file, named 12CPU1.BAS, provides two **Type** statements that hold information returned by the Windows functions, as well as three declaration statements.

Note: Remember that each declaration is actually entered on a single line in the program, even though in book listings they are divided into shorter segments.

```
Option Explicit

Public Type SystemInfo
  dwOemId As Long
  dwPageSize As Long
  lpMinimumApplicationAddress As Long
  lpMaximumApplicationAddress As Long
  dwActiveProcessorMask As Long
  dwNumberOfProcessors As Long
  dwProcessorType As Long
  dwAllocationGranularity As Long
  dwReserved As Long
End Type

Public Type MemoryStatus
  dwLength As Long
  dwMemoryLoad As Long
  dwTotalPhys As Long
  dwAvailPhys As Long
  dwTotalPageFile As Long
  dwAvailPageFile As Long
  dwTotalVirtual As Long
  dwAvailVirtual As Long
End Type

Declare Sub GetSystemInfo Lib
         "kernel32" (lpSystemInfo As SystemInfo)
Declare Sub GlobalMemoryStatus Lib
         "kernel32" (lpBuffer As MemoryStatus)
Declare Function GetVersion Lib
         "kernel32" () As Integer
```

GetSystemInfo() returns information from the kernel32 library concerning the microprocessor type and number. The **GlobalMemory Status()** function is a new 32-bit function used to retrieve memory information capabilities of the system. The **GetVersion()** function returns version information on the Windows product. From this information we can determine the major and minor version numbers for the operating system. The version number is returned as a 32-bit value. The returned value contains the major version value (such as 4) in the low byte of the integer and the minor version (such as .0, .1 or .2) in the next byte of the integer. The upper 8 bytes are used for the build information. Decoding will be required to separate this information.

Additional information regarding Windows functions can be obtained through various programming books, such as *The Visual C++ Handbook* or *The Borland C++ Handbook* (by William H. Murray and Chris H. Pappas, Osborne/McGraw-Hill 1996).

All information is processed when the form is loaded. Information is returned as text to several **Text Box** controls.

*Note: This information could have been returned as the captions to **Label** controls.*

The first section of code merely dimensions several variables, makes assignments, and loads an icon for the application. The icon is selected from the large icon library supplied with Visual Basic 5.

Note: Remember that if you are using a different icon library path, you need to change the code before executing the program.

```
Private Sub Form_Load()
  Dim YourSystem As SystemInfo
  GetSystemInfo YourSystem
  Dim YourMemory As MemoryStatus
  GlobalMemoryStatus YourMemory
  Dim majorver As Integer, minorver As Integer

  'Prepare an icon
  Icon = LoadPicture("c:\Vb5\Graphics\Icons\Computer\pc04.ico")
      .
      .
      .
```

The first information returned will involve the version number. As you examine the following piece of code, notice the masks used to separate the major and minor version numbers.

Note: Remember that the major version number is the lower byte of the integer and the minor version number is stored in the next byte of the integer. The build version is stored in the upper bytes of the integer.

```
      .
      .
      .
'Determine System Information
  minorver = (GetVersion() And &HFF00) \ &HFF
  majorver = GetVersion() And &HFF
      .
      .
      .
```

The microprocessor type can be determined by using a series of **If** statements. The **If** clause is coupled with the information returned to *dwProcessorType*. If a **TRUE** (-1) is returned for any of the following conditions, the processor will have been correctly identified.

```
        .

        .

        .

If YourSystem.dwProcessorType = 586 Then
    Text1.TEXT = "Intel Pentium Processor or clone"
    ElseIf YourSystem.dwProcessorType = 486 Then
      Text1.TEXT = "Intel 80486 Processor or clone"
        ElseIf YourSystem.dwProcessorType = 386 Then
          Text1.TEXT = "Intel 80386 Processor or clone"
            Else
              Text1.TEXT = "Unknown Processor Type"
  End If
        .

        .

        .
```

While it is possible to test for processors down to the 8086 (the original PC microprocessor), Windows 95 and Windows NT will run on only 80386 and later machines. If you are running this application, you must be using an 80386 or higher processor!

It is also possible to find the number of microprocessors present in a system. This system information was returned to *dwNumberOfProcessors*.

```
        .

        .

        .

'Determine Number of Processors
  Text2.TEXT = YourSystem.dwNumberOfProcessors
        .

        .

        .
```

The Windows version information, which was obtained at the start of this code, is now assembled into a complete string containing the major and minor version information.

```
        .
        .
        .
    'Determine Windows version
    Text3.TEXT = Str$(majorver) + "." + LTrim$(Str$(minorver))
        .
        .
        .
```

The total physical memory is returned to *dwTotalPhys* in bytes. A kilobyte is 1024 bytes, so the following code will return the number of kilobytes present in the system's RAM.

```
        .
        .
        .
    'Determine memory information
    Text4.TEXT = YourMemory.dwTotalPhys \ 1024
End Sub
        .
        .
        .
```

Figure 12.2 shows the system information reported for one of our Dell Pentium computers.

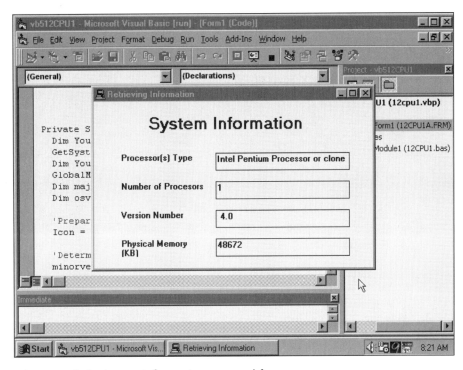

Figure 12.2 System information returned for a computer system.

READING KEY STATUS

Visual Basic 5 provides the **KeyDown()**, **KeyUp()**, and **KeyPress()** functions for obtaining information from the keyboard. Windows provides several expanded keyboard functions. In this project, 12Key2, the Windows **GetKeyState()** function will be used to return information on the status of Num Lock, Caps Lock, and Scroll Lock at execution time. Most keyboards have lights to show the status of these keys, but often you will need to detect their values under software control.

Figure 12.3 shows a very simple form for reporting this status information. **On** and **Off** values will be returned as captions to **Label** controls.

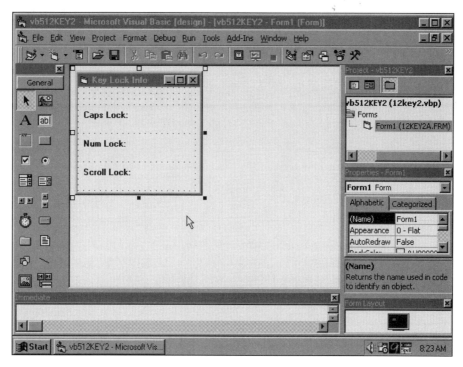

Figure 12.3 A form used to report the status of the Num Lock, Caps Lock, and Scroll Lock keys.

The Code for Keyboard Information

This is a simple but useful application, requiring a call to a Windows function, **GetKeyState()**. This function is declared, on a single line, in the **general declaration** section of the application's code.

Note: The long declaration line had to be broken in the following listing.

```
'declarations are entered on a single line
Private Declare Function GetKeyState Lib
        "User32" (ByVal I As Long) As Long
```

The program reads keyboard information upon execution (i.e., when the form is loaded). In addition, the variable *keylock* is dimensioned and a Visual Basic 5 icon is identified as the application's icon.

Note: Remember that your icon must reside in the path pointed to by this line of code.

```
Private Sub Form_Load()
  Dim keylock As Integer

  'prepare icon
  Icon = LoadPicture("c:\Vb5\Graphics\Icons\Computer\key01.ico")
      .

      .

      .
```

The **GetKeyState()** function accepts the decimal or hexadecimal virtual key code as a parameter. The value returned is an integer that can be interpreted as an ON (-1) or OFF (0).

```
      .

      .

      .

  'Report Caps Lock State
  keylock = GetKeyState(20)
  If keylock Then
    Label4.Caption = "On"
    Else
    Label4.Caption = "Off"
  End If

  'Report Num Lock State
  keylock = GetKeyState(144)
  If keylock Then
    Label5.Caption = "On"
    Else
    Label5.Caption = "Off"
  End If
```

```
'Report Scroll Lock State
keylock = GetKeyState(145)
If keylock Then
   Label6.Caption = "On"
   Else
   Label6.Caption = "Off"
End If
End Sub
```

A simple series of **If...Else** statements return the correct caption for each key lock assignment.

Viewing Key Lock Information

Figure 12.4 shows a sample set of values for one execution of the application.

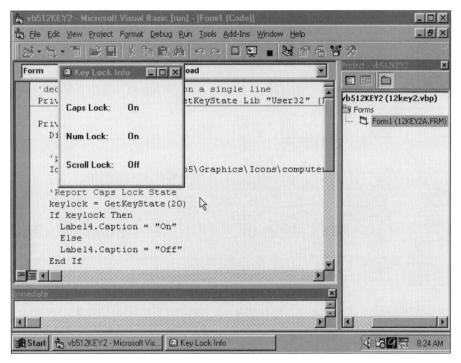

Figure 12.4 Reporting Num Lock, Caps Lock, and Scroll Lock information.

The technique used in this project can be extended to include other keyboard keys such as ESCAPE, TAB, and ENTER.

Viewing the Time and Date

The 12Time3 project is almost too simple! Visual Basic 5's **Timer** control is used by this application to update a digital clock and date display on the window. The form, shown in Figure 12.5, contains only the **Timer** control and two **Labels**.

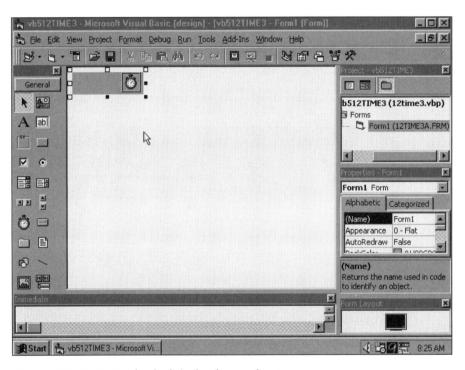

Figure 12.5 A simple clock/calendar application.

Once the timer icon is placed on the form, the timer interval is set to 1000. Recall from the previous chapter that the timer's interval is specified in milliseconds. By using 1000, the timer increments the time value once a second.

The code for the application consists of just two lines:

```
Private Sub Timer1_Timer ()
  Label1.Caption = Time$
  Label2.Caption = Date$
End Sub
```

Each time **Timer1** "ticks," new values of time and date are returned. These string values are printed dynamically as the caption values for **Label1** and **Label2**.

Figure 12.6 shows a screen with the time and date showing as an icon in the lower right corner of the screen.

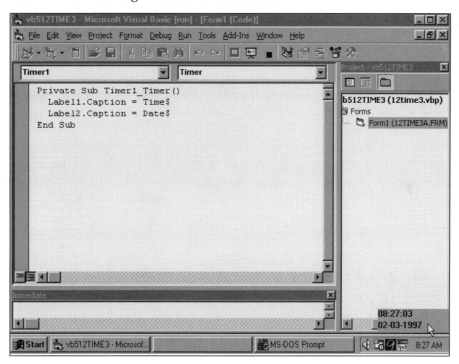

Figure 12.6 Displaying the current time and date on the screen.

Sizing and placing the form can be done when the form is created or under software control. For this application, we shrunk and moved the form to this position when the form was created. It would also be possible to use the Visual Basic 5 color palette to match the form's color to that of the screen. In this example, the border was removed from the form to give it a natural iconic appearance.

EXAMINING DEVICE CAPABILITIES

Applications written for Windows 95 and Windows NT automatically take advantage of hardware drivers developed for monitors, printers, plotters, etc. This total system integration is one of Windows' prized features. For example, if you develop an application that draws a circle on the screen, Windows will make sure that it can be drawn on CGA, EGA, VGA, or SVGA screens without additional intervention from the programmer. This translates into more time for developing applications and less time working with input and output devices. The downside, of course, is that someone must write a Windows-compatible driver for each hardware device. Hopefully, that has been done for the hardware components connected to your system!

For any given computer system, it is possible to obtain information on a device's capabilities. For example, you may wish to find the aspect ratios between vertical and horizontal pixels on a given monitor. Also, you may wish to inquire whether a plotter is directly capable of drawing circles. This information can be obtained with a single call to the Windows **GetDeviceCaps()** function.

This application, 12DEV4, will decode a subset of the total information that is available. Figure 12.7 shows the layout of the form used to report this information to the user.

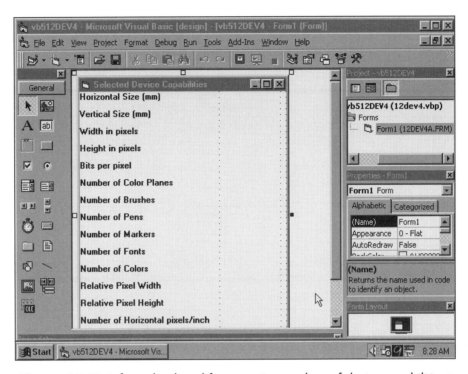

Figure 12.7 A form developed for reporting a subset of device capabilities to the user.

Using the GetDeviceCaps Function

The **GetDeviceCaps()** function returns a simple long value for any requested device parameter passed when the function is called. **GetDeviceCaps()** is declared, on a single line, in the **general declarations** section of the application's program code. Remember, this single line is broken, because of its long length, in the following listing.

```
'declarations are entered on a single line
Private Declare Function GetDeviceCaps Lib
            "Gdi32" (ByVal hDC As Long,
            ByVal nIndex As Long) As Long
```

This function is part of the Graphics Device Interface (Gdi.dll) library. As such, it is passed a handle to the Device Context (hDC) and an integer value (nIndex) that serves as an index for the information desired.

This information is processed when the application is executed and the form is loaded on the screen. Remember to check your system's location for the icon that is used in this project.

```
Private Sub Form_Load ()
  Dim newdata As Integer

  'prepare icon
  Icon = LoadPicture("c:\Vb5\Graphics\Icons\Computer\pc03.ico")

  'horizontal size in millimeters
  newdata = GetDeviceCaps(hDC, 4)
  Label16.Caption = Str$(newdata)

  'vertical size in millimeters
  newdata = GetDeviceCaps(hDC, 6)
  Label17.Caption = Str$(newdata)

  'horizontal width in pixels
  newdata = GetDeviceCaps(hDC, 8)
  Label18.Caption = Str$(newdata)

  'vertical height in pixels
  newdata = GetDeviceCaps(hDC, 10)
  Label19.Caption = Str$(newdata)

  'number of bits per pixel
  newdata = GetDeviceCaps(hDC, 12)
  Label20.Caption = Str$(newdata)

  'number of color planes
  newdata = GetDeviceCaps(hDC, 14)
  Label21.Caption = Str$(newdata)

  'number of brushes
  newdata = GetDeviceCaps(hDC, 16)
  Label22.Caption = Str$(newdata)
```

```
'number of pens
newdata = GetDeviceCaps(hDC, 18)
Label23.Caption = Str$(newdata)

'number of markers
newdata = GetDeviceCaps(hDC, 20)
Label24.Caption = Str$(newdata)

'number of fonts
newdata = GetDeviceCaps(hDC, 22)
Label25.Caption = Str$(newdata)

'number of supported colors
newdata = GetDeviceCaps(hDC, 24)
Label26.Caption = Str$(newdata)

'aspect for x
newdata = GetDeviceCaps(hDC, 40)
Label27.Caption = Str$(newdata)

'aspect for y
newdata = GetDeviceCaps(hDC, 42)
Label28.Caption = Str$(newdata)

'logical horizontal pixels/inch
newdata = GetDeviceCaps(hDC, 88)
Label29.Caption = Str$(newdata)

'logical vertical pixels/inch
newdata = GetDeviceCaps(hDC, 90)
Label30.Caption = Str$(newdata)
End Sub
```

Figure 12.8 is a report of the device capabilities for an SVGA monitor attached to a Dell Pentium computer using a Number 9 graphics card.

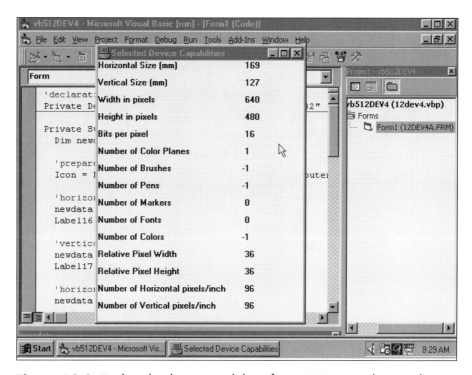

Figure 12.8 Finding the device capabilities for an SVGA graphics card and monitor.

A Drawing Marvel: Mouse-A-Sketch

No book dealing with the graphical Windows environment would be complete without a sketching program. Visual Basic 5 makes the development of this application very easy. If you leaf through your Visual Basic 5 manuals or help screens, you will find an example of a program that allows you to draw on a form with the mouse. Our Mouse-A-Sketch program, 12DRAW5, offers significant enhancements to this simple example. These enhancements include a palette of 16 colors, three brush widths, and a new canvas option. Each enhancement is offered through a menu that the user can select with a hot key or mouse.

Figure 12.9 shows the Mouse-A-Sketch form.

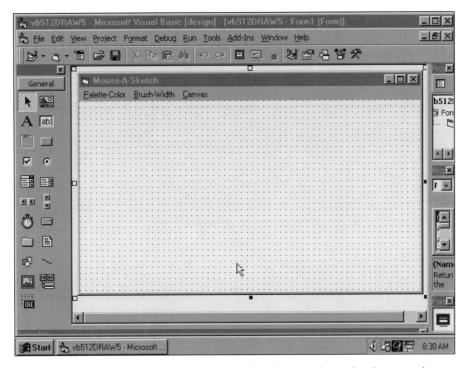

Figure 12.9 The Visual Basic form used by the Windows sketching application that allows several user options.

Coding a Sketching Program

When the Mouse-A-Sketch form is loaded at run time, the drawing width is set to 2 (narrow) and the drawing color to Quick Basic's black (**QBColor(0)**). An icon from Visual Basic 5's Icon Library is also loaded at this time. Remember to check the location of your system's icon for this application.

```
Dim MouseASketch As Integer

Private Sub Form_Load ()
   DrawWidth = 2
   ForeColor = QBColor(0)
   Icon = LoadPicture("c:\Vb5\Graphics\Icons\Writing\pens03.ico")
End Sub
```

Paint is placed on the canvas when either mouse button is pushed. The brush draws objects in the selected color and brush width as the mouse is moved. This code is fairly simple to implement.

```
Private Sub Form_MouseDown (Button As Integer, Shift As
                                  Integer,
                                  X As Single, Y As Single)
  MouseASketch = -1
  CurrentX = X
  CurrentY = Y
End Sub


Private Sub Form_MouseUp (Button As Integer, Shift As Integer,
                             X As Single, Y As Single)
  MouseASketch = 0
End Sub


Private Sub Form_MouseMove (Button As Integer, Shift As
                                  Integer,
                                  X As Single, Y As Single)
  If MouseASketch Then
    Line -(X, Y)
  End If
End Sub
```

If a mouse button is down, the variable *MouseASketch* is set to TRUE (-1) and painting can take place. If a mouse button is not pushed, *MouseASketch* is FALSE (0) and no painting takes place. The **Line()** function is used to draw lines on the canvas from the last x, y coordinate points to the present x and y positions. When a button is pushed, Visual Basic 5's *CurrentX* and *CurrentY* values are set to the present x and y values returned by the mouse.

If you examine the form shown in the previous figure, you will notice three menu options: Palette-Color, Brush-Width, and Canvas. The Palette-Color menu, shown in Figure 12.10, is being created in the Visual Basic 5 Menu Design window.

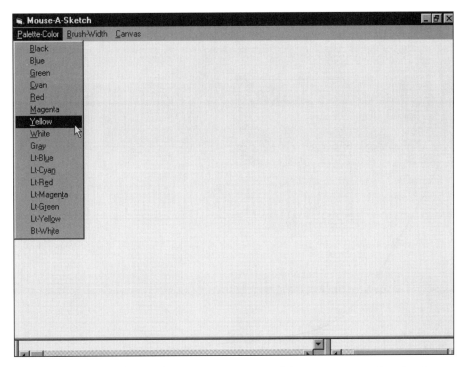

Figure 12.10 Palette color options are part of the menu created in the Menu Design window.

```
Private Sub CtlBlack_Click ()
  ForeColor = QBColor(0)
End Sub


Private Sub CtlBlue_Click ()
  ForeColor = QBColor(1)
End Sub


Private Sub CtlBWhite_Click ()
  ForeColor = QBColor(15)
End Sub


Private Sub CtlCyan_Click ()
  ForeColor = QBColor(3)
End Sub
```

```
Private Sub CtlGray_Click ()
  ForeColor = QBColor(8)
End Sub

Private Sub CtlGreen_Click ()
  ForeColor = QBColor(2)
End Sub

Private Sub CtlLBlue_Click ()
  ForeColor = QBColor(9)
End Sub

Private Sub CtlLCyan_Click ()
  ForeColor = QBColor(11)
End Sub

Private Sub CtlLGreen_Click ()
  ForeColor = QBColor(10)
End Sub

Private Sub CtlLMagenta_Click ()
  ForeColor = QBColor(13)
End Sub

Private Sub CtlLRed_Click ()
  ForeColor = QBColor(12)
End Sub

Private Sub CtlLYellow_Click ()
  ForeColor = QBColor(14)
End Sub

Private Sub CtlMagenta_Click ()
  ForeColor = QBColor(5)
End Sub

Private Sub CtlRed_Click ()
  ForeColor = QBColor(4)
End Sub

Private Sub CtlWhite_Click ()
  ForeColor = QBColor(7)
End Sub
```

```
Private Sub CtlYellow_Click ()
  ForeColor = QBColor(6)
End Sub
```

As you examine these color controls, notice that the *ForeColor* value is altered by setting it to a QuickBasic color value. A wider range of color values is available, for the truly professional painter, by specifying RGB parameters.

Brush widths are set in a similar manner. In this example, the *DrawWidth* parameter is set to 2, 8, or 14. The range of brush widths can easily be expanded or altered to suit your painting needs.

```
Private Sub CtlNarrow_Click ()
  DrawWidth = 2
End Sub


Private Sub CtlMedium_Click ()
  DrawWidth = 8
End Sub


Private Sub CtlWide_Click ()
  DrawWidth = 14
End Sub
```

The final menu option allows the artist the ability to erase a messy painting with the click of a mouse button. This is far better than cutting off an ear in a fit of anger! A new canvas is obtained with a call to the **Cls()** function.

```
Private Sub CtlNCanvas_Click ()
  Cls
End Sub
```

Painting with a Mouse

Figure 12.11 shows our best attempt at a reasonable drawing with the Mouse-A-Sketch program. Of course, the true beauty of this painting cannot be appreciated in a black-and-white screen dump. You'll have to load the program and try a painting yourself.

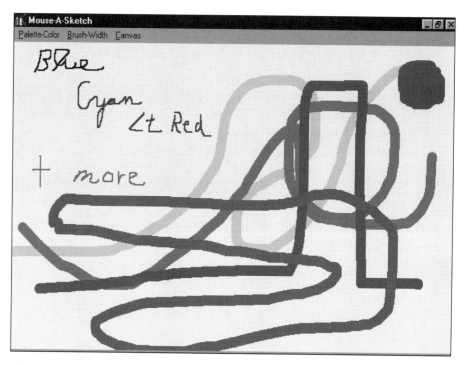

Figure 12.11 A masterpiece created with the Mouse-A-Sketch project.

AN ALARM AND TICKER TAPE DISPLAY

In an earlier example you learned how easily timers can be added to an application's code. The Visual Basic 5 manuals show how an alarm clock can be created with a single timer. Most alarm clock applications display a message on the screen at the designated alarm time.

This project will extend the idea of a computer alarm clock by using a ticker tape style message. In this example, two timers will be used. The first timer will function as the alarm controller. At the designated time, a form will pop up at the bottom of the screen. In the form will be a white tape, displaying a moving message. The speed at which the ticker tape message traverses the windows is controlled with the second timer.

The form used for initializing the ticker tape program named 12TICK6, is shown in Figure 12.12.

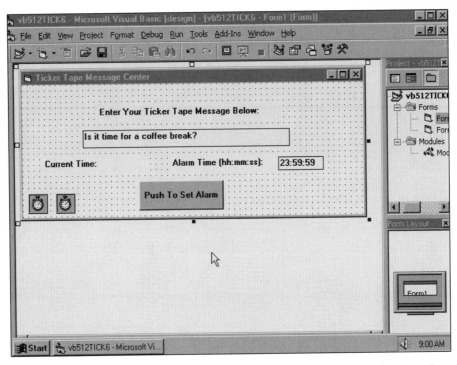

Figure 12.12 The form used to set the alarm time and message for the ticker tape project.

Crafting the Ticker Tape Application Code

Two forms and two timers are used for the ticker tape application. The form shown in the previous figure allows the user to enter the alarm time and a ticker tape message. The second form is used to display the message on the screen at the selected time. The second form is created and moved to the bottom of the screen. It is sized to occupy the total width of the screen and vertically to permit one line of text to be printed. No sizing buttons are included with this form.

This project will move text across a screen at a time interval determined by the second timer. The text, visible on the screen, increases in length with each tick of the timer. Eventually, the whole message will be visible. The position of the message is controlled by specifying X and Y values. A popular Windows function, **TextOut()**, provides this type of programming flexibility.

The MODULE1 file is named 12TICK6.BAS. This file is used for declarations needed by the project. Remember that declarations must be entered as a single line, not broken as they are shown in the following listing.

```
Option Explicit

Public I, J, SFont As Integer
Public TickerRun, Length As Integer
Public TickerTime As String
Public NStr As String

Declare Function TextOut Lib "gdi32"
            Alias "TextOutA" (ByVal hDC As Long,
            ByVal X As Long, ByVal Y As Long,
            ByVal P As String, ByVal N As Long) As Long
```

TextOut() is declared as a function since it returns a long value. The Alias is needed to accommodate Unicode provisions. **TextOut()** is part of Windows Gdi32.dll library of functions and is passed five parameters when called.

Two variables that control the movement of the ticker tape message are initialized by using **Form_Click()**. A flag, *TickerRun*, is used to show when the message has been displayed. It is initially set to FALSE (0).

```
Private Sub Form_Click ()
   I = 0
   J = 0
   TickerRun=0
End Sub
```

The alarm time and message are saved in *TickerTime* and *NStr* when the **Command Button** is clicked. **Form1** is also hidden at this time. The user will hear nothing more from this application until the designated time has been reached. At that given time, **Form2** will pop onto the screen.

```
Private Sub Command1_Click ()
 TickerTime = Text2.Text
 NStr = Text1.Text
 Form1.Hide
End Sub
```

Timer1 controls not only when the alarm clock goes off but also the "current time" displayed on **Form1**. *TickerTime* is compared to the current time reported by the system (**Time$**). If the current time is greater than or equal to the alarm time, the speaker is beeped, Form2 is displayed on the screen and the *TickerRun* variable is set to TRUE (-1).

```
Private Sub Timer1_Timer ()
   Label3.Caption = Time$
   If TickerTime = "" Then Exit Sub
   If Time$ >= TickerTime And Not TickerRun Then
      Beep: Beep
      Form2.Show
      TickerRun = -1
   End If
End Sub
```

The **AND** statement is included to prevent this portion of code from being executed each second, once the alarm time is reached. Remove this statement and the speaker will beep once a second as the message is scrolled across the screen.

While **Timer1** was waiting to display the ticker tape form, **Timer2** was running in the background. Recall that **Timer2** decides the speed at which the message is moved across the screen. Information regarding the font is read first.

```
Private Sub Timer2_Timer()
   Form2.FontSize = 12
   Form2.FontBold = -1
   Form2.FontItalic = -1
      .
      .
      .
```

The horizontal position of the message is determined by using a combination of the form width (about 9600 for a VGA screen) and how often the timer has ticked (*I*). The length of the string is found with the **Len()** function.

```
        .
        .
        .
'determine horizontal position of ticker string
  XPos = (Form2.Width \ 15) - (I)
  If XPos <= -(Len(NStr)) * 12 Then
    I = 0
    J = 0
  End If
        .
        .
        .
```

In order to see the message trail on the screen, *XPos* is allowed to be as small as or smaller than the message length.

Each time the timer ticks, a new block (or partial block) of the message is displayed. A simple clear screen (**Cls**) is used to prevent **TextOut()** from writing over previously displayed text.

```
        .
        .
        .
Form2.Cls

  'determine what part of string will be shown
  If J >= Len(NStr) Then
    J = Len(NStr)
  End If

  r% = TextOut(Form2.hDC, XPos, 10, NStr, J)

  J = J + 1
  I = I + 1
End Sub
```

In a ticker tape display, only part of the message is displayed at the start and end of the window. How much of the message is displayed is controlled by the variable *J*. *J* is incremented with each timer tick, displaying more characters, until the whole message is on the screen. *J* is set back to zero once the whole message has been scrolled.

The message will be displayed repeatedly once the alarm time has been reached. The program will end when the form is closed. Figure 12.13 shows a computer screen with the default ticker tape message running. Can't you just smell the coffee?

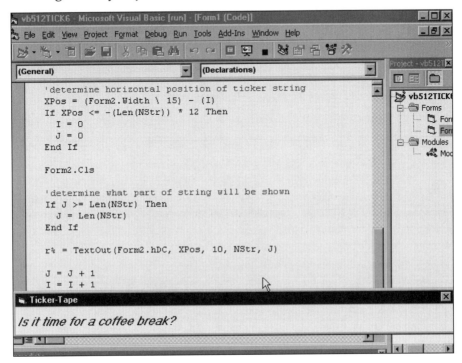

Figure 12.13 A ticker tape message displayed as an alarm message at a designated time.

ONE MORE STEP

As we close this chapter let us tempt you with a project you can develop on your own. How close do you think you are to a screen blanking routine for Windows 95 or Windows NT? Pretty close! In the previous example, the alarm from the first timer could be used to show a form that is black and completely fills the whole screen. If you remove the border and show only the ticker message, the only feature you must add is a method for detecting a keypress or mouse movement. Are you ready to get started?

Chapter 13

Financial Applications

We have all been involved with financial calculations for loans, account interest, and so on. When you were a child your financial concerns were probably limited to the distribution of your weekly allowance. As an adult you have learned that good money management helps secure stability now and for the future. This chapter contains five Visual Basic 5 financial projects that you will find useful for personal or business applications.

The first project determines the future value of an account if equal periodic deposits are made. The second project determines the maximum amount that can be periodically withdrawn from an account over a given term. This project assumes a zero balance at the end of the specified term. The third project allows you to determine the depreciation amount on a purchase, year after year. The fourth project calculates the payment on a loan, given the loan amount and term. The fifth project calculates a mortgage (loan) amortization table.

The five projects also introduce you to some new and powerful Visual Basic 5 programming concepts. You will learn how to save information to a file, send data to a multiline text box, and use the Windows 95 and NT clipboard to transfer data between various Windows 95 and NT applications. These new features will enhance all of the Visual Basic 5 projects you develop in the future.

Once you study the five projects and new programming concepts, use the projects as templates for your own financial applications.

REGULAR DEPOSITS IN AN ACCOUNT

Your mother always told you to put money away for a rainy day. Did you do it? What if you put $4 away each month from your sixth birthday until you were 76? What would the account be worth? What if your employer deducts $200/month from your paycheck and places it in a retirement account paying 10.5 percent interest? What will that retirement account amount to after 25 years? If these questions are of interest to you, this Visual Basic 5 project will be of value.

This project, 13FV1, is the simplest application in this chapter, since you have mastered all of the Visual Basic 5 programming techniques in earlier chapters. The data entry form, **Form1**, is shown in Figure 13.1.

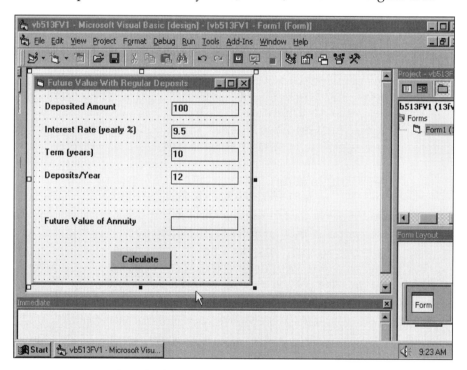

Figure 13.1 Finding the future value of an investment.

This form uses text boxes to enter and report values. The data entry boxes contain default values that can be edited in the normal manner. Perhaps you would like to include a Clear command button that would clear all default values with just a click. All money values are declared as type **Currency** in order to increase precision.

Developing the Future Value Code

In the general declarations section of **Form1**, the following declarations have been made for the variables used by this project.

```
Public Deposit As Currency
Public Rate As Currency
Public TotalYears As Integer
Public NumDepYr As Integer
Public AnnunityFinalValue As Currency
```

The currency data type is used because currency variables are stored as 64-bit numbers in an integer format. They are scaled by a factor of 10,000, giving a fixed-point number with 15 digits on the left of the decimal point and four digits on the right of the decimal. Values can be represented in the range from -922,337,203,685,477.5808 to 922,337,203,685,477.5807. This data type is used for calculations where accuracy is important.

Calculations are made when the Calculate button, **Command1**, is pushed. The first task is to retrieve data from the various text boxes.

```
Private Sub Command1_Click ()
  'retrieve form data
  Deposit = Val(Text1.Text)
  Rate = Val(Text2.Text)
  TotalYears = Val(Text3.Text)
  NumDepYr = Val(Text4.Text)
     .
     .
     .
```

The interest value, *Rate*, is converted to a decimal value and adjusted for the number of deposits/year. The value of the account, *AnnuityFinalValue*, is determined with an equation that compounds the interest.

```
      .
      .
      .
  'make calculations
  Rate = Rate / 100 / NumDepYr
  AnnuityFinalValue = Deposit * ((1 + Rate) ^ (TotalYears *
                        NumDepYr)  1) / Rate

  'report value in formatted form
  Text6.Text = Format$(AnnuityFinalValue, "$###,###,##0.00")
End Sub
```

 Note: The equation for the calculation of the AnnuityFinalValue *should be on one programming line when you enter this code.*

The value of the investment is printed in a formatted form that includes a dollar sign. To round out this application, an icon is selected from the stock icons provided with Visual Basic 5. Make sure your icon's location is correctly stated in your project.

```
Private Sub Form_Paint ()
  'load icon from library
  Icon = LoadPicture("c:\Vb5\Graphics\Icons\Office\graph03.ico")
End Sub
```

If your icons are stored in a different subdirectory, change this section of code before running the application. This might be a good place to use the IconWorks sample application provided with Visual Basic 5. Perhaps a large "$" would work well as your custom icon.

Invest Regularly and Reap the Benefits

Figure 13.2 shows the future value of an annuity calculated with the default values given in the data entry form.

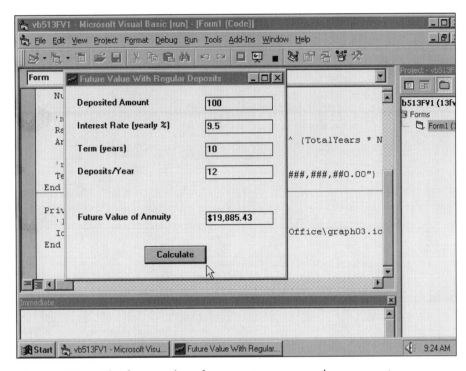

Figure 13.2 The future value of an investment using the program's default values.

We know you're very interested in finding out the answers to our original investment questions given at the beginning of this section. What would your account be worth if you had put $4/month in a savings account for 70 years at 7 percent interest? You might be surprised at the results shown in Figure 13.3. Listen to your mother the next time!

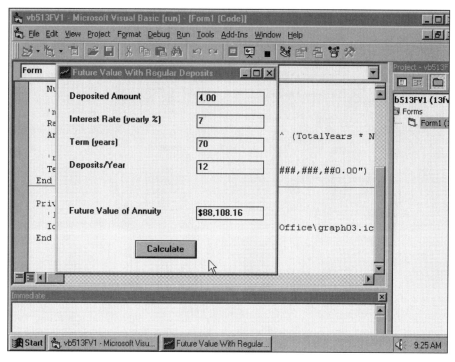

Figure 13.3 The future value of saving $4/month for 70 years.

Your employer has generously removed $200/month from your paycheck and placed it in a retirement account paying 10.5 percent. If you work for 25 years, what will your retirement be worth? Could you live on the amount shown in Figure 13.4?

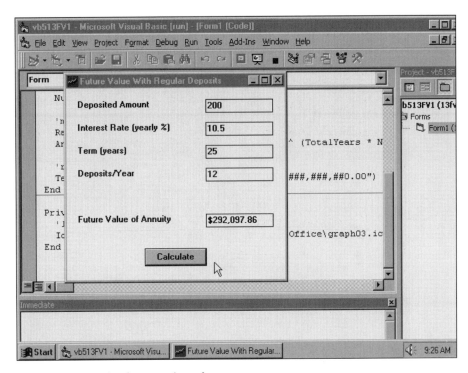

Figure 13.4 The future value of a retirement account.

REGULAR WITHDRAWALS FROM AN ACCOUNT

In the last section you learned how to calculate the amount of a retirement account based on regular deposits by your employer. Let's assume that this account has a future value of $400,000 when you retire at age 65. If you must spread this money over 15 years (assume you'll live to 80), what is the maximum amount of money that you can regularly withdraw from the account?

In this project, 13RW2, you will learn how to develop an application for calculating the maximum withdrawal allowed on an account if the money is to last for a specified term. Sooner or later, you're going to have to worry about your retirement!

This project parallels the last example in terms of simplicity and Visual Basic 5 programming features. The data entry form (**Form1**) is shown in Figure 13.5.

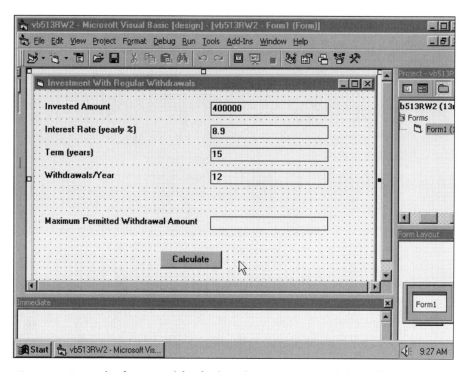

Figure 13.5 The form used for finding the maximum withdrawal amount from an account.

Developing the Project Code for Regular Withdrawals

In the general declarations section of **Form1**, the following declarations have been made for the variables used by this project.

```
Public Investment As Currency
Public Rate As Currency
Public TotalYears As Integer
Public NumWithYr As Integer
Public MaxWith As Currency
```

Again, the currency data type is used because currency variables are stored as 64-bit numbers in an integer format.

The data entry and withdrawal calculations are very similar to those in our last example. The maximum amount that can be regularly withdrawn from the account is formatted and returned to a text box on **Form1**.

```
Private Sub Command1_Click ()
  'retrieve form data
  Investment = Val(Text1.Text)
  Rate = Val(Text2.Text)
  TotalYears = Val(Text3.Text)
  NumWithYr = Val(Text4.Text)

  'make calculations
  Rate = Rate / 100 / NumWithYr
  MaxWith = Investment * (Rate / ((1 + Rate) ^
            (TotalYears * NumWithYr) - 1) + Rate)

  'report value in formatted form
  Text5.Text = Format$(MaxWith, "$###,##0.00")
End Sub
```

 Note: The formula for calculating MaxWith *should appear on one programming line when you enter this code into your project.*

An icon is loaded from the library of supplied icons. Note that the icon is loaded when the form is painted. Another option is to load the icon when the form is loaded. Be sure to enter the correct path to your icon on this line.

```
Private Sub Form_Paint ()
  'load icon from library
  Icon = LoadPicture("c:\Vb5\Graphics\Icons\Writing\note18.ico")
End Sub
```

Visual Basic 5 supplies a large number of icons; look around for one that suits your needs.

Stretching Out a Retirement Pension

Can you live on your retirement pension? Figure 13.6 shows the amount that can be regularly withdrawn from an account over a 15-year period.

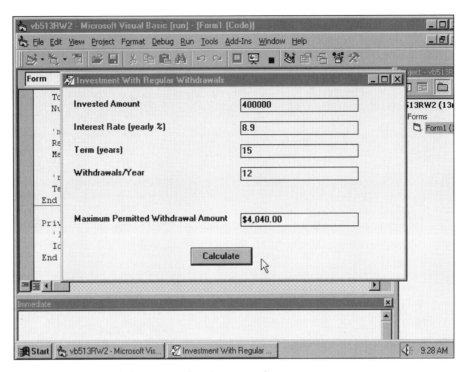

Figure 13.6 Withdrawing a fixed amount from an account over a 15-year period.

Figure 13.6 shows the maximum amount that you could regularly withdraw from an account initially containing $400,000 over a 15-year period. Could you live on a retirement amount this size? Remember, if the cost of living doubles during the 15-year period, this money will be worth half of its present purchasing power. Could you live on that amount? It gives you something to think about, doesn't it?

DEPRECIATION OF AN ASSET

With shiny new red paint and hot custom wheels, who would ever have thought that before you got it home it would lose 21 percent of its purchased value? The lesson you should have learned about the value of assets from your 1962 red-flyer wagon is now transposed to cars.

In the next project, 13Depr3, you will learn a simple technique for calculating the depreciation value of an asset for each year the asset is in use. The program calculates the depreciation value for a given year by multiplying the asset's value at the start of the year by the depreciation percentage.

This project also teaches several new Visual Basic 5 programming concepts. For example, you will learn how to save your output to a text file, how to print output to a multiline text box, and how to use copy and paste commands for sharing information between Windows 95 and NT applications.

Figure 13.7 shows the data entry form, **Form1**, with a checkbox for selecting file output.

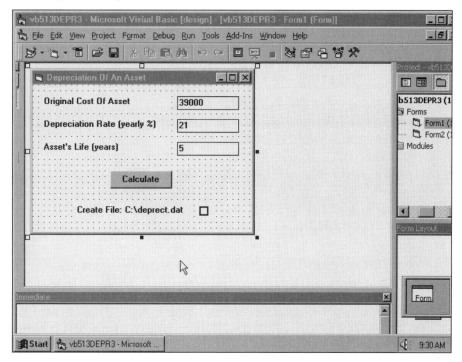

Figure 13.7 The form for finding a table of depreciation values.

This project allows you to save the data in an optional text file. For this example, the file is named deprect.dat and is saved to the C:\ root directory. If you are energetic, add code that will use a text box to allow the user to enter the drive and file name.

Attaching Code to the Form

The complexity of the project's code results from the added Visual Basic 5 features, not the program code itself. Since file, text box, and cut-and-paste features are going to be added, most of the variables used by the project are declared **global**. This is done in the **global declaration** section of the project's code.

```
Global AssetValue, Rate, Lifetime As Currency
Global Depreciation, Temp As Currency
Global I As Integer
```

A **Currency** data type is again used for precision.

All project action is initiated by a click on the Calculate button shown on the form. This button has the control name **Command1**.

```
Private Sub Command1_Click ()
  'retrieve form data
  AssetValue = Val(Text1.Text)
  Rate = Val(Text2.Text)
  Lifetime = Val(Text3.Text)
  Rate = Rate / 100

  'show form in window
  Form2.Show
     .
     .
     .
```

The first action taken is to retrieve the default or user-entered values from the form's text boxes. Remember, this information must be converted to numeric format with the use of the **Val** function. Next, the focus is shifted to **Form2**. This form is used for data output and contains a multiline text box, drawn at design time. This text box occupies the entire form's size. As a matter of fact, the multiline text box uses a sizing technique so that when the form is sized, the text box is also sized.

Regardless of what is happening on the output form sent to the window, a check must be made to see if the user would also like a copy saved to a file. Your Visual Basic 5 manuals give a complete description of the various options for creating files. We chose to generate a sequential file (a text file) for this application. Text files are typically used to store ASCII data and can be printed to the screen or line printer with simple command-line instructions.

If the checkbox on the data entry form is checked, the user is requesting a file be generated.

```
        .
        .
        .
'if a file copy is requested, then generate
If Form1.Check1.Value = 1 Then
  'open sequential file for output
  Open "C: \Deprect.Dat" For Output As 1
    .
    .
    .
```

To save data to a file, it is necessary to open the file with the **Open()** function and identify several parameters. This file will be located in the root directory on the C:\ drive and will be named Deprect.Dat. As we mentioned earlier, you can allow the user to name the location and file by including another text box on the data entry form. This file will be opened for data output and is given an identification number of 1.ng another text box on the data entry form. This file will be opened for data output and is given an identification number of 1.

Printing information to a sequential text file is almost as easy as sending it to a printer. The **Print #** statement is used, followed by the file's identification number. All information following that statement is channeled to the file.

```
        .
        .
        .
'send information to file
Print #1, "Asset Value"; Tab(20); AssetValue
Print #1, "Depreciation Rate"; Tab(20); Rate
Print #1, "Asset's Life"; Tab(20); Lifetime
Print #1,
Print #1, "Year"; Tab(15); "Depreciation Amount"
Print #1, "---------------";
Print #1, "--------------- "
Print #1,
For I = 1 To Lifetime
```

```
            Temp = AssetValue * Rate
            Depreciation = Temp * (1 - Rate) ^ (I - 1)
            Print #1, I;
            Print #1, Tab(18);
            Print #1, Format$(Depreciation, "$###,##0.00")
        Next I
        Close #1
    End If
End Sub
```

When the final bit of information has been sent to the file, the **Close** # statement is issued to close the file. Figure 13.8 shows the information sent to a file using the default values on the form.

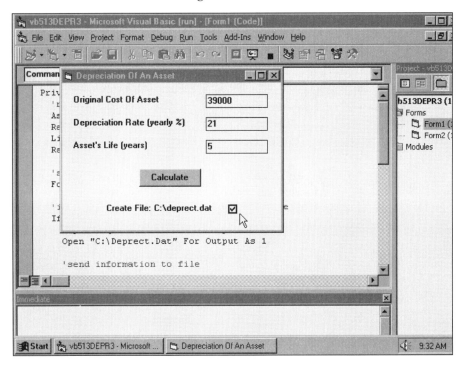

Figure 13.8 Depreciation data for an asset sent to a sequential text file.

While we are still using the data entry form (**Form1**) it is a good place to load an icon from the Visual Basic 5 icon collection.

```
Private Sub Form_Paint ()
  'load icon from icon library
  Icon = LoadPicture("c:\Vb5\Graphics\Icons\Misc\misc30.ico")
End Sub
```

Output is always sent to the output form, **Form2**. This form contains a multiline text box encompassing the whole form and a drop-down menu that permits cut, copy, and paste options. This form, along with the default depreciation values and menu options, is shown in Figure 13.9.

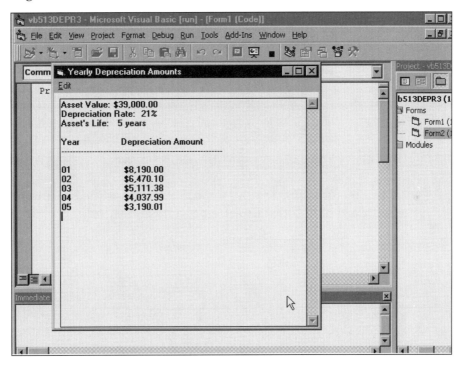

Figure 13.9 A table of depreciation can be printed in a multiline text box.

A multiline text box permits the table of asset depreciation values to be displayed. Multiline text boxes can use horizontal and vertical scroll bars and permit the use of cut, copy, and paste edit features.

Once the menu is created with the help of the menu design window, menu items are added and identified. These features are shown in Figure 13.10.

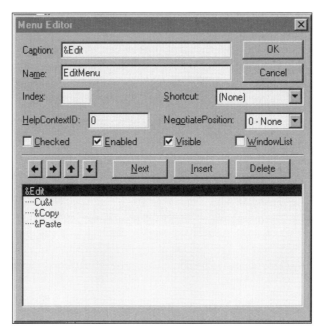

Figure 13.10 Using the menu design window to create a custom menu.

The menu items, for this example, are identified in the following code. Each block of code describes a menu feature.

```
Private Sub MCopy_Click ()
  Clipboard.SetText Text1.SelText
End Sub

Private Sub MCut_Click ()
  Clipboard.SetText Text1.SelText
  Screen.ActiveControl.SelText = ""
End Sub

Private Sub MPaste_Click ()
  Text1.SelText = Clipboard.GetText()
End Sub
```

Each menu item is activated with a click of the mouse button. The copy option transfers the highlighted text on the currently active screen to the clipboard. The cut option performs in an identical fashion but also replaces the text being copied with a null string. The paste option transfers the text in the clipboard to the portion of the active screen containing the cursor.

Once data is copied to the clipboard, it can be transferred to another location in the same application, pasted to an entirely different Visual Basic 5 application, sent to a Microsoft Word document, or moved to a Microsoft Excel spreadsheet.

The depreciation table data is printed to the multiline text box when the data output form is loaded. As with all text boxes, a command such as Text1.Text will accept string information. There is just one catch, however. The text box can accept only one string. That means that the entire table must be sent at one time in the form of a single string.

To accomplish this feat, our application generates various pieces of the final table and concatenates the information onto an ever increasing string, **MStr$**. When the whole string is finished, it is sent to the text box with a single command.

```
Private Sub Form_Load ()
   'make calculations and print answers to multiline text box
   NL$ = Chr$(13) + Chr$(10)
   MStr$ = "Asset Value: $"
   MStr$ = MStr$ + Format$(AssetValue, "###,##0.00") + NL$
   MStr$ = MStr$ + "Depreciation Rate:   "
   MStr$ = MStr$ + Format$(Rate, "##%") + NL$
   MStr$ = MStr$ + "Asset's Life:   " + Str$(Lifetime)
   MStr$ = MStr$ + " years" + NL$ + NL$
   MStr$ = MStr$ + "Year                  Depreciation Amount"
   MStr$ = MStr$ + NL$ + "---------------- "
   MStr$ = MStr$ + "--------------- " + NL$ + NL$
   For I = 1 To Lifetime
      Temp = AssetValue * Rate
      Depreciation = Temp * (1 - Rate!) ^ (I - 1)
      MStr$ = MStr$ + Format$(I, "00")
      MStr$ = MStr$ + "                        "
      MStr$ = MStr$ + Format$(Depreciation!, "$###,##0.00") + NL$
   Next I
   Text1.Text = MStr$
End Sub
```

Word wrapping is possible, along with the use of vertical and horizontal scroll bars. In order to force carriage returns and line feeds within the text box, the values for each are encoded in a string named **NL$**. Each **NL$** you see in the listing will force a carriage return and line feed within the multiline text box of the output form, **Form2**.

If the size of the form is changed, the size of the multiline text box will change accordingly. This is achieved by simply checking for form resizing. When a form is resized the new text box dimensions are set, just a little shy of the full form's height and width.

```
Private Sub Form_Resize ()
  Text1.Height = ScaleHeight - 130
  Text1.Width = ScaleWidth - 130
End Sub
```

In this example, a margin of 130 twips was allowed at the right and bottom of the output form. This gives the appearance of a border around the whole form.

Asset Depreciation and Data Sharing

Assume you have purchased equipment for your business that has a life expectancy of five years. The equipment, valued at $28,000, depreciates at a rate of 12 percent per year. Use this project to determine the depreciation for each year. Figure 13.11 is the depreciation table printed to the output form.

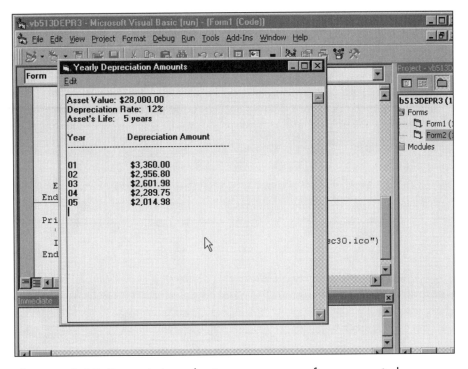

Figure 13.11 Depreciating a business asset over a five-year period.

This project concerns depreciating special equipment used in a business over a five-year period. The original cost of the equipment was $28,000 and it depreciates at 12 percent each year.

One of the truly remarkable features of this program is that all or portions of the depreciation table can be exported to other Windows 95 and NT applications. These applications include, but are not limited to, Microsoft Word and Microsoft Excel.

Figure 13.12 shows the depreciation table of the last example pasted onto a Microsoft Word document.

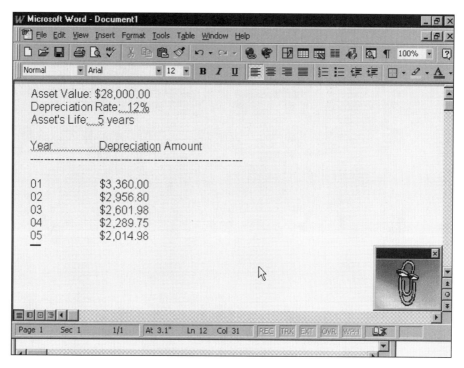

Figure 13.12 Using cut-and-paste features to transfer information to Microsoft Word.

With cut-and-paste options, data from specialized Visual Basic 5 applications can be transferred with ease. This also means that once the data has been transferred, you can employ the advanced features of Microsoft Word or even Microsoft Excel for forecasting and charting.

PAYMENT ON A LOAN

Sticker shock! It has happened to everyone purchasing a new car. We're sure there are people reading this book who remember being able to purchase a VW Beetle for under $3000. Well, that's not true anymore. Sticker shock is a term that refers to the shock purchasers go into when looking at the price of new cars.

Well, the sticker shock isn't nearly as bad as the *payment shock*. The *payment shock* occurs after you make the new car decision and sit down with the loan officer to discuss monthly payments. You know how it goes, you tell the loan officer, "I'd like to pay the car off in three years."

The loan officer tells you the payment, and you exclaim, "Wow, the payments are that high?" You then remark, "How about six years?"

The next project, 13Pay4, will help you plan ahead. Hopefully, you'll avoid the *payment shock* by being prepared with facts and figures. The sticker price might be $32,000, but what is that going to cost each month?

Here is how the application works. On the data entry form, shown in Figure 13.13, enter the data regarding the pending purchase.

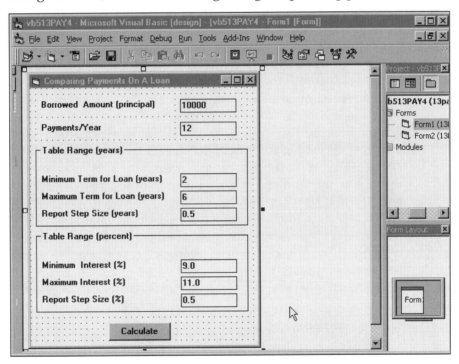

Figure 13.13 The form used for calculating payments on a loan.

The data entry form requests the principal and the number of payments per year. Next, enter a range of values for the term of the loan and another range of values for the interest rate. You'll be surprised how a half percent in interest can affect your monthly payment.

When the Calculate button, **Command1**, is pushed, a table of payments will be displayed on the screen. Now it is possible to see how changing the term from three to six years will affect your payment. It will also show you that shopping for a good interest rate will pay off in overall lower monthly payments.

Developing Code for Payments on a Loan

Most of this application's variables have been declared in the MOD-ULE1 file, named 13PAY4.BAS, because the project uses several forms and subroutines.

```
Public Temp1, Temp2, Principal, BInt, FInt, SInt As Currency
Public I, J. Column, SYears, PayYear, BYears, EYears As
Currency
```

When the Calculate button, **Command1**, is pushed, data is entered from the data entry form and converted to numeric format with the use of the **Val** function. Payments will be presented in tabular form with varying interest and terms. As such, several variables are needed for these calculations whose purpose might not be readily apparent. *BYears* represents the beginning year for the loan term. *EYears* represents the ending year. *SYears* represents the size of the step, in years, between output rows. For example, if *BYears* was 3 and *EYears* was 6 a step size (*SYears*) of 0.5 would produce a table with seven rows.

The interest variations are handled in a similar manner. *BInt* represents the first column of interest values, *FInt* the final column, and *SInt* the step size between columns. Thus, if you're interested in payments on a loan where the interest can vary between 9 and 12 percent in 1/2 percent steps, your final table will have seven columns with different payment values. (Sounds like we're going to need scroll bars for this project!)

```
Private Sub Command1_Click ()
  'retrieve data from the form
  Principal = Val(Text1.Text)
  PayYear = Val(Text2.Text)
  BYears = Val(Text3.Text)
  EYears = Val(Text4.Text)
  SYears = Val(Text5.Text)
  BInt = Val(Text6.Text)
  FInt = Val(Text7.Text)
  SInt = Val(Text8.Text)
      .
      .
      .
```

Both horizontal and vertical scroll bars will be used to allow the user to glide through large tables. The next piece of code requests a font size and then determines the scroll bar changes as a function of the font size.

```
         .
         .
         .

'set font and scroll properties
Form2.FontSize = 8
Form2.VScroll1.LargeChange = FontSize * 120
Form2.VScroll1.SmallChange = FontSize * 23
Form2.HScroll1.LargeChange = FontSize * 120
Form2.HScroll1.SmallChange = FontSize * 23


'show the output form
Form2.show
End Sub
```

Once the scroll bar information is found, the focus is shifted to the second form, where all output occurs.

This project also uses an icon from the stock icon library. As you can imagine, by this point we're getting desperate for icons that might in some way relate to the project. A letter icon was chosen to represent bill-paying time.

```
Private Sub Form_Paint ()
  'load the icon from the icon library
  Icon = LoadPicture("c:\Vb5\Graphics\Icons\Mail\mail03.ico")
End Sub
```

Calculations for the payment table are handled in a subroutine described in the general code section of the seccond form, **Form2**. This subroutine, named **CalPay**, is called whenever the scroll bars are used to change position within the payment table.

```
Private Sub VScroll1_Change ()
  Call CalPay
End Sub


Private Sub HScroll1_Change ()
  Call CalPay
End Sub
```

```
Private Sub HScroll1_GotFocus ()
  Call CalPay
End Sub

Private Sub VScroll1_GotFocus ()
  Call CalPay
End Sub
```

Form resizing can also create a problem. If the scroll bars aren't moved with code, they'll stay at the same position when the form is enlarged or shrunk. They can be resized by knowing the form's new *ScaleWidth* and *ScaleHeight*.

```
Private Sub Form_Resize ()
  VScroll1.Move ScaleWidth - VScroll1.Width, 0,
      VScroll1.Width, ScaleHeight - HScroll1.Height
  HScroll1.Move 0, ScaleHeight-HScroll1.Height,
      ScaleWidth-VScroll1.Width
End Sub
```

Note: The VScroll.Move *and* HScroll.Move *code must be on one program line when you enter this code in your project.*

The real action takes place in the **CalPay** subroutine.

```
Private Sub CalPay ()
  ScaleTop = VScroll1.Value
  ScaleLeft = HScroll1.Value
  Cls
    .
    .
    .
```

The first block of program code is responsible for printing the table heading on the screen. The first vertical column will be Years, and all remaining columns will be the varying interest rates. The number of output columns is variable and depends on the data entered by the user.

```
    .
    .
    .
  Column = 1
  Print "Years";
```

```
For J = BInt To FInt Step SInt
   Print Tab(12 * Column); Format$(J / 100, "##.0#%");
   Column = Column + 1
Next J
Print : Print
      .
      .
      .
```

The payment data is generated with the use of two loops. The first loop, controlled by *I*, increments the years, while the second loop, controlled by *J*, increments the interest values. Each value output to the table requires a separate calculation.

```
      .
      .
      .
For I = BYears To EYears Step SYears
   Print I;
   Column = 1
   For J = BInt To FInt Step SInt
      Temp1 = (J / 100) * Principal / PayYear
      Temp2 = (J / 100) / PayYear + 1
      Payment = Temp1 / (1 - 1 / Temp2 ^ (PayYear * I))
      Print Tab(12 * Column);
      Print Format$(Payment, "$###,##0.00");
      Column = Column + 1
   Next J
   Print
Next I
End Sub
```

Viewing Loan Payment Options

Figure 13.14 shows the payment table for the default values shown earlier in the data entry figure.

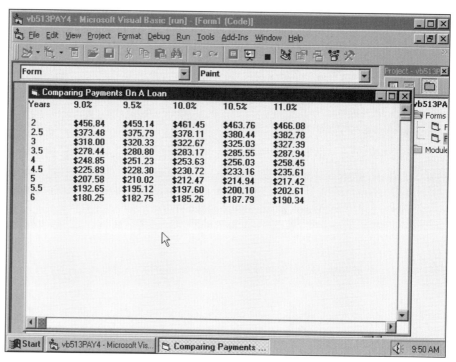

Figure 13.14 Calculating a loan payment for the program's default values.

Although these values appear interesting, we know you are more interested in the payments on the $32,000 car mentioned earlier. Assume that the value, interest, and terms for this car are represented by those in Figure 13.15.

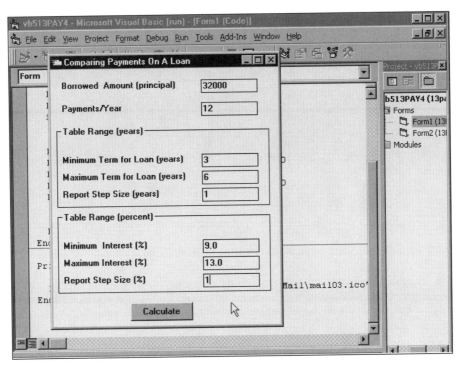

Figure 13.15 Values used to find payments on a new car.

The loan payment table, for the values selected, is shown in Figure 13.16. Do you see any payments in the table that you can afford? It looks as if we'll all have to change professions and come up with a new hit song just to make the car payments!

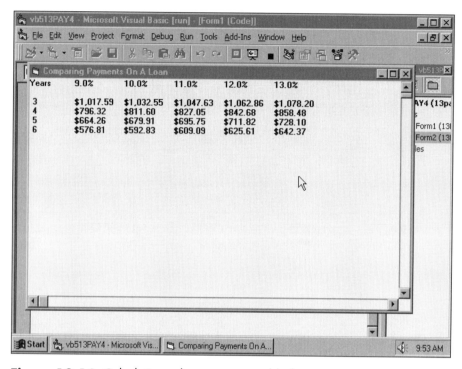

Figure 13.16 Calculating a loan payment table for a new car.

A MORTGAGE AMORTIZATION TABLE

Mortgage amortization tables allow you to view your mortgage or loan account status as you make regular payments. The next project, 13Mort5, will print a complete table on the screen, allow the user to request a hard copy from the printer, or permit the table to be saved to a file in the root directory of the C:\ drive.

The project can be used for any loan or mortgage when regular payments are made on an account with compound interest. If you have a mortgage on a home or vacation home, the interest paid may be deductible on your federal and state income taxes. Simply tally the interest for the payments you made in a given year to find out what may be deductible. If you own a small business, equipment purchased for the business can be depreciated and the interest deducted from your new profits, in many cases. The mortgage amortization project can help you plan your financial strategies before taxes are due.

The data entry form, **Form1**, is shown in Figure 13.17. You'll notice two checkboxes, contained in a frame, that allow the user to select two options: output to file or output to printer.

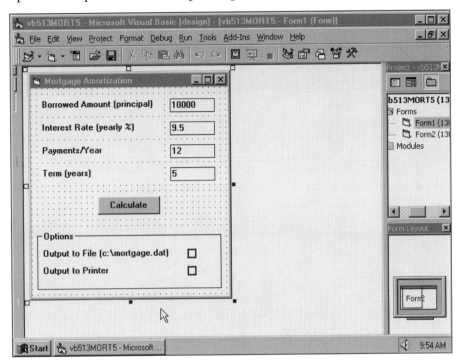

Figure 13.17 A form with file and print options for the mortgage amortization project.

Coding the Mortgage Table

The mortgage amortization project used multiple forms and subroutines. **Global** variables were used for situations in which data is being passed back and forth between forms.

```
Global Principal, Rate, Payment As Currency
Global Interest, Amortized, TInt, Balance As Currency
Global I, PayYear, Term As Integer
```

As with past applications in this chapter, information is gathered from the user regarding the borrowed amount, interest rate, number of payments per year, and the term of the loan. This information is processed when the user clicks the Calculate button, **Command1**, on the data entry form.

```
Private Sub Command1_Click ()
   'retrieve data from input form
   Principal = Val(Text1.Text)
   Rate = Val(Text2.Text)
   PayYear = Val(Text3.Text)
   Term = Val(Text4.Text)

   'determine periodic payment
   Rate = Rate / 100
   Temp1! = Rate / PayYear + 1
   Temp2! = PayYear * Term
   Payment = Rate * Principal / PayYear / (1 - 1 / Temp1! ^
            Temp2!)

   'view output table
   Form2.Show
End Sub
```

Notice, in the previous code, that the payment (*Payment*) for the period indicated is also calculated. Part of each payment is used to reduce the principal owed and pay the current interest charge. As you know, loans initially apply more of the payment to the interest and less to the principal.

This program also uses an icon from the Visual Basic 5 icon library.

```
Private Sub Form_Paint ()
   'load icon from icon library
   Icon = LoadPicture("c:\Vb5\Graphics\Icons\Mail\mail12.ico")
End Sub
```

Three output possibilities are available for the data generated. The data can be sent to the window, the printer, or a file. When the data is sent to a window, scroll capabilities must be included because mortgage tables can grow quite large for 20- or 30-year mortgages with monthly payments. The output will be narrow enough not to require a horizontal scroll bar. Output calculated for the window is done in a subroutine named **CalMortWindow**, found in the general code section of **Form2**. This is code that you have seen in many earlier projects.

```
Private Sub VScroll1_Change ()
  Call CalMortWindow
End Sub

Private Sub VScroll1_GotFocus ()
  Call CalMortWindow
End Sub

Private Sub Form_Resize ()
  VScroll1.Move ScaleWidth - VScroll1.Width, 0,
      VSCroll1.Width, ScaleHeight
End Sub
```

The subroutine that makes mortgage calculations for the window uses several **Print** statements to send formatted output to the screen.

Once the periodic payment is known, from **Form1**'s calculation, the payment can be divided into portions applied to the interest and principal. Once this is done, a running record can be sent to the screen.

```
Private Sub CalMortWindow ()
  'set scroll and draw parameters
  ScaleTop = VScroll1.Value
  AutoRedraw = -1
  Cls
  Balance = Principal
  TInt=0

  'print mortgage table to window
  Print "Borrowed Amount"; Tab(20);
  Print Format$(Principal, "$###,##0.00")
  Print "Interest Rate"; Tab(20);
  Print Format$(Rate, "#0.0#%")
  Print "Payments/Year"; Tab(20); PayYear
  Print "Term (years)"; Tab(20); Term
  Print
  'print column titles to window table
  Print "Period"; Tab(10); "Payment"; Tab(22);
  Print "Interest"; Tab(34); "Amortized"; Tab(46);
  Print "Balance"; Tab(58); "Total Interest"
  Print
  'print table to window
  For I = 1 To Term * PayYear
    Print I;
```

```
      Print Tab(10); Format$(Payment, "$###,##0.00");
      Interest = Balance * Rate / 12
      Print Tab(22); Format$(Interest, "$###,##0.00");
      Amortized = Payment - Interest
      Print Tab(34); Format$(Amortized, "$###,##0.00");
      Balance = Balance - Amortized
      Print Tab(46); Format$(Balance, "###,##0.00");
      TInt = TInt + Interest
      Print Tab(58); Format$(TInt, "###,##0.00");
      Print
   Next I

End Sub
```

This code prints a form, **Form2**, listing the payment number, payment amount, interest, amortized amount, balance on the account, and total interest paid to this point. Figure 13.18 shows a portion of the mortgage table printed with the default parameters.

Mortgage Amortization

Borrowed Amount	$10,000.00
Interest Rate	9.5%
Payments/Year	12
Term (years)	5

Period	Payment	Interest	Amortized	Balance	Total Interest
1	$210.02	$79.17	$130.85	9,869.15	79.17
2	$210.02	$78.13	$131.89	9,737.26	157.30
3	$210.02	$77.09	$132.93	9,604.33	234.38
4	$210.02	$76.03	$133.98	9,470.35	310.42
5	$210.02	$74.97	$135.04	9,335.30	385.39
6	$210.02	$73.90	$136.11	9,199.19	459.30
7	$210.02	$72.83	$137.19	9,062.00	532.12
8	$210.02	$71.74	$138.28	8,923.72	603.86
9	$210.02	$70.65	$139.37	8,784.35	674.51
10	$210.02	$69.54	$140.48	8,643.87	744.05
11	$210.02	$68.43	$141.59	8,502.28	812.48
12	$210.02	$67.31	$142.71	8,359.57	879.79
13	$210.02	$66.18	$143.84	8,215.74	945.97
14	$210.02	$65.04	$144.98	8,070.76	1,011.01
15	$210.02	$63.89	$146.12	7,924.64	1,074.91
16	$210.02	$62.74	$147.28	7,777.35	1,137.64
17	$210.02	$61.57	$148.45	7,628.91	1,199.22
18	$210.02	$60.40	$149.62	7,479.28	1,259.61
19	$210.02	$59.21	$150.81	7,328.48	1,318.82
20	$210.02	$58.02	$152.00	7,176.48	1,376.84
21	$210.02	$56.81	$153.20	7,023.27	1,433.65
22	$210.02	$55.60	$154.42	6,868.85	1,489.25
23	$210.02	$54.38	$155.64	6,713.21	1,543.63
24	$210.02	$53.15	$156.87	6,556.34	1,596.78
25	$210.02	$51.90	$158.11	6,398.23	1,648.68
26	$210.02	$50.65	$159.37	6,238.86	1,699.34
27	$210.02	$49.39	$160.63	6,078.24	1,748.73

Figure 13.18 A portion of a mortgage payment table using the program's default values.

This mortgage amortization table uses the default data values and prints to **Form2** on the screen. Notice the vertical scroll bar for viewing additional data.

The decision to send output to the printer and/or file is made by the user on the data entry form. The implementation of this decision is done when **Form2** is loaded.

```
Private Sub Form_Load ()
  FontSize = 8
  VScroll1.LargeChange = FontSize * 120
  VScroll1.SmallChange = FontSize * 23

  'write to a file if requested
  If Form1.Check1.Value = 1 Then
    Call CalMortFile
  End If
  'print to printer if requested
```

```
   If Form1.Check2.Value = 1 Then
     Call CalMortPrint
   End If
End Sub
```

When data is to be sent to a sequential (text) file, the file must be opened to receive output from the program by using the **Open()** function. In this case, the data will be sent to a file in the root directory of the C:\ drive named mortgage.dat.

```
Private Sub CalMortFile ()
   Balance = Principal
   TInt=0


   'if requested, send mortgage table to file
   Open "c:\mortgage.dat" For Output As #1
   Print #1, "Borrowed Amount"; Tab(20);
   Print #1, Format$(Principal, "$###,##0.00")
   Print #1, "Interest Rate"; Tab(20);
   Print #1, Format$(Rate, "#0.0#%")
   Print #1, "Payments/Year"; Tab(20); PayYear
   Print #1, "Term (years)"; Tab(20); Term
   Print #1,
   'print column titles to window table
   Print #1, "Period"; Tab(10); "Payment"; Tab(22);
   Print #1, "Interest"; Tab(34); "Amortized"; Tab(46);
   Print #1, "Balance"; Tab(58); "Total Interest"
   Print #1,
   'print table to window
   For I = 1 To Term * PayYear
     Print #1, I;
     Print #1, Tab(10); Format$(Payment, "$###,##0.00");
     Interest = Balance * Rate / 12
     Print #1, Tab(22); Format$(Interest, "$###,##0.00");
     Amortized = Payment - Interest
     Print #1, Tab(34); Format$(Amortized, "$###,##0.00");
     Balance = Balance - Amortized
     Print #1, Tab(46); Format$(Balance, "###,##0.00");
     TInt = TInt + Interest
     Print #1, Tab(58); Format$(TInt, "###,##0.00");
     Print #1,
```

```
  Next I
  Close #1
End Sub
```

Each **Print #** statement in the previous listing uses the identification number (**1**) assigned to the file when it is opened. The balance of the code in the listing is identical to the code for sending information to the window. Before ending this subroutine it is necessary to close the file with a call to **Close #**.

A similar portion of code is used for sending information to the printer if the print option is checked. Information is directed to the printer by using **Printer.Print**.

```
Private Sub CalMortPrint ()
  Balance = Principal
  TInt=0


  'print mortgage table to printer
  Printer.Print "Borrowed Amount"; Tab(20);
  Printer.Print Format$(Principal, "$###,##0.00")
  Printer.Print "Interest Rate"; Tab(20);
  Printer.Print Format$(Rate, "#0.0#%")
  Printer.Print "Payments/Year"; Tab(20); PayYear
  Printer.Print "Term (years)"; Tab(20); Term
  Printer.Print
  'print column titles to window table
  Printer.Print "Period"; Tab(10); "Payment"; Tab(22);
  Printer.Print "Interest"; Tab(34); "Amortized"; Tab(46);
  Printer.Print "Balance"; Tab(58); "Total Interest"
  Printer.Print
  'print table to window
  For I = 1 To Term * PayYear
    Printer.Print I;
    Printer.Print Tab(10); Format$(Payment, "$###,##0.00");
    Interest = Balance * Rate / 12
    Printer.Print Tab(22); Format$(Interest, "$###,##0.00");
    Amortized = Payment - Interest
    Printer.Print Tab(34); Format$(Amortized, "$###,##0.00");
    Balance = Balance - Amortized
    Printer.Print Tab(46); Format$(Balance, "###,##0.00");
    TInt = TInt + Interest
```

```
      Printer.Print Tab(58); Format$(TInt, "###,##0.00");
      Printer.Print
   Next I
   Printer.EndDoc
End Sub
```

In order to clear the print buffer and force the printer to print all of the mortgage table, a call is made to **Printer.EndDoc.**

A Possible Income Tax Deduction

In the last figure you viewed a portion of a mortgage table as it was sent to the window. The next figure will show data as it appears in the file, mortgage.dat.

Imagine that you have borrowed $55,000 to purchase two cars for your business. The interest rate is 10.25 percent and the term of the load is five years. Figure 13.19 is a portion of the sequential file that was generated for this project.

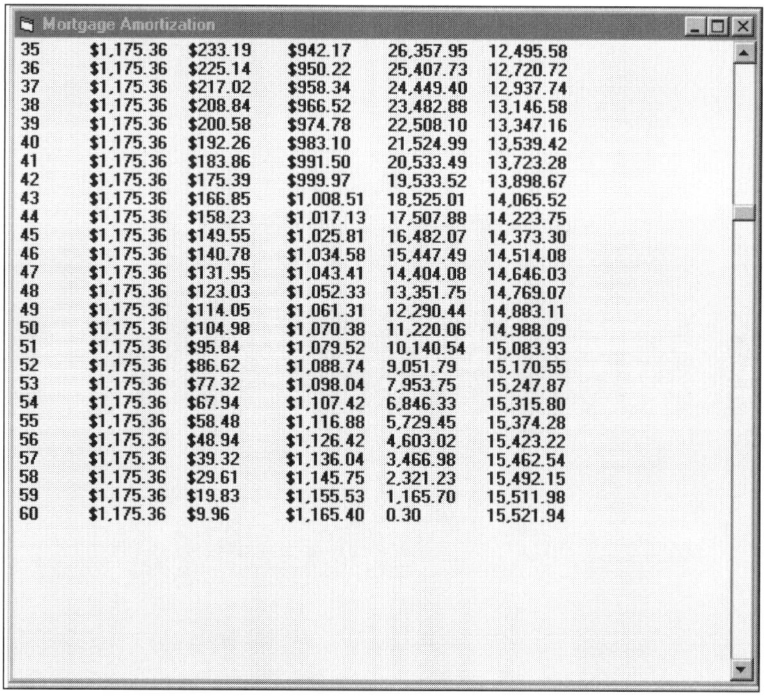

35	$1,175.36	$233.19	$942.17	26,357.95	12,495.58
36	$1,175.36	$225.14	$950.22	25,407.73	12,720.72
37	$1,175.36	$217.02	$958.34	24,449.40	12,937.74
38	$1,175.36	$208.84	$966.52	23,482.88	13,146.58
39	$1,175.36	$200.58	$974.78	22,508.10	13,347.16
40	$1,175.36	$192.26	$983.10	21,524.99	13,539.42
41	$1,175.36	$183.86	$991.50	20,533.49	13,723.28
42	$1,175.36	$175.39	$999.97	19,533.52	13,898.67
43	$1,175.36	$166.85	$1,008.51	18,525.01	14,065.52
44	$1,175.36	$158.23	$1,017.13	17,507.88	14,223.75
45	$1,175.36	$149.55	$1,025.81	16,482.07	14,373.30
46	$1,175.36	$140.78	$1,034.58	15,447.49	14,514.08
47	$1,175.36	$131.95	$1,043.41	14,404.08	14,646.03
48	$1,175.36	$123.03	$1,052.33	13,351.75	14,769.07
49	$1,175.36	$114.05	$1,061.31	12,290.44	14,883.11
50	$1,175.36	$104.98	$1,070.38	11,220.06	14,988.09
51	$1,175.36	$95.84	$1,079.52	10,140.54	15,083.93
52	$1,175.36	$86.62	$1,088.74	9,051.79	15,170.55
53	$1,175.36	$77.32	$1,098.04	7,953.75	15,247.87
54	$1,175.36	$67.94	$1,107.42	6,846.33	15,315.80
55	$1,175.36	$58.48	$1,116.88	5,729.45	15,374.28
56	$1,175.36	$48.94	$1,126.42	4,603.02	15,423.22
57	$1,175.36	$39.32	$1,136.04	3,466.98	15,462.54
58	$1,175.36	$29.61	$1,145.75	2,321.23	15,492.15
59	$1,175.36	$19.83	$1,155.53	1,165.70	15,511.98
60	$1,175.36	$9.96	$1,165.40	0.30	15,521.94

Figure 13.19 A portion of a mortgage table for a car loan.

This project assumes that 12 payments are made each year. If you would like to include the data sharing capabilities of this project with Microsoft Excel via the cut-and-paste options of the clipboard, you'll have to rewrite a portion of the code to send the information to a multiline text box. An example of this technique can be seen in the third project of this chapter, 13Depr3.

WHAT'S COMING?

Many times it is necessary to keep records of various items. This could be as simple as a recipe collection or as complicated as a real estate agent's book of houses. Regardless of the complexity, collections of related items form databases.

In the next chapter you'll learn how to create simple databases and search and retrieve information from them.

Chapter 14

Creating and Accessing Databases

It was the need to work with related columns of data, such as mortgage amortizations and loan information, that led to the development of spreadsheet programs such as Microsoft Excel. Computer users often have the need to store client information in other forms, too. This information can include names, addresses, telephone numbers, social security numbers, pay rates, and hours worked. Information of this type can be stored in a database. Programs such as Access, dBase, and Paradox are commercial products designed for this task. Students taking computer science courses learn how to develop simple database applications in courses dealing with data structures. In this chapter, we'll take a look at several simple database applications designed specifically with Visual Basic 5 in mind. Once you understand how databases work, we'll show you Visual Basic 5 tools that allow access to commercial databases, such as Microsoft Access.

Database programs can very quickly become overwhelmingly complicated, but we've created three projects to aid in your understanding. Our first project involves the ominous "black book" purportedly carried by single adults, containing the phone numbers of numerous dates and associates. This project, like the ad for a $5000 car, contains no frills and has been purposely kept as simple as possible. Sequential file access is used in this example. You'll also learn the advantages and disadvantages of sequential file access when this project is discussed.

The second project builds a personnel database of employee records. Although this application is somewhat similar to the first example, it contains many more data fields. This project is your first Visual Basic 5 exposure to random-access files. Random-access files are the file access of choice for more involved applications. This section will point out advantages and disadvantages of random-access files, while still keeping the application relatively simple.

The third application will highlight a major advantage of Windows 95 and NT—their graphical mode. This database application will keep records and pictures of various vacation packages for a travel agent. Another advantage of random-access files will be illustrated, since this application will contain a hashing function that allows you to search the database for the vacation package of your choice.

Once you study the three database examples, you can use the projects as templates for your own database applications. Haven't you always wanted to organize that photograph or CD-ROM collection?

The fourth application illustrates how to access information in Microsoft's Access database program. In order to run this example, you will need to have Microsoft Access installed on your computer.

A BLACK BOOK

The little black books containing telephone numbers are really simple databases used by all adults in various forms. The difference is that one group calls them black books while other groups call them telephone lists or address books. Regardless of how they are referred to, databases containing names and telephone numbers of clients and friends are very important in our daily lives.

The first project, 14Name1, will create a simple telephone number database using sequential file access. Figure 14.1 shows the form used for data entry.

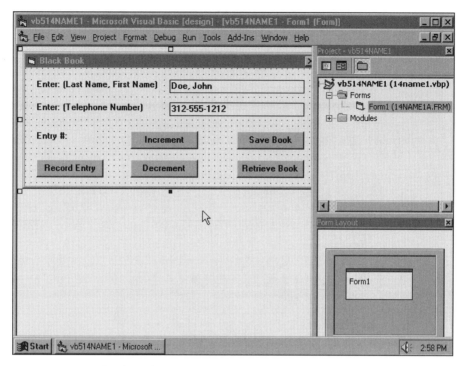

Figure 14.1 The form for a telephone number database.

Examine the data entry form and notice that only two data items can be entered: Name and Telephone Number. Entries are stored in the database by clicking the Record Entry command button. Users can increment up or down the database by clicking or the Increment or Decrement command button. The whole database can be saved to a file, named BlackBk.Dat. Likewise, a file by that name can be retrieved at a later date for additional data entries or deletions.

Sequential File Access

In order to be useful, databases must save information to a file. File information can be saved in a variety of ways, including sequential, random, and binary formats. Sequential files contain information in ASCII or plain text form. This means text and numeric information is stored as a series of ASCII characters. Random-access files contain items in fixed-length records. The records can contain text and numeric information in the specified format (i.e., text and binary formats). Binary files save information as a sequence of binary bits. You will find that sequential and random-access files will be your favorite format when developing database applications.

Sequential file access allows the user to access plain text files in which all information is stored as ASCII character data. Sequential files use **Open**, **Close**, **Line Input#**, **Print#**, and **Input$** statements for opening, accessing, and closing files. As the name implies, all data is stored in a sequential series of character bits. This format makes file access very simple. The general file access technique is to open a file, read/write or append information, and close the file. The file access action starts at the beginning of a file and progresses to the end of the file.

More information on and examples of sequential file access can be found in your Visual Basic 5 manuals, on-screen help, and in most QuickBasic books.

Another related topic that you might want to study when designing databases is error detection. Error detection is necessary to make file I/O reliable and safe.

Developing the Database Code

This database example will require a simple record type, as shown in the global declaration section of program code.

```
Type RecordType
  Name As String * 25
  Tele As String * 25
End Type


Global I As Integer, Total As Integer
Global MyData(50) As RecordType
```

MyData is the static array associated with this record type. Fifty locations are reserved for the list of names and telephone numbers. Since both *Name* and *Tele* hold strings of character information, the program could be easily modified to accommodate any type of information you desire. For example, you might want to add addresses instead of telephone numbers.

Upon loading the form, the array index number, *I*, and the total number of entries, *Total*, are initialized to 0. The index number is displayed on the form each time a new entry is made into the array.

```
Private Sub Form_Load ()
 I = 0
 Total = 0
 Label4.Caption = Str$(I + 1)
End Sub
```

Information is placed in the database by clicking on **Command1** (Record Entry). As you can see from the following code, the name information from **Text1** is stored at the current index position, *I*, in the *MyData* array. Likewise, the telephone number in **Text2** is stored in the next immediate location. Both entry fields (**Text1** and **Text2**) are then cleared in preparation for the next name and telephone entry. The total number of entries (*Total*) and the index (*I*) are incremented. The index position reported to the user is one higher than the actual array position, since the array is indexed from 0. No one wants to be a zero!

```
Private Sub Command1_Click ()
 'get information into present record
 MyData(I).Name = Text1.Text
 MyData(I).Tele = Text2.Text
 Text1.Text = ""
 Text2.Text = ""
 I = I + 1
 Total = Total + 1
 Label4.Caption = Str$(I + 1)
End Sub
```

During data entry, the user can increment through all names and telephone numbers by clicking on **Command2** (Increment). Incrementing through the database is possible until the next index number (*I* + 1) is greater than the total number of entries.

```
Private Sub Command2_Click ()
 'increment through record entries
 If I + 1 > Total Then Exit Sub
 I = I + 1
 Text1.Text = MyData(I).Name
 Text2.Text = MyData(I).Tele
 Label4.Caption = Str$(I + 1)
End Sub
```

A user can also decrement through the names and telephone numbers by clicking on **Command4** (Decrement). Decrementing through the database is possible until the next index number ($I - 1$) is less than the first database entry (location 0).

```
Private Sub Command4_Click ()
 'decrement through record entries
 If I - 1 < 0 Then Exit Sub
 I = I - 1
 Text1.Text = MyData(I).Name
 Text2.Text = MyData(I).Tele
 Label4.Caption = Str$(I + 1)
End Sub
```

Up to this point, all information is being held in volatile random-access memory (RAM). It is called volatile because if you turn your computer off or if a power failure occurs, the information in memory will be lost. This type of accident can be prevented by simply saving the entire database to a file. In order to keep this example as simple as possible, the file's path, name, and extension are entered at design time by the programmer. You may opt to use a Visual Basic 5 **InputBox** to request this information from the user. The second project in this chapter will illustrate how this is done.

The **Open** statement is used to open and/or create a sequential file named BlackBk.Dat in the root directory of drive C. Since information is sent to this file, the file mode is **Output**. Because Visual Basic 5 allows multiple files to be opened, a file identification number is used for future references (**#1**). If you examine the syntax for the **Open** statement, in your Visual Basic 5 manual or online documentation, you'll learn that no other parameters are required to open a file for sequential file access.

The **Print** # statement is used to print the ASCII character information to the file, one entry at a time. A **For** loop is used to index from the first entry to the total number of entries in the current database. When all information has been entered, the file is closed with a **Close** statement.

```
Private Sub Command3_Click ()
 'open sequential file for output
 Open "C:\BlackBk.Dat" For Output As #1
```

```
'send information to file
For I = 0 To Total
  Print #1, MyData(I).Name
  Print #1, MyData(I).Tele
Next I
Close #1
End Sub
```

Once the data is saved to a file, it is safe. If you turn your computer off or if a power failure occurs, this information will still reside on drive C. The entire database can then be retrieved back into this Visual Basic 5 application ready for your use. Once the program is running, simply click on **Command5** (Retrieve Data Bank). The program is instructed to look for a file by the name, BlackBk.Dat, and to read its data into the array.

```
Private Sub Command5_Click ()
  'open sequential file as input source
  Open "C:\BlackBk.Dat" For Input As #1

  'read information from file
  I = 0: Total = 0
  Do While Not EOF(1)
    Line Input #1, MyData(I).Name
    Line Input #1, MyData(I).Tele
    I = I + 1
    Total = Total + 1
  Loop
  I = 0: Total = Total - 1
  Close #1
End Sub
```

Notice, in the previous listing, that the file is now opened as an input file, since it will supply information to the project. The index, *I*, and number of entries, *Total*, are initialized to zero and file input is read until the end-of-file (EOF) is encountered for file #1. The **Line Input** is used for sequential files and permits information to be read from a file until a carriage return is encountered. This delimiter divides the data string into separate elements for array storage. Finally, the file is closed after all the data has been read.

In sequential mode, if a new set of names and numbers is saved to the file, the previous contents are overwritten and destroyed. The replacement file, by default, will contain only elements from the new list.

Creating a List of Names and Numbers

The database we created for this example contains a list of 10 names and telephone numbers. Figure 14.2 shows the fifth entry in this database.

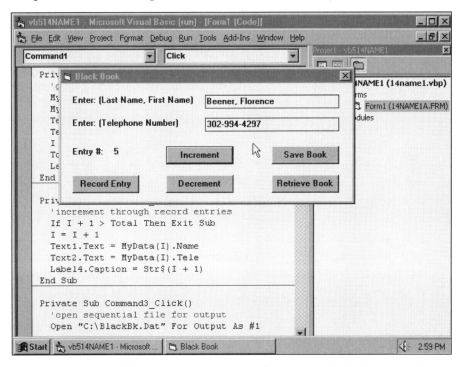

Figure 14.2 The fifth entry in a database of names and telephone numbers.

This database serves as a great start for understanding more complicated projects. It also works well for the job it was intended to perform. However, this database project is limited by design. Maybe you can anticipate some of the shortcomings? First, it would be helpful to store information in a file that we could name at run time. That way, multiple input and output files could be used. Second, this project provides no means of searching for a particular telephone number or name. If the database had 1000 entries, and if those entries had not been sorted, it would take quite a bit of time to locate a specific name or number. And speaking of sorting, it might be a nice feature to sort the database by names or area codes. It might be required of a user to store actual numeric data (as opposed to ASCII characters used to represent numbers in sequential access files). This might be required for a person's salary, number of hours worked, and so on. Sequential file access will not work well for us here.

Even though this is a simple and useful example, those questions were intended to prepare you for what is coming in the next two projects.

A COMPANY'S DATABASE

In the last project you learned how to create a simple database for saving character information to a sequential file. That project has two shortcomings that we want to overcome in this example. First, only text information can be saved. If integer data is to be saved, for example, it will have to be converted back and forth between character strings and integers. The second problem, with the first project, is that you couldn't specify the file in which to save or retrieve the data at run time.

In the project developed in this section, 14Pers2, a more complete database will be created using random-access files. For this example, imagine that a company wishes to develop a personnel file with a record for each employee. We created a data entry form, shown in Figure 14.3, for this company. Notice that the command buttons appear as they did in the last example. In this database the number of items entered (fields) in the database has increased.

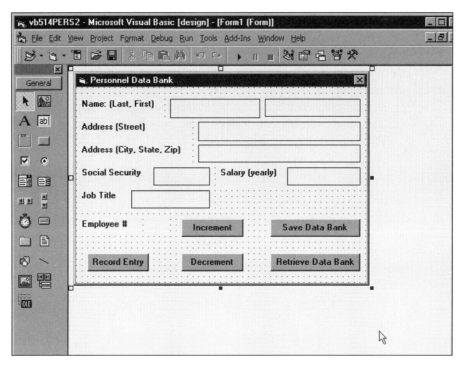

Figure 14.3 The data entry form for another database.

By using random-access files our project can mix various forms of data, such as text and numbers. For example, name and address information will still be saved as character string information but the salary value will be saved as a currency value (**Currency**) and the array index value (*I*) as a number (**Integer**).

Random-Access File Advantages

In the last example, you learned that to be effective, databases must save record information to files. The first project in this chapter used sequential file access because both data fields contained ASCII character strings and because we wanted to keep the application as simple as possible. For increased efficiency, especially where the record fields can contain character and numeric values, random-access files are the best choice.

Random-access files allow the user to access both plain text and binary information. Statements such as **Open**, **Close**, **Put**, **Get**, and **Len** are used for opening, accessing, and closing random-access files.

The **Get** and **Put** allow an optional record number to be specified in their command syntax. This makes random-access files ideal for situations in which insertion, deletion, sorting, and hashing must be done within the database. Our third database example will make use of some of these special features.

If you have not worked with random-access files before, be sure to see your Visual Basic 5 manuals, online documentation, or any QuickBasic book for additional information.

Developing the Personnel Database Code

The global declarations section for this project contains a data type for the new database. The *DataBank* declaration contains locations for a record number (*RecordNum* As **Integer**), last name (*LName* As **String**), first name (*FName* As **String**), street address (*Add1* As **String**), city and state (*Add2* As **String**), social security number (*SS* as **String**), salary (*Salary* As **Currency**), and job title (*Title* As **String**).

```
Type DataBank
  RecordNum As Integer
  LName As String * 50
  FName As String * 50
  Add1 As String * 50
  Add2 As String * 50
  SS As String * 15
  Salary As Currency
  Title As String * 30
End Type


Global MyFile As String
Global I As Integer, Total As Integer
Global PerData(50) As DataBank
```

Also notice in the previous listing that the *MyFile* variable will be used to hold the location, file name, and extension of the database file created by the user. *PerData* is an array, of type *DataBank*, that sets aside room for information on 50 employees.

```
Private Sub Form_Load ()
  I = 0
  Total = 0
  Label8.Caption = Str$(I + 1)
End Sub
```

The array index, *I*, and total number of entries, *Total*, are set to 0 when the form is loaded. The array index ranges from 0 to *Total*, and the employee number reported to the screen ranges from 1 to *Total* + 1.

Notice in the next listing that data is processed as long as the **Text1** field is not empty. If **Text1** contains data, a click of **Command1** (Record Entry) sends the data to the various array elements. As in the last project, once the data is placed in the array, the various text fields are cleared with a **null** string ("").

```
Private Sub Command1_Click ()
  'get information into present record
  If Text1.Text = "" Then Exit Sub
  PerData(I).RecordNum = I + 1
  PerData(I).LName = Text1.Text
  PerData(I).FName = Text2.Text
  PerData(I).Add1 = Text3.Text
  PerData(I).Add2 = Text4.Text
  PerData(I).SS = Text5.Text
  PerData(I).Salary = Val(Text6.Text)
  PerData(I).Title = Text7.Text

  'prepare for next set of values
  I = I + 1: Total = Total + 1
  Label8.Caption = Str$(I + 1)
  Text1.Text = ""
  Text2.Text = ""
  Text3.Text = ""
  Text4.Text = ""
  Text5.Text = ""
  Text6.Text = ""
  Text7.Text = ""
End Sub
```

The user can increment through the various records in the database with a click of **Command2** (Increment). From the current index position, contained in *I*, each click of the command button will bring the next higher database record into view on the form.

```
Private Sub Command2_Click ()
 'increment through present record entries
 If I + 1 > Total Then Exit Sub
 I = I + 1
 Label8.Caption = Str$(PerData(I).RecordNum)
 Text1.Text = PerData(I).LName
 Text2.Text = PerData(I).FName
 Text3.Text = PerData(I).Add1
 Text4.Text = PerData(I).Add2
 Text5.Text = PerData(I).SS
 Text6.Text = Str$(PerData(I).Salary)
 Text7.Text = PerData(I).Title
End Sub
```

Decrementing through the database is also straightforward. Decrementing starts at the current index position, *I*, and proceeds downward to 0.

```
Private Sub Command3_Click ()
 'decrement through record entries
 If I - 1 < 0 Then Exit Sub
 I = I - 1
 Label8.Caption = Str$(PerData(I).RecordNum)
 Text1.Text = PerData(I).LName
 Text2.Text = PerData(I).FName
 Text3.Text = PerData(I).Add1
 Text4.Text = PerData(I).Add2
 Text5.Text = PerData(I).SS
 Text6.Text = Str$(PerData(I).Salary)
 Text7.Text = PerData(I).Title
End Sub
```

When data entry is completed, the database will still be contained in the array, *PerData*, in random-access memory (RAM). To be a useful database this information must be saved to a file. An **InputBox**

prompts the user for a path, file name, and extension when
Command4 (Save Data Bank) is clicked.

The **Open** statement is used to open or create the file specified as a
string in *MyFile*. If the user opts for the default file name and extension, information will be saved to PerData.Dat in the root directory of
the C drive. Make note of the syntax for the **Open** statement. Random
file access requires a **Len** value, which is determined, in this case, by
finding the length of the first record. All database entries in a random-
access file are the same length. With random-access files, it is possible
to address individual record elements. For example, a file could be created of just the salary values from the array. In this example, however,
all of the elements of each record are saved to the file.

```
Private Sub Command4_Click ()
 'open random access file to store data
 Msg$ = "Enter the path and file name for this session."
 MyFile = InputBox$(Msg$, "Write Data", "C:\PerData.Dat")
 Open MyFile For Random Access Write As #1 Len = Len(PerData(0))

 'send information to file
 For I = 0 To Total
  Put #1, , PerData(I).RecordNum
  Put #1, , PerData(I).LName
  Put #1, , PerData(I).FName
  Put #1, , PerData(I).Add1
  Put #1, , PerData(I).Add2
  Put #1, , PerData(I).SS
  Put #1, , PerData(I).Salary
  Put #1, , PerData(I).Title
 Next I
 Close
End Sub
```

As you examine the previous listing, notice that a **Put #1** statement
is used. The missing parameter between the two commas is an
optional record number. In Visual Basic 5, if that value is missing, the
data specified is written to the next record or byte occurring after the
last **Put** statement. As you examine the various **Put** statements, recall
that *RecordNum* is an integer and *Salary* is a currency type.

Data is retrieved by reading the file with a series of **Get** statements. The program reads the file until the end-of-file (EOF) is located. The syntax for the **Get** statement is similar to that for the **Put** statement.

```
Private Sub Command5_Click ()
 'open random access file and retrieve information
 Msg$ = "Enter the path and file name for this session."
 MyFile = InputBox$(Msg$, "Read Data", "C:\PerData.Dat")
 Open MyFile For Random Access Read As #1 Len = Len(PerData(0))

 'read information from file
 I = 0: Total = 0
 Do While Not EOF(1)
  Get #1, , PerData(I).RecordNum
  Get #1, , PerData(I).LName
  Get #1, , PerData(I).FName
  Get #1, , PerData(I).Add1
  Get #1, , PerData(I).Add2
  Get #1, , PerData(I).SS
  Get #1, , PerData(I).Salary
  Get #1, , PerData(I).Title
  I = I + 1
  Total = Total + 1
 Loop
 I = 0: Total = Total - 1
 Close
End Sub
```

The advantages of random-access files will be more apparent if additional calculations are done on the numeric data they contain. For example, if a database is created with an hourly pay rate and the number of hours worked, it will be possible to generate a weekly paycheck. Taxes and other deductions can also be calculated and stored in this manner. There are other advantages to random-access files, which we'll point out in the next project.

Database Entries for a Small Company

Figures 14.4 and 14.5 show several personnel entries from a small company's database.

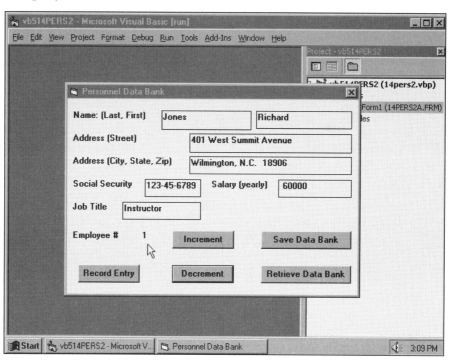

Figure 14.4 An initial entry in an employee database.

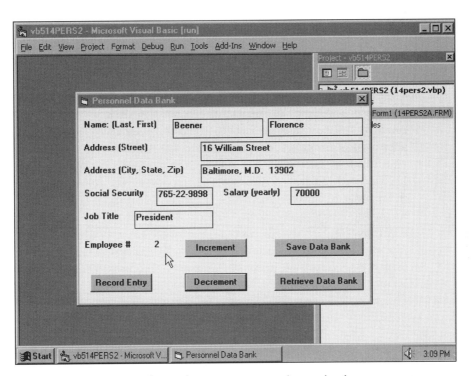

Figure 14.5 A second sample entry in an employee database.

The use of random-access files allows entries to be stored as text or binary data. In this example all data is stored as a sequence of ASCII characters except the Employee #, which is an integer, and Salary, which is a **Currency** type. In this project, unlike our telephone directory project, employee ID numbers are saved as part of each employee's record.

Take the time to experiment with this database example. Convert the yearly salary field to an hourly pay rate (make it a single-precision field). Add an additional field that will specify the hours worked in a given week (another single-precision field). Now add one final field, "Weekly Earnings" (before taxes). To generate the amount for this field, multiply the hourly rate by the number of hours worked. For real fun, determine how overtime can be calculated at time and a half for over 40 hours.

A Travel Agency Reservation System

For large databases, it is not always possible to read an entire database into memory. This can be due to the size of each entry or the overall quantity of information stored on disk. Under these circumstances it is better to leave the entire database on the disk, physically accessing only the information needed to answer a particular question. Random-access files are specifically set up to meet this need.

A random-access record has two very specific characteristics. First, it is a fixed-length record. This is necessary so that as you insert and delete records throughout the file each entry will fit between all surrounding entries. The second characteristic involves a search key. This is a data field that will be used to locate a particular record. The following listing shows the modest modifications needed to update the global declarations of our last example, named 14Real3.

```
Type ReservationType
  InUse As Integer
  ReservationNum As Integer
  LName As String * 20
  FName As String * 20
  Add1 As String * 20
  Add2 As String * 20
  Phone As String * 12
  Cost As Currency
  Agent As String * 15
  VacationPict As String * 17
  Package As String * 280
End Type


Global ARecord As ReservationType
Global Const MaxRes = 100
Global Const MaxPackNum = 2000
```

The *InUse* variable keeps track of which of the records has been used. *VacationPict* holds the path and file name for the vacation package's screen image and *Package* holds the verbal description of the package. *ARecord* will be used to access disk information efficiently by allowing its global structure to pass information throughout the application.

The reservation number, *ReservationNum*, will be used to locate each vacation package. The entire file has room enough for 100 reservations (*MaxRes*), with each vacation package having a valid number in the range 1001 to 2000.

The global declarations no longer contain an array-of-records. This is because all of the information for the database will be stored directly on the disk. Instead of using an index into an array-of-records to store and retrieve data, the application will use a physical disk record address.

Figure 14.6 shows the data entry form for our third database example.

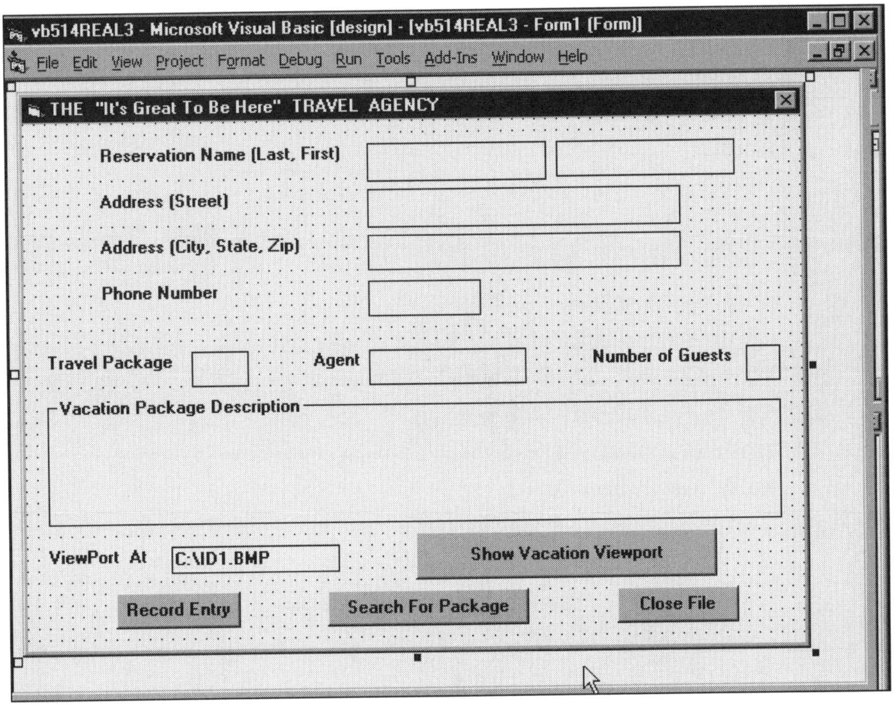

Figure 14.6 The form used for the third database project.

The program stores and retrieves all the information necessary to keep track of individual vacation plans, including a person's name, address, phone, travel package number, travel agent's name, number of guests, description of the vacation, and the location of a screen image related to the particular travel package.

Coding Considerations

The project begins by invoking the **Form_Load** event procedure. In order to concentrate on those features specific to random-access files, all of the code has been streamlined. The **Open** procedure is hard-wired to the file C:\VACLST.DAT for this reason. See the second example, again, for techniques that will allow the user to enter a unique file name. Also, notice how the **Len** function has been invoked on *ARecord* to tell the application how long each record is. The **Open** function will automatically open an existing file or create a new one if necessary.

```
Private Sub Form_Load ()
 Open "C:\VACLST.DAT" For Random As #1 Len = Len(ARecord)
End Sub
```

Very few modifications were made to the **Command1_Click** event used in the previous project. Most of the changes merely involve the new data fields associated with the new record structure, shown next:

```
Private Sub Command1_Click ()
 'get information into present record
 If Text1.Text = "" Then Exit Sub
 If Text10.Text = "" Then Exit Sub
 ARecord.ReservationNum = Hash(Val(Text10.Text))
 ARecord.InUse = -1
 ARecord.LName = Text1.Text
 ARecord.FName = Text2.Text
 ARecord.Add1 = Text3.Text
 ARecord.Add2 = Text4.Text
 ARecord.Phone = Text5.Text
 ARecord.Cost = Val(Text6.Text)
 ARecord.Agent = Text7.Text
 ARecord.VacationPict = Text8.Text
 ARecord.Package = Text9.Text
 Put #1, ARecord.ReservationNum, ARecord
```

```
Text1.Text = ""
Text2.Text = ""
Text3.Text = ""
Text4.Text = ""
Text5.Text = ""
Text6.Text = ""
Text7.Text = ""
Text8.Text = "C:\ID1.BMP"
Text9.Text = ""
Text10.Text = ""
End Sub
```

Text10.Text is reserved for the vacation package number that is entered by the user. Since this is the search key used to locate the physical record, it is critical that the user has entered this information. Pressing the **Record Entry** command with a missing search key aborts the subroutine. See Figure 14.7 for a sample reservation request.

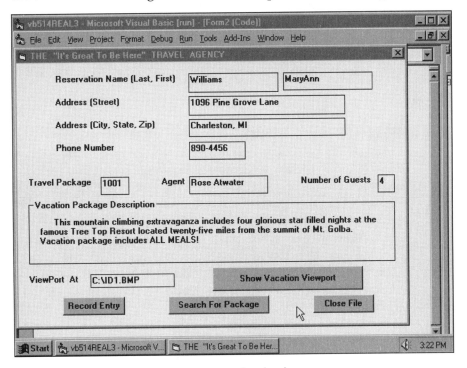

Figure 14.7 Entering a reservation in the database.

The program invokes a simple hash algorithm to map the package number down to a physical disk record address, assuming the user has entered a valid vacation package number.

```
Function Hash (PackNum As Integer) As Integer
 Dim TempIndex As Integer, OriginalIndex As Integer
 Dim Value As Integer, Found As Integer
 If PackNum = MaxPackNum Then
  TempIndex = MaxRes
 Else
  TempIndex = PackNum Mod MaxRes
 End If
 Get #1, TempIndex, ARecord
 If ARecord.InUse = -1 Then
  OriginalIndex = TempIndex
  While Not Found
   Value = Value + 1
   TempIndex = OriginalIndex + Value * Value
   Get #1, TempIndex, ARecord
   If ARecord.InUse <> -1 Then Found = -1
  Wend
 End If
 Hash = TempIndex
End Function
```

A problem has surfaced. How do you map a value from between 1001 and 2000 down to an index between 1 and 100 (*MaxRes*)? One approach would be to look at only the last two digits of the vacation package. For example, 1001 would map to disk record 1, 1099 would map to record number 99.

A simple way to accomplish this mapping would be to divide the package number 100 and use the remainder as the record index. Therefore 1001 **Mod** 100 yields 1, and 1099 **Mod** 100 yields an index of 99. This approach, however, can lead to a problem when the last two digits of vacation packages match (for example, 1234 and 1334). Here both packages would map to the same index of 34.

A better approach is to use a hash function to resolve these differences. The **Hash()** function uses the last two digits of a vacation package's number, because these digits vary most frequently as the numbers sequence through the valid range of package numbers

(1001–2000). If there is a collision, as with 1234 and 1334, the algorithm goes into a simple quadratic rehash algorithm to solve the conflict.

The Hash() function begins by taking care of that unique situation in which the vacation package number equals the *MaxPackNum*. The maximum valid package number allowed is 2000. When this is divided by 100 (*MaxRes*) a 0 value is returned. This incorrect hash value is modified to reflect the true location of the vacation package.

Most of the time the algorithm will calculate a hash index and do an initial **Get** from the file. The **Get** statement uses the file number, **#1**, and the calculated index, *TempIndex*, to fill *ARecord* with the disk record's current contents. The *InUse* field of the record will be a -1 only if the record has previously stored data.

If the record already has data in it, the **Hash()** function must locate the next closest empty record. It does this by incrementing and successively squaring a **Value** to add to the *OriginalIndex*. To optimize the search a Found flag is set to True (-1) as soon as an empty record is found.

Take, for example, the following four vacation package numbers: 1234, 1334, 1434, and 1534. Our algorithm at this point would have computed a *TempIndex* of 34 for all four. The quadratic rehash code resolves the conflict by assigning the four index values presented in Table 14.1.

Table 14.1 Using a Quadratic Rehash Code

Vacation Package Number	OriginalIndex	Quadratic Resolution
1234	34	
1334	34	34 + (1 * 1) = 35
1434	34	34 + (2 * 2) = 38
1534	34	34 + (3 * 3) = 43

The **Hash()** function terminates by returning a valid record index to **Command1_Click**.

At this point **Command1_Click** picks up by marking the current record used (*ARecord.InUse = -1*), assigns each record field the appropriate data, and then writes the information to the file with the **Put** statement. Notice that this statement needs to know the file, **#1**; which random-access record to access, *ARecord.ReservationNum*; and the record whose contents will be copied to disk, *ARecord*. **Command1_Click** finishes by cleaning up **Form1**'s interface and getting it ready for the next entry.

Searching for an existing vacation package is no more difficult than inserting one, with only a few exceptions. The process begins by asking the user for the package to search for; this is accomplished with **Command2_Click**. The subroutine aborts if the user has not entered the necessary search criterion, namely the *LName* (**Text1.Text**) and *Travel Package* (**Text10.Text**) number:

```
Private Sub Command2_Click ()
 'find information for present record
 Dim ReStorePackNum As String
 If Text1.Text = "" Then Exit Sub
 If Text10.Text = "" Then Exit Sub
 ReStorePackNum = Text10.Text
 ARecord.ReservationNum = HashFind(Val(Text10.Text))
 Text1.Text = ARecord.LName
 Text2.Text = ARecord.FName
 Text3.Text = ARecord.Add1
 Text4.Text = ARecord.Add2
 Text5.Text = ARecord.Phone
 Text6.Text = Str$(ARecord.Cost)
 Text7.Text = ARecord.Agent
 Text8.Text = ARecord.VacationPict
 Text9.Text = ARecord.Package
 Text10.Text = ReStorePackNum
End Sub
```

The *ReStorePackNum* variable is needed to print the current vacation package number in **Text10.Text**, since it is wiped out by **Text1**'s **Change** event procedure:

```
Private Sub Text1_Change ()
 Text2.Text = ""
 Text3.Text = ""
 Text4.Text = ""
 Text5.Text = ""
```

```
Text6.Text = ""
Text7.Text = ""
Text8.Text = "C:\ID1.BMP"
Text9.Text = ""
Text10.Text = ""
End Sub
```

The **Change** event is used to erase a previous client's reservation information when entering a new client's information. However, it works to our disadvantage here, because the minute the valid record is located and displayed, the **Change** event is invoked, wiping out **Text10.Text**. Notice that each vacation package is assigned a default screen image, C:\ID1.BMP, until the user changes it.

The function **HashFind()** modifies the **Hash()** function strictly for the purpose of locating existing reservations. The minor changes have been highlighted:

```
Function HashFind (PackNum As Integer) As Integer
 Dim TempIndex As Integer, OriginalIndex As Integer
 Dim Value As Integer, Found As Integer
 Dim PaddedLName As String * 20
 PaddedLName = Text1.Text
 If PackNum = MaxPackNum Then
  TempIndex = MaxRes
 Else
  TempIndex = PackNum Mod MaxRes
 End If
 Get #1, TempIndex, ARecord
 If ARecord.LName <> PaddedLName Then
  OriginalIndex = TempIndex
  While Not Found
   Value = Value + 1
   TempIndex = OriginalIndex + Value * Value
   Get #1, TempIndex, ARecord
   If ARecord.LName = PaddedLName Then Found = -1
  Wend
 End If
 HashFind = TempIndex
End Function
```

PaddedLName is necessary for the *LName* comparison. Since *ARecord* has defined *LName* as a fixed-length string of 20 characters, that is the way they are stored on the disk. So, for example, the name

```
"Williams"
```

is really stored as

```
"Williams          "
```

To complicate matters, if the user enters "Williams" into **Text1.Text**, the field is stored *without* padding. The string comparison part of the **HashFind()** function would not see

```
"Williams"
```

as being equal to

```
"Williams          "
```

By assigning **Text1.Text** to a fixed-length string, *PaddedLName*, the stored string will match the user's entry.

Once the valid record has been found and read into *ARecord*, **Command2_Click** can take care of assigning the information to **Form1**. Figure 14.8 is an example of what you should be seeing on your screen.

Figure 14.8 A sample vacation viewport.

The travel agency program gets its visual appeal from **Form2**, which displays the selected travel package's screen image whenever the user selects the Show Vacation Viewport option **Command4**, as seen previously in Figure 14.8.

```
Private Sub Command4_Click ()
 Form2.Picture = LoadPicture(ARecord.VacationPict)
 Form2.WindowState = 2 'Maximized
 Form2.Show
End Sub
```

The algorithm assigns the current record's vacation picture, *VacationPict*, to **Form2**'s **Picture** property, sets the **WindowState** to full-view, and then displays the image. **Form2** has a return option, **Hide**, that hides the form from view. The form could have been unloaded, **UnLoad**, if the application were memory intensive:

```
Private Sub Command1_Click ()
 Form2.Hide
```

```
End Sub
```

The travel agency program terminates with a **Close** command, **Command3**, which closes the random-access file and **Ends** the program:

```
Private Sub Command3_Click ()
 Close #1
 End
End Sub
```

To try our example database, use any of the entries presented in Table 14.2.

Table 14.2 Database Examples

Last Name	Package Number
Ivan	1001
Sneakers	1002
Tango	1003
Shadow	1004
Beener	1005

Type the last name, exactly as shown, and enter the vacation package number. Then request that the database find the record. If your database file and bitmaps reside on the root C:\ directory, you should see one of five bitmapped images.

If you have access to a scanner, you can develop your own vacation packages from photographs you have taken. If not, use our images and experiment with the power of random-access records.

ACCESSING A COMMERCIAL DATABASE

Accessing information in a commercial database application, such as those created by Microsoft Access, is a snap. This is especially true if you create your Visual Basic 5 project with the Visual Basic Application Wizard.

In this section, we will create a Visual Basic 5 project that will access a sample database, Northwind.mdb, included with the Microsoft Access product. You will need to have both Microsoft Access and the sample database installed on your computer. The location of the database on our computer is found at:

c:\msoffice\Office\Samples\Northwind.mdb

This sample database contains a large amount of information about the Northwind Company. Our Visual Basic 5 project will be designed to access just the employee information from the Northwind database.

Figure 14.9 shows the complete employee list, for Northwind, while in Access.

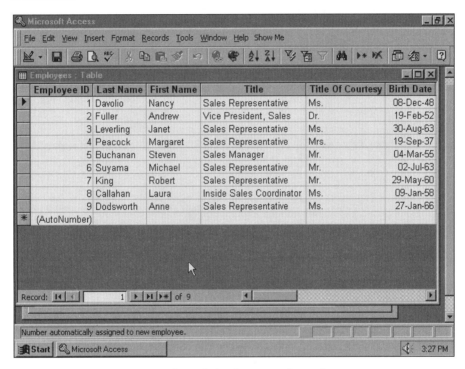

Figure 14.9 Access's Northwind database employee list.

Figure 14.10 shows the details on one of Northwind's employees from the employee list.

Figure 14.10 Details on one of Northwind's employees.

You will be able to use the Visual Basic 5 Application Wizard during design time to access other types of databases. The best news is that you really don't have to understand too much about databases to build powerful Visual Basic 5 projects.

Project Design

Let's walk through the design phase of our Visual Basic 5 project, step by step. The project will be named DataAccess1.

1. Start Visual Basic 5, and request the Application Wizard to aid you in building the project.

2. Answer the Application Wizard questions, as follows:

    *   Select a Single Document Interface, as shown in Figure 14.11. Clear all menu options, as shown in Figure 14.12.

    *   This project will not need a resource file for strings, as shown in Figure 14.13.

    *   This project will not need to access the Internet, as shown in Figure 14.14.

    *   No standard forms will be required with the project, as shown in Figure 14.15.

    *   Select the database options as shown in Figure 14.16.

    *   Select the Employee table by clicking the right-direction button as shown in Figure 14.17.

    *   Name the Visual Basic project, as shown in Figure 14.18.

    *   Click on Finish to complete the Application Wizard design process.

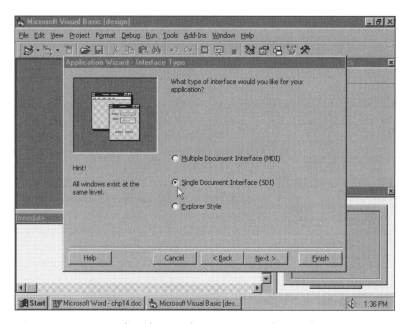

Figure 14.11 Select the Application Wizard's Single Document Interface option.

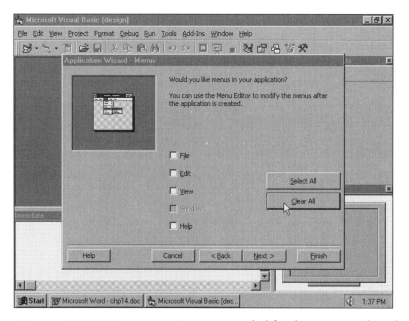

Figure 14.12 No menu options are needed for this project. Clear the menu options.

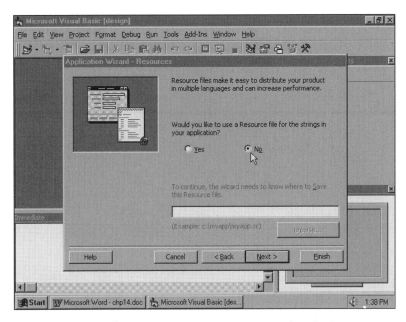

Figure 14.13 There are no resource strings. Select the No option.

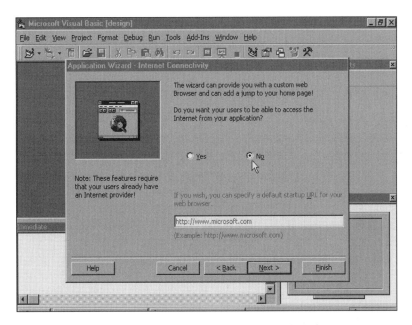

Figure 14.14 No Internet access is needed. Select the No option.

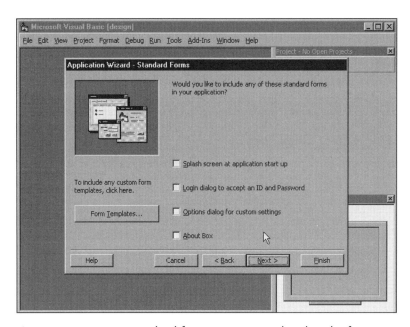

Figure 14.15 No standard forms are required. Select the features as shown.

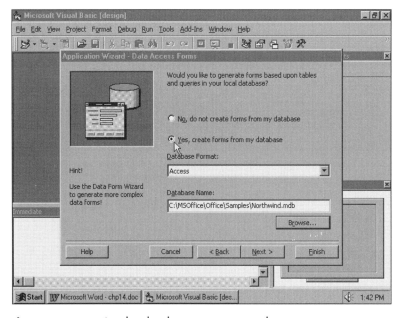

Figure 14.16 Set the database options, as shown.

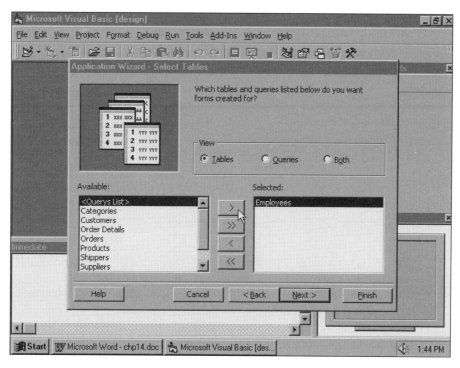

Figure 14.17 This project will access employee information. Set your options as shown.

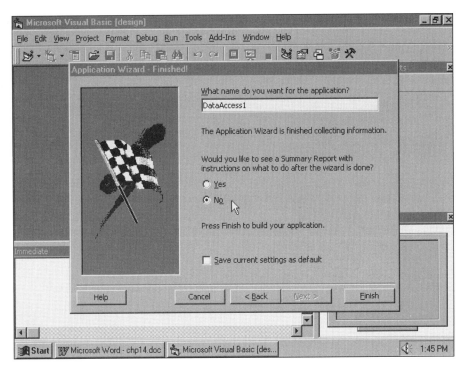

Figure 14.18 Name your project DataAccess1.

Almost by magic, the complete Visual Basic form and code will be generated before your eyes. Figure 14.19 shows the data access form for this Visual Basic project.

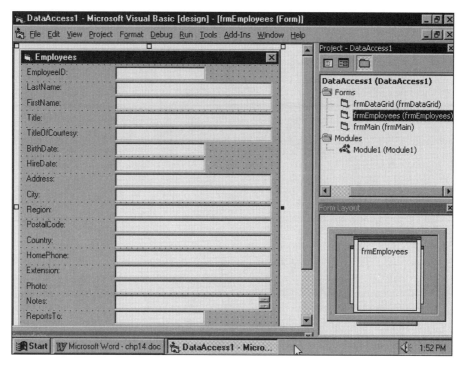

Figure 14.19 The Visual Basic Application Wizard's data access form.

When you choose to run the Visual Basic 5 project, you will see an initial screen similar to Figure 14.20.

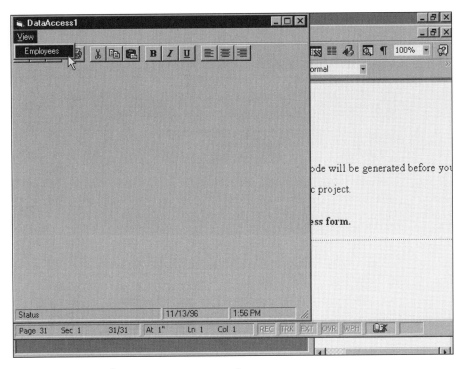

Figure 14.20 The DataAccess1's initial screen.

The database will be accessed by selecting Employees from the menu list, as shown in the previous figure.

Figure 14.21 shows the details for one employee in the database.

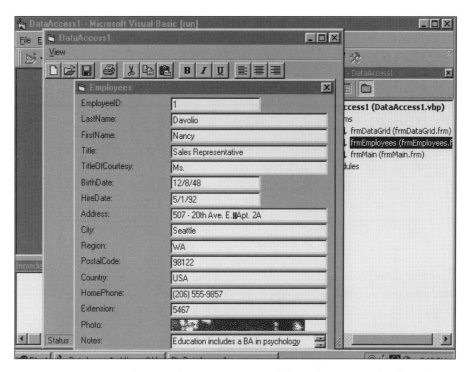

Figure 14.21 Employee information retrieved from the Access database by our Visual Basic 5 project.

As an exercise, why not use the Visual Basic Application Wizard to create another project that will allow you to access a different table of information in the Northwind Company?

WHAT'S COMING?

In the next chapter you will learn how to plot data on pie, bar, and line charts. These projects will give your data the look of a professional presentation and can serve as the gateway to a complete data graphing package.

Chapter 15

Line, Bar, and Pie Charts

Charts and graphs are used to represent data visually for presentations and reports. In this chapter you will learn how to create professional quality line, bar, and pie charts. Each project is complete and ready to use. As you study the code in this chapter, perhaps you can think of some additional customizing touches for each project.

In Chapter 11 you learned simple techniques for creating a bar chart. The programming was easy and straightforward—and the resulting bar chart had several limitations. In the past several chapters new Visual Basic 5 topics, such as saving bitmap files and copying and pasting to the clipboard, have been presented. Many of these new ideas will be used in the projects of this chapter. In addition, you will learn how to evaluate and scale data, label axes, print titles, create legends, draw pie wedges, and so forth.

Once you have mastered the charting concepts in this chapter, you will be ready to use powerful ActiveX controls. ActiveX controls, discussed in Chapter 17, allow you to perform charting with only a minimal amount of program code. With Visual Basic 5 at your command, it is an exciting time to be a 32-bit Windows programmer!

A LINE CHART

A line chart will serve as our first charting project. When a project, such as 15LCht1, is initiated, many decisions have to be made about its function and purpose. In contemplating the design for the line chart project we decided on the following specifications. The line chart project will:

- allow the user to enter chart labels.
- allow the user to enter coordinate (x, y) values for several data points.

Once all the values have been entered, the project will:

- divide each axis with several tic marks.
- draw a line between subsequent data points entered by the user.
- draw a symbol (+) at the location of each data point.
- draw and x and y axes on a form.
- draw the chart labels using Windows 95 and NT Graphics Device Interface (GDI) function calls.
- print the Max and Min values for each axis.
- scale the data points to the chart size.

Figure 15.1 shows the data entry form for this project.

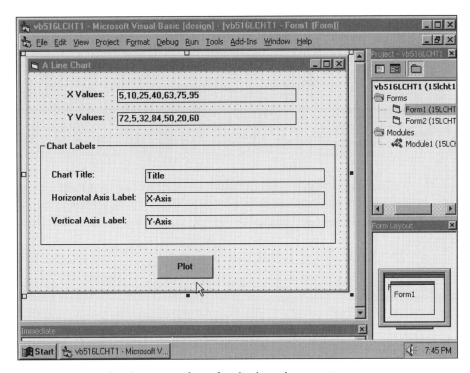

Figure 15.1 The data entry form for the line chart project.

Each data point has an X and a corresponding Y coordinate point. They must be entered in pairs. Chart labels are optional, but this project provides three default values: Title, X Axis, and Y Axis. The chart can be drawn by clicking on the command button, **Plot**.

Developing the Line Chart Code

The project coding starts with the identification of the global variables in the MODULE1 file named 15LCHT1.BAS. Global variables will be shared between the various forms and procedures.

```
DefInt A-Z
Global I, J, TNums, SPos, FPos, NLen
Global NArray(50, 50) As Single
Global ScaledNArray(50, 50) As Single
Global PtXMax As Single, PtYMax As Single
Global X1 As Single, Y1 As Single
```

```
Global X2 As Single, Y2 As Single
Declare Function TextOut Lib "gdi32" Alias "TextOutA"
    (ByVal hDC As Long, ByVal X, ByVal Y,
    ByVal sP As String, ByVal N) As Long
```

 Note: Remember that the declaration for the **TextOut***() function, shown in the previous listing, must be entered on one program line.*

Programming for this project take place in two forms, **Form1** and **Form2**. **Form1** is the data entry and data scaling form, while the chart is calculated and drawn on **Form2**.

The Line Chart Data Entry Form The chart is created when the command button is pushed on the data entry form (**Form1**). Actually, pushing this button initiates a series of events: **ProcessData**, **ScaleData**, and Form2.Show.

```
Private Sub Command1_Click ()
 'load icon
 Icon = LoadPicture("c:\Vb5\Graphics\Icons\Office\graph05.ico")

 ProcessData

 ScaleData

 Form2.Show

 ChartLabels
End Sub
```

From previous chapters, you should be familiar with the technique for entering a group of numbers in a text box. This example reads *X* and *Y* data pairs from separate text boxes, converts them to numeric values, and stores them in a two-dimensional array, *NArray*.

```
Private Sub ProcessData ()
 'numbers in string equal commas+1
 TNums = 1
 For I = 1 To Len(Text1.Text)
  XCh$ = Mid$(Text1.Text, I, 1)
```

```
   YCh$ = Mid$(Text2.Text, I, 1)
   If XCh$ = "," Then TNums = TNums + 1
 Next I


 'convert each group to an X number
 XNewStr$ = Text1.Text + ","
 SPos = 0
 J = 0
 For I = 1 To TNums
   FPos = InStr(SPos + 1, XNewStr$, Chr$(44))
   NLen = (FPos - SPos) - 1
   NArray(I, J) = Val(Mid$(XNewStr$, SPos + 1, NLen))
   SPos = FPos
 Next I


 'convert each group to a Y number
 YNewStr$ = Text2.Text + ","
 SPos = 0
 J = 1
 For I = 1 To TNums
   FPos = InStr(SPos + 1, YNewStr$, Chr$(44))
   NLen = (FPos - SPos) - 1
   NArray(I, J) = Val(Mid$(YNewStr$, SPos + 1, NLen))
   SPos = FPos
 Next I
End Sub
```

The array information is then scaled so that the maximum value entered is the chart's upper value. This means all other values are scaled as a fractional part of the maximum value. The alternative to this approach is to allow the user to enter the data range for numbers. Both have their advantages and disadvantages. The latter technique forces the user to make additional decisions at data entry time but does provide more flexibility in the outcome of the chart. The following technique for scaling data points has been used in several examples.

```
Private Sub ScaleData ()
 'find Maximum X & Y point in array
 PtXMax = NArray(0, 0)
 PtYMax = NArray(0, 1)
 For I = 1 To TNums
  If PtXMax < NArray(I, 0) Then
   PtXMax = NArray(I, 0)
  End If
  If PtYMax < NArray(I, 1) Then
   PtYMax = NArray(I, 1)
  End If
 Next I
     .
     .
     .
```

The code in the following listing is unique to this chapter. The program scales each array point to the maximum data point and also to the size of the axis it is plotted on. This project uses an x axis and y axis with a 1000-point extent.

For example, if the user enters the values 10, 20, 30 as original data, the values will be processed in the following manner:

First, the program will select 30 as the maximum data value. All other points are then proportionally scaled to this value.

```
10 * 1000 / 30 = 333.33

20 * 1000 / 30 = 666.67

30 * 1000 / 30 = 1000.00
```

On the line chart, 30 will be scaled and drawn to the maximum scale size of 1000 units. This technique works for any values entered by the user.

```
     .
     .
     .
 'scale all X & Y values in array to chart size
 For I = 1 To TNums
```

```
        ScaledNArray(I, 0) = (NArray(I, 0) * 1000 / PtXMax)
        ScaledNArray(I, 1) = (NArray(I, 1) * 1000 / PtYMax)
    Next I
End Sub
```

The Line Charting Code A custom coordinate system is used for drawing the line chart. The 0 point on the *x* axis is 200 units from the left edge. The *y* axis is created so that chart values increase positively from the bottom of the screen. The 0 point on the *y* axis is 300 units from the bottom of the window. Can you figure this out from the following chart constants?

```
Private Sub Form_GotFocus ()
  'set chart constants
  ScaleLeft = -200
  ScaleTop = 1400
  ScaleWidth = 1400
  ScaleHeight = -1700
    .
    .
    .
```

An *x* axis and a *y* axis are needed for the line chart. These are drawn (1000 units) in the appropriate direction from the chart origin (0, 0). One reason for using a custom coordinate system is to avoid the need to offset each data point on the chart. If the origin of the chart is 0, 0, then every data point can be drawn directly.

```
    .
    .
    .
  'draw horizontal and vertical axes
  Line (0, 0)-(1000, 0)
  Line (0, 0)-(0, 1000)
    .
    .
    .
```

This chart will place tic marks on each axis. Tic marks are small symbols used to divide an axis. For this project tic marks are used to divide both the *x* axis and *y* axis every 100 units.

```
    .
    .
    .
'draw tic marks
For I = 100 To 1000 Step 100
  Line (I, -5)-(I, 15) 'x tic
  Line (-5, I)-(6, I) 'y tic
Next I
    .
    .
    .
```

A **For** loop is used to plot each point and then draw a line between successive points. As you can see, a dash-dot line style is chosen instead of the default solid line style for drawing each line.

```
    .
    .
    .
DrawStyle = 3 'dash-dot style
'draw lines between data points
For I = 1 To TNums - 1
  X1 = ScaledNArray(I, 0)
  Y1 = ScaledNArray(I, 1)
  X2 = ScaledNArray(I + 1, 0)
  Y2 = ScaledNArray(I + 1, 1)

  Line (X1, Y1)-(X2,Y2), QBColor(1)
Next I
    .
    .
    .
```

Small marker symbols are drawn after the lines are drawn. These little (+) symbols are created with short solid line segments at the location of each data point.

```
    .
    .
    .
DrawStyle = 0
'draw a "+" marker at each point plotted
For I = 1 To TNums
 X1 = ScaledNArray(I, 0)
 Y1 = ScaledNArray(I, 1)
 Line (X1 - 9, Y1)-(X1 + 11, Y1), QBColor(11) 'x width
 Line (X1, Y1 - 15)-(X1, Y1 + 15), QBColor(11) 'y width
Next I
    .
    .
    .
```

The **TextOut()** Windows GDI function is used to draw the chart
labels. In the first portion of code, a font size of 40 is requested.
Windows 95 and NT will supply the font that most closely matches the
request. In other words, ask for what you want, but be prepared to
work with the font Windows 95 or NT supplies!

 *Note: Several **TextOut()** function calls, in the following listing, have been
wrapped to a second line of code. They should be entered on a single
program line.*

```
    .
    .
    .
'chart title
 FontSize = 40
 FontName = "Courier New"
 sStr$ = Form1.Text3.TEXT
 r% = TextOut(Form2.hDC, 320 - (Len(sStr$) * FontSize / 2),
          15, sStr$, Len(sStr$))
```

```
'horizontal axis label
FontSize = 10
sStr$ = Form1.Text4.TEXT
r% = TextOut(Form2.hDC, 320 - (Len(sStr$) * FontSize / 2),
             400, sStr$, Len(sStr$))

'vertical axis label
sStr$ = Form1.Text5.TEXT
r% = TextOut(Form2.hDC, 5, 230, sStr$, Len(sStr$))

'max and min X values
sStr$ = Str$(PtXMax)
r% = TextOut(Form2.hDC, 90, 375, "0", 1)
r% = TextOut(Form2.hDC, 535 - (Len(sStr$) * FontSize / 2),
             375, sStr$, Len(sStr$))

'max and min Y values
sStr$ = Str$(PtYMax)
r% = TextOut(Form2.hDC, 60, 350, "0", 1)
r% = TextOut(Form2.hDC, 35, 100, sStr$, Len(sStr$))

End Sub
```

The remaining text is printed to the window in a 10-point font. This font label information is printed on the line chart, **Form2**, as it is produced.

Now that you've examined the code, let's look at some interesting line charts.

Drawing Unique Line Charts

The line chart project has features and code that are simpler than those for the bar and pie charts. Despite this simplicity, the line chart produced with this project is still presentation quality.

Figure 15.2 shows a line chart drawn with the default values that appeared in the data entry form, shown earlier.

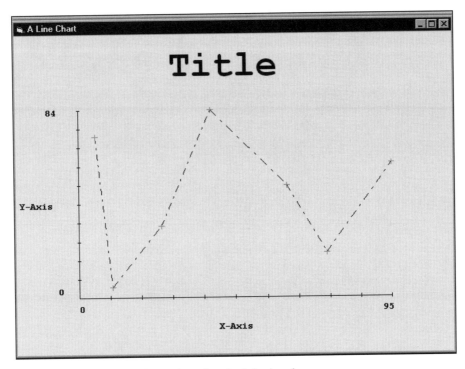

Figure 15.2 A line chart plotted with default values.

Figure 15.3 shows a unique line chart with custom labels and several data points.

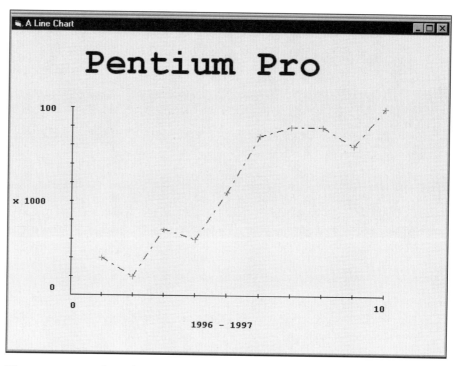

Figure 15.3 A line chart plotted with unique data values.

What could you add to this project to customize this code? It might be important for you to be able to plot negative points, too. How could you alter the line chart to accommodate both positive and negative X and Y values?

A Bar Chart

The bar chart project, 15BCht2, will incorporate many features of the last program and add several new and powerful options. The bar chart project will:

- allow the user to enter bar labels for an optional legend.
- allow the user to enter a chart title.
- allow the user to enter a number of bar height values (up to 15).

Once all bar chart values are entered, the project will:

- allow the user to save the chart to a bitmap file.
- allow the user to clip and paste chart information using the Windows 95 and NT clipboard.
- divide each axis with several tic marks.
- divide the bar width evenly so that the bars fill the chart horizontally.
- draw an optional legend to the right of the bar chart.
- draw an x and a y axis on a form.
- draw the chart labels.
- draw the Max and Min values for the vertical axis.
- scale the vertical heights to the chart values.

Does the thought of implementing all these features scare you? Remember, many of these features have been used separately or together in earlier chapters. In this project they will be combined.

Figure 15.4 is the data entry form for the bar chart program. If the user enters more than 15 values, the extra numbers will be ignored.

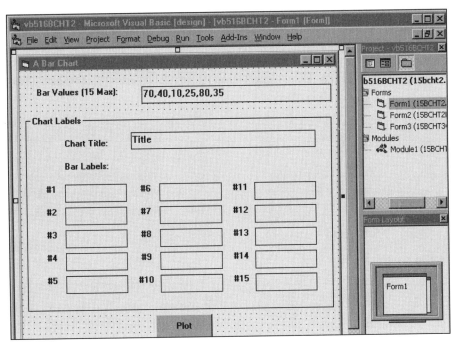

Figure 15.4 The data entry form for the bar chart project.

The project will check the first bar label text box to see if the user has entered a value. If a value exists in that text box, a bar chart legend will also be drawn on the chart.

Developing the Bar Chart Code

This project contains a good portion of code that has been used numerous times. You've already seen much of this programming code in earlier projects.

The global variables for this project are entered in the MODULE1 file named 15BCht2.BAS, shown in the next listing.

```
DefInt A-Z
Global I, TNums, SPos, FPos, NLen
Global NArray(15) As Single, ScaledNArray(15) As Single
Global BarMax As Single
Global X1 As Single, Y1 As Single
Global X2 As Single, Y2 As Single
Global Leg(15) As String
Global Title As String
```

The Bar Chart Data Entry Form   The values entered on the data entry form are processed when the command button, **Plot**, is clicked. This initiates a series of actions: **ProcessData**, **ScaleData**, and Form2.Show. When the focus is turned to **Form2**, the bar chart is actually calculated and drawn.

```
Private Sub Command1_Click ()
 'load icon
 Icon = LoadPicture("c:\Vb5\Graphics\Icons\Office\graph07.ico")

 ProcessData

 ScaleData

 Form2.Show
End Sub
```

This code for processing the data is very similar to that of the last example, with the exception that the data entry array, *NArray*, is one-dimensional. The array is one-dimensional because the width of each bar is derived, not entered by the user.

```
Private Sub ProcessData ()
 'numbers in string equal commas+1
 TNums = 1
 For I = 1 To Len(Text1.Text)
  YCh$ = Mid$(Text1.Text, I, 1)
  If YCh$ = "," Then TNums = TNums + 1
 Next I


 'limit the number of bars
 If TNums > 15 Then TNums = 15


 'convert each group to a bar magnitude
 YNewStr$ = Text1.Text + ","
 SPos = 0
 For I = 1 To TNums
  FPos = InStr(SPos + 1, YNewStr$, Chr$(44))
  NLen = (FPos - SPos) - 1
  NArray(I) = Val(Mid$(YNewStr$, SPos + 1, NLen))
  SPos = FPos
 Next I


 'prepare title and legend labels
 Title = Text2.Text
 Leg(1) = Text3.Text
 Leg(2) = Text4.Text
 Leg(3) = Text5.Text
 Leg(4) = Text6.Text
 Leg(5) = Text7.Text
 Leg(6) = Text8.Text
 Leg(7) = Text9.Text
 Leg(8) = Text10.Text
```

```
 Leg(9)  = Text11.Text
 Leg(10) = Text12.Text
 Leg(11) = Text13.Text
 Leg(12) = Text14.Text
 Leg(13) = Text15.Text
 Leg(14) = Text16.Text
 Leg(15) = Text17.Text
End Sub


Private Sub ScaleData ()
 'find maximum bar magnitude in array
 BarMax = NArray(0)
 For I = 1 To TNums
  If BarMax < NArray(I) Then
   BarMax = NArray(I)
  End If
 Next I


 'scale bar values in array to chart size
 For I = 1 To TNums
  ScaledNArray(I) = (NArray(I) * 1000 / BarMax)
 Next I
End Sub
```

Data values are scaled in a manner similar to the technique used for the line chart. Here the *BarMax* value is used.

The optional legend values are transferred from the 15 text boxes to a simple array of strings. The use of an array will simplify drawing the legend on the bar chart.

The Bar Charting Code   The **BarPlot** subroutine contains several groups of familiar code. The first group sets the chart's scale, several charting parameters, and draws the coordinate axes with tic marks.

```
Private Sub BarPlot ()
 'set chart constants
 ScaleLeft = -100
```

```
ScaleTop = 1400
ScaleWidth = 1600
ScaleHeight = -1700

Cls
AutoRedraw = -1
DrawWidth = 1

'draw horizontal and vertical axes
Line (0, 0)-(1000, 0) 'x axis
Line (0, 0)-(0, 1000) 'y axis

'draw tic marks
For I = 100 To 1000 Step 100
  Line (I, -5)-(I, 15) 'x tic
  Line (-5, I)-(6, I) 'y tic
Next I
    .
    .
    .
```

The Visual Basic 5 **Line()** function is used to draw each bar and then fill it with the specified color. The *X1* and *Y1* values specify the lower left coordinates of each bar, while *X2* and *Y2* specify the upper right coordinates. *X1* starts at the chart's origin (0,0) and is incremented as each bar is drawn. *Y1* does not change because the bar is always drawn from the *x* axis. (Note: *Y1* is set to 5, which is very close to the *x* axis, so that the bars do not draw over the axis.) The *x* axis is 1000 units long, so if there are *TNums* bars, each bar's width is found by dividing 1000 by *TNums*. Smart? Color values for each bar are chosen by incrementing the values available with the **QBColor()** function.

```
    .
    .
    .
'draw a bar for each data value
X1 = 0: Y1 = 5
BoxWidth = 1000 / TNums
X2 = BoxWidth
```

```
For I = 1 To TNums
  Y2 = ScaledNArray(I)
  Line (X1, Y1)-(X2, Y2), QBColor((I + 8) Mod 15), BF
  X1 = X2
  X2 = X2 + BoxWidth
Next I
```

    .

    .

    .

A legend is created on the bar chart just to the right of the graph. Small rectangles are used to form the legend. These small rectangles replicate the colors of the bars they represent. Legend labels are printed to the right of these icons. The legend labels are read from the array of strings, *Leg()*.

    .

    .

    .

```
'print legend boxes and labels
If Leg(1) <> "" Then
  X1 = 1100
  Y1 = 1000
  FontSize = Height / 600
  For I = 1 To TNums
    Line (X1, Y1)-(50 + X1, Y1 + 50),
         QBColor(I + 8) Mod 15), BF

    Print " " + Leg(I)
    Y1 = Y1 - 75
  Next I
End If
```

    .

    .

    .

 Note: The **Line()** *function in the previous listing must be entered on one program line.*

The bar chart title is drawn with the **Print** command. The parameters for location, font, and color are set before the command is called.

   .

   .

   .

```
'print bar chart title
If Title <> "" Then
  X1 = 700
  Y1 = 1400
  ForeColor = QBColor(12)
  FontSize = Height / 200
  LabelWidth = TextWidth(Title) / 2
  LabelHeight = TextHeight(Title) / 2
  CurrentX = X1 - LabelWidth
  CurrentY = Y1 + LabelHeight
  Print Title
End If
```

   .

   .

   .

The final information printed to the chart is for the maximum and minimum y axis values. The minimum value is always 0, and the maximum value is determined from *BarMax*, the size of the largest data value entered by the user.

   .

   .

   .

```
'print max and min bar height values
ForeColor = QBColor(0)
FontSize = Height / 600
MaxStr$ = Str$(BarMax)
CurrentX = -75
CurrentY = 1025
Print MaxStr$
```

```
 CurrentX = -75
 CurrentY = 25
 Print " 0"
End Sub
```

The menu options for the bar chart are handled by a small group of routines: **MCopy_Click**, **MPaste_Click**, and **MSave_Click**.

```
Private Sub MCopy_Click ()
 'copy image to clipboard as a bitmap
 Clipboard.SetData Form2.Image, 2
End Sub


Private Sub MPaste_Click ()
 'paste a bitmap picture from clipboard
 Form2.Picture = Clipboard.GetData(2)
End Sub


Private Sub MSave_Click ()
 'show form for name and file path
 Form3.Show
End Sub
```

The bar chart can be sized to the current window in this project. To do this, the **BarPlot** procedure, just discussed, is nested in the **Form_Resize** subroutine.

```
Private Sub Form_Resize ()
 Icon = LoadPicture("c:\Vb5\Graphics\Icons\Office\graph07.ico")
 Call BarPlot
End Sub
```

Saving Your Bar Chart to a File In order to be able to save this chart, a third form is used with the bar chart project. When the user selects the Save option from the bar chart's menu, a dialog-type box appears. This form, shown in Figure 15.5 allows the user to specify the path and file name for the bitmap image to be saved.

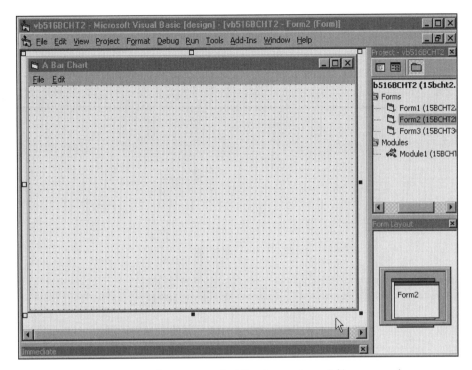

Figure 15.5 An extra form is needed for the path and file name when saving a file.

```
Private Sub Command1_Click ()
  If Form3.Text1.Text <> "" Then
    FileSave$ = Form3.Text1.Text
    SavePicture Form2.Image, FileSave$
  End If
  Form3.Hide
End Sub
```

Drawing Unique Bar Charts

Figure 15.6 shows a plot of the default values provided on the data entry form. Impressive, but not exciting!

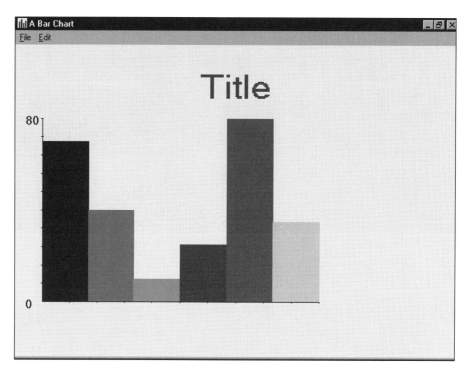

Figure 15.6 A bar chart plotted with default values.

Figure 15.7 shows how a chart title and legend information can dress up an otherwise drab chart. Of course, you shouldn't believe everything you view on a bar chart!

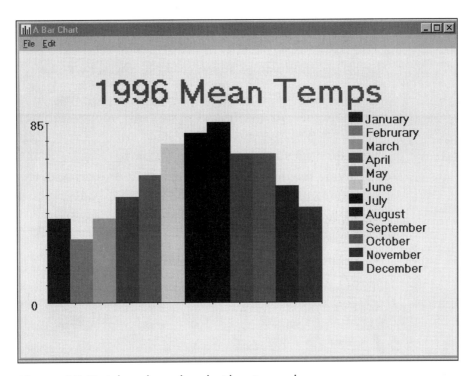

Figure 15.7 A bar chart plotted with unique values.

A PIE CHART

A pie chart presents some interesting programming considerations. Visual Basic 5 does not have a **Pie()** function. How do you form pie wedges? How do you get the pie wedges to form a whole pie? Even Microsoft has several different approaches to solving this problem. Their techniques vary in Visual Basic 5, Visual C++, and Visual J++. For Visual Basic 5, pie wedges can be created with the use of the **Circle()** function.

In the next project, 15PCht3, you'll learn how to scale a set of values so that they produce a proper set of pie wedges. The slices will be fitted proportionally inside the whole pie.

The pie chart project will:

- allow the user to enter pie labels for an optional legend.
- allow the user to enter a chart title.

- allow the user to enter a number of pie wedge values (up to 12).

Once all pie chart values are entered, the project will:

- allow the user to save the chart to a bitmap file.
- allow the user to clip and paste chart information from the Windows clipboard.
- color each slice with a different color.
- divide the pie into a maximum of 12 proportional values.
- draw a whole pie chart scaled to the window.
- draw an optional legend to thght of the pie chart.
- draw the legend labels.
- print an optional pie chart title.

Figure 15.8 shows the data entry form for this project.

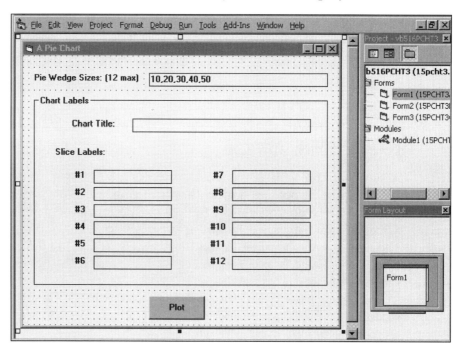

Figure 15.8 The data entry form for the pie chart project.

Coding the Pie Chart

The pie chart application uses three forms. The following is a list of global variables found in the MODULE1 file named 15PCht3.BAS.

```
DefInt A-Z
Global I, TNums, SPos, FPos, NLen
Global LabelWidth, LabelHeight
Global NArray(20) As Single, ScaledNArray(20) As Single
Global SAngle As Single, FAngle As Single
Global PWTotal As Single, X1 As Single, Y1 As Single
Global Leg(20) As String
Global Title As String
```

As in the previous example, the string array *Leg()* will be used for legend labels.

The Pie Chart Data Entry Form The pie chart project is started by entering values on the data entry form and clicking the command button, **Plot**. The information is processed in a manner similar to the past examples.

The value for PI is entered in the general declarations section for the first form.

```
Const PI = 3.141


Private Sub Command1_Click ()

  'load icon image
  Icon = LoadPicture("c:\Vb5\Graphics\Icons\Office\graph11.ico")
  ProcessData

  ScaleData

  Form2.Show
End Sub


Private Sub ProcessData ()
  'numbers in string equal commas+1
  TNums = 1
  For I = 1 To Len(Text1.Text)
```

```
  PCh$ = Mid$(Text1.Text, I, 1)
  If PCh$ = "," Then TNums = TNums + 1
Next I

'limit number of wedges
If TNums > 12 Then TNums = 12

'convert each group to a pie wedge number
PNewStr$ = Text1.Text + ","
SPos = 0
For I = 1 To TNums
  FPos = InStr(SPos + 1, PNewStr$, Chr$(44))
  NLen = (FPos - SPos) - 1
  NArray(I) = Val(Mid$(PNewStr$, SPos + 1, NLen))
  SPos = FPos
Next I

'prepare title and legend labels
Title = Text2.Text
Leg(1) = Text3.Text
Leg(2) = Text4.Text
Leg(3) = Text5.Text
Leg(4) = Text6.Text
Leg(5) = Text7.Text
Leg(6) = Text8.Text
Leg(7) = Text9.Text
Leg(8) = Text10.Text
Leg(9) = Text11.Text
Leg(10) = Text12.Text
Leg(11) = Text13.Text
Leg(12) = Text14.Text
End Sub
```

Did you notice that the value we chose for pi was specified to just a few decimal places? As a matter of fact, if rounded properly it would have been 3.142. The value 3.141 was chosen so that our whole circle was just a bit shy of 360 degrees or 2 x pi radians. We needed the closing angle to be larger than the starting angle. This would not be true if we returned, full circle, to 0 degrees. If you think this is a little underhanded, read the details on the use of the **Circle()** function in your Visual Basic 5 manuals.

```
Private Sub ScaleData ()
 'add all pie slice sizes together
 PWTotal = 0
 For I = 1 To TNums
  PWTotal = PWTotal + NArray(I)
 Next I


 'scale all pie slices to fit in whole pie
 For I = 1 To TNums
  ScaledNArray(I) = NArray(I) * 2 * PI / PWTotal
 Next I
End Sub
```

The data is scaled to fit the circle by scaling all slices in proportion to the total of all individual slice values. An appropriate angle is then assigned to these calculated values. For example, suppose a user enters the following data values: 10, 20, 30. The data is processed in the following manner:

```
10 + 20 + 30 = 60   (total of all slice values)
10 / 60 = .166667  ->    .166667  x (2 x PI) = 1.047
20 / 60 = .333333  ->    .333333  x (2 x PI) = 2.094
30 / 60 = .5       ->    .5       x (2 x PI) = 3.141
```

The sum of the final values should be the number of radians in a full circle (2 x PI = 6.282).

```
1.047 + 2.094 + 3.141 = 6.282
```

You will find that this technique works for any set of data values entered by the user.

The Pie Charting Code The origin (0, 0) for this coordinate system is placed at the center of the pie. (The origin is 0, 0 when the legend is not printed.)

```
Private Sub PiePlot ()
 'set chart constants
 ScaleLeft = -800
 ScaleTop = 800
 ScaleWidth = 1600
 ScaleHeight = -1600

 Cls
 AutoRedraw = -1
 DrawWidth = 1
 FillStyle = 0
    .
    .
    .
```

The **Circle()** function must use a value, other than zero, to work properly. The first value is set to a very small number.

```
    .
    .
    .
'a small seed number is needed
'for the initial angle
SAngle = 0.0000001
    .
    .
    .
```

If a legend is being drawn, the pie is shifted slightly to the left of center screen with the following code. This is a neat little trick, isn't it?

```
    .
    .
    .
 SAngle = 0
 If Leg(1) = "" Then
   X1 = 0
 Else X1 = -250
 End If
    .
    .
    .
```

Specifying values for the **Circle()** function is actually simple—once you have done it a few times. The following **For** loop aids in drawing the pie slices and selecting the fill color. The brighter QuickBasic colors start at an index value of 8, so this pie chart starts its color selection there. A Modulo operator is necessary in case more than eight pie wedges are required.

```
    .

    .

    .

For I = 1 To TNums
  FillColor = QBColor((I + 8) Mod 16)
  FAngle = SAngle + ScaledNArray(I)
  Circle (X1, 0), 400, , -SAngle, -FAngle
  SAngle = FAngle
Next I

    .

    .

    .
```

As you examine the previous code, notice that the starting points for the circle are fixed (except the offset value). The radius is 400 and the outline color value is black, the default. A wedge will be drawn when using the **Circle()** function, since *SAngle* is smaller than *FAngle*. The negative sign (-) in front of each value extends a line from the tip of the curve to the center of the circle. Just what is needed for a pie slice!

Legend values and a chart title are drawn next, if requested by the user.

```
    .

    .

    .

'print legend boxes and labels
If Leg(1) <> "" Then
  X1 = 250
  Y1 = 400
  FontSize = Height / 600
  For I = 1 To TNums
    FillColor = QBColor((I + 8) Mod 16)
```

```
   Line (X1, Y1)-(X1 + 50, Y1 + 50),
      QBColor((I + 8) Mod 16), BF
   Print " " + Leg(I)
   Y1 = Y1 - 75
 Next I
End If

'print pie chart title
If Title <> "" Then
 ForeColor = QBColor(11)
 FontSize = Height / 200
 LabelWidth = TextWidth(Title) / 2
 LabelHeight = TextHeight(Title) / 2
 CurrentX = -LabelWidth
 CurrentY = LabelHeight - ScaleHeight * 9 / 16
 Print Title
 End If
End Sub
```

Since sizing affects the chart, the **PiePlot()** function just discussed is called from the **Form_Resize()** subroutine.

```
Private Sub Form_Resize ()
 Icon = LoadPicture("c:\Vb5\Graphics\Icons\Office\graph11.ico")
 Call PiePlot
End Sub
```

The menu options for saving the bitmap file or clip and pasting from the clipboard are handled with a small additional amount of code.

```
Private Sub MCopy_Click ()
 'copy image to clipboard as a bitmap
 Clipboard.SetData Form2.Image, 2
End Sub

Private Sub MPaste_Click ()
 'paste a bitmap picture from clipboard
```

```
Form2.Picture = Clipboard.GetData(2)
End Sub


Private Sub MSave_Click ()
 'show form for name and file path
 Form3.Show
End Sub
```

Saving Your Pie Chart to a File If the File | Save option is selected, an additional form permits the user to specify the path and file name for the bitmap file.

```
Private Sub Command1_Click ()
 If Form3.Text1.Text <> "" Then
  FileSave$ = Form3.Text1.Text
  SavePicture Form2.Image, FileSave$
 End If
 Form3.Hide
End Sub
```

Once the file is saved, the form is hidden.

Drawing Unique Pie Charts

Figure 15.9 shows a plot of the default values provided on the data entry form. Notice that without a legend, the pie is centered on the form. Also, note the bright colors. Well, at least try to imagine that those shades of gray represent rich and vibrant colors.

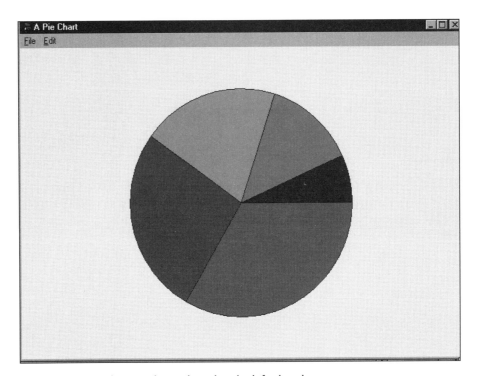

Figure 15.9 The pie chart plotted with default values.

Figure 15.10 is a pie chart created with a chart title and legend. Notice in this figure that the pie chart is offset to the left in order to provide additional room for the legend.

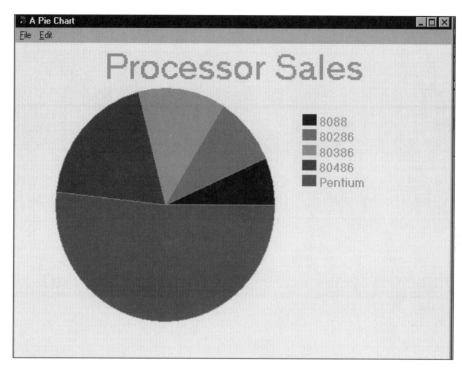

Figure 15.10 The pie chart plotted with unique values.

WHAT'S COMING?

You have learned how to access a few WIN32 API functions throughout the previous chapters. In Chapter 16, a more detailed approach will be undertaken to examine the techniques and advantages of accessing these powerful Windows functions. You'll learn how to perform graphics feats not possible with Visual Basic 5 graphics functions.

And remember: Chapter 17 will introduce you to ActiveX controls. With ActiveX controls, adding graphs to your Visual Basic 5 projects couldn't be easier!

Chapter 16

Accessing the Win32 API

In Chapter 11 you learned how to access the Win32 API (Application Program Interface) in order to tap into powerful Windows GDI (Graphics Device Interface) graphics primitives. In this chapter, you'll discover additional features of the Win32 API.

In Visual Basic 5, the key to successful access to the Win32 API is through the Win32api.txt file. If you performed a default installation of Visual Basic 5, this file is probably located in the C:\VB5\Winapi subdirectory. The Win32api.txt file is a hefty text file of over 680 KB containing Declares, Constants, Types, and other important information for making use of the Win32 API. This file translates to over 300 pages of text if you bring the file into a word processor to view.

THE WIN32 API INTERFACE

The Win32api.txt file is critical for a successful interface with numerous Win32 API functions. However, because the size of this file is so large, Microsoft has provided an API Viewer that allows you to browse the Win32api.txt file. As a matter of fact, the API Viewer, api-load.exe, can be used to view Jet Database files, too. This file is located in the same subdirectory as the Win32api.txt file. While in the API Viewer, you can use the clipboard to copy portions of the file for subsequent pasting into your Visual Basic 5 project.

Note: The apiload.exe program allows the conversion of text files to Jet Databases. This conversion is provided because it is much faster to display the information in a database than when opening it as a text file. Text files can be converted to Jet Database files by loading the text file and selecting the File | Convert... menu option.

A Quick Tour of Win32api.txt

Normally you will not print a copy of the Win32api.txt file, in its entirety, because of its enormous size. However, to give you an idea of the contents of this file, the following listing contains a small portion of the file for you to study. Here is a small portion of the Win32api.txt file, taken from the beginning of the listing, that illustrates the use of Type definitions.

```
'_____
'
'   WIN32API.TXT — Win32 API Declarations for Visual Basic
'
'        Copyright (C) 1994 Microsoft Corporation
'
'
' This file contains only the Const, Type,
' and Declare statements for Win32 APIs.
'
' You have a royalty-free right to use, modify, reproduce and
' distribute this file (and/or any modified version) in any way you
' find useful, provided that you agree that Microsoft has no
' warranty, obligation or liability for its contents. Refer to
' the Microsoft Windows Programmer's Reference for further
' information.
'
'_____
```

```
' Type definitions for Windows' basic types.
Public Const ANYSIZE_ARRAY = 1
Type RECT
     Left As Long
     Top As Long
     Right As Long
     Bottom As Long
End Type

Type RECTL
     Left As Long
     Top As Long
     Right As Long
     Bottom As Long
End Type

Type POINTAPI
     x As Long
     y As Long
End Type
     .
     .
     .
```

If you have programmed with Windows API functions, you are familiar with such types as RECT, RECTL, and so on. They're all here in the Win32api.txt file; just copy and paste those that you need.

The following listing, also taken from the Win32api.txt file, illustrates several constant declarations.

```
     .
     .
     .

Public Const DELETE = &H10000
Public Const READ_CONTROL = &H20000
Public Const WRITE_DAC = &H40000
Public Const WRITE_OWNER = &H80000
Public Const SYNCHRONIZE = &H100000
```

```
Public Const STANDARD_RIGHTS_READ = (READ_CONTROL)
Public Const STANDARD_RIGHTS_WRITE = (READ_CONTROL)
Public Const STANDARD_RIGHTS_EXECUTE = (READ_CONTROL)
Public Const STANDARD_RIGHTS_REQUIRED = &HF0000
Public Const STANDARD_RIGHTS_ALL = &H1F0000
    .
    .
    .
```

Constants, such as those just listed, make programming with Windows API functions much easier. By using declared constants, you are freed from having to remember specific numeric values.

The most important use of the Win32api.txt file is for access to the hundreds of declaration statements for Win32 API function calls. The next listing shows several declarations used to provide file access through the Win32 API.

```
Declare Function GetFileInformationByHandle Lib "kernel32"
  Alias "GetFileInformationByHandle" (ByVal hFile As Long,
  lpFileInformation As BY_HANDLE_FILE_INFORMATION) As Long

Declare Function GetFileType Lib "kernel32" Alias "GetFileType"
  (ByVal hFile As Long) As Long

Declare Function GetFileSize Lib "kernel32" Alias "GetFileSize"
  (ByVal hFile As Long, lpFileSizeHigh As Long) As Long

Declare Function WriteFile Lib "kernel32" Alias "WriteFile"
  (ByVal hFile As Long, lpBuffer As Any, ByVal
  nNumberOfBytesToWrite As Long, lpNumberOfBytesWritten As Long,
  lpOverlapped As OVERLAPPED) As Long

Declare Function GetFileTime Lib "kernel32" Alias "GetFileTime"
  (ByVal hFile As Long, lpCreationTime As FILETIME,
  lpLastAccessTime As FILETIME, lpLastWriteTime As FILETIME)
  As Long
```

```
Declare Function SetFileTime Lib "kernel32" Alias "SetFileTime"
  (ByVal hFile As Long, lpCreationTime As FILETIME,
  lpLastAccessTime As FILETIME, lpLastWriteTime As FILETIME)
  As Long

Declare Function GetDriveType Lib "kernel32" Alias
  "GetDriveTypeA" (ByVal nDrive As String) As Long
```

File access is important. If Visual Basic 5 doesn't provide the built-in power you need, you'll be able to use the powerful Win32 API functions declared in this file.

Many times your Visual Basic 5 project will need to manipulate fonts. The declare statements contained in the Win32api.txt file allow access to two very popular Windows functions, **CreateFontIndirect()** and **CreateFont()**. Their declarations are shown in the following portion of code.

.

.

.

```
Declare Function CreateFontIndirect Lib "gdi32" Alias
  "CreateFontIndirectA" (lpLogFont As LOGFONT) As Long

Declare Function CreateFont Lib "gdi32" Alias "CreateFontA"
  (ByVal H As Long, ByVal W As Long, ByVal E As Long, ByVal O
  As Long, ByVal W As Long, ByVal I As Long, ByVal u As Long,
  ByVal S As Long, ByVal C As Long, ByVal OP As Long, ByVal CP
  As Long, ByVal Q As Long, ByVal PAF As Long, ByVal F As
  String) As Long
```

.

.

.

Did you ever wonder how it might be possible to rotate strings or individual characters in a string in Visual Basic 5? The answer is in the use of these two functions! We'll illustrate the **CreateFont()** function later in the chapter, with an actual example.

Here is another portion of the Win32api.txt file showing a variety of Windows GDI functions.

```
Declare Function CreateHatchBrush Lib "gdi32" Alias
  "CreateHatchBrush" (ByVal nIndex As Long, ByVal crColor As
  Long) As Long

Declare Function CreatePalette Lib "gdi32" Alias
  "CreatePalette" (lpLogPalette As LOGPALETTE) As Long

Declare Function CreatePen Lib "gdi32" Alias "CreatePen" (ByVal
  nPenStyle As Long, ByVal nWidth As Long, ByVal crColor As
  Long) As Long

Declare Function CreatePenIndirect Lib "gdi32" Alias
  "CreatePenIndirect" (lpLogPen As LOGPEN) As Long

Declare Function CreateRectRgn Lib "gdi32" Alias
  "CreateRectRgn" (ByVal X1 As Long, ByVal Y1 As Long, ByVal X2
  As Long, ByVal Y2 As Long) As Long

Declare Function CreatePatternBrush Lib "gdi32" Alias
  "CreatePatternBrush" (ByVal hBitmap As Long) As Long

Declare Function CreateRoundRectRgn Lib "gdi32" Alias
  "CreateRoundRectRgn" (ByVal X1 As Long, ByVal Y1 As Long,
  ByVal X2 As Long, ByVal Y2 As Long, ByVal X3 As Long, ByVal
  Y3 As Long) As Long

Declare Function CreateSolidBrush Lib "gdi32" Alias
  "CreateSolidBrush" (ByVal crColor As Long) As Long

Declare Function Ellipse Lib "gdi32" Alias "Ellipse" (ByVal hdc
  As Long, ByVal X1 As Long, ByVal Y1 As Long, ByVal X2 As
  Long, ByVal Y2 As Long) As Long

Declare Function ExtFloodFill Lib "gdi32" Alias "ExtFloodFill"
  (ByVal hdc As Long, ByVal x As Long, ByVal y As Long, ByVal
  crColor As Long, ByVal wFillType As Long) As Long
```

```
Declare Function FillRgn Lib "gdi32" Alias "FillRgn" (ByVal hdc
   As Long, ByVal hRgn As Long, ByVal hBrush As Long) As Long

Declare Function FloodFill Lib "gdi32" Alias "FloodFill" (ByVal
   hdc As Long, ByVal x As Long, ByVal y As Long, ByVal crColor
   As Long) As Long

Declare Function GetROP2 Lib "gdi32" Alias "GetROP2" (ByVal hdc
   As Long) As Long

Declare Function GetBkColor Lib "gdi32" Alias "GetBkColor"
   (ByVal hdc As Long) As Long

Declare Function GetBkMode Lib "gdi32" Alias "GetBkMode" (ByVal
   hdc As Long) As Long
```

 Note: Remember that Visual Basic 5 requires that these declarations be typed on one program line, not wrapped as they are shown in the previous listings.

If you have programmed in Windows with C or C++, many of these function names are familiar to you. As a matter of fact, you already saw some of them illustrated in programming code in Chapter 11. You'll see them illustrated again in this chapter.

Making Sense of Win32api.txt Declarations

As you viewed the listings in the previous section you may have been asking yourself several questions. How do you know which declaration or group of declarations you need to use in order to perform a particular operation? There are hundreds of them. How do you understand what those declarations mean once you do select the proper function? Both of these questions will be answered in the following sections.

Which Function to Use If you viewed the Win32api.txt file, in its entirety, you may be overwhelmed by its size and the total number of declarations contained in the file. Be assured you are not alone!

Have you ever heard anyone say, "How can I look up a word in a dictionary if I can't spell it?" The implication is, you can't find the word unless you know how to spell it. Working with the Win32 API can be a similar adventure: how can you know which function to use if you don't know the name of the function?

If you plan to go at the Win32 API big time, we recommend that you invest in a reference book that deals specifically with the Windows API. However, if you plan only to dabble with a few select Windows functions, almost any Windows programming book will illustrate enough of their use for you to get the knack of using them. Once you select the proper function, a trial-and-error approach will usually work in terms of parameter passing.

Understanding Declarations There is a lot of information packed into each declaration statement. This information can help you tremendously, especially if you are using the trial-and-error approach, when passing parameters. Let's use the Ellipse function declaration as an example.

```
Declare Function Ellipse Lib "gdi32" Alias "Ellipse" (ByVal hdc
  As Long, ByVal X1 As Long, ByVal Y1 As Long, ByVal X2 As
  Long, ByVal Y2 As Long) As Long
```

The function name is **Ellipse**. The function name is followed by information on which API library contains this function. In this case, the **Ellipse()** function is in the "gdi32" library. The function's alias refers to any other name by which this function might be known. For most Windows functions, the alias will be identical to the function name. However, examine the **CreateFont()** function shown earlier. Its alias is "CreateFontA." **CreateFontA()** is a Unicode variant of **CreateFont()**, which allows specific language substitutions to be made in programs written to accommodate them.

Most function parameters are passed by value. The **Long** represents a 32-bit data type in Windows. There are five values that are to be passed to the **Ellipse()** function and a single return value. The first parameter (hdc) is the handle to the Windows device context. This handle points to the device where subsequent drawing will be done. This is usually the CRT but can also be a printer or plotter. The remaining parameters describe the bounding rectangle for the ellipse. Most

Windows GDI primitives are drawn within a bounding rectangle. The bounding rectangle is an invisible rectangle used to bound the graphics figure. In this case, the bounding rectangle uses upper left coordinates at *X1,Y1* and lower coordinates at *X2,Y2*. The return value is True if the function is successful and False if it is not successful.

Once the function is declared in your project, by doing a cut and paste from the Win32api.txt file, it is a simple step to draw an ellipse. An ellipse could be drawn in Visual Basic 5 with just this portion of code and the parameters shown.

```
Private Sub Command1_Click ()
 'draw an ellipse
 r% = Ellipse(Form1.hDC, 190, 190, 275, 250)
End Sub
```

MANIPULATING FONTS WITH THE WIN32 API

In the General Declarations section of your Visual Basic 5 code, enter the following definitions and declarations. Remember, you can simply copy and paste the function declarations from the Win32api.txt file.

```
DefLng A-Z
Dim WT, CS, OP, CP As Long

Private Declare Function CreateFont Lib "gdi32" Alias
   "CreateFontA" (ByVal H As Long, ByVal W As Long, ByVal E As
   Long, ByVal O As Long, ByVal WT As Long, ByVal I As Long,
   ByVal U As Long, ByVal S As Long, ByVal CS As Long, ByVal OP
   As Long, ByVal CP As Long, ByVal Q As Long, ByVal PAF As
   Long, ByVal F As String) As Long

Private Declare Function SelectObject Lib "gdi32" (ByVal hdc As
   Long, ByVal hObject As Long) As Long

Private Declare Function TextOut Lib "gdi32" Alias "TextOutA"
   (ByVal hdc As Long, ByVal x As Long, ByVal y As Long, ByVal
   lpString As String, ByVal nCount As Long) As Long
```

Next, in your project's Paint procedure, enter the following code.

```
Private Sub Form_Paint()
hnFont = CreateFont(30, 30, 0, 0, FW_Normal, False, False,
  False, Default_Charset, Out_Default_Precis,
  Clip_Default_Precis, Default_Quality, 34, "Arial")
hoFont = SelectObject(hdc, hnFont)
r% = TextOut(hdc, 85, 460, " Rotating Fonts", 15)

hnFont = CreateFont(30, 30, 450, 0, FW_Normal, False, False,
  False, Default_Charset, Out_Default_Precis,
  Clip_Default_Precis, Default_Quality, 34, "Arial")
hoFont = SelectObject(hdc, hnFont)
r% = TextOut(hdc, 85, 460, " Rotating Fonts", 15)

hnFont = CreateFont(30, 30, 900, 0, FW_Normal, False, False,
  False, Default_Charset, Out_Default_Precis,
  Clip_Default_Precis, Default_Quality, 34, "Arial")
hoFont = SelectObject(hdc, hnFont)
r% = TextOut(hdc, 85, 460, " Rotating Fonts", 15)
End Sub
```

Again, remember that all of the parameters for the **CreateFont()** function must be entered on a single program line.

In the previous lincs of code, you will notice the use of several font constants, such as Default_Charset, Default_Quality. The following listing gives a brief description of the available font constants.

```
' weight values
FW_DONTCARE            0
FW_THIN                100
FW_EXTRALIGHT          200
FW_LIGHT               300
FW_NORMAL              400
FW_MEDIUM              500
FW_SEMIBOLD            600
FW_BOLD                700
FW_EXTRABOLD           800
FW_HEAVY               900
FW_ULTRALIGHT          FW_EXTRALIGHT
FW_REGULAR             FW_NORMAL
FW_DEMIBOLD            FW_SEMIBOLD
FW_ULTRABOLD           FW_EXTRABOLD
FW_BLACK               FW_HEAVY


' CharSet values
ANSI_CHARSET           0
UNICODE_CHARSET        1
SYMBOL_CHARSET         2
SHIFTJIS_CHARSET       128
HANGEUL_CHARSET        129
CHINESEBIG5_CHARSET    136
OEM_CHARSET            255


' OutPrecision
OUT_DEFAULT_PRECIS     0
OUT_STRING_PRECIS      1
OUT_CHARACTER_PRECIS   2
OUT_STROKE_PRECIS      3
OUT_TT_PRECIS          4
OUT_DEVICE_PRECIS      5
OUT_RASTER_PRECIS      6
OUT_TT_ONLY_PRECIS     7
OUT_OUTLINE_PRECIS     8
```

```
' ClipPrecision
CLIP_DEFAULT_PRECIS     0
CLIP_CHARACTER_PRECIS   1
CLIP_STROKE_PRECIS      2
CLIP_MASK               0xf
CLIP_LH_ANGLES          (1<<4)
CLIP_TT_ALWAYS          (2<<4)
CLIP_EMBEDDED           (8<<4)

' Quality values
DEFAULT_QUALITY         0
DRAFT_QUALITY           1
PROOF_QUALITY           2

' PitchAndFamily pitch values (low 4 bits)
DEFAULT_PITCH           0
FIXED_PITCH             1
VARIABLE_PITCH          2

' PitchAndFamily values (high 4 bits)
FF_DONTCARE             (0<<4)
FF_ROMAN                (1<<4)
FF_SWISS                (2<<4)
FF_MODERN               (3<<4)
FF_SCRIPT               (4<<4)
FF_DECORATIVE           (5<<4)

' Stock fonts for use with GetStockObject()
OEM_FIXED_FONT          10
ANSI_FIXED_FONT         11
ANSI_VAR_FONT           12
SYSTEM_FONT             13
DEVICE_DEFAULT_FONT     14
DEFAULT_PALETTE         15
SYSTEM_FIXED_FONT       16
```

```
' tmPitchAndFamily flags
TMPF_FIXED_PITCH      0x01
TMPF_VECTOR           0x02
TMPF_DEVICE           0x08
TMPF_TRUETYPE         0x04
```

These constants are used as parameter values for various font functions and structures.

Your Visual Basic 5 project should be ready to execute. Run your project. Your screen should look like Figure 16.1.

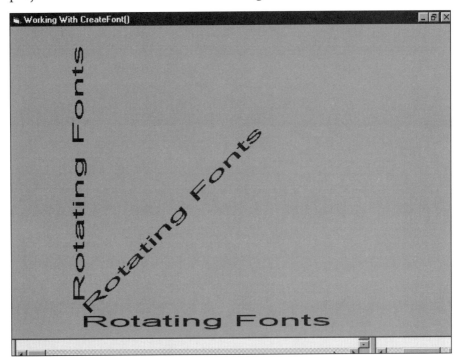

Figure 16.1 The CreateFont() Win32 API function is used to rotate fonts.

What's Ahead?

In this chapter you learned general techniques for accessing hundreds of Win32 API functions. As you write Visual Basic 5 projects that include Win32 API functions, your ability and understanding of using these functions and passing parameters will increase.

In the final chapter of this book you'll learn how to use Common and ActiveX controls and interface applications with them.

Chapter 17

Common and Custom Controls

Microsoft Windows allows programmers to use a variety of controls. Controls fit into three broad categories: standard, common, and custom controls. Almost every Windows programmer is familiar with standard controls. Standard controls form the backbone of all programming work and are the easiest controls to implement and use. Common and custom controls allow unique and specific control design to be added to your projects.

Standard controls include CheckBox, ScrollBar, CommandButton, TextBox, and so on. You have worked with this type of control from the start of this book. These are the controls that are found in the default Visual Basic toolbox. Standard controls are easy to implement and use because Microsoft has predesigned both the controls and the controls' interface properties.

Common controls include a group of controls that present the user with a common user interface. This type of control can be further subdivided into two groups: CommonDialog controls and Windows common controls. You may be familiar with several CommonDialog controls from previous Windows programming. This group of controls includes Color Dialog, Font Dialog, Help Dialog, and Print Dialog. The Windows Common control group includes TabStrip, Toolbar, StatusBar, ProgressBar, TreeView, and Slider. Common controls are a little harder to implement than standard controls, because the controls themselves tend to be more complicated. Common controls, like standard controls, are predesigned with the control's interface properties available to the designer. We'll show you the steps necessary to implement a common control in a project. You'll find that most common controls behave in a similar manner.

The third group of controls, custom controls, provides the programmer with the ability to produce bold new control design. If you are designing a custom control, it will be up to you to design the control and write the code for the control's interface properties. Many private companies are creating custom controls. By purchasing a commercial custom control, you can save time and development money. Custom controls tend to be even more complicated than common controls. Many custom controls are also available to the programmer in specific versions of Visual Basic 5. The Enterprise edition of Visual Basic 5 includes a Calendar control, Chart control, Grid control, Multimedia control, and so on. These may also be available in the version of Visual Basic 5 that you are using. To see if they are included in your version, open Visual Basic 5 and use the Project | Components... file selection to view included components and controls. Although it is beyond the scope of this book to investigate custom controls in depth, we'll take a look at a simple custom control later in this chapter.

COMMON CONTROLS

In this section you will learn a technique for adding common controls to an application. We'll work with two separate examples, one involving the CommonDialog File dialog box and the other the Color Dialog box. With the knowledge you gain from these examples, you'll be able to experiment with other CommonDialog controls.

The Common File Dialog Box Control

Let's create a simple application that will take advantage of the CommonDialog File box control. Here is a step-by-step approach:

- Open a new Visual Basic 5 project and name it Co17Cr2.prj.
- Add a CommandButton anywhere on Form1.
- Use the Project | Components file option to view the list of available components (controls).

- Select Microsoft Common Dialog Control 5.0 by clicking the mouse on the appropriate checkbox, as shown in Figure 17.1.

- When you click the OK button, the CommonDialog control icon will be added to the toolbox, as shown in Figure 17.2.

- Drag the CommonDialog control icon to the form. Place it anywhere on the form.

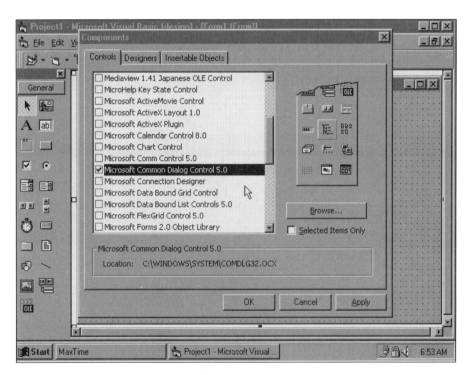

Figure 17.1 Use the mouse to check Microsoft Common Dialog Control 5.0.

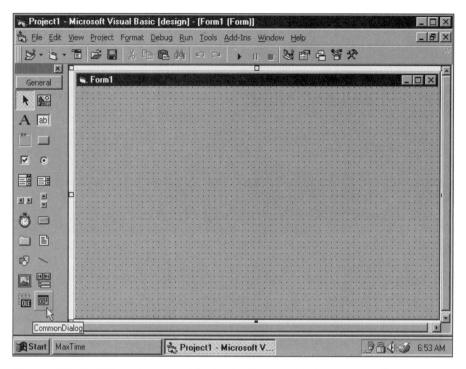

Figure 17.2 When the control is checked, it is added automatically to the toolbox.

That's all there is to it, except writing the necessary code to access data from this dialog box. We'll use the CommandButton's click event to trigger the dialog box action. Add the following code to your project:

```
Private Sub Command1_Click()
    CommonDialog1.Flags = cdlCFEffects Or cdlCFBoth

    'Display the Font CommonDialog box
    CommonDialog1.ShowFont
    Font.Name = CommonDialog1.FontName
    Font.Size = CommonDialog1.FontSize
    Font.Bold = CommonDialog1.FontBold
    Font.Italic = CommonDialog1.FontItalic
    Font.Underline = CommonDialog1.FontUnderline
```

```
FontStrikethru = CommonDialog1.FontStrikethru
ForeColor = CommonDialog1.Color

'Insert a Cls to erase previous entry
'Cls
String1$ = "Click on TEST to pick a font"
Form1.Print String1$
End Sub
```

Change the captions on your form and CommandButton to match those of Figure 17.3.

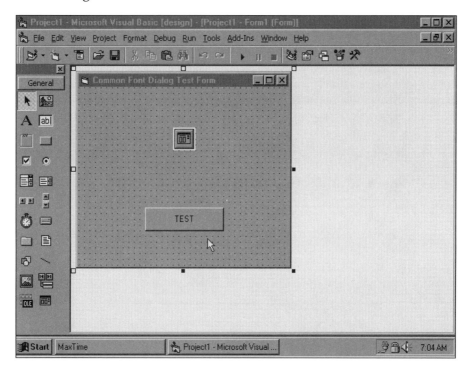

Figure 17.3 The form and CommandButton, showing appropriate captions.

Now, run the application. When you click the mouse on the TEST button, you will see the Common Font Dialog box, shown in Figure 17.4.

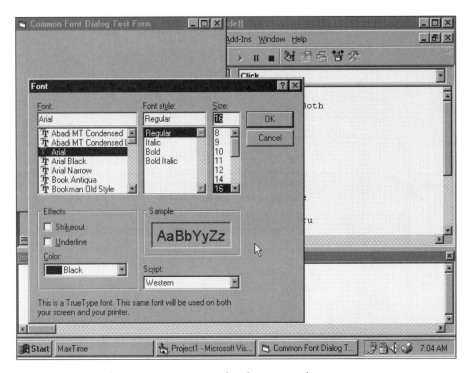

Figure 17.4 The Common Font Dialog box control.

You can now change the font family, size, color, and so on. Wasn't this easy? Figure 17.5 shows some experimenting that we did with this project.

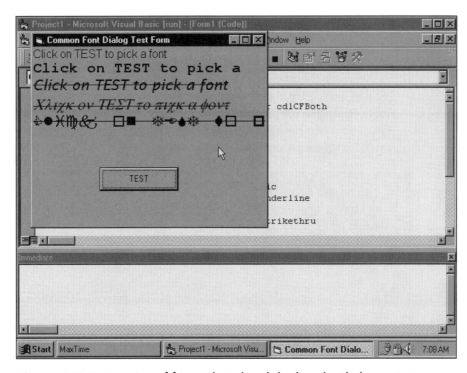

Figure 17.5 A variety of fonts selected and displayed with this project.

If you are a careful reader, you are probably screaming, "Wait a minute—where did some of that code come from?" The code we're referring to appears to the right of the equal sign in the following portion of the code listing:

```
CommonDialog1.Flags = cdlCFEffects Or cdlCFBoth
    .
    .
    .

CommonDialog1.ShowFont
Font.Name = CommonDialog1.FontName
Font.Size = CommonDialog1.FontSize
Font.Bold = CommonDialog1.FontBold
Font.Italic = CommonDialog1.FontItalic
Font.Underline = CommonDialog1.FontUnderline

FontStrikethru = CommonDialog1.FontStrikethru
ForeColor = CommonDialog1.Color
```

The first part of the listing sets the control's flags before calling the ShowFont method. Additional information on these flag values can be found by using the Help | Search Reference Index… menu selection. Enter Flags as the topic to search for, then select Font Dialog from the suggested list of topics.

The remaining values in the listing represent the control's property values. They can be found listed in the Properties box for this control. Figure 17.6 shows a portion of this listing.

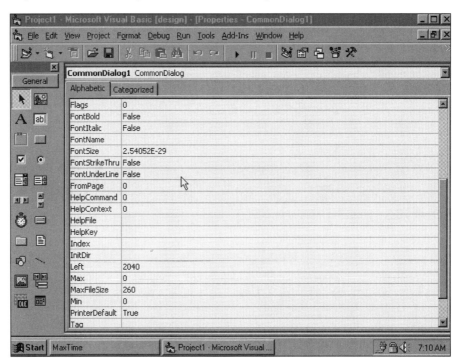

Figure 17.6 Properties for the Common Font Dialog box.

Again, if you need additional detail on any property use the Help | Search Reference Index… menu option to look up that property.

This is the key to becoming successful with common controls. Understand which properties are available for your use, then use the Help facility to learn more about the properties.

The Common Color Dialog Box Control

Let's create another simple application that will take advantage of the Common Color Dialog box control. First, repeat all six steps given in the previous section for adding a CommonDialog box control.

That's all there is to it, except writing the necessary code to access data from this dialog box. We'll use the CommandButton's click event to trigger the dialog box action. Add the following code to your project:

```
Private Sub Command1_Click()
    CommonDialog1.Flags = cdlCCRGBInit
    'Show the CommonDialog Color box
    CommonDialog1.ShowColor
    'Use selected color for form's background color
    Form1.BackColor = CommonDialog1.Color

    Cls
    String1$ = "Push TEST to select a background color"
    Form1.Print String1$
End Sub
```

Change the captions on your form and CommandButton to match those of Figure 17.7.

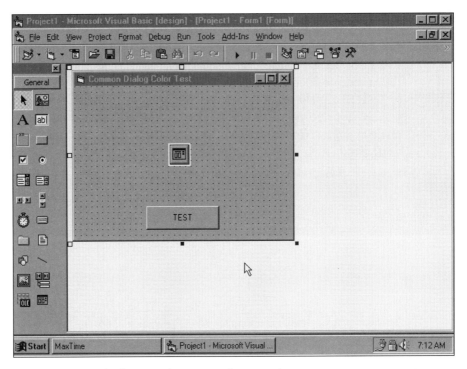

Figure 17.7 The form and CommandButton, showing appropriate captions.

Now run the application. When you click the mouse on the TEST button, you will see the Common Color Dialog box, shown in Figure 17.8.

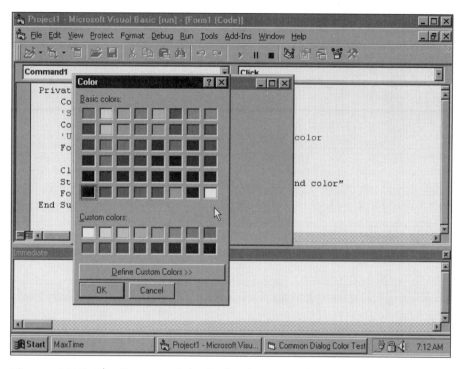

Figure 17.8 The Common Color Dialog box control.

You can now change the background of the form. Give it a try. Figure 17.9 shows the background of Form1 changed to a light blue.

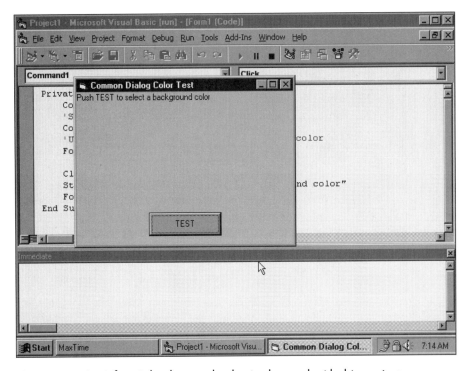

Figure 17.9 A form's background color is changed with this project.

In the previous section, we told you how to find information on the CommonDialog box control properties. Why not experiment with another common control, such as the Print Dialog box, to increase your skills?

CUSTOM CONTROLS

As we mentioned earlier, there is commercial value in producing good custom controls. Open any magazine dealing with Visual Basic and you'll see advertisements for a wide variety of controls. These include spreadsheet controls, calendar controls, scheduling controls, and so on. Often these controls sell for several hundred dollars! A commercial custom control will have value to you if you don't have the development time to devote to creating a specific control yourself. Of course, if no commercial control is available, your only alternative is to develop the control yourself. If you choose this path, you must design the control and the control's interface. This can take weeks of work.

Microsoft refers to 32-bit versions of custom controls as ActiveX controls. When designed properly, ActiveX controls can migrate across all compiler and commercial Microsoft applications. This includes the entire Microsoft Office suite.

If you are interested in creating your own custom controls, you should obtain the Visual Basic 5 Custom Control Edition (CCE) from Microsoft. This is a version of Visual Basic 5 identical to the version you are currently using, except it can be used only to create ActiveX custom controls. You may be able to download this version from Microsoft's Web site at no charge. Although it is beyond the scope of this book to teach how to create custom controls, we can take time to investigate a custom control included in many versions of Visual Basic 5. Custom controls are not part of the standard Visual Basic 5 interface and must be provided in separate files. These files use an OCX file extension.

 Note: Earlier versions of custom controls used a VBX file extension.

If you buy or create a custom control, you will use the OCX file to access the control and control properties.

Custom Calendar Control

Let's create a simple application that will take advantage of the custom Calendar control provided with many versions of Visual Basic 5. To see if your version contains this OCX control, use the Project | Components file option. If the OCX control is provided, you will be able to check Microsoft Calendar Control 8.0 in the list provided. Here is a step-by-step approach to adding this control to the toolbox:

- Open a new Visual Basic 5 project and name it Cu17Cal3.prj.
- Add a CommandButton anywhere on Form1.
- Use the Project | Components file option to view the list of available components (controls).

- Select Microsoft Calendar Control 8.0 by clicking the mouse on the appropriate checkbox, as shown in Figure 17.10.

- When you click the OK button, the Calendar control icon will be added to the toolbox, as shown in Figure 17.11.

- Drag the Calendar control icon to your project's form.

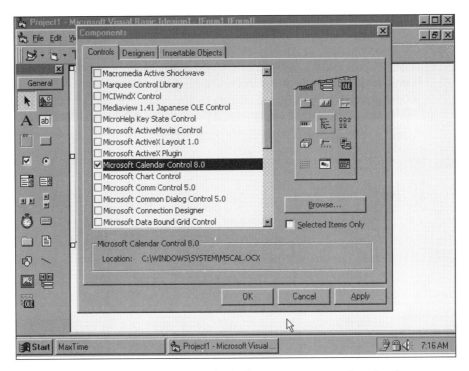

Figure 17.10 Use the mouse to check the custom Microsoft Calendar Control 8.0.

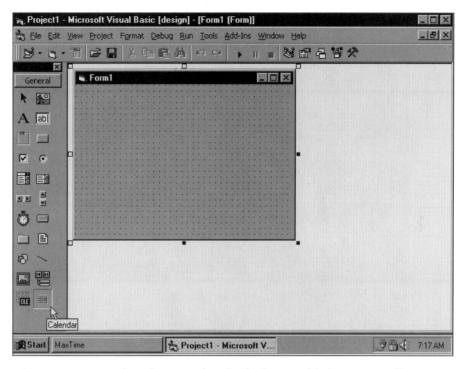

Figure 17.11 When the control is checked, it is added automatically to the toolbox.

Size the form, CommandButton, and calendar to match those of Figure 17.12. Change the captions on the form and CommandButton to match those shown in Figure 17.12, too.

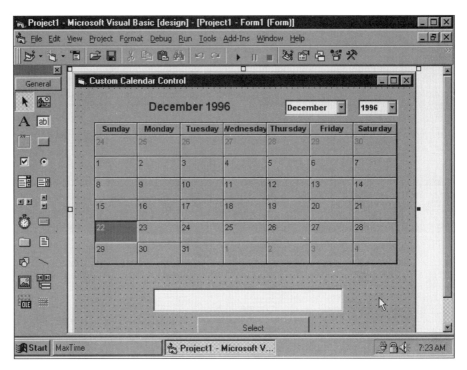

Figure 17.12 Adjust your form and controls to take on this appearance.

The properties for the custom Calendar control can be found listed in the Properties box for this control. Figure 17.13 shows a portion of this listing.

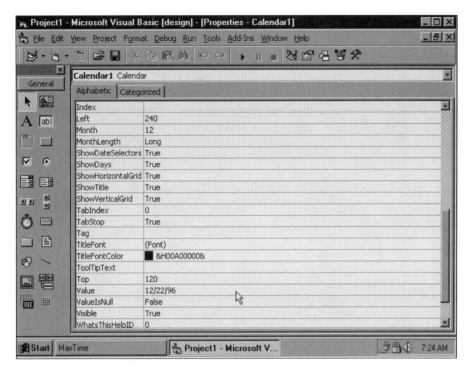

Figure 17.13 Properties for the custom Calendar control.

If you need additional detail on any property, that information must be provided by the manufacturer of the custom control. Usually, you will not be able to use the Help | Search Reference Index... menu option as we did for common controls.

Add the following code to the CommandButton click event:

```
Private Sub Command1_Click()
  MonthDayYear = Calendar1.Value

  Cls
  Text1 = "The selected day is " & MonthDayYear
End Sub
```

The Calendar1.Value property returns the selected month, day, and year in an xx/xx/xx format. This information is then printed in an appropriate TextBox control. Figure 17.14 shows a typical screen.

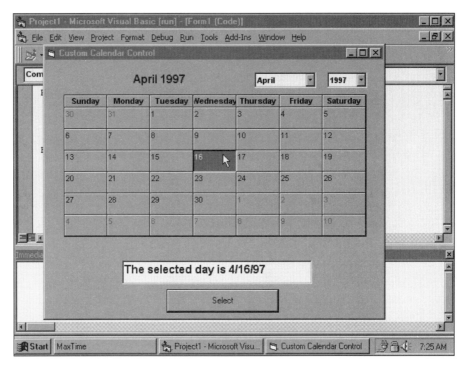

Figure 17.14 Calendar control information printed to the project's TextBox control.

What would be required to have this project return the number of days between the day the user selects and the end of the month? If you are going to take the challenge, don't forget leap year.

The Calendar control is a fairly simple custom control to implement and use in a project. Some controls, such as scheduling and spreadsheet controls, require much more time to master. If you would like to experiment with a custom control, we recommend trying Microsoft Multimedia Control 5.0 or Microsoft PictureClip Control 5.0 as your next step. Approach the use of either of these controls in the same manner as that of the Calendar control in this section.

WHAT'S NEXT?

You have made it to the end of the book! This is not where learning ends, only the point where additional learning begins. If you're hungry for more, you'll find whole Visual Basic books written on many of the individual topics touched on in this book. Congratulations on your newly developed programming skills!

INDEX

Numbers/Symbols

^, 392
!, 392
1/4" control, 38
80386, 2
80486, 2

A

Access Key Assignment for TextBox and
    PictureBox Controls, 186-187
access keys (using), 185-187
Access (Microsoft), 401
accessing Win32 API, 475-507
Activating Help, 5-6
ActiveControl, 70
ActiveForm, 70
ActiveX, 501
AddItem, 209, 215
additional controls, 43-44
Alarm, 356-361
align controls to grid, 35
Alignment, 70, 111
ALT, 166
altering interface properties, 69-95
amortization table, 390-399
AM/PM, 243
ANSI_
    CHARSET, 485
    FIXED_FONT, 486
    VAR_FONT, 486
appearance (visual), 34

application (creating), 13-16
application
    program interface, 5
    Wizard (VB), 57-66, 430-437
applications (menu-driven, developing),
        163-181
Arc(), 321-326
Archive, 70
arcs, 269-272
argument passing (call-by-value), 144-145
arithmetic operators, 135
arrays, 130-131
As, 129, 130-131, 142, 180-181, 193, 217
asset depreciation, 372-382
assignment statement, 130
attaching code to objects, 102
autoalignment, 35
AutoRedraw, 71, 267, 393, 457, 468
Autosize, 71
AVI files, 327-330

B

B, 268-269
BackColor, 71, 183, 184, 317, 497
background color, 499-500
bar chart. *See* charts
base change calculator, 274-281
BASIC, 2
Beep, 168, 199, 359
BF, 268-269
bitmap, 303
BorderStyle, 71, 110

509

G

About AP PROFESSIONAL

AP PROFESSIONAL, an imprint of Academic Press, a division of Harcourt Brace & Company, was founded in 1993 to provide high quality, innovative products for the computer community. For over 50 years, Academic Press has been a world leader in documenting scientific and technical research.

AP PROFESSIONAL continues this tradition by providing its readers with exemplary publications that bring new topics to light and offer fresh views on prominent topics. Often, today's computer books are underdeveloped clones, published in haste and promoted in series. Readers tend to be neglected by the lack of commitment from other publishers to produce quality products. It is our business to provide you with clearly written, educational publications that contain valuable information you will find truly useful. AP PROFESSIONAL has grown quickly and has established a reputation for fine products because of this commitment to excellence.

Through our strong reputation at Academic Press, and one of the most experienced editorial boards in computer publishing, AP PROFESSIONAL has also contracted many of the best writers in the computer community. Each book undergoes three stages of editing (technical, developmental, and copyediting) before going through the traditional book publishing production process. These extensive measures ensure clear, informative, and accurate publications.

It is our hope that you will be pleased with your decision to purchase this book, and that it will exceed your expectations. We are committed to making the AP PROFESSIONAL logo a sign of excellence for all computer users and hope that you will come to rely on the quality of our publications.

Enjoy!

Jeffrey M. Pepper
Vice President, Editorial Director

Related Titles from AP PROFESSIONAL

WAYNER, *Digital Cash*

WAYNER, *Disappearing Cryptography*

WAYNER, *Java and JavaScript Programming*

WEISKAMP, *Complete C++ Primer, Second Edition*

YOUNG, *Introduction to Graphics Programming for Windows 95*

YOUNG, *Windows Animation Programming with C++*

Ordering Information

 **AP PROFESSIONAL**
An imprint of ACADEMIC PRESS
A division of HARCOURT BRACE & COMPANY

ORDERS (USA and Canada): 1-800-3131-APP or APP@acad.com
AP Professional Orders: 6277 Sea Harbor Dr., Orlando, FL 32821-9816

Europe/Middle East/Africa: 0-11-44 (0) 181-300-3322
Orders: AP Professional 24-28 Oval Rd., London NW1 7DX

Japan/Korea: 03-3234-3911-5
Orders: Harcourt Brace Japan, Inc., Ichibancho Central Building 22-1, Ichibancho Chiyoda-Ku, Tokyo 102

Australia: 02-517-8999
Orders: Harcourt Brace & Co., Australia, Locked Bag 16, Marrickville, NSW 2204 Australia

Other International: (407) 345-3800
AP Professional Orders: 6277 Sea Harbor Dr., Orlando, FL 32821-9816

Editorial: 1300 Boylston St., Chestnut Hill, MA 02167 (617) 232-0500

Web: http://www.apnet.com/approfessional

About the CD-ROM

The CD included with this book is meant to run on PC compatibles. It consists of video instruction as well as programming code from the book. The video instruction presents an overview of Visual Basic 5 and covers the conceptual details discussed in the book. As such, it creates a unique combination with the text. The video portion of the CD requires Windows 3.1, Windows 95, or Windows NT. It also requires a sound card for the audio track. To run the video, run the SETUP.EXE program from the CD drive. It will take roughly 5 MB, but will run quickly. If for any reason that fails, you can run the APVB5.EXE file from your CD drive.

If you have any further questions or problems regarding the CD-ROM please contact LearnKey, Inc., at (801) 674-9733.